Working in Law

Working in Law

A guide to qualifying and starting a successful legal career

Charlie Phillips

trotman t

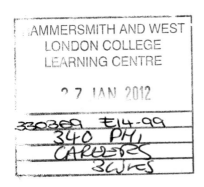
Working in Law 2012: A guide to qualifying and starting a successful legal career
This first edition published in 2011 by Trotman Publishing, a division of Crimson
Publishing Ltd., Westminster House, Kew Road, Richmond, Surrey TW9 2ND.

© Trotman Publishing 2011

Author Charlie Phillips

British Library Cataloguing in Publication Data
A catalogue record for this book is available from the British Library.

ISBN 978 1 84455 418 8

Typeset by IDSUK (DataConnection) Ltd
Printed and bound in Great Britain by Ashford Colour Press, Gosport, Hants

Contents

Contents

Acknowledgements

I would like to thank all the contributors who gave their time to talk about their experiences, and whose insight makes this book a true insiders' view: Fredericka Argent, Ed Chivers, James Evans, David Swain, Daniel Turnbull, Gadi Oron and Katherine Pymont. Thank you also to those I spoke with who preferred to remain anonymous, but whose views and experiences are no less valuable in giving an overview of what to expect when embarking on a career in law.

A special thank you to Walter Bilas and Joanne Rourke for their meticulous review of the text, and comments. Your encouragement and support throughout this project really have been a great help.

Likewise, my thanks are due to Beth Bishop and Jessica Spencer at Trotman for their input and professional guidance, which have been invaluable.

Special thanks to my wife Indre for her support not only during the process of writing this book, but all along my journey to qualification as a solicitor in the first place.

Author's note

A book on law would not be complete without a disclaimer, so: every effort has been made to ensure that this book is accurate and up to date. However, things change, and deadlines, course contents, legal provisions, rules and regulations are likely to change every year. The book is for general guidance only, and readers must check the current state of play, and satisfy themselves of the accuracy of anything set out in the book before taking action. Please note that the text is accompanied by information provided by training institutions, employers and institutions.

Finally, it is impossible to pack every bit of useful information into a book like this, and invariably some things have been left out. The intention was to ensure that what is covered in the book is relevant to the greatest number of people. Additional information, and resources useful to law students and trainees are

Acknowledgements

available on my website (www.charliephillips.info). Suggestions for improvements or additions are welcome!

Charlie Phillips
London, 2011

Introduction

I f you're considering a career in law, then you have already made a good decision. There is a vast range of opportunities available to people with legal qualifications: law is a wide open field, with huge potential for people from all walks of life. In this book we will look in detail at each stage of the qualification process, to help you navigate your way through and decide which areas of law and legal work are best for you. In addition to the facts, you will hear from people who have completed their qualifications, and have gone on to successful legal careers, giving you first-hand insight into what a career in law could really entail.

A career in law can be rewarding, but success will come with overcoming the challenges you'll face along the way. We'll set out what you need to succeed in your chosen discipline — be that as a solicitor, barrister, paralegal or part-qualified lawyer — and how to get there.

In order to get into the legal profession, many people believe that all they need to do is a law degree, another course or two, then perhaps a bit of training. Unfortunately, the truth is slightly more complex than that, and we'll look at the qualifications you'll need in detail in Part 3. It's also not true that you need to have studied a law degree to become a lawyer. There are alternative ways in. Law is, however, a qualification-based profession, so there are several academic and other qualifications you need to get before you can pass from one stage to the next.

A time of diversification

In a period of economic uncertainty and recession, with spending cuts affecting the private and public sectors, it's no surprise that opportunities across the legal profession have become more limited than in previous years. Nevertheless, the number of people looking to a legal career seems to be continually on the increase, leading to many more qualified people than there are jobs for them to take. But even if it looks as though the odds may be stacked against you, remember: there are vacancies out there, and employers are looking for good candidates to fill them. Approach them the right way, and you will succeed.

More people are coming into law from diverse backgrounds than ever before; with many of them offering qualities other than just a set of compulsory academic qualifications. This has led to a genuine increase in diversity across the profession, with more opportunities opening up for people who, in years gone by, may have struggled to get a look in. This means that contrary to the gloom that the legal profession faced after the recent recession, from another perspective, there has never been a better time to get into law, as the profession adjusts to include a more diverse workforce. The increase in applicants has contributed to a view that flexibility within the profession has to be encouraged. For example, it's perfectly acceptable to work as a paralegal, or in another part-qualified legal position for a while, before going on to do a training contract or pupillage. In fact, some – perhaps most – employers won't take you seriously without at least some 'hands on' legal experience.

A broad range of opportunities

There is a wide range of alternative career options available in law, other than the traditional solicitor or barrister routes. These alternatives are open to people with many levels of legal qualification, be that a law degree or conversion degree, or one of the more advanced legal qualifications we will look at later. If you don't manage to get all the way to where you want, there will always be other opportunities that present themselves along the way, to which any legal skills or qualifications will be very well suited. You will find that it's not uncommon to decide that law is generally right for you, but that other professions actually appeal to you more. There is nothing to stop you adjusting your direction as you go, and a legal qualification will always be useful. Were it not for gaining a legal qualification in the first place, you might not have come across these alternatives, and you may not have gained the context in which to come to a firm decision as to which direction to take. We will look at some of the possible career options available to people with legal qualifications in Chapter 5. We've also included a glossary of useful and common terms associated with the world of law, so if you aren't familiar with a term we use in the book, see page 263.

PART 1
Heading into law

1

About working in law

The law covers every aspect of our lives in one way or another, so it's no surprise that working within law presents a wide range of possible career options. You may think the only choice you have to make is between being a solicitor or a barrister, but your options are actually far wider.

The first questions you might be asking yourself are: Why do I want to be a lawyer? Do I have the right academic background to start? Which area of law do I want to work in? We'll look at these, and end this chapter with an overview of the climate of the legal profession today.

Why choose a legal career?

You will probably not be reading this if you are not already at least partially convinced that a career in law is for you. However, it's a good idea to revisit your reasons for making the decision to pursue this career path initially, as this will play a large part in defining where you will end up.

For future solicitors, the pace of life and potentially high salaries of the City may be particularly appealing to some. Others will be looking to work in a particular area, perhaps family law or property, which may offer the opportunity to work as part of the community, rather than part of a commercial enterprise. For barristers, the attraction may be in the independence, responsibility and authority that come with the job, be that at the commercial or criminal bar. With their reputation for intellect, it's perhaps no surprise that there's a good deal of prestige attached to being a barrister.

Here are some of the other main reasons for choosing a career in law.

Intellectual challenge

The strict academic qualifications needed for entry to the profession set the tone for what a lot of the work of a qualified lawyer entails. Wherever you end up, you will need to have a good grasp of the main areas of law, as well as the soft skills that good all-round experience will give you.

All legal practitioners need to keep up their own areas of expertise, but will usually need to draw on a working knowledge of a number of other areas in order to advise their clients effectively. All successful lawyers share a common desire to keep up with developments in law, and read around and discuss the subject with colleagues; to absorb and share knowledge just as much as they are required to focus on a particular matter at a particular time.

Barristers versus solicitors

Barristers are known for being experts on technical aspects of law. They are generally called upon to give their expert opinion on the merits of a case, and to assess the strengths and weaknesses, likelihood of success and potential strategy of a case. This can only be done with a very finely tuned expert knowledge of any number of different areas of substantive law, as well as rules governing court procedure, evidence, disclosure and so on – before they even get on their feet to represent their client in court. In addition to knowledge of the various legal areas, effective advocacy requires impeccable verbal presentation, sharp reactions and reasoning skills, knowledge of every last detail of a set of complex facts, and powers of persuasion to reach a successful outcome for the client.

For solicitors, the work is often no less intellectually demanding. A solicitor will very often be required to sift through sets of complex facts to pull out the key areas around which a legal argument can be constructed. Commercial considerations relevant to the matter will also need to be considered. While a barrister's work will usually be in the context of contentious matters that may ultimately reach court, a solicitor working on predominantly non-contentious matters will also deal regularly with detailed technical and factual scenarios.

Salary

You may be enticed into law by the promise of a large salary. Statistics show that salary levels vary greatly within the profession, depending on each lawyer's level of qualification, experience and area of practice. It is true that high salaries are available in some parts of the legal profession, but only a few of the very highly qualified and experienced lawyers earn that much, and it goes without saying that you'll have to work extremely hard over a number of years to get there. Commercial law generally pays better than working in criminal or other state-related sectors of law, as the work relates closely to profit-driven business in one form or another.

Perhaps not surprisingly, the highest salaries are to be found in the commercial City of London law firms and barristers' chambers, with their counterparts in other commercial centres around the country coming a close second. For solicitors, salaries in regional commercial law firms and chambers generally tend to be lower than in London, but will often be at the higher end of the salary range when compared with other professions. 'High-street' firms may focus on a broader range of matters perhaps than the more specialist commercial firms. On a pure salary basis, these firms will pay less than the larger commercial law firms, but will instead offer other incentives – close contact with colleagues and clients, a good deal of responsibility from an early stage, and a sense of contributing to the community.

Making a difference

For many, the attraction of a career in law lies in the possibility of making a positive difference, perhaps to individuals, or to society as a whole. Common to all areas of legal practice are fundamental principles of justice, and in certain areas of legal practice this is particularly prevalent. Criminal law is perhaps the clearest example. Representing a defendant, either as solicitor or barrister, will pit the lawyer against the state, in whose name the case has been brought in the interests of wider society. Environmental law is another area where lawyers have a very real opportunity to shape the course of projects with far-reaching implications on the environment, particularly in areas such as mineral exploration, oil and gas. Areas of property law can also have a significant social angle, such as advising large-scale construction projects, or proposing/opposing planning applications. Human rights law, employment and personal injury law are other areas where it is possible for the lawyers' input to have a positive social effect.

Diversity of career options

Legal work offers a wide range of options, both at the start and as you progress and gain legal experience. Wherever you start off working in law, you will always come across new legal issues, areas of law you have less experience with, and which may present opportunities for you as your career develops.

Your contribution counts

Regardless of your level of qualification, it is very rewarding to see your work being used and valued, perhaps in its own right, or as part of a broader matter. A high level of productivity will be required from you in any area of law you work in, and very seldom will you be expected to be an observer. Feeding into this productivity gives you the opportunity to make your mark, and see your contribution count.

Career resilience and employability

Any legal qualification helps put you ahead of your non-qualified peers. Competition for qualified roles is tough, and we will look at this in more detail later, but legal qualifications are viewed positively because they are relevant to many employers. This is very helpful as you apply for any role, either now or in the future. Legal qualifications and experience can be portable from one area of work to another, which can be a great advantage when approaching the job market.

Dynamic working environment

Any legal matter may change and take an unexpected direction as it progresses, requiring agility and the ability to react and adapt strategy accordingly. This makes for an interesting and vibrant working environment. When this is added to the changing backdrops of updated legislation and new case law, and the challenges posed in reacting to or working around these developments, it is easy to see why many people are attracted to the dynamic nature of legal work.

International angle

There is an international angle to most, if not all, legal matters. UK legislation in all areas is shaped by developments in Europe, while cross-border trade plays an increasingly important role in the global economy. Whether you decide to specialise in international law or not, it is likely you will come across international issues in many areas of legal work.

Status and perceived value

Obtaining any legal qualification requires dedication, hard work and a certain amount of intellect. As such, there is some kudos and status attached to them. There is much more to this than vanity, however. From a professional perspective, the positive perception of legal qualifications can be very useful, as there is a common understanding of one's level of knowledge or experience, which is easily communicated. This helps in the workplace, and boosts employability.

The qualities you need for law

Handling responsibility

You can expect to be given a good deal of responsibility from the start of your legal career, and the rewards and accountability that come with it. An introduction to the kinds of responsibility you might expect as a lawyer may come during some of the assessments during the Academic and Vocational stages of training (see Chapters 6 and 7). Written exams and other assessments such as mock client interviews, or applications to court, are a good indicator of the level of personal responsibility you will take as your career progresses: you will often be expected to prepare and present aspects of a matter on your own, and while you will usually receive a good level of support, the ability to handle work autonomously is an essential skill.

Willingness to learn

Good research, reasoning and written skills are essential for any lawyer, as are good verbal presentation, personal organisation, self-motivation and persistence. There is a steep learning curve at the start of any legal career, and you never stop learning as your career progresses. It is important to develop the ability to take criticism well, and treat this as an essential part of the process. Most legal roles will provide training and development that will seek to enhance these 'soft' skills, in addition to developing more technical legal skills.

Intellectual ability

In order to gain the qualifications needed to go from one stage of training to the next, all lawyers need a good level of academic and intellectual ability. It is not enough simply to have passed the exams, however. Legal work can be complex and challenging, and it is essential to have an interest in keeping up with the more 'academic' aspects of the law, as well as the more practical ones.

Capacity for hard work

You won't be slaving away in the office until 3a.m. every day, but you will be expected to work hard. Be realistic about this from the outset: the academic qualifications require a lot of effort, so does the professional training, and that's before you qualify. On qualification, a new set of factors come into play, requiring a new set of skills that take time to develop. It doesn't always come easily, so be prepared to work hard, as that's the way to get ahead.

Working with people

Perhaps the most important aspect of a lawyer's work is the ability to work with people, and the importance of good communication cannot be over-emphasised. You need to develop professional relationships with a wide range of people at all levels, and be able to get on with people, understanding differing view points and levels of experience.

Commercial awareness

Most legal work contains a commercial or financial element, and the majority of commercial legal work focuses exclusively on this. It is therefore essential to have a good sense of commercial awareness (which we look at more on page 147). You also need to understand the value of offering good service to your clients, and be keen to get some satisfaction out of offering excellent service.

Integrity

The legal system is, at its most fundamental level, intended to serve the interests of society, and lawyers have a duty to further this interest. Professional conduct across the profession is set out in a number of rules, and it is essential to understand these obligations. Different areas of law face different ethical or professional challenges, and a good sense of integrity goes a long way to approaching potential issues in the most appropriate way. You'll be placed in positions of trust as well as responsibility, which can require skills that can't be learned from textbooks.

Common sense and self-awareness

It may sound obvious, but an essential requirement for all lawyers is common sense. Throughout your career you will be faced with situations where you may not immediately have a clear idea of what you should do, or what the most suitable option is to take. Very often, however, using your common sense is all you need to get yourself through a seemingly difficult situation. The same approach applies to studying, making job applications, interviews, or when tackling any other aspect of the qualification process. You are often being assessed on how you approach an issue, rather than your technical legal skills.

An overview of the academic requirements needed

Now we've looked at some of the reasons you might want to work in law, and the personal attributes you need, we'll look at the fundamental academic requirements that are essential when embarking on a legal career.

Regardless of which route you decide to take in law, the starting points are very similar. There are a number of entry requirements for each of the academic qualifications, which must all be completed successfully before candidates can continue to the next level. It's worth mentioning this right at the start for a couple of reasons.

- These are strict requirements. While it's sometimes possible to start a qualifying law degree or equivalent conversion course without A levels, the remaining academic and vocational steps are compulsory requirements for full qualification.

- In order to get a training position within a solicitors' firm or barristers' chambers, you will need a law degree or conversion, and the relevant vocational qualifications: either the Legal Practice Course (LPC) for solicitors, or the Bar Professional Training Course (BPTC; formerly the Bar Vocation Course) for barristers.

Sticklers for results

The fact that all this academic training is required should give an indication of the nature of the work you'll be doing once you are working in law. When assessing new recruits, lawyers, who tend to be naturally risk averse, will view academic achievements as a fairly reliable way of benchmarking the extent to which a candidate is likely to be a successful fit into their team. The higher the academic achievements, the lower the potential risk of taking on that candidate. There will always be exceptions to this, but it gives employers a starting point, and it's one that applies to everyone.

The stages of qualification

The main stages of qualification for solicitors and barristers can be broken down into five main areas.

1. Your previously existing academic qualifications (GCSEs, A levels, etc.).

2. The 'Academic Stage' for all lawyers.

3. The 'Vocational Stage' for solicitors and barristers.

4. Professional training (training contract or pupillage).

5. Post-qualification requirements.

	Stage 1			Stage 2	Stage 3	
A levels, GCSEs or equivalent	'Academic Stage' of training			'Vocational Stage' of training	Professional training	Post-qualification
	Law degree or conversion degree: Graduate Diploma in Law (GDL) (if non-law degree)		Solicitors*:	Legal Practice Course (LPC)	Training contract	Continuing professional development
			Barristers:	Bar Professional Training Course (BPTC)	Pupillage	Continuing professional development

* Legal executives: the Institute of Legal Executives (ILEX) route is also available to gain equivalent qualifications to each of stages 1–3 (see below).

Stage 1: The 'Academic Stage'

Undergraduate-level law degree, or equivalent conversion degree

Law degree courses

If your first degree is in law from a recognised course provider, then great: you will now have what is referred to as a 'qualifying law degree'. You will have had three years working through the various legal subjects, and you can now progress directly to the Vocational Stage of qualification, via the Legal Practice Course (LPC) or Bar Professional Training Course (BPTC) (see below).

Law conversion degrees

If you have a degree in a subject other than law, you will need to complete the Graduate Diploma in Law (GDL), or less commonly the Common Professional Examination (CPE), which are both often referred to as a 'conversion degree'. These courses compress the key contents of a three-year law degree into one academic year (or two years part-time).

A conversion degree is a convenient way of getting onto the legal ladder. There are advantages and disadvantages to both the conversion degree and the qualifying law degree routes, but in practice, it doesn't matter which you take. As long as you have a relatively solid understanding of the course material (and some good grades!) then you'll be fine. You're at the start of a long journey, so in just the same way that no one expects you to be an expert driver just after passing your driving test, neither will anyone expect you to an authority on any aspect of law before you have even started the Vocational Stage – not at this stage, at least.

The Academic Stage qualifications are looked at in more detail in Chapter 6.

Stage 2: The 'Vocational Stage'

Vocational courses for solicitors and barristers

Once you have your qualifying law degree or conversion qualification, the next step of the academic process is to complete a vocational course. These courses are different for solicitors and barristers, and it is at this stage that their routes to qualification split: you have to decide on one or the other. We discuss the difference between training and working as a solicitor and barrister in depth in Chapter 5, if you haven't already made up your mind on which route to pursue.

Solicitors' Vocational Stage of training

The LPC builds on the main theoretical legal areas covered on a law degree, and sets them in a more practical context. The LPC is split into compulsory areas, and optional areas. It is at the stage of choosing these options (known as 'electives') that you will effectively start to specialise, as you will need to make some decisions to narrow the course options to fit the areas of legal practice that you are most interested in.

Barristers' Vocational Stage of training

Barristers will need to complete the BPTC. The objective of the BPTC is similar to that of the LPC, in that it equips students with the skills necessary for practice as a barrister, by building on the knowledge acquired during the Academic Stage of training. There are compulsory and optional elements to the BPTC, with the emphasis being on case preparation, giving advice on cases and claims, and advocacy (representing clients in courts and tribunals).

The Vocational Stage qualifications are looked at in more detail in Chapter 7.

Stage 3: Professional training

With your Academic and Vocational stages done, the next step to qualification is either the solicitors' training contract, or barristers' pupillage. These are similar to apprenticeships, as the trainee or pupil gains essential hands-on experience by assisting qualified lawyers over the course of several months, learning to apply the theoretical knowledge gained so far in the context of real-life legal practice. There's more on this in Chapter 10.

Solicitors' professional training

The solicitors' training contract generally takes two years. Trainee solicitors will usually be employed by a solicitors' firm on a fixed-term contract, and will be exposed to a range of work by assisting qualified solicitors in different departments. The time spent in each department is known as a 'seat'.

In addition to the practical work, all trainees must pass a Professional Skills Course (PSC). This ensures that all solicitors receive training in important aspects of legal practice such as money laundering and the ethical aspects of a solicitor's work. The PSC involves a couple of written tests, and some role-play-type assessments, but is not nearly as intensive as the GDL or LPC. A couple of alternative routes to qualification exist, such as that offered by the Institute of Legal Executives (ILEX). Again, we'll look at these in more detail in Chapter 7.

Barristers' professional training

Once a future barrister has passed the BPTC, they will need to complete a 'pupillage' in order to become fully qualified. A pupillage usually takes one year, and is divided into two six-month periods, spent assisting a junior barrister with five or more years of experience. The first six months is usually spent in a non-practising capacity, shadowing and assisting the pupil supervisor. The second six months involves the pupil playing a much more active role, continuing to assist the supervisor, but also running matters of their own, with appropriate supervision. After successfully completing pupillage, a barrister is fully qualified, and entitled to set up his or her own practice, taking a room in a set of barristers' chambers (known as taking a 'tenancy').

We will look at all this in a lot more detail in Part 3, so don't worry if it sounds complex. The main point at this stage is to understand that there are a number of academic hurdles to get over. Making sure you have a realistic chance of getting through these – and that you have the time and the stamina required – is very important.

Research for the future

When it comes to applying for professional training positions, your credibility as an applicant will increase dramatically the more real-life legal experience you have, so get out there and find some! It's essential to start forming your own view of what the legal profession is all about, and how you may fit into it.

At this early stage of your career search, the main aim is to learn the landscape of the profession, how solicitors and barristers work, how the support roles work, and what happens day to day in the life of someone already in the position you one day hope to reach yourself.

- Research areas you're interested in and read as much as you can on the subject (this book is a good start).

- Speak to your college or university law tutors and careers advisers.

- Look around for any contacts in law you have already, and ask whether you can do a work placement, or shadow them.

- Familiarise yourself with the official regulators and bodies, as you will deal with them throughout your career (see page 271)

Career progression

Which specific areas of law appeal to you, and what do you know about the careers and positions that relate to those areas? You may be thinking that there are only two paths to choose from: solicitor or barrister, but in reality there is a wide range of options available for both, in private practice (in a law firm for solicitors, or in chambers for barristers) or working in-house for a non-legal organisation.

There are fairly well-defined career paths available in most areas of legal practice, allowing you a certain level of control over where your future may lie. Of course, there are no guarantees, but you are more likely to know what your long-term prospects as a lawyer might be than in other, less qualification-driven walks of life. Below we look at how your qualifications and career progression could work out.

Solicitors in private practice law firms

For solicitors, each full year following qualification counts towards an overall tally of post-qualification experience or PQE. For the first year following qualification, solicitors are referred to as 'newly qualifieds' or NQs. Within law firms, less-experienced solicitors of up to around five years' PQE are often referred to as 'associates' or 'assistants', as well as just 'solicitors'. With a few more years' PQE, they may become 'senior associates', at which point they will usually be looking at being made a partner. Partnership is generally as high as it gets within many law firms. Partners share overall responsibility for the performance of the firm, which means taking a share of the profits (and taking home more than salaried staff), but also sharing the liability for the firm's performance. This may mean taking the occasional pay cut during tough times, or being ultimately responsible for anything done in error or negligence within the firm, subject to the firm's insurance cover.

Barristers

Practising barristers working from chambers are self-employed from qualification all the way through their career. In essence, these barristers fall into two categories according to experience: 'junior' or Queen's Counsel (QC). A junior may have many years of qualification (or 'call'), and an experienced junior barrister can be referred to as a 'senior junior'. QCs are barristers who have been selected on the basis of exceptional ability, and represent the most senior level of the profession. QCs are often selected as judges, and it is also possible for QCs to sit as judges, at the same time as continuing their barrister's practice.

In-house lawyers

For many solicitors and barristers, life in a firm or practising at the Bar is not as appealing as working in-house. Every organisation, in every sector, is faced with a range of legal issues every day. These may include employment law issues with staff, property questions with leases or ownership of premises, or commercial contract points, and may perhaps lead to litigation if there is a dispute. Depending on the nature of the organisation, there will often be a range of regulatory rules to consider, governing everything from health and safety to local council rules. In-house lawyers deal with all the day-to-day legal issues that their organisation faces, and the variety of this kind of work can be very appealing. Of course, it's impossible for any one lawyer – or even a team of in-house lawyers – to be experts in every field, so the expertise of external lawyers is often drawn upon for more specialist or business critical matters. In-house lawyers tend to enjoy the detailed knowledge of the business that they gain from effectively only having one client, and can become leaders in their field.

Part-qualified lawyers: legal executives and paralegals

Legal executives usually work in a particular area of law, and their work is similar to that of a junior solicitor. The ILEX offers a set of qualifications for legal executives (see Chapter 7). One of the principal remits of ILEX is to offer its members flexible legal training and professional development. ILEX helps its members achieve the full range of qualifications required for each level of the profession, from diploma and A level, to part qualification as legal secretaries or paralegals, and up to fully qualified status.

Paralegals often assist solicitors with fee-earning work, but are not trainees or qualified solicitors. There is no formal level of qualification required to become a paralegal, and the Law Society does not directly regulate their activities, so there can be a great deal of flexibility to a paralegal role. Many view paralegal work as an opportunity to gain valuable hands-on legal work experience, working in a firm with the ultimate objective of gaining a training contract, and to progress from there on to qualification. Others are career paralegals, who have amassed a huge amount of experience in a particular area of law, and make their paralegal work an end in itself.

In Part 2 we will look at the process of getting qualified, from making the early decisions right up to what happens at qualification and beyond. There's no doubting that it can be tricky at times, but the rewards are well worth the effort you put in. The key to success lies in assessing your options realistically at the outset, and we will help you do exactly that.

Do I need previous work experience?

In more specialist areas of law, previous experience is a definite advantage. The fact that the GDL allows a law degree to be fit into one year, makes it relatively quick for those wishing to qualify with experience in other areas to do so. Previous working experience in the area of law in which you wish to practise will put you in very good stead. There are numerous examples of specialist lawyers working in all manner of areas, who came to law from previous careers, in areas such as financial regulation, the media, information technology (IT), and many more. Of course, some organisations offer the opportunity to train in-house, and qualify internally. While not strictly necessary, previous legal work experience will count very favourably, and will help both employer and employee get the most out of the investment in training and qualification.

The competitive climate

The law is a competitive and specialist profession. Standards are high, as are the potential rewards, but so is demand for the opportunities available. There are more people than ever coming into law, with more applicants applying for the same places on courses, and going on to apply for the same training contract or pupillage positions. Your challenge is to be the best of the bunch, and you should have this in your mind from the outset.

Solicitors are on the increase

The number of newly qualified solicitors is still increasing, despite economic pressures: 7% more qualified solicitors were registered in December 2010 than at the same time in 2009. While this increase demonstrates that more people are progressing through the various stages of training to ultimately gain full qualification, the availability of jobs for them to take has not necessarily increased at a matching rate. The long-term effects of this are hard to assess, but it is possible that increased competition will reduce job opportunities within the profession.

Solicitors passing the professional stage

Each year, more than 14,000 full- and part-time LPC places are available, with an average of over 9,000 students passing the LPC. In 2010, the LPC pass rate was 89.7%. Assuming you have the required grades for entry, you shouldn't have any problems getting a place.[1]

In 2010, 4,874 training contracts were registered with the Law Society, down approximately 1,000 on the previous year.[2] As a very rough average, there were therefore only enough training positions available in England and Wales for 54% of the people who passed the LPC.

According to the *AGR Graduate Recruitment Summer Survey 2011*, there were on average 65.5 applications for every training contract position.

Retention rates for solicitors

Be very careful when you look at published or quoted retention rates of trainees at law firms, particularly the larger ones. It doesn't look good when a firm does not keep on the very people they have invested time and money in training up. If trainees are not kept on, awkward questions are asked: Is the firm doing badly? Are they taking on the wrong people at trainee level? Is their training policy flawed? The result is that firms will tend to put a positive spin on their trainee retention figures, regardless of the real reasons. 'Trainee retention' does not mean 'trainees that were given qualified solicitors' roles immediately on qualification'. A firm may only give qualified roles to three out of six trainees, and may offer paralegal or business development roles to the others. The fact that job offers were made to all of them means the firm can say they had 100% retention, when in reality, only 50% were offered fully qualified roles. Nevertheless, an offer of a part-qualified role means the firm doesn't want to lose you, and your role will probably develop into a fully qualified role over time.

Barrister positions remain competitive

The situation for prospective barristers has always been tough, and their profession has not seen the same increases in numbers reaching qualification in recent years as for solicitors. As has long been the case, the likelihood of an applicant to the BPTC going all the way to securing tenancy remains low. As a general guide, the Bar Council states that the BPTC is completed by approximately 1,500 students each year, while the number of pupillage places available across the country recently dipped to below 500. Even when pupillage is secured, not all barristers go on to secure tenancy. While this may sound gloomy, remember that there *are* pupillage positions out there, and with the right approach and commitment, suitably qualified candidates are very much in demand.

Professional stage (barristers)

Entry requirements are relatively strict. There are approximately 3,000 applications for 1,800 places on the BPTC, and The Bar Council's Bar Standards Board is planning on introducing both an aptitude test and an English language test for BPTC applicants whose first language is not English or Welsh. See Chapter 7 for more details on the aptitude test.

Most years, fewer than 500 newly qualified barristers take up tenancy after pupillage, while just over 200 take up jobs as employed barristers. The success rate of BPTC applicants ultimately continuing to pupillage and then taking up tenancy is only 17%. Adding employed barristers into the equation, the figures look slightly better: 24%.[3]

Given the investment in time and money required just to get through the BPTC, do think about the success rates for barristers, and plan your future accordingly. The statistics alone should not put you off, but keep in mind alternative career options along the way (see Chapter 12).

Case study

A BPTC student yet to secure pupillage warns of the need to be informed from the outset

It pays to be realistic before starting out, because entering the legal profession is a costly business! In order to become a barrister you have no choice but to complete the BPTC, but it is recommended that you do not consider it unless you have pupillage secured.

This makes sense for two reasons: first, there is a chance (albeit a small one) that the chambers will reimburse you, at least in part, for your BPTC fees; and second, the training you have had is fresh in your mind, which may give you some confidence when starting pupillage.

Since September 2010, anyone graduating from Bar school no longer has the right to call themselves a 'non-practising barrister' – they can only give themselves the barrister title if they complete pupillage. This means that if you are a student who does not have pupillage, you are paying £15,000 to attend Bar school with no employment or title at the end of it.

The Law Society of England

Becoming a solicitor

Solicitors combine legal expertise and people skills to provide expert confidential legal advice and assistance, in direct contact with clients.

Becoming a solicitor can be competitive and expensive. Those willing to invest time and effort will enter a career that can be incredibly rewarding, but the qualification process requires academic and financial commitment and will take at least five years. Approximately 8,000 individuals qualify each year.

If you are interested in becoming a solicitor you should do your research. Talk to people in the profession and seek some work experience. This will help you to decide whether you and the profession are right for each other, as well as demonstrating to recruiters that you are serious about a career in law.

A wide range of career options

Solicitors have a variety of career options: in private practice; within a business or organisation; in local or central government; or in court services.

Routes into the profession

There are three main routes to qualifying as a solicitor.

1. The law graduate route

The majority of solicitors qualify by this route. The key stages are:

- Qualifying Law Degree – three years
- Legal Practice Course – one year
- Training Contract – two years

A 'qualifying' law degree meets the requirements of the Solicitors Regulation Authority and the Bar Standards Board and is valid for entry to the Legal Practice Course for up to seven years after graduation.

2. The non-law graduate route

Approximately 20% of solicitors qualify by this route. The key stages are:

- Degree in any subject – three years
- Common Professional Examination/Graduate Diploma in Law – one year (for non-law graduates).
- Legal Practice Course – one year
- Training Contract – two years

Find out more on the above routes to qualification at the Solicitors Regulation Authority website www.sra.org and the Law Society careers website http://www.lawsociety.org.uk/careersinlaw/becomingasolicitor.page

3. The Institute of Legal Executive (ILEX) routes

Qualification through ILEX routes takes longer than by other routes and is designed to enable individuals to study while working. As an ILEX Fellow you may work as a Legal Executive, or you may go on to qualify as a solicitor. In some circumstances you may be exempted from the training contract. Find out more at www.ilex.org.uk

Training contract

After academic and vocational stages comes practice-based training, or a 'training contract'. Stiff competition means training contract applications are usually made during the second year of university. Trainees apply, under supervision, skills and knowledge acquired during academic and vocational stages. Most training contracts are in private practice, but also are offered within local and central government, commerce and industry, Crown Prosecution Service, Magistrates' Court Service and other organisations. Details of employers authorised to take on trainee solicitors can be found at www.lawsociety.org.uk under 'Find a solicitor'.

Support for junior lawyers

The Junior Law Division (JLD) of the Law Society represents all student members of the Law Society enrolled through the SRA, trainees, and solicitors with up to five years' active experience. It provides its members with support, advice, information and networking opportunities and provides a voice for students and trainees through lobbying and campaigns. A mentoring scheme matches members to more experienced fellow solicitors for advice and support on work related issues. Student members can enrol through the Solicitors Regulation Authority while trainee solicitors are enrolled automatically.

Preparing students for gaining entry to the solicitors' profession

A free careers event for undergraduates is held biannually, covering all aspects of preparation for a career in the solicitors' profession including tips on gaining relevant experience, completing applications and interview techniques. The range of career options are also represented by the many employers who participate.

Diversity Access Scheme

The Law Society Diversity Access Scheme aims to improve social mobility in the legal profession by supporting promising entrants who face significant social, educational, financial or personal obstacles to qualification, for example homelessness, time in local authority care, overcoming coercion into arranged marriage or severe physical disabilities. All have shown tenacity, courage and commitment in the pursuit of their career. The Diversity Access Scheme has helped 101 students to date

Changes in Legal Education and Training

Three legal regulators, the Solicitors Regulation Authority, Bar Standards Board and ILEX Professional Services, are currently reviewing legal education and training in England and Wales. An independent Research Team is expected to make recommendations by December 2012.

Visit www.letr.org.uk for more information, or to stay up-to-date with the progress of the review. You can also send any comments to the Law Society, at educationandtraining@lawsociety.org.uk.

Profile: Law Society of Scotland

Heather McPhee, Development Officer, Education and Training at the Law Society of Scotland discusses the route to qualification

Being a Scottish qualified solicitor is held in high regard throughout the business world and by solicitors from other countries. The standard of education and professionalism which solicitors must attain, and which continues throughout the working life of a solicitor mean that it is recognised as a highly respected profession which can lead to a varied career, whichever career path is chosen.

Scots law (the LLB) can be studied as a first degree in 10 higher education institutions in Scotland. This can take two, three or, more commonly, four years. The single honours law degree, which is taken by the majority of students, takes four years. The ordinary degree takes three, and the accelerated ordinary degree, for those with a first degree in another discipline, takes two. It is also possible to study law as a joint honours degree at several institutions.

The alternative to gaining an LLB is by completing a three-year pre-diploma training contract with a Scottish solicitor and sitting the society's professional exams. Those who take this route must still obtain the Diploma in Professional Legal Practice and undertake a two-year post-diploma traineeship.

The route to qualification as a solicitor in Scotland is undergoing significant changes from 2011. The LLB will be replaced with a new 'Foundation programme' at eight of the 10 institutions offering the LLB. The Foundation programme will be offered at the same level as the LLB, with the benefits of more flexibility in the programme to deliver subjects required for entry to the solicitors' profession.

Students wishing to qualify as a solicitor in Scotland then undertake Professional Education and Training (PEAT). The first stage, the vocational element, PEAT 1, is also known as the Diploma in Professional Legal Practice. PEAT 1 is the post-graduate Vocational Stage which has been developed to teach the practical knowledge and skills necessary for the working life of a solicitor. Up to 50% of the content of PEAT 1 is elective, meaning that students have a real choice regarding the areas of law they might later wish to practise in.

The final stage in the route to qualification is PEAT 2, the Professional Education and Training Stage 2, which is the two-year work-based or in-office stage and shares the outcomes of PEAT 1. This is where the knowledge, skills, attitudes and values taught in PEAT 1 are honed in the working environment. During PEAT 2, trainees need to undertake 60 hours of trainees continuing professional development and will work towards meeting the standard of the 'qualifying solicitor'.

The Law Society is here to support solicitors throughout their career, from giving information to school leavers about careers in law, to giving professional guidance and support.

Case study

Thomas Murdock is working as a trainee at Tods Murray LLP. He describes why he chose this career, and life as a trainee solicitor

I was looking for a career that would be challenging, to provide many opportunities that would allow me to use my brain and think logically, and ultimately be rewarded for doing so. I think it's an exciting time to begin a career in law – lawyers are changing the way they practise and having to evolve.

I found the interview and application process tough, but I don't think there's ever been an easy path to becoming a lawyer. You have to really want to do it, and be committed to it. If you aren't, it's fairly obvious to prospective employers. There are of course a few Einsteins out there in huge demand for their sheer academic ability, but for the majority of applicants success will come from having a wide skills base and being a great communicator.

The best possible advice I could give would be that you have to make your own luck – create your own opportunities. Follow up any and all contacts you may have. Think creatively about how you can get involved with firms, and importantly, show your enthusiasm.

In terms of a typical day as a trainee, I'll arrive at my desk for 9a.m., and I'll usually have lots of emails to work through. I'll then prioritise my work – at any one time I'll usually have between five and 20 tasks on the go, so it's a case of juggling these. Afternoons are often spent tying up loose ends and delivering Companies House forms. Unless I'm working on something with an urgent close, I'll usually leave around 5:30p.m.

My first seat was in the banking department, which has given me a breadth of work, from discharging standard securities for large lenders, preparing the monthly banking update, to undertaking due diligence reports for opinions. I was also involved with an assignation portfolio of 900 standard securities, which although hard work, proved great experience.

My current seat has been in commercial property. It's been a particularly varied and fast-paced seat, with calls to clients from day one. I've had experience of leasing, drafting rent review memoranda, and buying and selling commercial and residential property for large companies and individual clients. My next seat is litigation.

The firm has provided opportunities to get involved outside of my own department. I've drafted an agreement for a comedy promoter and I'm advising a record company about to broadcast music videos on Connecticut PBS. I've also written newspaper articles, been a guest lecturer at Edinburgh Napier University, and attended client-development events and conferences.

2

What working in law is really like

Popular myths about working in law

Legal qualifications have meaning and value because they are subject to carefully regulated standards. The academic courses and exams are not easy, and the Vocational and Professional stages of training are also taxing. Competition is tough – for training contracts and pupillages in particular – so it is inevitable that a number of myths have sprung up about working in law, which aren't all that helpful. Here are some of the more popular myths, and how they measure up to reality.

'Everyone doing law has 15 A* at GCSE and 5 A* at A level'

You will find that the majority of applicants don't have such illustrious credentials. You will inevitably need to have solid, consistent grades, but a full house of nothing but the very highest scores may suggest you're only good on paper, and that you've spent your life holed up, studying alone. You need to have some extra-curricular and commercial experience on hand, to show a more balanced skill set. You'll need good grades, but grades alone don't tell an employer anything about your personality and people skills, which are essential elements for any lawyer.

'Everybody in law went to Oxford or Cambridge'

There are far more people working in law than there are Oxbridge graduates, so this clearly isn't true. While it's important to get consistently good grades, it's also vital to get a 2.i to get a look in at most firms and chambers. A 2.i from a lesser-known university is still a 2.i, and it will be up to you to demonstrate in applications and interviews how much you applied yourself, and how much you got out of your time, wherever you studied. An Oxbridge graduate with a 2.ii still has a 2.ii. They will find it much harder to progress in law without a well thought-out strategy, not least because the majority of online application forms simply won't let you progress unless you can tick the '2.i' box. It can be done, but it's a lot harder.

Regardless of where you studied at undergraduate level, you must focus hard on getting the best grades you can, particularly on your law conversion, LPC or BPTC. Your legal grades can be viewed as far more relevant than where you happen to have studied at undergraduate level.

'There are so few training contracts to go round that it's hardly worth applying'

It's true that there are not many training contracts and pupillages available, and far fewer than there are applicants to fill them. Nevertheless, the positions do exist, and are waiting to be filled by people with the right skills and qualifications. It's not easy, but with the right strategy you can hugely increase your chances of putting in good applications, getting interviews and ultimately securing that elusive place. In Chapter 11 we will concentrate on strategy and tactics which will help you get a training contract or pupillage, and in Chapter 12, we will look at the alternative routes to qualification that are available for those for whom the traditional route is not working out, or for whom it just isn't appropriate.

'Day-to-day work in law is a nightmare, with very long hours, late nights and weekends all thrown in'

You will be expected to work as long and as hard as anyone else; indeed at junior level you may be required to work longer and harder than your more qualified colleagues. You have the disadvantages of lack of experience, legal knowledge and context, and early on in your career, you may not even know where things are in the office, or who the right person is to ask when you're not sure of something. All this adds to a challenging working environment. Occasionally you may have to stay late, and it has been known that some overnight and weekend work can be involved. One thing always holds true however – no one likes working late, including supervisors. If the work is urgent or important enough to justify long or out-of-hours work, then this is an opportunity to demonstrate commitment. Make sure you get the context and background to the work from supervisors or colleagues. You'll learn more from the experience and you'll be more useful to your colleagues, and you can take a lot of positive value from what might otherwise not perhaps have been such a positive experience.

'As a junior lawyer, you only do menial work, such as photocopying'

All legal work is varied, even at junior level, but you have to start somewhere. Having said that, there are great variances in what is expected at the very start. For barristers, the nature of their work means they are expected to hit the ground running, perhaps more than for trainee solicitors. Trainee solicitors may well start off by being given work that probably doesn't need to be done by someone on their way to a high-level legal qualification. However, there are good reasons for being given menial work, at least initially. Usually, it is simply because something is needed urgently, and you are there to do it.

A supervisor should be able to count on the reliability, attention to detail and overall competence that a trainee solicitor can offer, to ensure that whatever they are given will be done well and on time. Some firms start trainees off low, to test their aptitude (and attitude!). The better you do, the more likely you are to get better quality work that is more appropriate to your level of ability. Lawyers are naturally cautious. They are not going to set you, as a newly arrived trainee, on the most important client matter they are working on, until they know with a good degree of certainty what your skills and abilities are, and that they can rely on you. It's up to you to fast track your way to this level of responsibility. This can be done, and often a lot quicker than you may think.

'You're only a real lawyer if you work in a firm or chambers. In-house doesn't count'

A perception may exist that in-house legal positions have less appeal than positions in a specialist legal practice. However, you only have to look at the roles and responsibilities of senior lawyers at some of the country's biggest companies to know that this is of course a myth.

Solicitors in private practice, and barristers in chambers, are legal specialists, but very often in-house counsel have superior knowledge of their sector than many private-practice lawyers. Day-to-day contact with their sector can give in-house lawyers the edge on legal and commercial issues affecting their business.

'It's worth paying for all the course fees, because you make a killing when you qualify'

The salaries on offer in law vary greatly depending on which route you take, and are not always as high as you might expect, given the level of qualification needed. Your legal courses will always cost money, and there is no guarantee of success at the end. However, every qualification you gain puts you a step ahead, so the sensible thing is to plan each stage of your qualification carefully. Don't stretch yourself on the assumption that things might work out in the end. Instead, make sure you can justify each course, and each week of work experience, or time spent in junior level roles that you may get along the way to build your CV.

Of course, you may need to take out a loan, or otherwise subsidise your course fees (we will talk about that in more detail later on), but the important thing is to ensure that you get something positive for yourself out of each stage of your training, without needing to rely on specific job offers, or input from third parties.

The truth about salaries

The attraction of high salaries may draw a lot of people to law, but the reality can be very different. Salaries vary greatly depending on what type of work you do, what type of firm or organisation you work for, and where in the country you work. You should do as much research as you can in the areas you are most interested in, to get the most accurate information on what the salaries might be, and to make sure your expectations are realistic.

Be aware that the law evolves, and with this comes the risk that some areas of law become less widely applicable over time, less commercially viable, and therefore less profitable. The law is not immune to outside pressures, and was affected just as badly by the 2008/09 recession as any other service industry. Many law firms were forced to consolidate their operations, and in many cases had to make redundancies.

A City solicitor tells you what you need to know about salaries

'Don't expect an easy ride: people see the big salaries, but that isn't always the case, particularly as you make your way up the ladder. The glamorous image that people have through watching *Ally McBeal* just isn't the case.

'As you work your way through law, legislation is constantly changing, which means that areas of the law that might have been lucrative in the past may no longer be. You never know the changes that may come along as the law changes. For example, the *Jackson Review* may well impact on litigation work, and it's unclear what changes to litigation work may be introduced.

'Similarly, the introduction of licensed conveyancers has changed the property law/conveyancing market. You no longer have to pay qualified solicitors' rates to get conveyancing work done, which has reduced the value of this kind of work. And when a recession hits, the legal market can be badly affected. I know of several firms where entire departments were made redundant.

It's getting better now, but you have to bear in mind that even full qualification is no guarantee of a job for life.'

Trainee solicitors

Until September 2011, the Law Society minimum salary for trainees working in London was £18,590, and £16,650 for those working outside of London. Many commercial firms, however, pay their trainees well above the Law Society minimum, with some firms (inside or outside of London) paying around £25,000 and some of the larger City firms paying upwards of £35,000.

Again, do your research. Many firms publish their trainee salaries on their websites, as part of their strategy to recruit the best applicants. If it is difficult to find out how much you are likely to be paid, then it is reasonable to ask a firm what the expected or current salary ranges are. You may not feel comfortable asking about this in an interview, but there should be an opportunity to ask human resources (HR) or another representative along the application process. This could be done either when making initial enquiries, or perhaps when following up on an application. If a firm is reluctant to give you an indication of salaries in writing (including by email), then you may have more luck making a phone call and asking for a 'ball park' estimate, on the understanding that this is just to help you get an idea of what to expect.

Paid to take a year out?

There was a lot of press activity in 2009 and 2010, when trainees at some larger firm were paid sums of around £10,000 just to defer their training contracts for a year. It's as well to treat this as an unexpected upside to the recession. At the time, it was cheaper for these large firms to pay their (relatively numerous) trainees a sum that was much less than their salaries would have been over the same time period than to take them on as trainees. Since then, more drastic measures have been put in place by firms to reduce their trainee intakes. In some cases trainee recruitment has been frozen altogether, until the economy stabilises. This has had a big impact on the number of training places available. The paid deferral phenomenon looks to have been a one-off – so if you're successful in getting a training contract, make sure you snap it up. Don't set your sights on getting paid to take a year out.

Qualified solicitors

A newly qualified solicitor in a regional firm or smaller commercial practice may expect to earn around £20,000 to £35,000. Starting salaries for newly qualified solicitors in larger commercial firms and those in the City will be from £35,000 to £50,000, with the larger City firms paying up to £60,000 or more. Salaries at American firms based in the UK will be higher still: some trainees are paid £40,000 or more, while their starting salaries are reputedly as high as £90,000.

There is considerable variation in salary range for more senior or experienced solicitors. Senior solicitors in commercial firms who are not yet at partner level may earn between £40,000 and £90,000 or more, depending on expertise and area of work. Partners may expect to earn from £80,000 to £100,000 or more, with anything up to seven figures being possible, particularly at the larger City and American firms.

Pupil barristers

The minimum salary for pupil barristers is £10,000 for the year of their pupillage, although some barristers' sets may pay a lot more than this, upwards of £40,000 for the year.

This does not look like a lot of money when the outlay on course fees alone – before you even set foot in chambers on the first day of your pupillage – is between £25,000 and £35,000.

Practising barristers

The salaries available to barristers range greatly according to the type of work, and level of experience. As a very rough guide, a barrister may expect to earn between £10,000 and £90,000 in the first year of qualification. For some criminal work, a junior barrister may earn as little as £50 per day.

As a barrister's level of experience grows, so their clients and cases will increase in value: a barrister with five years' experience may expect to earn between £40,000 and £200,000, while salaries for those with 10 or more years' experience might range from around £65,000 to over £1,000,000.[4]

Employed barristers will have their salaries determined by their employer according to market rates, with less variation than their self-employed counterparts. Starting salaries may be around the £25,000 mark, in line with other junior-level skilled professional roles, and may rise to more than £130,000 or more, depending on experience and sector.

3

Reality check: is it right for you?

Before we embark on the nitty gritty of qualifications and work, first let's make sure that you're ready to go, and check that nothing will stand in your way at this stage. As we've shown, working in law is extremely competitive, which is why you need to be 100% committed at the outset, to ensure you have the best possible chances of success.

Make your career path realistic

Whichever route you take into law, there will be challenges and, probably, setbacks along the way to qualification. Competition is tough, and it will be rare for an applicant to sail through the various stages of qualification, directly into a training position with no rejected applications, and on to a qualified position as a solicitor or barrister. You may not end up working in the area you had your sights set on initially. However, there is always something to be learned from a setback, which will contribute to your overall experience. In order to maintain efficiency, and maximise your chances of success (and keep the setbacks to a minimum), you must take the time to assess carefully all the options available to you, and to set and adjust your targets appropriately and realistically as you go, according to your own individual strengths and weaknesses.

Assessing where you're coming from

The way in which you enter the profession of law can have a direct effect on your experience in this profession, so read through the section below to see how this may affect you.

Law graduates

Graduates with qualifying law degrees will have spent three years studying the theory and legal principles that underpin English law. While the course content is similar to that of the Graduate Diploma in Law (GDL), a three-year law degree allows for subjects to be considered in more detail, with more time for consolidation. The availability of alternative routes to law is a relatively recent development. Many people at senior level will have come to the profession after an undergraduate law degree, and some employers also may prefer applicants who have a law degree. The logic is that it is an advantage to have had three years to absorb the subject matter, rather than a few months during a conversion degree. Most employers have no preference as to which route applicants have taken, however.

If you go straight from school to a law degree, and progress through the various stages of training with no gaps, it's possible to become a qualified lawyer in your early to mid-twenties, allowing you to gain those all-important initial years of post-qualification experience, relatively early on.

Non-law graduates

Not everyone considers law as an option when deciding which degree to do, while others may only see a legal qualification as an advantage, after graduating in a subject other than law, or after working for a while. The conversion route prevents you having to spend six years at university (three in your first subject, then three in law), then another year on a vocational course, and then a further couple of years completing the professional stages of training before you qualify.

The GDL effectively removes two years from the time required for a non-law graduate to qualify, and while it's fair to say that fitting a degree into one year can be a fairly intense experience, the fact you do not have to take another three-year degree more than makes up for any downsides.

Law degree or conversion?

There is a view that it's impossible to cover and understand adequately the principle legal foundations in one year, and that it's better to have a longer period of exposure to the subject matter of law. Conversely, there is an argument that having experience in addition to a law degree is more useful than only having expertise in one area.

An employer's view: a law firm's HR department gives you their perspective

'From an employer's perspective, it may be an advantage for an applicant to have gained knowledge or qualifications in areas other than law. Applicants who have taken the conversion route may be able to offer this, having alternative academic experience, and possibly some work experience too. An essential element of any lawyer's work is having a practical, commercial insight into their clients' work, and previous experience may give you some insight into the commercial context of the legal issues faced in a particular industry or sector. This is particularly the case in specific areas, for example technology or clinical law, if you have an IT or medical degree. On the other hand, those who have done an undergraduate law degree will have detailed knowledge of the course material, and may well have covered one or two subjects in detail, perhaps in a dissertation or project. This can be very useful, particularly if it relates to areas we work in.'

In summary, the two systems exist to cater for people in different circumstances, so it's not possible to say one route is 'better' than another – it depends entirely on the individual. The important thing is to make sure you get through the Academic Stage with the best possible grades, regardless of which route you happen to take, before going on to the Vocational Stage.

Mature applicants

If you are coming to law with experience after school or university, you can set yourself apart by drawing on that experience, and using it to your advantage, at each stage of the qualification process. All previous working experience is valuable, whichever route you take to law, and whichever area you end up working in. Of all the people who have come to law after doing something else before, very few have failed to find a legal role they are suited to, and which they find more rewarding than what they were doing before. Previous work experience gives you commercial knowledge, develops your interpersonal skills, and may give you some legal knowledge and a working context to fit it to. These things only come with experience, and should be to your advantage. Those coming to law from other backgrounds face different (and sometimes additional) challenges to those who are not, yet some of the best lawyers around are those who had previous experience before qualification.

Are your academic results sufficient?

Over half of all law degree students who graduated in 2009 did so with either a 2.i or a first. This means that at any given time, there is a huge number of people with very good academic credentials in circulation, all looking to fill the vacancies available.

The result of this is that, unfortunately, most employers in law will not consider you unless you have at least a 2.i in your first degree (law or otherwise), and sometimes at least a Commendation or equivalent at the Legal Practice Course (LPC) or the Bar Professional Training Course (BPTC; formerly the Bar Vocation Course) level. If this wasn't bad enough, many employers – especially mid- to large-sized commercial firms – will request your exam grades from GCSE to the present, including assessments and marks gained during your degree, and during any of the legal courses you have done so far.

The important thing to remember is that employers see a lot of high-quality applications. They are offering applicants a rare and desirable opportunity to progress in their chosen career, and do not owe the applicants anything. With so many people for employers to choose from, you need to make sure that your application is as strong as it possibly can be, to give an employer no reason to reject it at first glance. We will look at applications in much more detail in Chapter 7.

To make matters worse, many employers (particularly law firms) only accept applications online, and will not allow applicants to progress unless they first confirm that they have at least a 2.i degree and a minimum of 320 UCAS points at A level (or equivalent). If you don't meet these minimum requirements, the system will not permit you to go further. There are things you can do in this situation, however, and we will look at these in Chapter 7 also.

Do not be discouraged if you have one or two 'blips' on your CV. There are ways to approach this, and even to turn them to your advantage when making applications, which we will look at later.

Thinking about your finances

Financial aspects of further study

Tuition fees vary from provider to provider, and you should check the prospectus of your chosen university or college for up-to-date details of course fees for the courses you intend to enrol on.

The cost of the conversion courses ranges from around £7,500 to nearly £9,000 – and remember, you can only enrol if you have a first degree, so you will already have racked up the costs of a few years at university before you start the conversion course.

The LPC starts at around £10,000 and can go up to more than £13,000 for some London-based course providers.

The BPTC fees can be as high as an eye-watering £16,000. When you consider that each of these courses are only one year long (full-time), or two years part-time, the financial outlay on fees is significant.

The Law Society of England and Wales estimates that the overall cost of a degree and/or the Graduate Diploma in Law (GDL) and LPC, including living expenses, will be between £25,000 and £50,000. Living expenses vary greatly on a case-by-case basis, but according to the National Union of Students' figures,[5] the average cost of student living for the academic year 2010/11 was £16,613 in London, with living costs outside of London being approximately £1,090 lower.

Funding

Sources of funding that are available to all students include student loans, local authority maintenance grants (which, unlike student loans, do not have to be paid back), bank loans and professional or career development loans.

The Law Society operates two schemes that offer financial assistance towards the cost of LPC course fees for future solicitors: a Bursary Scheme, and Diversity Access Scheme. Both schemes offer financial support to individuals in a position of serious financial hardship. The Bursary Scheme is available to individuals with exceptional academic ability and potential as a solicitor, while the Diversity Access Scheme is aimed at individuals who face exceptional obstacles in qualifying as a solicitor. The application process is strict, and only a small number of awards are made relative to the number of applicants each year. More information on these, and other schemes, is available on the Law Society's junior lawyers website.[6]

You should check with your course provider if they offer any scholarships or other assistance, as many offer generous scholarships across many of the courses they provide. Overseas students may be eligible for assistance through the British Council, and there are various other scholarships set up privately to assist applicants who satisfy certain eligibility criteria.

For barristers, the four Inns of Court (Inner Temple, Middle Temple, Gray's Inn and Lincoln's Inn) offer scholarships to BPTC and GDL students. Contact each Inn for information on how and when to apply.

Financial aspects of training

The illustrations above demonstrate just how much of a financial commitment is required in order to gain the entry-level qualifications to law. Even in the event that you secure funding from a firm or chambers to cover some or even all of your course fees, it may still be a struggle to make ends meet. This is particularly the case if you are studying full-time, and are therefore unable to find paid work that adequately covers your living expenses.

It is critical that you plan each step of the qualification process carefully well before you start. You need to work out a detailed budget for exactly what the fees and other expenses will be for each qualification you are planning. This will allow you to come to a balanced conclusion as to whether you feel the amount you will have to spend will be justified at each stage, given the lack of guarantees of a job at the end of it all.

Even if your ultimate objective is to become a fully qualified solicitor or barrister, it is well worth treating each stage of qualification as its own individual unit. Each level of qualification has value in its own right, and will open doors to areas of legal work that would otherwise be shut.

Timing and managing your qualification progress

If you have yet to secure a training contract or pupillage having completed your LPC or BPTC, you may find yourself in a position where there will be a gap between the end of the LPC or BPTC, and the start of your training contract or pupillage. It will be a disappointment not to be able to progress directly from one stage to the next, but this can be turned to your advantage. A year or two in a part-qualified legal role will build on the skills gained at any level of qualification. It cannot be underestimated how important practical legal experience is particularly when approaching prospective employers for training positions – being forced to take some time between each stage of qualification may in fact be the perfect opportunity to gain this experience.

Working in a part-qualified legal role between one stage of training and the next has a number of other advantages. It will help ease the financial strain, and possibly allow you to save for the next set of course fees or living expenses. Your contact base will increase greatly through the real-life work experience your position will offer you, and a year or two of 'proper' legal work also gives you the opportunity to prove your worth to your employer over a reasonably long period of time. Even if there are no opportunities to go up to the next level with them, your colleagues will almost certainly know people in other firms, chambers or companies who may be able to offer you something. Your work experience will show you off as a credible candidate, with a good level of understanding of the areas of law that you are looking to progress into.

If you have secured a training position, it will of course be easier for you to map out the likely route that you will take to qualification, and to plan your time accordingly. Even so, you need to keep a careful eye on your finances.

> You should be aware that time limits apply to the validity of some academic and vocational qualifications. For solicitors, the Academic Stage qualifications (law degree or conversion) will be valid for seven years, while there is no expiry date for LPC. The BPTC is valid for five years after completion.

The bottom line

Is (your chosen area of) law right for you, and do you have a realistic chance of succeeding?

The only guarantee that you can bank on at the start of your legal training is that it will take a lot of effort, time and financial outlay to progress through each stage of the qualification process. This is the case regardless of which direction you want your legal career to take. When assessing your chances of success, a good starting point is to look at your Academic Stage and Vocational Stage qualifications as one set of credentials in their own right, and take the professional training (training contract or pupillage) as a separate process altogether.

The academic courses are rigorous, time consuming and costly. It is, however, entirely within your control as to how well you perform. Assuming you have the necessary credentials to get onto the courses initially, it will be down to you to manage your time, put the work in, and make sure you get the highest grades you can. You are responsible, which means your fate is not subject to factors beyond your control (except perhaps the inevitable bad exam paper!). Even if it looks unlikely, for whatever reason, that you will progress through to full qualification, your legal qualifications will always be on your CV, and will always be useful.

Training contracts and pupillages are notoriously difficult to obtain. The number of training places has always been fewer than the number of applicants to fill them, but the situation has worsened since the recession of 2009/10. There has been a decline in the number of training contracts and pupillages available but a steady increase in the number of people applying for them. Every application you make will find itself among many other equally (or more) convincing applications. You will then have to get through interviews and further assessments, where other factors will come into play and will influence your chances of success, just like any other job application.

If you assess what your options might be with the skills and experience gained at each stage of the qualification process (as well as viewing the process as a whole), you will be at an advantage over those whose only goal is becoming a fully qualified solicitor or barrister. If you set your sights on full qualification only, you are limiting your options, and greatly increasing the likelihood of disappointment. We will look at ways to deal with the challenges to be overcome during the application process in Chapter 11, but you will help yourself enormously if you plan for contingencies along the way, by thinking flexibly from the start, and with realistic expectations.

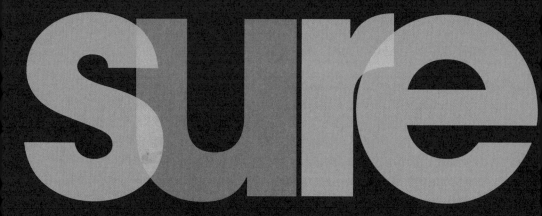

sure

To be a successful lawyer of tomorrow you need the best training available today

Our highly structured programmes are unlike others. Taught by qualified lawyers using a high proportion of face-to-face tuition and supported by cutting-edge multi-media tools, our training will hone your professional skills so that from day one you will think and act as a lawyer. That's why we find more work for future lawyers than any other law school.

If you're serious about law, qualify with the leaders in law.

The full range of courses to prepare you for your legal career:
GDL/LPC/BPTC/JD/LL.M
Flexible full-time, part-time and S-mode options available nationwide

The College of Law

believing in your future

To find out more join the Future Lawyers Network
at **college-of-law.co.uk/futurelawyers23**
or call **0800 289997**

Profile: The College of Law

Maximising your chances of success

Everyone knows that it's a competitive job market for graduates. According to the Association of Graduate Recruiters' summer 2011 survey, there are around 83 applications for every graduate level vacancy: and in law, around 65.5 applications for each training contract vacancy.

At The College of Law, we have identified '10 steps to a career in law' to help you keep one step ahead of the competition, and maximise your chances of success.

Step 1: Understand the legal market
Why do you *really* know about the legal market? Research the two main arms of the profession (solicitors and barristers) and the differences and similarities between them: different types of legal employer and the many different practice areas. Keep up to date with changes to the legal profession, ranging from the Legal Services Act to globalisation; from emerging markets to the role of technology in the delivery of legal services.

Step 2: Assess your employability
Find out what legal employers are looking for. Many legal recruiters expect a consistently good academic record: relevant work experience; commercial awareness and a range of skills and abilities such as oral and written communication, numerical and verbal reasoning, negotiating, and being a team player.

Step 3: Plan your career
You will make an easier transition to a career in law if you give yourself enough time to plan your career properly, as targeting your efforts will save you a good deal of time and effort in the long run.

As many law firms and chambers recruit two to three years in advance you need to start planning early, as you will be juggling three different 'timetables': an academic timetable; a 'work experience' timetable and a recruitment timetable.

Step 4: Research employers
Legal recruiters tell us that the single biggest reason that applications fail is because the candidate has failed to target properly. So to 'market' yourself to a recruiter, you must thoroughly research them to understand what the organisation is about, and what they're looking for in their recruits.

Step 5: Gain experience and make contact
Employers want to see that you are committed to a career in law, and have a real understanding of what that might mean. The best way to demonstrate it is by securing legal work experience, and most students now start law school with some work experience under their belt.

If you're off to the Bar, then you'll need to arrange a mini-pupillage or two. If you are intending to be a solicitor, many of the larger firms are increasingly treating their work experience schemes as an integral part of the recruitment process, and competition for formal 'vacation schemes' is fierce.

Step 6: Draft a legal-specific CV and covering letter
Make sure that you *target* your CV to each individual employer you are applying to (this is where your research in Step 4 comes in). Identify what the employer wants, and think about how your unique blend of skills and experience meets those requirements. While your CV must be professional, easy to read, and no more than two sides long, remember that style is no substitute for content, which is where Step 5 is essential.

Step 7: Make convincing applications
As with CVs, targeting each answer to the particular recruiter is key: it's easy to spot 'generic' applications and it doesn't impress! A good application form can take many hours to complete, and it is best to start early, leave the form, and come back to it with fresh eyes. Don't leave your application to the last minute before submitting though: employers have been known to bring forward a closing date if they are inundated with applications – and do keep a copy!

Step 8: Prepare for interview
The old adage 'failing to prepare is preparing to fail' should be your motto here. As a basic checklist you should: re-read your application form/CV and anticipate likely questions; go back over your research (student directories, legal press online, and the website); and prepare a few questions to ask the employer. If you are able to access a careers service, book an appointment for a mock interview.

Step 9: Prepare for assessment centres
Some firms (usually the larger ones) hold 'assessment centres'. You will be given details of what to expect, but they usually consist of an interview, a presentation and a range of tests and activities, such as an 'in-tray' exercise, a group exercise, situational judgement tests or psychometric tests looking at your verbal or numerical reasoning. This may sound daunting, but you can practise many of these tests online; and good old common sense will stand you in good stead.

Step 10: Manage your career
Finally, not only should you *plan* your career, you should also actively *manage* your career. Constantly reassess the early decisions and career plan you made – as you progress through your research and the recruitment process you will probably define and re-define your plan many times. In a competitive market you may need to be pro-active and flexible, and adjust your plan accordingly.

Maximise your chances – join the Future Lawyers Network

www.college-of-law.co.uk/futurelawyers23

PART 2
How the legal world works

4

Areas of law

Every lawyer in England and Wales begins by mastering the seven foundation subjects, which together make up the basis of English law. These are the most fundamental aspects of English law, and while they may appear relatively abstract and unrelated, they all link to each other in different ways, and can appear together in any number of different contexts. They are all equally important at the start, even if some of them may appear to have no possible bearing on your future career, or may seem particularly obscure. One or other of these legal areas will apply to virtually every legal situation. As such, the foundation areas crop up time and again in your career, no matter which direction you take. We will look at how these areas of law interact with each other, and relate to particular areas of legal work, later in the chapter.

The foundation subjects are:

- contract law

- constitutional and administrative law

- criminal law

- equity and trusts

- European Union law

- land law

- tort law.

They are taught as separate subjects on all law degree or conversion courses. As your career progresses you will see how they crossover, but for now, here is a summary of what each foundation subject is all about. It is important to note that there are differences between the legal systems of England and Wales, and the systems of the other countries that make up the UK: Scotland and Northern Ireland. While there is a good deal of crossover between the systems, this book deals with qualification under the law of England and Wales.

Contract law

Contract law deals with the principles that govern agreements between parties that can be legally enforced. Contracts are formed all the time – every time you buy something or use most kinds of service, you will have entered a formal contact. Contract law therefore affects almost every aspect of our lives, in one way or another. Contracts come about in many ways (for example, a contract does not have to be in writing), and certain elements need to be present before a legally enforceable contract can be said to exist.

In addition to understanding the requirements for forming a contract, the extent to which a contract can be limited or extended in scope is also important: Can a party exempt certain things from being included in a contract? What if this might be considered unfair to the other party to the same contract? The study of contract law also looks at how the courts will analyse points of law where disputes have arisen between parties, and the courts' ability to step in to resolve the dispute through remedies for breach of contract.

Constitutional and administrative law

Constitutional law is the foundation for allowing society to be legitimately governed. You will look at the background and sources of the English constitutional system as it exists today, as well as the main constitutional concepts:

- the rule of law (the concept that no person is above the law)

- separation of powers (the status of government being separate from the monarchy, both of which are in turn separate from the judiciary)

- parliamentary sovereignty (where the decisions of Parliament are the supreme legal authority).

Administrative law takes the principles of constitutional government, and applies them to society. This includes the rights of individual citizens within the state apparatus, and covers human rights, freedom of association and assembly, freedom of expression and privacy. Police powers over the citizen make up an important part of this area of law, including issues such as police powers of arrest, detention, and search, and citizens' rights granted under statute, such as the Criminal Justice and Police Act 2001.

Judicial review is another key element of administrative law. This is the process available to citizens to challenge the validity of a decision made by a public body (perhaps a government department, local council or other state institution) through the courts. As the judiciary is independent of government, judges are in a position to impose remedies where necessary. Specific criteria apply in challenging a decision through the judicial review process, which are looked at by reference to cases and decisions made over the years.

Criminal law

Criminal law is the subject of news headlines, courtroom dramas and crime documentaries, but what is 'crime'? This area of law concentrates on the measures in place to control society through an analysis of the key principles that make up 'criminal law', and a review of certain offences and their consequences. The subject matter is gritty and often uncomfortable, but fundamental questions are raised as to what should be considered a 'crime', and as to the morality of society's right to impose punishment on its own members.

The elements required to constitute a crime are the building blocks of criminal law. These start with the basic requirement for there to be a combination of 'guilty act' or *actus reus*, and 'guilty mind' or *mens rea* on the part of the offender. Elements of the most common offences against the person and against property are also covered: non-sexual offences such as wounding or murder, sexual offences such as rape, theft, deception and criminal damage.

Next, what happens when a crime has been committed, and the person who committed the crime has been identified? Treatment of the offender is considered, and includes offenders' liability, their capacity or incapacity to commit the offence, how the law treats attempted crime, and the defences available to those accused of certain offences.

Equity and trusts law

Equity is, very broadly, a system of rights and remedies that exists alongside other areas of law. The purpose of equity is to serve interests of justice and fairness, in cases where other legal remedies have not been able to do so adequately. Equitable remedies can be available in situations that relate to ownership of property, and are particularly important in the creation and implementation of trusts.

This may at first seem to be a technical and obscure area of law, but in fact it is applied in all kinds of day-to-day situations: gifts, charities, pensions, investments and insurance are all areas that fall within the scope of the law of equity and trusts, and which play a vital role in most people's everyday lives.

European Union law

There are 27 member states in the European Union, all of which are governed by one unifying system of laws to encourage and maintain certain rights and freedoms for the wider benefit of all Member States. This system shapes Member States' interaction with their neighbouring territories, particularly regarding trade and commerce. European Union law covers the historical development of the European Union and its institutions, and how European law is implemented in the national courts of Member States.

The key areas of European law considered in detail on the course are:

- competition law

- free movement of goods and workers

- freedom of establishment of businesses and services

- freedom from discrimination.

Land law

Land law is considered by many law students to be particularly useful in its practical application in day-to-day life. Whether you are buying or selling a flat or house, renting, or living at home, knowledge of land law is an extremely useful tool in understanding property ownership, in terms of what you may or may not do with property, and how property may be affected by the rights of others.

The course does not deal with the technical or practical aspects of conveyancing. This is practical legal work usually done by solicitors, and is therefore covered on the solicitors' Legal Practice Course (see Chapter 7).

Land law as a foundation subject deals with the main legal concepts governing the ownership and use of land:

- registered and unregistered land

- freehold and leasehold

- obligations of landlord and tenant

- obligations under leasehold covenants

- trusts over land, licences, and third-party rights in land (mortgages and charges, easements and freehold covenants).

Law of tort

The law of tort is used to impose liability and remedies for a broad range of acts resulting in 'harm' to related parties, but which may not be covered by liability in contract, or other areas of law. Tort is a strand of law that has developed through the courts rather than through legislation and statute. As a result, much of the material covered is based in case law, requiring analysis of factual and legal points that have arisen and been decided by the courts in all kinds of contexts.

A fundamental area of tort law is the concept of negligence, and the existence of a duty of care between neighbouring parties. This is a relatively recent legal concept, as industrial progress in the nineteenth century increased cases of death and injury to members of society. With this came a need to develop the law to protect society by balancing the benefits of industrial and economic progress with the risk of harm or damage to people and property. As a result, case law developed and consolidated into the legal framework of tort law, to allow cases in which harm had been suffered to be decided with some consistency.

Various aspects of negligence are considered, including duty of care and breach of duty, economic loss, psychiatric illness, and the liability of employers and occupiers of premises. Negligence is probably the broadest area of tort, while trespass, defamation, nuisance and aspects of consumer protection also fall within it. Tort matters are usually contentious in nature, involving a claimant and defendant, so the various defences and remedies available are also looked at.

How legal work relates to what you are taught

Before we get into the specifics of qualification, it is worth having a look now at how the legal theory generally relates to legal practice. A good way to explain the relationships between what you learn at the Academic and Vocational stages of qualification, and how this relates to legal work, is to look at some example scenarios.

These scenarios are taken from real-life situations, and while they only provide a small snapshot of the kinds of legal problems that may occur in practice, they are a useful illustration of how some of the different areas of law interact, and come into play in different situations. These are the kinds of issues you will come across as you work in any legal environment, and are an indication not only of what to expect in legal practice, but also perhaps in interviews or applications.

Scenario 1

A building company finishes a large development for a client several months later than the agreed date, and the work is dangerously substandard.

Some of the legal issues involved are listed below.

- Contract law: What were the terms of the agreement in place between the company and the client? This will define what was agreed, and the options available to both parties.

- Property law: Aspects of property and construction law will come into play in analysing the extent to which the finished project is, or is not, fit for purpose.

- Tort: If the poorly completed work is dangerous, might the building company be liable to anyone who might be injured as a result of its failure to complete the work adequately?

- Litigation and strategy: There will need to be careful consideration of the strategy to take, depending on which side you are advising. Is settlement an option? Can the work be redone or remedied in some way? Would financial compensation be available? Would it be an adequate remedy for the problem? What if the client had contractual obligations of its own to sell or rent the development to a third party, but has been unable to do so?

Scenario 2

An employee is sacked from their job for alleging that his manager's son, also an employee had been stealing money from the company.

Some of the legal issues involved are listed below.

- Criminal law: There are allegations of theft – how might these be pursued? By whom? What sort of problems are likely to be faced if a criminal investigation takes place?

- Contract law: The employee and employer are both bound by the terms of the contract of employment – what does that contract say?

- Employment law: Eligibility to pursue a legal claim through the employment tribunals is subject to criteria which would need to be satisfied. The claims and remedies available are prescribed by employment legislation, which in turn is shaped by European and Constitutional legal principles. This might include 'whistleblowing': does the possibility that the employee is acting in the public interest help him in any way?

- Litigation and strategy: Who are you acting for? The employee, the manager, the son, the company? Should the employee claim against the employer by litigation in an employment tribunal? How much money is the claim worth? Are there any other ways to resolve the situation? What would be the benefits and downsides to each option? Might another route to settlement be a better option?

Scenario 3

A company director wants to merge his company with another.

In a situation like this, some of the legal issues that would be involved are listed below.

- Property law: Does either company own or lease premises? How will ownership be allocated following the merger? Will the current premises still be required? Will any property need to be sold, bought or leased?

- Employment law: Are staff employed by either company? How may their positions be affected by the merger? What are the employees' rights, and the employer's obligations in a situation like this?

- Company and corporate law: How would the shareholdings be allocated, to ensure control of each company is maintained as agreed between the parties? What documentation needs to be prepared? What other administrative work or registrations need to be done? What is the proposed timescale for the merger? Will this impact on how the process is to be managed by the legal teams involved?

- EU and international law: What if the other company is based outside of the UK, perhaps in the EU? If both companies operate in the same sector, might there be competition issues if both were to merge?

Scenario 4

A couple decide that they want to buy a flat occupied until recently by an elderly resident, who has since died. They would need to consider the following legal questions.

- Probate and administration of estates: Who now owns the property? If it was the resident, did she have a will in place? Have executors been appointed, and probate granted? Are they in a position to sell the property?

- Property law: Is the flat freehold or leasehold? Are any parts of the property shared with anyone else? Are there any restrictions on how they might use the flat? How will their ownership of the flat be shared, once they take possession of it? Do the couple require a mortgage? If so, will it be in one of their names, or both? What are the implications of this?

- Contract and tort: What if the couple moves in, and find that the surveyor they used did not pick up on some important defects to the flat, which will cost a lot of money to remedy? What provisions are in their contract with the surveyor? Might the surveyor have worked negligently?

- Litigation and strategy: As with some of the other scenarios, the couple would need advice on which options are available to them if a dispute arose, and if they wished to be compensated for any losses incurred, as would other parties involved in the sale.

Contentious or non-contentious?

In any of these scenarios, a solicitor may be acting for either party. This would be the case for the transactional, non-contentious arrangements, or if a dispute were to occur. If a dispute has arisen, input from a barrister may be required to manage the litigation or dispute resolution process. If this was to happen, the legal team will need to consider additional points.

Will it be necessary to prepare for a court or tribunal hearing? The pros and cons of this approach will need to be weighed up, as court preparation and procedures are time consuming and expensive.

Is it likely that a settlement might be reached? This is always an option, and is often better than going all the way to court. If so, which dispute resolution method might be best? Mediation? Arbitration? There are different rules and procedures for each, which will need to be considered in light of the facts of the case, and explained to the client to help them decide upon the best strategy.

We will look at this in more detail in Chapter 5.

Summary

You can see that while the foundations of law can be viewed as separate entities in theory, when it comes to real-life legal problems, there will almost always be several areas of law involved, each overlapping with the other, depending on the nature of the matter. Certain areas may appear together frequently, and may be relatively straightforward to deal with. Other situations may place more rarely seen areas of law together, which may pose a challenge to finding an adequate solution. This may require more specialist input, from a specialist lawyer, barrister, or perhaps patent attorney, or other adviser operating in a particular area of law. Keep these different disciplines and areas in mind as you go through your training, as opportunities within them may expand your target area for potential career options.

And where do you fit into all this as a working lawyer? We look at this in more detail in the next chapter.

5

Legal roles and lawyers' areas of practice

The legal profession is generally divided into two parts: solicitors and barristers. While solicitors and barristers both start off studying the same foundation subjects at the Academic Stage, they are each required to do different vocational courses (the LPC and BPTC), and will go on to do entirely different professional training (solicitors' training contracts, and barristers' pupillages). So, what are the differences between the two professions?

Solicitors

A solicitor is anyone who has gone through one of the recognised routes to qualification, and who is, or has been, in possession of a Solicitors Regulation Authority (SRA) practising certificate. Once the various stages of training are all complete, a solicitor must apply to have his or her name entered on the SRA roll of solicitors, and apply for their first practising certificate in order to become qualified and eligible to practise as a solicitor.

The solicitor's role is to work directly with the client, taking their instructions, advising the client on legal aspects to a matter, and managing certain administrative aspects of matters as they progress. Importantly, solicitors are in a position to act on their client's behalf, as an attorney, which a barrister is not. A solicitor will be responsible for reviewing and drafting legal documentation (contracts, deeds, witness statements, pleadings, etc.), preparing evidence, and liaising with barristers where necessary, in disputes or litigation proceedings.

Private practice and in-house

Solicitors will either be employed in private practice law firms, or in-house in other organisations. Those working in private practice will often develop expertise in certain areas of law, or certain areas of commercial or other activity, and will be particularly familiar with the kinds of legal problems that occur in those contexts.

Solicitors working in-house can be required to work on any legal issue that their employer may come into contact with. Issues may concern the core business or activity of the organisation, or any number of other legal problems, perhaps in employment, dealing with a lease of premises, corporate matters such as finance arrangements, or a company merger or acquisition. No solicitor is expected to know all there is to know about such a wide array of law, so in-house solicitors frequently use the services of private practice lawyers to deal with issues requiring specialist input. If a legal issue is particularly complex, obscure or unusual, a private practice solicitor may in turn consult a barrister for additional expert advice, as necessary.

Contentious and non-contentious work

Solicitors' work will generally be contentious or non-contentious in nature, and these categories are often used to describe the nature of any matter a solicitor is working on.

Contentious work

Contentious work is concerned with prevention and resolution of legal disputes. Whenever something goes wrong with a legal arrangement between any parties, a contentious situation arises. There are several methods available to resolve disputes other than going to court, and the parties will generally want to avoid the cost, stress and potential negative publicity of going all the way to formal court litigation. However, this will be the final option if all other routes to resolution fail. The solicitor's job is to give the best advice to their client on the legal issues, and to set out the options available to reach an appropriate resolution of the dispute.

Contentious work centres on the legal issues behind a case, analysing the facts in detail to ascertain the client's position, and analysing the opposing party's position to assess the merits of both sides' arguments. Excellent working knowledge of the law, and the ability to apply the law to the facts of a contentious matter are essential. Negotiation skills are also crucial when working with the opposition's legal representatives. The same goes for the skills involved in dealing with clients, who may be under considerable stress as a result of being caught up in a legal dispute.

Since the processes of dispute resolution are formal and prescribed, detailed knowledge of the various procedures is also required, to formulate the best strategy for a given matter, and guide a case through to a successful conclusion.

In the past, solicitors were obliged to use a barrister for advocacy in cases other than relatively minor criminal cases in the magistrates' courts, and lower value or less complex civil cases in county courts. While the solicitors' and barristers' professions remain as two distinct areas of practice, solicitors are now able to become 'solicitor advocates', allowing them to represent clients directly in any court or tribunal, without incurring the additional expense of hiring a barrister. Training is available for solicitors wishing to qualify as solicitor advocates – see Chapter 10 for more details.

Non-contentious work

Non-contentious work is characterised by advising on aspects of legal arrangements being put in place between parties, to ensure legal and other regulatory compliance. The solicitor's role is to ensure that legal matters are managed properly, and agreements are constructed in such a way that if a dispute was to arise, appropriate protection for the client has been factored into the agreement. In some ways, non-contentious legal work can be viewed as 'prevention', while contentious work and dispute resolution are more akin to a 'cure'.

Non-contentious work involves managing administrative aspects of matters, such as checking through all necessary paperwork, maintaining documentation, or ensuring that registrations and forms are filed correctly and on time. This may not always require detailed legal knowledge, but requires a solicitor's input to ensure that all legal obligations are covered, and are understood by the client.

Solicitors are often required to negotiate on the client's behalf, to ensure that the client receives the best possible terms. While no formal legal dispute may have occurred, it is a myth that complex, challenging and sometimes heated negotiations only occur in the context of disputes and litigation. The stakes can be high for both parties to a commercial deal or any other legal agreement, and there can sometimes be very little difference in pressure and excitement between negotiations in a non-contentious or contentious context.

Barristers

A barrister is an independent lawyer specialising in advocacy, litigation, and giving expert, objective advice on specific areas of law. They are most often engaged in contentious matters, generally leaving non-contentious legal work to solicitors. They usually take instructions from solicitors rather than from clients directly, leaving the administrative side of matters and direct client contact for the solicitors to manage.

The barrister's profession has a long history, and has developed into the expert profession it is today after being shaped by developments to the courts system, and litigation practice in general, over several hundred years. This is sometimes reflected in the language used within it, and in the traditions that continue to be observed. For example, a barrister can only call him or herself a 'barrister' if they have been 'called to the Bar' by an Inn of Court, meaning that they have completed the Academic Stage of legal training (a law degree or conversion course), are a member of a particular Inn and, from September 2010, have completed pupillage. 'Bar' is the original word used collectively to describe all qualified barristers, while the 'Inns of Court' were originally private buildings where lawyers would live and work. Today, the Inns are professional organisations which regulate the barristers' profession, and provide educational, research and other essential resources. Barristers are referred to as 'counsel', and this term is used much more commonly than the word 'barrister' in day-to-day legal business.

Qualified barristers are generally self-employed, but often share offices, administration teams and other services in 'chambers' with other barristers specialising in compatible areas of law. Barristers working from chambers are referred to as 'tenants', and may only become tenants after completing a pupillage. Within chambers, senior barristers often use the services of more junior tenant barristers or pupil barristers to assist on larger matters, but as barristers working from chambers are self-employed, the decision of who works with who will be made according to the skills and experience of individuals. There is nothing to stop barristers working with colleagues from other chambers, if this would be best for a particular matter.

Court appearances are probably the best known, and perhaps highest profile aspect of a barrister's work. This involves putting submissions to the judge, guiding the judge and, where applicable, the jury, through evidence and legal points, and responding to the opposing counsel's argument. The objective is of course to make as persuasive a case as possible, and to obtain a ruling in the barrister's client's favour.

Barristers are involved in a number of other areas, as well as appearing 'on their feet' in court. Some of these are described below.

Written opinions

Solicitors may require expert advice on a particular legal point. Advice is usually given in writing, and is referred to as 'counsel's opinion'. Counsel's opinion may be sought in a contentious matter, for advice on litigation strategy, or how the law might be interpreted in the context of the facts of a particular matter. Barristers may also be consulted in non-contentious matters, perhaps to clarify how particular areas of law may affect a commercial transaction, or when complex or unusual facts make interpretation of the law particularly difficult.

Conferences

When a barrister meets with the solicitor who has instructed him or her perhaps also with the solicitor's client, the meeting is referred to as a 'conference'. The solicitor will usually provide the barrister with the background materials to the matter under discussion, and in conference, the barrister will go through the various issues with the solicitor, and will advise on relevant legal or procedural points. It is generally the case that prior to litigation, one or two conferences with counsel will be needed. If a case goes to trial, there is often ongoing consultation with counsel, before, during and after the hearing.

Negotiation

When counsel has been instructed by each party to a dispute, it will frequently be appropriate for them to negotiate terms to reach a possible settlement. This might be the case when a matter reaches trial, if it becomes evident that settlement might be better for both parties, instead of continuing the trial. This would avoid the risk of an unpredictable decision, which may have a negative impact on both sides.

Drafting documentation

Barristers are often instructed to draft documents in the context of litigation, such as particulars of claim, defence, applications and other court documents. There is sometimes no formal requirement for a barrister to draft these documents, but their input may save time, and have other advantages in terms of efficient case management.

Legal research

The law is constantly changing as new legislation is brought in, and as cases are decided, which affects all areas of legal practice. Barristers keep fully up to date with developments in the law affecting their areas of expertise through regular legal research. Junior barristers gain valuable experience early on in their careers through assisting more senior counsel with legal research in complex areas of law, while also researching the law on matters they are handling themselves.

Employed barristers

In a similar way to solicitors, barristers can work in-house for specific organisations, including law firms, and around 20% of qualified barristers work in employed practice. A barrister working in-house will be referred to as an 'employed barrister' rather than a 'practising barrister'. Historically, once a barrister had completed the Bar Vocational Course, and been called to the Bar, they could become employed barristers right away, without completing a pupillage under a practising barrister. If not employed or taking up tenancy, the term 'non-practising barrister' was used to describe their status, but this is no longer the case. The recent introduction of the

Bar Professional Training Course (BPTC), and revised professional regulations, mean that the term 'barrister' is now reserved only for those who have gone through all stages of training, including pupillage.

Barristers' practice areas

Barristers work in all areas of the law, and while there is considerable crossover, their practice areas are usually divided into the following categories, with most barristers specialising in perhaps two or three areas:

- criminal law

- commercial law and chancery

- common law

- employment law

- family law

- personal injury and clinical negligence

- constitutional and administrative law

- European law.

The BPTC is structured according to these areas, so take a look at Chapter 7 to get a good idea of how the practice areas and BPTC course materials relate to each other.

Differences between a solicitor and a barrister

There are a number of characteristics that separate solicitors and barristers, once they have achieved their respective qualifications. We mentioned earlier that in most cases, barristers are not instructed by clients directly, and do not act as a client's attorney. They take instructions from solicitors, and will generally deal only through the solicitor.

Here are some other main differences between the two professions.

- The solicitor is responsible for paying the barrister's fees, although fees will be passed on by the solicitor to the client.

- On qualification, a barrister is permitted to conduct advocacy in all courts and tribunals. A solicitor's qualification does not permit this, in itself. In order to conduct advocacy in higher courts (known as 'higher rights of audience'), a solicitor is required to obtain additional qualifications.

- Barristers are experts in dispute resolution, and specialise in the practical conduct of litigation in and out of court. A solicitor will be required to ensure the barrister has all the factual and other details from the client, allowing the barrister to focus on the strategy and procedure of litigation, as well as the courtroom advocacy. Not all solicitors deal with litigation and dispute resolution.

- As we have seen, barristers work independently, grouping together to share certain offices in 'chambers', and to offer a range of related legal services as a 'set'. Solicitors may work alone as sole practitioners, but more frequently work in partnerships or as employees in firms, with shared responsibilities.

- Another difference between solicitors and barristers is how they are dressed for work in court: barristers are quite distinctive in wigs and gowns, while solicitors will usually wear a conventional suit (although solicitor advocates now have their own equivalent formal dress to barristers).

Other legal roles, in addition to solicitors and barristers

Many people come to law intending to qualify as a solicitor or barrister, but find that it is not possible to progress directly from one stage of qualification to the next. Others come to law intending to work in a particular area from the start, without intending to tick off all the various stages required for full qualification as a solicitor or barrister.

For most solicitors' and barristers' training positions, applications can only be submitted once a year. It is common therefore for people who have not yet secured a training contract or pupillage by the time they finish their LPC or BPTC, to fill a year or two with legal work which builds their experience, and puts the qualifications they have to good use. Luckily, the law is such a huge area that there are always positions to be filled by part-qualified lawyers. For those with no formal legal training, there are opportunities to gain experience and qualifications while working (see Chapter 7).

Below are some of the more common part-qualified and specialist roles, all of which can offer excellent insight into legal practice, helping you gain valuable points for your CV, or which can offer plenty of career options in themselves.

Part-qualified roles

Paralegal or legal assistant

Paralegal work is usually either offered through private practice solicitors firms, or in-house in the legal department of other organisations. While no formal qualifications are needed to work as a paralegal, most firms will usually prefer applicants with at least a law degree or conversion degree, and usually an LPC or Bar Vocation Course (BVC)/BPTC qualification too.

The majority of the work is spent assisting with practical aspects of matters being managed by more senior lawyers, potentially in any area of law. A paralegal working in litigation will manage the production and administration of case documents and bundles (sets of formal documents and files used in litigation). They will liaise with court and tribunal staff, barristers and their clerks on important administrative matters, and might assist with drafting and proofreading particulars of claim, witness statements and other court documents. Paralegal work in a non-contentious capacity might involve anything from drafting contracts or other agreements, assisting with legal research, taking and preparing notes in client meetings, writing articles, or dealing with forms or registrations for Companies House or the Land Registry.

Paralegal work offers excellent hands-on experience, and insight into day-to-day legal work. It is often seen as a vital bridge between academic legal study, and practical legal work, and can be the best way to get an idea of what you might experience as your legal career progresses. Most legal employers see experience gained as a paralegal or legal assistant as a very positive attribute on a CV. Working as a paralegal can introduce you to the firm or chambers you may wish to apply to, making you a 'known quantity' and possibly putting you at the top of the list for future positions that may come up, including training contracts or pupillages. This experience also broadens your range of subject matter to draw from in interviews and applications. We will look at how this experience can be put to use in getting a training position in Chapter 11.

Profile: National Association of Licensed Paralegals

NALP

A leading awarding organisation in the legal sector

The National Association of Licensed Paralegals (NALP), established in 1987, is the leading professional body for qualified legal practitioners – namely paralegals – whose skills are invaluable to many workplaces, such as law firms and the public sector, including the NHS.

The NALP is a government-approved awarding body regulated by Ofqual, the national qualification standards organisation, and is committed to providing students with a structured, career-based alternative into law practice.

The NALP is passionately committed to professional development and offers an inclusive career path accessible to paralegals seeking qualifications at every level – from an entry-level diploma to a postgraduate diploma and further specialist awards.

International

Interest in the NALP is growing not only in the UK but also overseas, with members and students spread across many countries, from the Cayman Islands to Japan.

Recognised qualifications

The NALP's Level 4 Diploma in Paralegal Studies is an ideal course to set students on the path to a successful career. Level 4 modules reflect the NALP's belief that it is vital for all paralegals to have a solid grounding in the English legal system and other substantive areas of law, together with knowledge of procedural law. This nationally recognised course is suitable for students who have completed their A levels.

The course can be studied by class attendance or by home learning, with flexible payment options. For less than half of a year's current university tuition fees, students can attain a recognised qualification that will launch them into a legal career.

Paralegals who pass this course become associate members of the NALP and can use the letters 'A.PLL' after their name.

To find out more about us, visit our website on www.nationalparalegals.co.uk

Testimonials

> 'The paralegal skills course I attended was so inspiring, mixed with the overall knowledge and practical ease of delivery that I made the decision to retain my life and my future for the better. The organisation is supportive, creative, diverse. I am

> *positive about my future as the NALP assists and encourages non-legal working individuals such as myself.'*

Deena Stephens, an NALP qualified paralegal

> *'It takes commitment and determination to get through, but it's worth it in the end. I studied as a distance learner because of my location. I would recommend the course to others, mainly because you don't have to be seated in a classroom to obtain this qualification.'*

Tia Whittaker, a litigation clerk and the first student from the Cayman Islands to gain the Higher Certificate (now called Level 4 Diploma in Paralegal Studies).

Legal executives

Legal executives work in many areas of law, frequently specialising in property matters and conveyancing, personal injury work, criminal and civil litigation, local authority work, corporate and commercial law, or the administrative side of legal practice.

Once certain qualifications are obtained from the Institute of Legal Executives (through a combination of legal work experience and exams – see Chapter 7), a legal executive is permitted to work in the areas of law covered by their qualification, allowing them to build up considerable expertise. They can do similar work to solicitors, often managing their own cases and matters, and may become leaders in their field. In private practice, legal executives may be fee earners, having their time billed to clients, thereby directly generating income for the firm. The main difference between a legal executive and a fully qualified solicitor (or barrister) is that they will not have gained the full range of experience required for formal qualification. This means there will be areas on which they will not be qualified to advise or work, or for which they or their employers might not be insured. In practice, a legal executive may do all the preparatory and practical work on a particular matter, with the work being reviewed and signed off by a partner, or other qualified lawyer. Otherwise, there can sometimes be little to differentiate an experienced legal executive from other fully qualified lawyers.

Case study

Katherine Pymont worked as a paralegal, and is now a trainee solicitor in the London firm Kingsley Napley

After getting very good grades on the GDL and LPC, my first legal role was as a legal assistant in the firm's criminal and regulatory department (now regulatory and professional discipline), assisting with regulatory prosecution work. This included consideration of papers received on instruction from clients, meeting with and taking statements from witnesses, preparing witness statements, drafting correspondence and liaising with witnesses and with the client. The work was challenging, interesting and varied, and no two days were the same.

One of the best things about working as a legal assistant at Kingsley Napley was the level of responsibility that I was given. I was expected to run my own case load, with my opinion being valued by the lawyer responsible for each case. The experience provided invaluable experience and I have recently started a training contract with the firm. I am sure that my time as a legal assistant contributed to securing my training contract

Daniel Turnbull, partner at City firm Stewarts Law LLP explains how paralegal work is valued, and helps with securing a training position:

'At my firm we advertise internally for training contracts, and trainees are often recruited from our team of paralegals. We have a unique approach in that we have approximately one paralegal per fee earner. This means there is usually quite a number of paralegals in our firm, many of whom are looking for training contracts. This is advantageous both for the firm, and for the staff themselves, and the system works well. The paralegals are very motivated, and they know that if they work well they will be rewarded. If they don't get a training contract on the first attempt, they can take a second or third opportunity to get there. I look around my office, and see paralegals who've been there two or even three years. All of them have been able to gain valuable experience in a City law firm, which will put them in very good stead for the future, whether they end up training and qualifying with us, or elsewhere.'

Specialist legal roles

Patent and trade mark attorney

Patent agents are members of the Chartered Institute of Patent Attorneys who specialise in patent law. They advise clients as to whether rights can be obtained and protected in relation to an invention, and if so, what the procedures will be, as well as advising on challenging or enforcing rights already in place. The technical and industrial nature of patent work is such that many employers view a science degree or other industrial experience as a distinct advantage, and since many registration systems are located outside the UK, a working knowledge of French, German or other languages can be useful.

Trade mark attorneys are members of the Institute of Trade Mark Attorneys, and specialise in the law protecting the identity of a product or service. A trade mark creates brand recognition and public confidence that the trade marked item is what it claims to be, and allows investment to be made in marketing the item. Trade marks are protected through a formal process, which gives the owner of the mark certain rights to prevent the mark being copied. Trade mark attorneys advise on all aspects of trade mark law, licensing of marks for use by parties other than the registrant, and on challenging or resisting a challenge to a registration, or potentially infringing use of a mark.

Licensed conveyancer

A licensed conveyancer is a lawyer with specific qualifications relating to property law, and who is entitled to act for a client when purchasing, selling or remortgaging property. Some licensed conveyancers are also qualified to provide probate services, as sale of property is a common element in dealing with a deceased person's estate. Several routes to qualification are available, which makes this area popular with people from any background. Once licensed, a conveyancer may work for an employer, either in private legal practice or in-house, or they may set up their own conveyancing practice. Licensing, regulation, education and monitoring of the profession are provided through the Council for Licensed Conveyancers.

Practice development lawyer/professional support lawyer

Practice development or support lawyers (PDLs or PSLs) often work in private practice law firms, and give assistance to the firm, or departments within in the firm, in a number of areas. These usually include researching and monitoring important developments in the law, managing legal training and professional development, writing articles and training materials, and assisting in practice management and business development. PDLs are usually qualified solicitors or barristers, but do not generally work on fee-earning matters, allowing them to focus on being expert consultants within their departments or firms, effectively acting as 'lawyers' lawyers'.

Costs lawyer

Costs incurred in contentious legal matters can be very significant, and in more complex cases, can be incurred over a long period of time. Costs often make up a critical part of the terms of any legal settlement, and may be disputed after the substantive legal claims have been decided in a case. The general rule in litigation is that the loser of a claim pays the winner's costs, but in practice it is very unlikely that the winner will recover 100% of their costs from the loser, particularly if costs are disputed.

Costs lawyers are members of the Association of Costs Lawyers, and specialise in dealing with aspects of legal costs and cost-related litigation. They may be required to draft a detailed bill of costs incurred during a case, for review if disputed by the paying party. Fees due to a solicitor by a client may also be subject to dispute, and a costs lawyer may advise either party on legal and procedural aspects to recovery or payment of fees. Costs lawyers also advise on budget management, particularly when litigation or dispute resolution procedures are likely to be lengthy and expensive. The work of a costs lawyer is a unique combination of litigation practice and procedure, financial acumen and numeracy that can play as important a part in proceedings as that of a solicitor or barrister.

Notary

Notaries are qualified lawyers providing specialist services of authenticating and certifying documentation, usually for use abroad, and often in the context of diplomatic or immigration work. Advances in technology mean that many parts of the world do not require documentation to be officially certified, so the work is relatively specialised, with notaries often requiring knowledge of specific laws in specific territories, in order to ensure the correct procedure is followed. Notaries may also offer general legal services similar to solicitors, with the exception of litigation work, and are governed by similar rules of professional conduct to solicitors.

Legal support roles

It is rare for any legal practice to operate without the assistance of support staff, including librarians, legal secretaries and human resources managers, many of whom hold legal qualifications as well as vocational qualifications relevant to their day-to-day role. More information on some of these roles is set out in Chapter 12.

How law firms and legal practices work

We have had a look at some of the key legal roles, so how do they work in practice? Solicitors and barristers work in different ways, so it is worth looking at each in turn.

Solicitors

As we have seen, solicitors usually work in partnerships, or 'firms'. You will come across many different law firms of all shapes and sizes as your career progresses, but they can generally be broken down into a few main categories: full service firms, high-street firms, and niche firms.

Full service solicitors firms

Full service law firms are divided into departments, each of which will deal with specific areas. There will be some crossover of work between the departments and teams of specialists, but the majority of work will be specific to each department. A large law firm may be divided into the following departments:

- antitrust/competition law

- banking/finance/investments

- corporate

- employment

- insurance

- intellectual property

- litigation

- personal injury

- real estate/property/construction

- regulatory law

- tax

- technology, media and telecommunications.

International firms, and the large- or medium-sized City-based firms, are often (but not always) structured this way, to reflect the nature of the work they tend to focus on.

High-street firms

High-street firms are usually much smaller than full service firms, and may focus less on areas of commercial law, and more on matters relating to individuals. There is sometimes more crossover of work between departments, with individual lawyers taking on a broader range of matters. High-street firms may offer some commercial services to local businesses, but all will specialise in personal, day-to-day legal issues that affect people, such as buying and selling property, dealing with disputes, writing wills, planning trusts and tax, advising on family or divorce law and occasionally taking on criminal cases.

Niche firms

Specialist, 'niche' firms fall some way between the two. These often cater to a particular industry, which may require more specialist lawyers, with deeper knowledge of their specific areas. Some are very small, being made up of only a few expert lawyers, while others can compete with equivalent departments at some of the larger firms, particularly in areas such as media and technology, employment or property law.

Barristers' sets

We saw earlier how most barristers have expertise in a few practice areas, often working in 'sets' with complementary skills. Barristers' sets are often structured in such a way that the set as a whole offers a wide range of services through the combination of areas of expertise of the set's members. Some sets will offer more general legal and litigation services, while others offer services tailored towards more specialist areas such as family law, intellectual property, or construction and engineering law.

Alternative and new ways of working

The traditional way in which lawyers generate income is through being instructed or retained on matters that require their expertise, with clients paying an hourly or daily rate for the lawyer's time. The rate is agreed in advance, but the exact amount of time to be spent (and therefore the final bill) will vary on a case-by-case basis, as a matter progresses. The final fee will only be known at the end of the matter, once the work is done. Professional obligations of honesty and acting in a client's best interest are in place to prevent abuse of the system, but it is still far from perfect.

Today's clients demand greater visibility on how lawyers charge for their work, and demand greater flexibility of approach. The legal market has developed, and a range of different types of law firm has appeared, to cater for the demands of the market. Regulation has also changed in recent years and has opened the legal world up to new business structures, which will alter the landscape of the profession in ways that will only become apparent in years to come.

Certain provisions of the Legal Services Act 2007 came into force in October 2011, permitting, among other things, law firms to seek external funding into their businesses, introducing external shareholders and investors into the legal profession. Traditional law firm partnerships or LLPs may no longer remain the predominant law firm structure. Instead, 'alternative business structures' (ABS) will be introduced, allowing non-legal companies such as banks or supermarkets to merge with legal providers. They will be able to offer legal services in the same way as they currently offer services not usually associated with their core business, and while it is too early to say whether ABS will ultimately prove to be a threat or an opportunity to the legal profession as a whole, it will certainly be interesting to see how the profession responds.

Some alternative legal business structures and organisations are given below, all of which operate in slightly different ways. In terms of employability, bear these organisations in mind, as they may offer opportunities, and more flexible ways of working, than those offered in the more traditional legal practices.

Co-operative legal services – the 'Co-op'

The UK's largest consumer co-operative has a long history, and operates in many areas, including food shops, funeral services, insurance, banking, farming and travel services, with an emphasis on value and social responsibility. Its legal service extends the Co-operative brand and ethos, offering services that will be found in many high-street law firms: personal injury advice, employment advice, property and conveyancing, will writing and probate. Some contentious services are offered on a 'no win no fee' basis, while other services are billed at fixed rates for the work done.

Which? Legal Service

This is a legal service offered by the well-known consumer watchdog, Which? The Which? Legal Service specialises in legal advice geared to individuals, as may be expected from its activities in other areas. The main services offered include advice on consumer rights, landlord and tenant issues, neighbour disputes, parking and clamping, and employment.

Clients pay for the service on a subscription basis, paying a monthly rate for unlimited contact with legal experts by phone and email, either during or out of office hours, depending on the level of subscription. Some self-contained areas of work are charged at a fixed fee.

Quality Solicitors

Quality Solicitors is an organisation looking to take advantage of looser regulation and increased opportunities for new business models through ABS to build a nationwide network of quality law firms operating under one recognised brand. Its aim is to offer consistently high-quality legal services through high-street practices that are already local market leaders. Local firms that meet the standards set by Quality Solicitors are recommended by the public, and invited to join the Quality Solicitors network. Quality Solicitors operates through over a hundred branches across England and Wales, and has plans to expand further in the coming years.

Lawyers On Demand

This is a City-based, corporate and commercial legal service, offered by law firm Berwin Leighton Paisner (BLP). A central group of qualified freelance lawyers are selected, trained and supported by BLP, to operate as a resource to be drawn on as and when the core resources of the firm need them. The use of freelancers reduces costs, while the support of a large City law firm guarantees the quality of services provided, and ensures that the best resources, training and support are in place for the freelance team. The service offers flexibility for clients and lawyers alike, as work may be allocated on the basis of a number of part-time hours per week for ongoing matters, while project specific work may allow time to be apportioned on the basis of a number of full-time weeks or months.

Keystone Law

This is one of a number of solicitors' firms using technology to offer corporate and commercial legal services from a 'virtual' firm. Each solicitor works remotely from wherever they choose, sharing central law firm services. This structure can operate very efficiently, with cost savings being reflected in competitive rates. The downside for those early on in their career is that this particular firm's recruitment policy is only to take on experienced solicitors, preferably with an existing client base, so there is no opportunity to train with the firm.

New approaches to legal recruitment: Law Absolute

As the legal market has consolidated over recent years in response to recent economic conditions, there has been increased demand for part-time and interim lawyers, and a corresponding increased availability of lawyers looking to fill non-permanent vacancies. Law Absolute is a recruitment agency specialising in placing lawyers in temporary positions in private legal practice, and in-house in the commercial and public sectors. In addition to placing qualified and experienced solicitors and barristers, Law Absolute also has newly qualified lawyers, paralegals, legal assistants, contract managers and legal secretaries on its books, and is well worth bearing in mind when it comes to looking for legal work as your career progresses.

Summary

These alternative structures aim to offer improved legal services to the market, but their range and flexibility have the additional benefit of offering more diverse and flexible ways of working for lawyers at every stage of their careers. While there is no evidence to suggest that traditional ways of working will ultimately be replaced by these new entrants to the profession, the alternatives are certainly on the increase. This will make legal services more competitive on value and quality, and will also offer a broader range of career possibilities outside of the traditional channels.

PART 3
Training and qualifying

6

The Academic Stage: getting the academic qualifications you need

In Chapter 1 we briefly looked at how the main stages of legal qualifications are divided, and how your career progression might evolve. In Chapters 4 and 5 we had a closer look at the main areas of law, and how work in legal practice relates to them.

In this chapter, we will look more closely at *how* you get the qualifications you need. Here we give you a brief guide to the main stages and requirements and a summary of the key stages of qualification, to help you navigate your way through. You should read this together with details given by specific course providers, and by the Solicitors Regulation Authority (SRA) or Bar Standards Board (BSB) – the boards responsible for regulating the profession. Deadlines and procedures are likely to change from year to year, so make sure you check that the information you have is up to date.

Qualifications required to become a solicitor or barrister

Remind yourself of the stages of qualification on page 11. To recap, a law degree is usually the required entry-level qualification for all future lawyers, regardless of the area in which they wish to go on to specialise. This initial qualification can be studied either as a first undergraduate degree, or as a postgraduate 'conversion' course, i.e. the Graduate Diploma in Law (GDL). Both undergraduate and conversion law courses are recognised by the SRA and BSB, and make up the 'Academic Stage' of qualification.

Once the Academic Stage is satisfied, the routes to qualification for future solicitors and barristers take different directions: this is the 'Vocational Stage'. To complete the Vocational Stage, solicitors are required to complete the Legal Practice Course (LPC), while barristers complete the Bar Professional Training Course (BPTC) formerly the Bar Vocational Course or BVC.

The Academic and Vocational stages are followed by professional training: either a solicitors' training contract, or barristers' pupillage.

Post-qualification: continuing professional development for solicitors and barristers

Practising solicitors and barristers are required to maintain their professional skills throughout their qualified career. There is a requirement to gain a certain number of continuing professional development (CPD) hours or 'points' throughout each year, according to each lawyer's level of experience. A proportion of each year's CPD points must come through participation in accredited courses or activities. The remainder can be made up from a wide range of other legally related activities, including teaching, writing articles, pro bono work or business development.

GCSEs and A levels

You may already have good grades at GCSE and A level, and an excellent academic record is the starting point for most legal careers, so it is important to be aiming high at the very start. Most course providers will not look at GCSE results, but some employers will, to assess the consistency of an applicant's CV. You may already have eight or more GCSEs – if they are all at grades A or B, this will usually be enough to satisfy most legal employers. At A level, the minimum that many firms and chambers will expect is two at grade A, and one at grade B.

If you do not have A levels, you should consider alternative qualifications, such as those offered by the Institute of Legal Executives (ILEX). The ILEX Level 3 qualification is equivalent to A level Law, and serves as both a stand-alone introduction to law, or as the first stage of full qualification. See Chapter 7 for more information on ILEX options; and dealing with missing or problematic exam grades is discussed later in this chapter.

Looking to improve your tea-making and photocopying skills?

Apply elsewhere

Joining us for a week's placement or full Gap Year means getting fully involved. Working on real projects, alongside real life lawyers, learning about commercial law today, in the real world. We'll expect you to ask questions and have opinions. Ideas even. It may not be the experience that decides your career – but then again, it just might.

www.pinsentmasons.com/workexperience

Pinsent Masons

Profile: Pinsent Masons LLP

Our programmes

School work experience programme

We want to give ambitious candidates from any background the chance to experience life at a top law firm – demonstrating your proactive approach and developing your CV for university applications.

It doesn't matter which subjects you are studying, or which degree you plan to study. In fact, some 50% of our graduate trainees join us having completed a degree in a subject other than law. We do ask that you like solving problems, are 16 or over, well organised, smartly presented, bright, articulate, and willing to ask questions and get involved.

Over the placement you will also have the opportunity to listen to a number of presentations from trainee lawyers and qualified lawyers on what it is like to work at Pinsent Masons and why they decided to become commercial lawyers.

Students on the programme commented:

> 'Fantastic work experience. The programme was pitched just right and has cemented my desire to study law. Attending seminars, etc. and working alongside trainees was invaluable. I didn't just learn; I felt I added value.'

Gap-year programme

Lasting eight months, our gap-year programme offers solid, first-hand experience of commercial law before you start university. So if you're serious about a career in law, it's a chance to build a CV that will help you stand out from your peers.

Your typical duties will include drafting and proofreading documents and letters, carrying out research, liaising with clients by phone, email and face-to-face meetings, and getting involved in community work. We're looking for commitment, curiosity and enthusiasm, as well as good organisational skills, a smart appearance and the ability to think on your feet.

A former student commented:

> 'I received a warm welcome when I arrived in my department, which was employment. We were given a departmental induction and then it was straight into live work such as taking witness statements and drafting agreements. Over the year, I was involved in a confidential case, which involved

> *attending court with the client, and I even got to write one of the monthly technical updates. It was great experience and I didn't realise how many doors it would open.'*

How to apply

The placements are specifically for AS and A level students (or the equivalent) and school leavers. You can apply from 1 September via our website where you can also find out more information (www.pinsentmasons.com/workexperience). The work experience programme typically has four intakes across the year and operates in all our UK offices. These are London, Birmingham, Leeds, Manchester, Edinburgh and Glasgow. The gap-year programme operates in Birmingham and Leeds only but some students have relocated to undertake a placement as it is paid.

Academic Stage of training: law degree or conversion

Objective

To complete the Academic Stage of training, you either need to have completed:

- a qualifying law degree

- a conversion law degree (GDL).

The Academic Stage of training requires both solicitors and barristers to have obtained the equivalent of a law degree at undergraduate level. The Academic Stage is overseen by a joint committee of the SRA and BSB, to ensure that qualifications comply with standards for both solicitors and barristers.

Qualifying law degrees

Most undergraduate law degrees are recognised as fulfilling the formal requirements of the Academic Stage of training, and are known as 'qualifying law degrees' because they reach the standards set by the SRA/BSB joint committee.

You should check with your university to make sure that the law degree you have done, or are considering, will qualify.

Entry requirements for a qualifying law degree

As specified by the university or training institution (usually ABB at A level or equivalent).

Profile: Aston Law

Where legal expertise meets commercial intelligence

Aston Law specialises in commercially intelligent legal education

Law is a very popular subject and is taught in most universities. With such choice it can be difficult deciding which law degree and which university most suits you and your career aspirations. At Aston Law we offer something unique and distinctive: the opportunity to gain a commercially intelligent legal education focusing on business and commercial law, from one of the UK's leading business schools.

Entry to the legal profession is highly competitive. Law graduates today need much more than legal knowledge to succeed. Our law degrees help our graduates stand out from the crowd. In addition to legal knowledge, our students gain highly sought-after business skills and real-world commercial experience during the optional placement year. Our students also benefit directly from the research of our experienced team of lawyers. We are passionate about the study of law and this is reflected in all that we do.

Law has been taught at both postgraduate and undergraduate level within Aston Business School for many years, giving Aston Law the necessary experience to provide a world-class programme that combines legal expertise with commercial intelligence. We encourage and support our students to invest in their own personal development, enhancing their employability in the years to come.

Our academic staff, many of whom are qualified lawyers, have considerable experience of teaching law. Students benefit from our active research and learn about the latest national and international developments from staff passionate about the subjects they teach.

Research-led teaching

Aston Law specialises in legal research that is vitally important to the management and success of businesses. Our research reflects current issues, such as the regulatory framework, restrictions on business contracting and the effective protection of intellectual property rights. Our research agenda is informed by the latest legislative and regulatory developments and Aston Law researchers have been cited in a number of important commercial cases, before the English courts and internationally. Our aims are to assist businesses in working in a legal environment and to aid the development of the law through proposals for reform and policy making. Our research strengths include: financial regulation and corporate governance, commercial contracting and consumer protection, and intellectual property rights.

The Aston Law LLB Law with Management

The LLB programme has been developed in consultation with legal practitioners to prepare you for a career in law. Legal practice has changed dramatically in the past 20 years and successful lawyers need more than legal knowledge to succeed. Our LLB will give you legal knowledge, business awareness and management skills. It also provides an excellent foundation for other careers and professions where legal knowledge is required. The placement year provides the opportunity to apply your knowledge in practice, develop skills and network professionally. Our LLB is different from many other law degrees and will help you stand out from other graduates in a highly competitive field.

The Aston Law LLM International Commercial Law

The Aston Law LLM provides an exciting and nurturing environment at a world-class business school. Graduates can expand their interest in key aspects of commercial law and business management with a clear international and comparative perspective. Engagement focuses on small interactive seminars. The programme is aimed at UK, EU and international students and is highly relevant for aspiring senior managers and legal practitioners. Structured support is given to students new to the common law.

Case study

Chris Benn is in his third year studying LLB Law with Management

I felt Aston was the right university for me when I attended an open day. I knew I would feel at home from the community spirit that echoed through the campus. In addition to the world-renowned reputation and invaluable placement year, Aston has a great deal to offer. As a campus university in the centre of Birmingham, everything I need is within close walking distance. The campus appealed due to the majority of first-year students living in the student residences. Birmingham has a great social scene and is a vibrant city to live in.

The Law with Management degree stood out due to its commercial relevance. The degree has enabled me to learn law in a commercial context, and see its application in a business environment. When applying for a placement this year I realised just how valuable this was in helping me stand out, as commercial awareness is increasingly expected by the legal profession. A significant factor in my decision to choose Aston was that class sizes are small, allowing greater interaction with the lecturers. The law lecturers all know me by name. This relationship means you are not afraid to seek help when you do not understand something, or need advice on future career direction. Having a personal tutor is invaluable and helps relieve some of the worries of being a law student.

I secured a placement in my second year. I am working in London, as the legal intern for the financial services company UBS. My placement gives me the chance to use my legal knowledge in a real business environment. It's the perfect placement for me and closely relevant to my studies.

I have never regretted my decision to choose Aston, and look forward to returning for my final year. I feel part of Aston and my experiences have been a great step forward towards my legal career.

Conversion degrees

If you do not hold a qualifying law degree, the Academic Stage of training can be satisfied by successfully completing a GDL 'conversion'. These courses take the key elements of the law degree, and fit them into a one-year postgraduate course for those studying full-time, or into two years for part-time students. It's not always necessary to have an undergraduate degree to do a law conversion course.

Entry requirements for the GDL conversion degrees

For future solicitors, any of the following may be acceptable to satisfy the SRA requirements:

- undergraduate-level degree in any subject from a UK or Republic of Ireland university

- undergraduate-level degree in any subject from a non-UK university, with an SRA Certificate of Academic Standing

- other degree-level qualification, with SRA Certificate of Academic Standing

- ILEX Level 3 and Level 6 qualifications.

For non-graduates, at least 10 years of academic, commercial or other professional or managerial experience is required.

For future barristers, the BSB requires any one of the following:

- UK honours degree at 2.ii level or above

- undergraduate-level degree in any subject from a non-UK university, with BSB Certificate of Academic Standing.

Non-graduates may also be accepted by the BSB Qualifications Committee on a case-by-case basis.

How to apply for the GDL

- Full-time course applications are not made direct to the course provider. All applications for full-time GDL courses must be made online via the Central Applications Board or CAB (www.lawcabs.ac.uk). A fee is required for applications to be processed.

- Applications for places on part-time courses, or courses taught through other study modes are made direct to the course provider.

- In addition to your academic results and other details requested on the CAB form, you will need to provide references. These should be from academic tutors, where possible.

When to apply for the GDL

- The GDL usually starts in September each year. You will usually be given some pre-course materials a few weeks before the course starts, so it's important to get your application submitted in good time.

- Applications are usually accepted from November of the year before you wish to start the GDL. You should aim to submit your application by January of that year.

- First-round selections of candidates take place at the start of February, with offers being made in early March. Course providers make second-round selections and offers in April.

- You must enrol on the GDL (that is, actually start the course) no later than two weeks after the course enrolment date. This is to prevent you falling behind.

- Application dates are subject to change every year, so make sure you check the deadlines at www.lawcabs.ac.uk and/or with your course provider of choice.

- Contact your referees as early as you can, and make sure you allow plenty of time (at least a month) for them to respond.

Where to study the GDL

GDL/CPE and LPC courses are taught at institutions around the country, and the CAB website lists all eligible course providers, with links to their websites. This is the best place to start your research into where to study. Some are traditional universities, where it is possible to study law at undergraduate level, and then to go on to take the LPC. These universities include Birmingham, Cardiff, Nottingham, and Westminster. Other course providers are more specialist, either providing professional/postgraduate training only, or legal training only. Some employers view these institutions as having the edge over their competitors, and it is true that some, such as the College of Law or BPP, have excellent reputations.

Note that the CAB system is purely an administrative service to manage applications for the GDL/CPE and LPC. The CAB does not make any decisions as to who is allocated a place on which course.

Note also that while a qualifying law degree is valid indefinitely, those with a GDL qualification must go on to the LPC (or BPTC) within seven years, after which the qualification expires.

The City Law School
CITY UNIVERSITY LONDON

World-class legal education
in the heart of London

Your route to Professional Legal Practice

The City Law School, part of **City University London,** is one of London's major law schools. With three levels of study: undergraduate, postgraduate and professional, we offer courses suitable for every step of your legal career.

Our high quality courses are delivered by leading academics and practitioners from around the world and each course is fully accredited by the relevant professional body.

Our 'real-world' experience and student focussed approach will ensure that you develop the legal knowledge and skills you'll need to excel in practice.

Undergraduate:
> LLB Law

Postgraduate:
> Graduate Entry LLB
> Graduate Diploma in Law
> LLM in EU Commercial Law
> LLM in International Banking and Finance
> LLM / M.Jur in International Commercial Law
> LLM in International Competition Law

> LLM in International Energy Litigation
> LLM in Maritime Law (UK)
> LLM in Maritime Law (Greece)
> LLM in Criminal Litigation
> LLM in Civil Litigation and Dispute Resolution
> PhD, MPhil or LLM by Research

Professional:
> Legal Practice Course
> Bar Professional Training Course
> LLM in Professional Legal Practice
> LLM in Professional Legal Skills
> CPD courses

FOR MORE INFORMATION AND TO APPLY CONTACT US:

☎ +44 (0)20 7040 3309

🖱 law@city.ac.uk

🖱 www.city.ac.uk/law

Please quote the following reference when contacting us: WL0711

www.city.ac.uk/law

Profile: The City Law School

A step in the right direction

Located in the heart of legal London, The City Law School provides legal training right where the law is being made. As one of the first major London law schools, it offers courses for every step of a student's legal career at undergraduate, postgraduate and professional level.

Based at Northampton Square in Clerkenwell and Gray's Inn in Holborn, the School offers the main professional courses for students aspiring to be solicitors or barristers: the LPC and the BPTC.

City's LPC prepares students for professional life by offering a broad range of vocational subjects, these are taught to replicate the demands and disciplines of being in practice. For students still looking for a training contract, there's the school's Training Contract Advisory Service, which gives specialist career advice about getting that first foot in the door.

As the original provider of training for barristers, the school's BPTC is taught at master's level and gives students the knowledge to go on to a career at the Bar. The course also provides students with a range of transferable skills that can be used in a wide range of non-legal professions. Students are provided with their best chance of success at the Bar by having access to a dedicated pupillage advisory service, which provides students with expert guidance about starting a career at the Bar.

For non-law graduates looking to start a legal career, the school offers the GDL – a conversion course that allows students to transfer into law. Started in 1976, the GDL was one of the first conversion courses in the country and teaches students the seven-core foundation modules from an undergraduate LLB in just one year.

All students can further bolster their professional connections by attending a range of events at the school, where they can meet members of both sides of the profession. Dean of The City Law School, Susan Nash, explains: 'We have great links with the legal profession in London due to our locality and history, which enables us to provide huge levels of interaction between our students and the profession.'

City is at the forefront of modern legal education; students on all courses are given one-on-one support and encouraged to learn by doing in a real-life environment. Susan adds: 'This is a place where you can get personalised, life-long learning. We can offer you an education that is as much about life experience as it is about academia.'

With this many acclaimed courses and a modern approach to learning, The City Law School really *is* the school for professionals.

Case study

Leon Pickering attended The City Law School and completed his GDL in 2008/09 and Bar Vocational Course in 2009/10

About me

I'm originally from Norwich and I went to Oxford University, initially intending to be an academic. I studied medieval English (MA, MPhil), however, friends of mine looked like they were having so much fun at the Bar that I jumped ship.

Why City?

I found City's location to be absolutely unparalleled – it's inside one of the Inns of Court at Gray's Inn. Studying for the BPTC in the very environment where I was going to go on to practise cannot be beaten.

Teaching and support

The teaching at the school is excellent. Advocacy training is perhaps one of the most entertaining (and surreal) learning experiences I have ever had! Everyone was very interested in who I was and what I wanted to do: it didn't feel like a sausage factory. I found the school's personal tutor system very useful and there is a strong pastoral support network, too.

Benefits

The School has its own library at Gray's Inn Place, which is very well stocked with practitioner books. I also had access to the huge law library at the university's main campus in Northampton Square, which is equipped with just about every academic text you could need. Lawbore Pro is also an absolutely fantastic resource – very similar to that available at leading law firms and chambers.

Law in London

London is where the biggest and most exciting law cases happen. Living in London makes it so easy to go on mini-pupillages and vacation schemes – or even pop into the Royal Courts of Justice or the Old Bailey for a day. Nowhere else can match this.

Future career

Thanks to some great support and advice I've been able to secure a pupillage at Ten Old Square. Following studying at City, I am confident that I will be able to hit the ground running.

What the GDL (or law degree) covers

The Academic Stage (i.e. law degree or GDL) covers the main areas of law that together make up the basis of all legal practice. We looked at the seven legal foundation subjects in Chapter 4, and these make up the majority of the course content.

Introductory course materials

You will usually be set some pre-course study materials before the GDL starts, including a course in legal method. This is taught and assessed early on in the GDL, well before the main foundation subject exams. Areas covered include an introduction to the English legal system, and interpretation and analysis of statutes and cases. These are areas that will crop up time and again throughout your legal career, so it is important to get a good grounding in the basics at an early stage. Some providers include an introduction to aspects of commercial law (for example general commercial practice and company law) at this point.

Core subjects

These are the foundation subjects of contract law, constitutional and administrative law, criminal law, equity and trusts, EU law, land law and tort law we covered on pages 47–48. The GDL covers these areas of law as separate academic subjects, setting out their background and development, and current status of the law in each area. In contrast to a traditional three-year law degree, the foundation subjects are all taught in parallel throughout the GDL, with each foundation course subject progressing simultaneously. For this reason, there are only certain areas that really link up towards the final stages of the GDL, and it can be very satisfying to have a 'eureka' moment, when things finally come together.

Generally the GDL courses are taught as a combination of lectures and smaller study group sessions. There is usually the equivalent of one lecture per week per foundation subject, and perhaps three or four small group sessions. It is important to consolidate material covered in each lecture, to be ready for the next one, and it is essential to be properly prepared for each small group session. For these, you will be expected to have done preparatory reading, and to have prepared written exercises for discussion in class, as well as preparing and taking part in occasional group tasks. Time constraints mean that the courses are structured such that you absolutely must do the preparatory work for all classes. You will not pick up all the information you need for the exams unless you have covered the preparatory material for each class, and done the follow-up work as the course progresses.

Coursework

The purpose of coursework is not so much to delve into a subject in detail, but rather to develop legal research skills. Two legal research assessments are generally set on the GDL. The first is a shorter written assignment which relates to one of the foundation subjects, with each student being allocated a particular question relating to an area of law. The second assessment is longer and more detailed, and usually takes the form of a dissertation or problem-based question, on an area of law that each student can choose according to their own interests.

Profile: Northumbria Law School

Northumbria is justifiably renowned for excellence in learning and teaching and offers a ground-breaking portfolio of programmes at undergraduate, postgraduate and professional levels. We focus on law in practice and are committed to ensuring that our students develop the knowledge and skills needed to become successful legal professionals. This commitment is demonstrated through our academic staff, the majority of whom have considerable and often continuing experience of practice. We provide an extensive careers and employability programme and our graduates are highly sought after by employers both regionally and nationally.

Undergraduate programmes

Our innovative LLB (Hons)/M Law Exempting programme allows students to achieve a qualifying law degree, a master's and exemption from the LPC. We are the only university in the UK to offer the LLB (Hons)/M Law Bar Exempting programme, an integrated master's degree incorporating the BPTC. For a small number of students there is also the possibility of following our LLB (Hons)/M Law Solicitor programme, a degree leading to full qualification as a solicitor.

In September 2010 the Law School launched a brand new, innovative qualifying law degree, LLB (Hons) Law with Environment – the only degree of its kind in the UK. Following the success of this programme, the school proudly introduced a suite of Law+ programmes, a range of specialist law degrees including LLB (Hons) Law with Property Management, LLB (Hons) Law with Business and LLB (Hons) Law with International Business.

Professional programmes

We are a leading provider of the GDL for non-law graduates looking to practise law, the LPC for aspiring solicitors and the BPTC for aspiring barristers. Our students have the opportunity to gain a Master's in Advanced Legal Practice whilst studying the LPC or BPTC – a qualification which will undoubtedly benefit students when they embark on their training contract or pupillage.

Postgraduate programmes

Northumbria has an enviable reputation for its practical, innovative master's programmes, which are accessible to a wide range of professionals. Various programmes can be studied on a full-time basis, although many students now opt to study via distance learning, which provides a flexible approach more suited to busy lifestyles. Our master's programmes include child law, commercial law, employment law and medical law to name but a few. An MSc in Business with Legal Management and an MBA in Legal Management are also available.

Location

The Law School is located on a modern, award-winning development in central Newcastle – City Campus East. Our students are taught in purpose-built accommodation which includes state-of-the-art lecture theatres, workshop rooms equipped with the latest technology and courtrooms modelled on those that students will experience as qualified practitioners.

The building also houses the school's internationally renowned Student Law Office, which provides our students with the opportunity to offer legal advice and representation to members of the public and thus experience life as a professional lawyer.

Case study

Rachel Sykes is a GDL and LPC graduate

I studied the GDL and LPC at Northumbria. The Law School was my first choice for the GDL after being impressed with the excellent facilities and friendly teaching staff I encountered during an open day, and I was rewarded with a fantastic year. My experiences were so positive I chose to remain at Northumbria to study the LPC.

The LPC is all about learning to apply your legal knowledge in a practical setting, and this is mainly achieved through participating in short group sessions and workshops. These sessions involve group work in 'firms' which provides a useful opportunity to interact with other students. Most importantly, the teaching staff at Northumbria are really supportive and approachable, and their experience in legal practice means they can explain how tasks fit into the context of life as a solicitor.

The LPC is designed to equip students for practice and is complemented by a good careers programme to help students achieve their career goals. There is support and advice with CV writing and a practice interview scheme, as well as a careers fair and regular presentations by firms. An added bonus is that Northumbria offers the opportunity for students to complete an LLM in Advanced Legal Practice while studying the LPC, an option I chose to undertake.

The quality of teaching and the support on offer at Northumbria are fantastic. I would thoroughly recommend the GDL and LPC to anyone.

Contact us

For further information on the range of programmes offered by Northumbria Law School, please visit www.northumbrialawschool.co.uk, call 0191 243 7035 or email la.marketingenquiries@northumbria.ac.uk

How the GDL works in reality

The vast majority of the subject matter is assessed by exams. For full-time students, this means one three-hour paper for each of the seven subjects, usually sat one per day across a two-week period. Exams are usually a combination of essay questions and problem questions, designed to test your knowledge of the legal principles of each of the foundation subjects. More practical considerations, such as how a legal problem might perhaps affect a client in daily life, are not covered on the GDL, and are reserved for the LPC or BPTC. Generally, each exam counts as 10% of the overall GDL grade – 70% of your GDL is therefore exam based, with only 30% available through coursework assessments.

The course contents of the GDL are similar to those of a full undergraduate law degree. The obvious advantage of fitting the course into the equivalent of one academic year is that it is possible to gain an initial legal qualification without having to make the financial and time commitment to law as a first degree. The disadvantages are that the GDL is very time pressured, and cannot offer the exposure over time to the various subjects you cover. If you go on to do the LPC or BPTC you may feel that you have not had the time to properly absorb the subject matter to the same extent as those who have spent three years studying the same foundation subjects on law degrees.

The point about pressure is worth emphasising. The formal time requirement for the GDL is 32 weeks of tuition, with each week taking in 45 hours of lectures, tutorials and private study. Most GDL courses start in September, with exams usually scheduled the following June. This means that in reality, all the teaching is squeezed into about nine months. All seven foundation subject exams are then sat in succession, usually one per day for four days in one week, followed by one exam per day for three days of the following week. When you add the coursework assessments and mock exams into the equation, you can see that these courses are quite intensive.

The GDL is intellectually and academically challenging, and the subject matter is very broad in scope. There is a lot of material to cover and to learn, and as we have seen, the vast majority is tested at the end by exams. You need to think carefully about whether this is right for you – most students manage the GDL well, albeit with some stressful times around exams and during some of the tougher course modules. However, the keys to success lie in being organised, focusing on the work you need to do, and being aware of the relatively short amount of time available to get on top of the subject matter. As one former GDL student puts it: 'Treat it like a full-time job – keep on top of things as you go through the course, and don't leave anything to the last minute. If you're not clear on something, speak to your tutors or classmates as soon as you can. That way you can't go wrong.'

Case study

David Swain is an associate solicitor at Simmons and Simmons, and studied for his GDL full-time

The GDL is a full-time commitment: you have lectures and classes all day, then you need to work in the evenings to catch up and prepare. You have to focus straight away, as you only have one year to get everything done. Everyone's in the same position though, and discussions between people in your group are very interesting. The work is condensed, and doing seven core subjects simultaneously can feel a bit overwhelming at times, especially when you are doing subjects that would be taught in different years on an undergraduate law degree. You have a lot of fun though, and it's generally easy to have a good work–life balance.

When it gets to exams it is quite intense, particularly as the exams are very close together. It's not like a modular degree course when different things are tested in different years. It is probably one of the more difficult sets of exams you can do, because even though the subjects fall under the umbrella of 'law' it is amazing how different they all are, with their own case law, statutes and so on.

Overall, managing the GDL workload gives you a good idea of what life in law is like, with tight deadlines, and working on several matters in parallel. You really get an understanding of how useful a network of friends and contacts can be – bouncing ideas off each other, working as a team, working with people. These are essential skills for any lawyer.

Modes of study available

The details of conversion courses and modes of study differ between course providers, but it is generally offered in three varieties.

One-year full-time

The one-year full-time course requires attendance at lectures and small group classes throughout the week, from September to June, with short breaks for Christmas and Easter. As mentioned earlier, the GDL is usually made up of 32 weeks of teaching, with around 45 hours of classes and lectures per week, with additional time needed for preparation between classes, and time for the introductory course, and written assignments.

The full-time GDL packs a great amount of course and assessment work into the shortest possible time, but allows you to concentrate on it exclusively. Your teaching time will be spent with a group of fellow students whom you will see regularly throughout the year, giving you a support network that might prove invaluable when it comes to revising and preparing for assessments!

Two years part-time

The two-year part-time courses require about 23 hours' attendance per week, split across study days which are held either during the day, in the evening, or at the weekend. Again, preparatory work is required between classes, with the part-time courses being designed specifically for those with other commitments. The seven foundation subject exams are done at the end of each of the two years, with exams in four subjects at the end of the first year, and the remaining three at the end of the second year.

Mixed

Some institutions offer the option to study the GDL over 18 months. Subjects are taught through a combination of online tutorials and attendance at a small number of study days (fewer than 10 in total) across the year, with supervision available as needed by individual students.

Part-time or full-time?

The general view is that the full-time GDL offers the highest amount of face-to-face contact with tutors and fellow students, and has the advantage of allowing the qualification to be obtained in the shortest possible amount of time. It is commonly accepted that balancing work, family or other commitments makes it harder for part-time students to focus on their academic work. When choosing a GDL provider, look out for those that offer a high ratio of tutor-to-student contact, a high ratio of lectures to small group classes, and those that can offer some flexibility through use of online resources. Part-time courses are popular and have good pass rates. It is possible to combine GDL study with other commitments, and to do well. Also, some providers include all course books and materials in the course fee, while others do not. Shop around, and be sure to look carefully at what each course provider offers, and how their courses are taught and assessed, to make sure your GDL provider is the best fit for you.

Overcoming problem areas in academic qualifications

You can see that the application system for courses and training positions across the legal profession is very heavily focused on academic grades. The general requirements for most employers will be 'A' grades at A level and GCSE, at least a 2.i in your degree, and at least a commendation on the GDL and/or LPC, or 'very competent' on the BPTC.

How earlier exam grades relate to legal practice

Many legal employers will require you to fill in an online application form, which will not let you progress unless you have submitted a number of UCAS points, usually equivalent to grades AAB at A level. If you have to apply through one of these sites, then the reality of the situation is that there is no way around this, if you do not have the required grades. Unfortunately, you do not meet their eligibility criteria. However, this is not to say that there are no potential employers out there for you. Work on getting the best possible law grades you can, and combine this with legal work experience: you will find that this will help outweigh lower grades from life before law. There are many excellent legal employers out there who may not have the marketing budgets of the big firms you've heard of, but who are no less capable of offering fantastic training and employment opportunities. Keep up your research and contacts, and keep your eyes open, as there are plenty of opportunities out there.

Course providers will be less concerned at the odd lower grade on your CV, although you should still check eligibility criteria with the college or university where you intend to study, to make sure you have what is required. Course providers are happy to discuss this with prospective candidates. Contact them if you are in any doubt, or discuss any questions or concerns you have at a course open day.

In reality, a lot of people experience the occasional blip in their academic career, and you might feel as though your grades, while generally good, do not tell the whole story, or that some lower grades reduce the overall quality of your academic record. If this is the case, then there are plenty of ways to go about addressing the issue, and ensuring your academic capabilities are seen in the most positive light. The following sections cover some of the most common issues, and ways they can be remedied.

Inconsistent grades at GCSE and/or A level

It is quite common for people to have a spread of grades, particularly when sitting a lot of exams in different subjects at the same time. Of course, your grades should indicate that you have the aptitude for law, and this may be shown by top grades in at least a few subjects. If your grades are good in some areas, but poor in others, then you should think about why this happened. Are there any reasons which properly explain why you did better in some subjects than in others? Can you work on this to prevent similar erratic results in the future? Remember that a career in law requires hard work, focus, concentration and stamina (as well as a lot of exams!), so you may need to look at how you approached the exams in which you did not do so well. Ask yourself if you would do things differently now, and if so, how? Even if your previous grades are not great, the clearest and best way to demonstrate to an employer that you have what it takes for law is to do well in your law exams and assessments. This is entirely within your control, and with hard work and dedication, you will be able to get some very strong grades.

No A levels

For any number of reasons, you may have either decided not to do A levels, or you may have chosen a career path that did not require you to do them, if perhaps some other experience or qualification was required. This is not a barrier to entry to law, as there are qualification systems available to allow you to bridge these gaps. In particular, the ILEX provides a range of options to gain equivalent qualifications, which are recognised by legal course providers and employers. Legal executive work is some of the best legal work experience there is, and this can be used to replace A levels, and to count directly towards qualification. Useful information on routes to qualification for those without 'traditional' academic qualifications is available from the ILEX (see page 135).

Again, your emphasis should be on getting the best grades you can in your legal studies, and to focus on getting good legal work experience. Many solicitors have come to law with no A levels, and have gone on to train, qualify and have very successful careers. It is possible to replace a set of exam grades you might have missed out on years ago with alternative legal qualifications. When combined with good, practical legal work experience, this can be a very attractive offering to an employer.

Mitigating circumstances

Legal employers do take mitigating circumstances into account, if this has been indicated by an applicant. It is worth bearing this in mind because all legal employers receive a high number of high-quality applications, and it would be perfectly possible for them to fill vacancies with the very best candidates, without even looking at people whose lower grades may be explained by perfectly valid reasons.

The important thing to remember is that an employer will only view 'mitigating circumstances' as situations that would genuinely prevent someone from performing to their optimum level through no fault of their own. This can't be used as a way to excuse poor performance because you had decided to concentrate on something other than your work, no matter how positive that other activity was. If you had a choice as to how you spent your time, this is unlikely to be considered a 'mitigating circumstance'. However, there are no hard and fast rules as to what 'counts', and you don't have to have been personally incapacitated. If, for example, a parent or other close family member was seriously ill or undergoing treatment while you were at university, then this may quite reasonably have prevented you from fully reaching your potential during your degree.

If you find yourself in this situation, then it is useful to include with your application a reference or explanatory statement from someone (preferably in a position of responsibility) who knew you at the time, as this will add credibility to your explanation. If you have any doubts as to how best to present this on a CV or application, you should speak to your careers adviser.

Not getting a 2.i or above in your first degree

If you were not awarded at 2.i or a First in your degree, then this will not generally prevent you from getting a place on the various law courses offered by most providers. Note, however, that the BSB requires at least a 2.ii before the GDL or BPTC in order to go on to qualify as a barrister. In any event, you should check each course provider's entry requirements before you apply. Use the CAB and BSB websites as a starting point.

Employers (law firms, sets of chambers, etc.) are inclined towards offering places to candidates at the higher end of the degree range. Like any employer, this is part of their remit to find the best people. Measuring candidates by academic results is a relatively consistent method of reducing the risk of taking on people who might not be suitable for the role, but this can be a relatively rough and ready benchmark of aptitude. Legal training positions invariably require more than just academic ability; grades alone may not reveal the full picture of an applicant's suitability.

However, sometimes the requirement to have a 2.i is not always a hard and fast rule. Sometimes a candidate with a lower degree, but very good additional attributes on their CV, may trump another applicant with little to offer other than good grades. Once again, you need to make sure your CV is continually being improved, adding work placements or vacation schemes, and achievements in other activities as you acquire them. A strong, updated CV demonstrates that your motivation and dedication count for more than one or two weak spots on the academic side. If mitigating circumstances applied to you, then say so. Otherwise, focus on building up your CV through good legal grades and relevant work experience. This will show your overall achievements in a more positive light than your previous academic grades may suggest.

Summary

Academic results are important in law, and you need to work hard to get the best grades possible in your law exams. These are directly relevant to your career, much more so than a bad GCSE grade in an unrelated subject, years ago. Aim high: try to get distinctions in all modules throughout your GDL, LPC and/or BPTC, and if you put the work in, you will do very well in at least some – if not all – areas. If your better grades match the areas of law you are interested in, then so much the better. This will make it much easier to sell yourself to firms or sets of chambers that may work in these areas. If you did well in areas you do not expect to practise in, keep an open mind. If your grades suggest strengths in areas of law you had not previously considered, then this may suggest an aptitude for these areas: perhaps you should investigate career possibilities in these areas? You may well find that opportunities come along as your contact with legal work continues, and in areas of law that you had not considered before.

When you have acquired your qualifying law degree or conversion, you have satisfied the Academic Stage of training, and are eligible to go on to the Vocational Stage of training for either solicitors or barristers.

7

The Vocational Stage of training

As we mentioned earlier (and see page 11), once the Academic Stage is completed, the training for solicitors and that for barristers take separate routes, specific to the skills required for each profession. We will look at each in turn, starting with the vocational training required for solicitors.

Vocational Stage of training: for solicitors

Before starting a training contract, all future solicitors must complete the Legal Practice Course (LPC). The LPC is the springboard for taking the theoretical law you have learned in the foundation subjects at the Academic Stage, and applying this to everyday legal situations that solicitors face in day-to-day working life.

The LPC builds on the law you have learned during the Academic Stage, and is the starting point for preparing you for life as a practising solicitor. The course contents are prescribed by the Solicitors Regulation Authority (SRA), with an emphasis on the practical application of the law to client-specific cases, and learning to advise clients appropriately. This is a move away from identifying and analysing points of law in isolation, as tends to be the case at the Academic Stage.

Objective

To complete the solicitors' Vocational Stage of training, you will need to have:

- completed the LPC

- enrolled with the SRA, with confirmation of completion of the Academic Stage of training.

LPC entry requirements

- Completion of the Academic Stage of training (through qualifying law degree or conversion, as above, or confirmation from the SRA that an overseas equivalent qualification is acceptable).

- Enrolment with the SRA as a student member.

- Written confirmation of completion of Academic Stage of training from SRA.

How to apply for the LPC

- As with the Graduate Diploma in Law (GDL), all applications for full-time LPC courses must be made online via the Central Applications Board (CAB; www.lawcabs.ac.uk). A fee is required for applications to be processed.

- Applications for places on part-time or alternative study mode LPC courses should be made direct to the course provider.

- There is no obligation to study the GDL and LPC at the same college or university, if both courses are offered. Many providers of both courses will offer guaranteed LPC places to their GDL students, as well as assistance in the application process. There are advantages to studying both GDL and LPC at the same place, and other advantages to changing course provider – the choice is yours.

When to apply for the LPC

- The LPC usually starts in September of each year, although alternative LPC structures may start earlier.

- The deadline for applications for the first round of LPC selections is the end of the November before you wish to start the LPC. First round selections of candidates take place at the start of December, with offers being made in early February.

- Applications received after early December are processed in a second round of selections, with a submission deadline of mid-March.

- Application dates are subject to change every year, so make sure you check the deadlines at www.lawcabs.ac.uk and/or with your course provider of choice.

Where to study the LPC

As with the GDL, institutions offering the LPC are listed on the CAB website. These are similar to those offering the GDL, and fall into the same categories of 'traditional' universities, or more specific professional or postgraduate training providers. The same considerations apply when selecting where to study the LPC as we looked at for the GDL on page 93.

How to enrol as a student member of the SRA, and obtain confirmation of completion of your Academic Stage of training

- Use the SRA's online registration system to apply for both enrolment and confirmation of the Academic Stage (www.sra.org.uk/students/student-enrolment.page). A fee is payable.

- Applications should be submitted to the SRA one month before the start of the LPC.

- Your Academic Stage course results should be submitted to the SRA two months after the start of the LPC at the latest, or within one month for students on shorter LPC courses. Your LPC course provider can help you with this.

- Note that the application for enrolment requires a declaration that you are of a suitable character to join the profession. All applicants are asked to provide information on convictions, bankruptcies, county court judgments, acts of plagiarism, other investigations to which they may have been subject, and to give information on anything else that might call their suitability into question.

- Note also that it is your responsibility to ensure you have enrolled with the SRA and obtained confirmation of completion of the Academic Stage. The SRA no longer sends reminders to potential LPC students, as in previous years.

When you have completed your solicitors' Vocational Stage of training, you are eligible to start your professional training, as a trainee solicitor.

LPC course content

The LPC is split into two parts: the compulsory stage and the elective stage. The compulsories are covered in the first few months of the LPC, with exams in late spring. The elective modules and exams take place in the summer.

There are additional compulsory assessments along the way, which take various forms, including legal research, interviewing clients, preparing simple accounts and face-to-face advocacy. We will look at those in a moment.

There are more than 15 exams and assessments in all throughout the LPC, with additional mock exams and assessments available to help you, so bear in mind that you need to pace yourself as the LPC progresses!

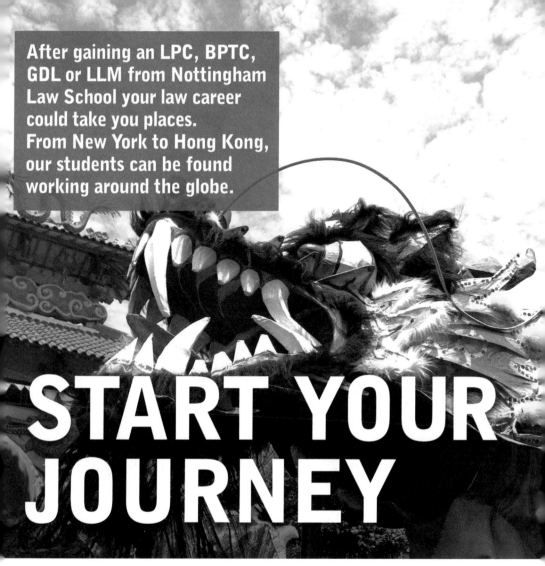 

Profile: Nottingham Law School

Nottingham Law School is one of the largest university law schools in the UK. We enjoy a national and international reputation for delivering high-quality education and training across a broad range of academic and professional law programmes: from undergraduate to research degrees.

Master in Laws (LLM) – build a programme that suits you

In the competitive area of law, it is apparent that graduates increase employability by undertaking postgraduate study.

The taught LLM programme at Nottingham Law School is an exciting and expanding area, offering a refreshing and flexible approach to postgraduate study. You can build an LLM programme to suit your individual requirements, choosing modules from 10 specialist areas that allow enhanced legal expertise and career progression. Subject areas include corporate, insolvency, health, sports and employment law, and all routes can be studied full-time or part-time.

Staff expertise

Nottingham Law School is one of the largest in the UK and has as extensive network of national and international professional contacts. Students can take advantage of the school's network to enhance their professional profile and you will also benefit from the expertise of our staff.

Your experience with us is dependent on the quality and dedication of your tutors. That's why we invest in high-quality, committed teaching staff, which is reflected in our reputation for world-class scholarly research. We have a number of internationally recognised experts in a wide range of legal areas. International insolvency law, criminal justice, legal education and health law are some of the areas where academic research excellence is recognised globally. Many of our staff are invited to take up roles with advisory and regulatory bodies both in the UK and abroad. Our expertise is valued throughout the world and many staff are employed as consultants.

International summer schools

You will also have an opportunity to attend one of our exciting international summer schools in Tallinn, Strasbourg, Berlin or Geneva. The summer schools were developed in collaboration with partners across the world for students to experience places of influential legal standing. If you take part in a summer school you will be taught various aspects of European and international law and will visit institutions such as the European Court of Human Rights.

Want to know more?

To find out more about the subject areas available or to request a master's in law brochure, visit www.ntu.ac.uk/llm.

If you have any queries please feel free to contact to us on +44 (0)115 848 4460 or email nls.enquiries@ntu.ac.uk.

Case study

Our LLM students come from a wide range of different backgrounds and put the knowledge gained through their course to a variety of uses. Mohamed Elmessiry, a LLM Human Rights and International Criminal Justice student and a Chevening Scholar, talks about the value of his LLM

I began my career as a volunteer with a non-governmental organisation (NGO) in Cairo that provides legal assistance to refugees in Egypt and later moved to Eastern Sudan as a resettlement consultant (team leader) with the United Nations Refugee Agency. I also worked as a coordinator with the American Bar Association's Rule of Law Project in Cairo, which seeks to establish continuing legal education and practical legal skills around the world.

All of this gave me invaluable human rights experience and inspired me to gain an LLM in Human Rights Law from a British university. I chose to study at Nottingham Law School because of the highly flexible modules, which has allowed me to build an LLM that best suits my career needs. Also, Nottingham Law School is one of the few UK universities that provide in-depth tuition in international criminal justice, and has a good community atmosphere and amazing library facilities.

The knowledge I have acquired on the course and the teaching methods have helped me to secure a placement with Amnesty International. The open discussion seminars and presentations gave me the skills I needed to present my ideas and opinions in a persuasive way, which really helped with the interview. The focus of my work with Amnesty International will be the protection of marginalised people who are victims of political or economic persecution.

The course I have undertaken at Nottingham Law School has given me pertinent and practical knowledge of human rights law and criminal justice which I will take back with me, both to use in my own work and to share with fellow and future practitioners.

Other successes

Mohamed is not the only one who has put his LLM to good use. Baker A Al-Haboob, who won the Paragon Law Prize for the best LLM student in 2009, has been appointed the 'Head of the Appeal Committee for the Resolution of Securities Disputes' in Saudi Arabia, and Tom Hughes, who gained a distinction in his LLM in International Criminal Justice and Human Rights in 2010, has obtained an internship with the International Tribunal for the former Yugoslavia. Tom says the LLM programmes at Nottingham Law School are a great building block to big possibilities.

Compulsory stage

The compulsory stage is made up of the areas that every solicitor is required to have covered, as prescribed by the SRA. These are split into the following four areas:

1. LPC core subjects:

    - business law and practice

    - litigation (civil and criminal)

    - property.

2. course skills

3. professional skills

4. elective subjects.

LPC core subjects

Business law and practice

This is important for all solicitors, regardless of the area of practice you end up in. The majority of clients you will come across will operate in a commercial context of one sort of another, and even if you decide to work in a less commercially focused area, such as criminal or family law, you will need to know how to run your own practice. This element of the LPC is designed to give you the insight you need into many of the issues affecting commercial enterprises, whether or not you will advise on them in practice.

The main areas covered in this module are:

- partnerships: formation and dissolution of partnerships, terms of agreement and liability

- companies: formation and management, shareholders' rights, directors' duties, funding and capital structures

- corporate security and insolvency: types of security, administration and receivership, company voluntary arrangements, liquidation, personal bankruptcy, disqualification of directors

- business relationships: employment, commercial contracts, trading relationships

- taxation: income tax, inheritance tax, capital gains tax, corporation tax, value-added tax (VAT)

- business accounts: book-keeping, profit and loss accounts, and balance sheets for sole traders, partnerships and companies, year-end adjustments and interpretation of accounts.

Litigation – civil

Solicitors working in all practice areas are required to have a good working knowledge of both civil and criminal litigation. Clearly this is crucial for those choosing to specialise in contentious work, but litigation can occur in any number of different contexts, and all solicitors should have a good understanding of how litigation works in practice, and what the procedures and considerations are in the context of legal disputes.

The civil litigation compulsory module covers high court and county court litigation under the Civil Procedure Rules (published in the *White Book*). The course covers important aspects of court procedure and the key skills required in the civil litigation process:

- pre-action considerations

- commencement proceedings

- interim matters

- evidence

- strategy and tactics

- trial and enforcement costs and funding

- jurisdiction

- non-litigation/alternative dispute resolution.

Litigation – criminal

This module is an introduction to the skills needed by solicitors involved in criminal work, and covers the procedures at all stages of a criminal case, from initial arrest of the suspect to disposal of the case. The course is usually taught around a series of scenario-based case studies.

Elements covered on the course include:

- advising the suspect at the police station

- detention, and dealing with the custody officer

- applying for legal aid

- bail applications

- where the case will be heard (magistrates' court, Crown Court, or other court)

- assessing the cases of the prosecution and defence; managing evidence

- sentencing

- professional conduct rules affecting criminal practice and advocacy

- human rights law, and the effect of the European Convention on Human Rights and Human Rights Act 1998 on aspects of criminal litigation.

In both civil and criminal litigation modules, you will find that the legal issues are not particularly complex or hard to identify, to the same extent they might have been at the Academic Stage. Instead, the emphasis at LPC level is on the wider issues around a case or claim, introducing you to more practical matters that a solicitor will deal with, over and above the 'black letter' law.

Property law and practice

Having covered the legal foundations of land law on your law degree or conversion course, the purpose of the LPC property module is to set the legal theories in the context of practical conveyancing, and the solicitor's role in buying and selling property. It provides very useful grounding for solicitors wishing to specialise in property work, but is useful for all solicitors, since many commercial transactions include a property element. Even if property law is likely to play a minor role in your qualified career, an understanding of the conveyancing process is useful in your life outside work, when buying, selling or renting your own property.

The main areas covered on the property law and practice module are:

- introduction to the conveyancing process, and the legal and practical skills required

- drafting contracts and transfers of property

- searches and enquiries

- e-conveyancing

- standard conditions of sale, and standard commercial property conditions

- problem areas such as the creation of new easements, covenants, new and existing mortgages

- commercial leases

- planning law

- VAT on property transfers

- financing property transfers

- the role of other professionals in the conveyancing process

- drafting leases

- introduction to the Landlord and Tenant Act 1954 Part 2

- professional conduct considerations in the conveyancing process

- residential transactions: SRA protocol and documents.

Life Changing

Make a start on your future with a law qualification from the University of Sunderland

- Foundation Degree in Law
- Business Law (Top Up)
- LL.B (Hons) with Paralegal Accreditation
- LL.M Criminal Law and Procedure
- LL.M Human Rights

 Best Law Department in th UK for Teaching Excellenc
Sunday Times University Guide 2012

Tel: 0191 515 3341
Email: emrteam@sunderland.ac.uk
Web: www.sunderland.ac.uk

 **University of Sunderland**

Profile: University of Sunderland

The Department of Law at Sunderland has grown in national and international recognition and popularity. We offer a range of courses from our LL.B, for those wishing to pursue a career in practice, to our LL.M suite, designed to enable students to gain a comprehensive understanding of their intended area of practice. We also offer the chance to combine the study of law with another subject. The Department of Law is currently ranked 'Best in the UK for Teaching Excellence' (*Sunday Times University Guide 2012*).

Undergraduate study

Our LL.B is an internationally recognised undergraduate qualification providing students with the Academic Stage of training required by the SRA to embark upon the LPC for those wanting to qualify as a solicitor, or the BPTC for those wanting to qualify as a barrister. The LLB is designed to allow students to take a two in one paralegal route. The LL.B is taught by a diverse teaching team and consequently offers students the chance to study a range of bespoke modules. For students who do not have the credits to apply directly to the LL.B we also offer the Foundation Degree in Law, which allows students to transfer onto Level 2 of the LL.B or onto Level 3 of the BA (Hons) Business Law (Top Up).

Postgraduate study

Our LL.M programmes (LL.M Criminal Law and Procedure and LL.M Human Rights) are designed predominately for those wishing to further their understanding of law to support subsequent career progression. A particular benefit of studying for a master's at Sunderland is the vibrant research environment. Our academic team has in-depth expertise in criminal law and procedure and human rights, which has inspired the master's programmes on offer. Our LL.M programmes equip students with in-depth legal understanding, and will assist in furthering your ambitions whether you aspire to practise in law, go on to further study or simply aim to improve your career prospects.

A few more reasons

- To date over £130 million investment on its two campuses, providing an excellent learning environment.

- Law students are eligible for associate membership of the Sunderland Law Society and the Mooting and Debating team.

- The Faculty's law court develops students' advocacy skills in practical and realistic surroundings, giving real-world experience.

- One of the first UK law schools to develop a Law on Film group, an idea originally pioneered at Harvard.

For further information please contact us on 0191 515 2311 or visit www.sunderland.ac.uk.

Case study

Lewis A. Kerr LL.B (Hons), G.PLL, LL.M, Barrister

I moved from my home city in 2005 after studying for my A levels in order to read law at the University of Sunderland. I settled on Sunderland after meeting the friendly teaching staff and viewing the excellent facilities on an open day. I was also impressed by what I had read about the North East, which is a hub for students from all over the country.

Reading law proved to be challenging but extremely rewarding. Thanks to the support I received, I did not feel disadvantaged in not having studied A level law and was able to progress well, something I attributed to being part of a close-knit department. I was given the opportunity to gain paralegal accreditation while studying on the LL.B programme and this proved beneficial in the next stages of my career.

The University's links with the Crown Prosecution Service (CPS) enabled me to gain employment with them and I began work in September 2008 following my graduation. At the same time, I began an LL.M in Criminal Law and Procedure and studied the programme alongside my work. While the workload was challenging, the support I received from the University of Sunderland was outstanding and I graduated with a distinction.

Working for the CPS inspired me to pursue a career at the Bar so I embarked upon the BVC (now BPTC) at another North East institution in September 2009. I could have moved to London to study but when you have moved to the North East and experienced the friendly community and excellent nightlife the tendency is not to leave!

My graduate and postgraduate degrees and my work experience all equipped me with the tools I needed to compete with the other BVC students and eventually, candidates for pupillage. The University of Sunderland is passionate about mooting and debating, and these skills are essential for any budding barrister or solicitor and therefore are a must for anyone ultimately intending to practise in law.

I was successful in obtaining pupillage in January 2011, and at the time of writing I am entering my second week of the practising half of pupillage. I have appeared in the Crown Court representing defendants in a number of serious offences and have even been quoted in the regional newspaper! It is challenging and rewarding work but my time at the University of Sunderland and the support I received there has stood me in good stead for whatever life can throw at me.

Course skills

The LPC core subjects mentioned above deal with the practice areas that most solicitors work with, although not all solicitors will be involved with all three areas all of the time. By contrast, the 'course skills' are taught as separate course elements, and introduce you to skills and considerations that every solicitor needs, in all areas of practice.

Advocacy

While 'courtroom' advocacy is more generally associated with the work of barristers, it is common for solicitors (particularly those specialising in litigation) to be required to make applications before a judge, to represent clients in tribunals, and to act as advocate in other contexts. On the LPC, advocacy techniques are taught in tutorials, with the assessments taking the form of a mock application before a judge.

You will either represent the claimant or respondent in a case, and will be expected to argue your case in front of a tutor or actor playing the part of the judge. A fellow student will represent the opposing party, and argue against you. The adversarial nature of the process might suggest that your performance is assessed on whether or not you successfully 'win' your application. In fact, what counts is demonstrating that you have researched your area well, put forward a convincing legal argument, and that you respond to, and question, your opponent's points convincingly.

Interviewing and advising

This is again taught in class, where you are given the opportunity to practise interviewing techniques with your colleagues, while the assessments take the form of a scenario prepared in advance. You are required to interview an actor or tutor playing the part of the client, and to provide on the spot legal advice to them, in the context of the information they have given you in the interview.

If you feel that face-to-face assessments are not your strongest area, then take advantage of any practice interview opportunities available from your course provider. These are sometimes video recorded, so you can see how you come across to your client – you may be surprised at what you see, and it can be very easy to spot areas for improvement, which can be a great help in approaching the assessments.

Drafting

A sizeable proportion of any solicitor's workload is taken up with drafting documents of one form or another. These might include legal agreements, court documents, written summaries of legal research and analysis, articles, policy guidelines or any number of other written pieces. For the LPC drafting assessment, you will be given a case study which requires a legal document to be produced.

Again, the legal issues are not particularly difficult to identify or understand at this stage; the scenario may perhaps require drafting a simple licence to occupy land for a specified period of time, or may be a detailed letter of advice to a client. What matters is to ensure that your drafting is well structured and succinct, using clear and unambiguous language, yet covers everything that the scenario requires.

Practical legal research

Good legal research skills are essential for all trainees, paralegals and qualified solicitors. Getting to grips with the array of legal resources available is something you need to master early on. Hard copy and online resources are both commonly used in practice, but have respective advantages and disadvantages, depending on the legal issue you are looking into. This element of the LPC covers both types of resource, with the emphasis on learning to navigate your way through them, to present clear, concise written summaries of your results.

A note on accounts and advocacy

It may seem strange that would-be solicitors are required to study areas more commonly associated with accountants and barristers, but these are core skills that will stand you in good stead wherever you end up in your legal career. When it comes to advocacy, all solicitors find that the advocacy modules provide good training for speaking and thinking on your feet, and are good preparation for life beyond qualification.

Solicitors also find that having some experience in accounts is handy later on in the training process and beyond. A good handle on financial reporting is useful in any area of law, so there is good reason for the accounts modules to be included in the LPC. Accounts assessments are not widely acknowledged as a student favourite, but they are pass/fail assessments whose individual marks do not count towards the overall LPC grade. Most candidates pass them first time, but if you need to retake either of the accounts exams (or other assessments), this is possible. Bear in mind that this may affect your ability to gain a commendation or distinction overall, regardless of whether you have attained the required marks to do so in other exams or assessments.

Case study

Dan Turnbull is a partner at Stewarts Law

I found the LPC quite straightforward, as I had worked in law for a long time before starting it. I had good background knowledge of some of the areas covered, and could easily place them in context. I liked the structured approach to the modules, and found it useful overall. The LPC teaches you to be structured in your thinking, and focused in your work, particularly in terms of how you prepare for exams.

Another thing the LPC teaches you is that you have to be prepared to put the work in. You can't just cram at the last minute, then turn up to the exams, and pass with good grades. The way the courses and the exams are put together means that you have to put the hours in. But if you do, it shouldn't be too difficult.

Other professional subjects

In addition to the course skills, a number of professional and regulatory areas are also covered on the LPC, as they affect many aspects of a solicitor's work.

Professional conduct and regulation

The SRA monitors the training and qualification of solicitors, and implements rules and regulations that govern the solicitors' profession as a whole. The SRA Code of Conduct 2011 is the foundation of the new 'outcomes focussed' regulatory system in which solicitors operate in England and Wales.

The code is based on 10 mandatory principles.

"You must:

1. uphold the rule of law and the proper administration of justice;

2. act with integrity;

3. not allow your independence to be compromised;

4. act in the best interests of each client;

5. provide a proper standard of service to your clients;

6. behave in a way that maintains the trust the public places in you and in the provision of legal services;

7. comply with your legal and regulatory obligations and deal with your regulators and ombudsmen in an open, timely and cooperative manner;

8. run your business or carry out your role in the business effectively and in accordance with proper governance and sound financial and risk management principles;

9. run your business or carry out your role in the business in a way that encourages equality or opportunity for diversity; and

10. protect client money and assets."[7]

The Code covers a wide range of potentially problematic areas that solicitors may face, such as conflicts of interest, confidentiality, referrals of business, publicity and issues specific to litigation work or selling property. The key elements of the Code are covered during the LPC, and issues of professional conduct can appear in any context in the course.

Another key area covered on this part of the LPC is financial regulation. Financial services and money laundering regulations (particularly the Financial Services and Markets Act 2000, or FSMA) have had a big impact on the profession, and the LPC introduces you to the main financial and regulatory issues that solicitors are likely to face. Solicitors' accounts are also taught and assessed as part of the professional conduct element of the LPC. This is assessed by an exam, which is usually sat relatively early on in the LPC year.

Wills and administration of estates

A number of issues, both legal and practical, will occur when dealing with ownership of property of a person who has died. These will differ according to whether or not there is a properly executed will in place. This LPC module introduces each stage of the estate administration process, from initial representation of the client to distribution of assets of the estate to beneficiaries and the final winding up of the estate.

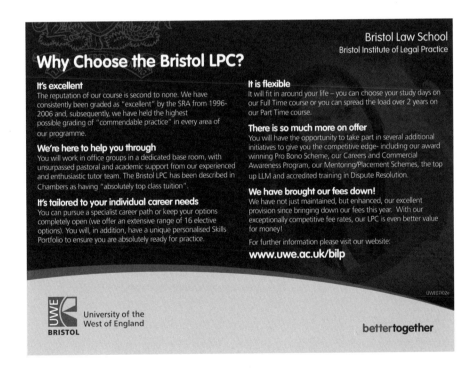

Profile: Bristol Institute of Legal Practice

Bristol Institute of Legal Practice (BILP) is the leading provider of professional legal education in the South West (and the dominant provider of professional legal education in Bristol). BILP is unique in offering the full range of professional courses: CPE, LPC, BPTC, PSC, CPD and additional bespoke training to local firms. BILP is known for its excellence in learning and teaching; all of BILPs courses are designed and taught by experienced practitioners teaching within their own subject areas. BILP's all-round excellence has been confirmed by the SRA year on year – BILP is one of only a very few LPC providers nationally to have consistently achieved the highest possible grading of 'excellent' from the SRA. At the last SRA assessment visit, BILP received the top grade of 'Commendable Practice' in all six areas of its LPC. BILP's reputation in the local market is also second to none.

Enhancing employability

BILP offers much to students in terms of enhancing employability and there is a very good track record of placing students who have not secured training contracts prior to joining (the true measure of success). Students benefit from its placement scheme, which is run in association with Bristol Law Society; BILP has also just introduced an innovative international placements scheme with partner firms in Germany. BILP's students also benefit from a mentoring scheme and a commercial awareness programme, including an innovative legal practice simulation where students are part of a virtual firm with real supervising principals/lawyers in practice with local firms. BILP students may also train to become accredited ADR mediators. BILP students are encouraged to put their excellent skills to good use with real clients by participating in its nationally acclaimed and award-winning Pro Bono Unit.

Professional courses

BILP's courses will provide you with a foundation for a career in law that is hard to match. Fresh and innovative, the emphasis is on learning by doing and providing you with the skills and knowledge to make sure you are prepared for practice within a supportive and friendly environment. On the LPC for example, BILP offers students a broad-based Stage 1 that is designed to prepare students for the full variety of practice, and students are not required to specialise too early. BILP then offers one of the widest selections of elective subjects for Stage 2 of any LPC provider: 16 electives ranging from corporate finance to IP, media and clinical negligence to name a few. All students can top up their LPC/BPTC with a top-up LLM in Advanced Legal Practice.

BILP is a large provider but it is small enough to be very personal. BILP students regularly report that they have not only done really well on their courses but that they have really enjoyed them and have felt nurtured rather than churned through a large professional legal education factory. BILP offers the full range in terms of flexible modes of study (full- and part-time) and a choice of timetabling options to suit you. The facilities are superb – from the newly refurbished dedicated teaching rooms to the fully equipped mock court rooms and a Reuters trading room.

Value for money

Since bringing down its fees for the LPC in 2010/11, BILP has not just maintained but enhanced its excellent provision and offers incredible value for money.

Contact us

For further information on our courses, for a brochure or to attend our law fair/open days visit www.uwe.ac.uk/bilp or email: bilpinfo@uwe.ac.uk.

Case study

Heather Shere-Massey LPC 2010/11

I have really enjoyed my LPC and my experience of studying at Bristol Institute of Legal Practice UWE has been a hugely positive one. There is great emphasis placed on careers support and specialist careers tutors provide careers support to students individually. I have had considerable help with my applications and as a result secured two placements and two training contract offers during the year. There is a much wider focus on raising business awareness and this has also been helpful. I have also taken part in a commercial pro bono project, one of the first of its kind, involving a community group acquiring a swimming pool from its local council. I had a significant amount of day-to-day client contact throughout the project which I have seen through to completion having registered the company or charity, negotiated service level agreement or lease and advised on directors' duties and employment issues.

The course is well structured and the teaching is superb; the focus is on the practical side of being a lawyer as well as providing the relevant knowledge. It has been very useful to gain insight from experienced practitioners who really know their stuff. The teaching is based around small workshop groups conducted face to face by experienced tutors and the work is the kind of practical work that is undertaken by trainees. We stayed in our workshop groups throughout Stage 1 and within these workshop groups we were split into smaller rotating office groups which means you quickly build great relationships and feel confident to practise skills such as negotiation at the workshop. The facilities are excellent, from the high-quality base rooms with computer access to real courtrooms for advocacy practice. There is an active social scene too and all the advantages of being on a University campus. I would not hesitate to recommend BILP UWE as an excellent choice to really prepare you for practice within a nurturing environment.

Compulsories: summary

The purpose of the compulsory stage of the LPC is to ensure that every solicitor is equipped with the core competencies required for a career in practice, no matter in which area you ultimately chose to specialise. The SRA approves individual teaching institutions on the basis that the required subjects are covered, and while there is some variance among institutions as to how the LPC is structured, the course content is very similar wherever you choose to study. Even though the course contents may be similar, you should still do your research before you select an LPC provider, to check how the course is structured, and see what else is on offer.

LPC elective stage

Once you have completed the compulsory stage of the LPC, you will go on to choose three further subjects from a number of different options ('electives'). The elective courses on offer will differ from one course provider to another, but the most common electives to be offered by most providers are:

- advanced commercial litigation/dispute resolution
- advanced commercial property
- banking and debt finance
- commercial law and intellectual property
- corporate acquisitions
- corporate finance
- employment law and practice
- family law
- insurance law
- welfare and immigration law
- personal injury and clinical negligence
- private client
- public companies and equity finance.

By the time you come to choose your LPC electives, you will probably have a relatively good idea of which areas of law appeal to you the most, and where you are most likely to want to work. The electives offer the opportunity to fine-tune your learning to fit these areas, as a first step in specialising your legal knowledge. The elective subjects often match departments within some law firms, and when you come to do your training contract, you will find that the course contents fit very well with the day-to-day work done in those departments. Course providers ensure that all course contents are kept up to date every year, so you will find that your notes and resources will be invaluable when you make the transition from study to practice, and start work as a trainee solicitor.

If you have a training contract in place by the time you choose your electives, then it makes sense to choose electives that match the work you will do with your firm. If you are yet to secure a training contract, then it is important to choose a set of electives that does not limit your future options. Specific electives to choose will depend on individual circumstances, but if you see yourself in any commercial firm, for example, then any of the litigation and finance focused options will be useful. Areas such as employment, family, personal injury and private client law are not practice areas covered by all firms, and may sit better with general practice or high-street firms. Choose options to build your knowledge in your areas of interest, but be aware that narrowing your options at this stage may make your CV less appropriate to a broader range of potential firms to train with.

A note on LPC electives, from a City solicitor

'Your choice of electives is important, and this can influence where you can apply to train. Some firms will require you to do certain electives: pretty much all the big international and City firms will require you to do a corporate/commercial elective, a banking/debt finance elective, and public companies and/or acquisitions. These firms expect you to do these options because these areas are core to their business. This in turn serves as a big clue as to what to expect from these firms, if and when you train there. At other firms the options are not set in stone, but it might be harder to convince a firm that you are the right choice to offer a training contract, if you have not chosen electives that coincide with that firm's main areas of work.'

Full-time or part-time?

The LPC can be studied as a one-year full-time course, requiring around 40 hours of study time per week, including attendance at a number of seminar style classes, plus attendance at lectures and/or viewing online video tutorials, which are becoming increasingly popular.

Part-time courses are also available. These usually span two years, and require around 20 hours of study time per week. Additional time is required for attendance at exams, assessments and assessment practice. As with the part-time conversion courses, part-time LPC courses are intended to offer flexibility, and are a good way to gain your qualification while managing other commitments.

Case study

Ed Chivers is a solicitor at Buss Murton Law, Tunbridge Wells

I did the GDL and the LPC. For me, the GDL was a return to academic education after a gap of a couple of years and I enjoyed it very much. It was both intellectually demanding and satisfying. As it was based around the theory of law rather than the practice of it, it suited my background well. I enjoyed the structure and the teaching, with discussion and debate built into it as a requirement of the course.

On the other hand, the LPC I did not enjoy so much, and I don't believe I learnt as much that has really helped me in my qualified career as I did on the GDL. However, there is flexibility in the system, particularly as to whether or not you do the 'right' electives. By way of example, I am now specialising in an area of law that I did not study at all on the LPC, and did not do as an elective. This has not been a problem, because my firm supported me through my training contract, plus it is only through working in law that you really learn about law and practice.

Case study

David Swain is a solicitor at Simmons and Simmons

The LPC is not very 'academic' as it is more about process and procedure of areas that all solicitors have to cover. Some people find it less interesting than their law degree or conversion for that reason. The LPC builds on your understanding of areas of law you might want to work in, but you should bear in mind at this stage that what you learn procedurally on the LPC is not exactly how things work in practice. In litigation for example, the LPC course sets out deadlines and procedures involved in taking a court action all the way from start to finish. In reality, the timescales in litigation can be very long, so it is unlikely that as a trainee you will see a case all the way through. This will probably not happen until you have qualified, and been working in a litigation department for perhaps a few years.

Because you are in a classroom, some areas of the LPC give a misleading impression of the work in real life, and do not show you how interesting or exciting some of the work can be. For example, it is only when as a trainee you go to the opponents' offices and serve a form on them, or when you go to the Royal Courts of Justice with a claim form and fee to commence a serious action that you realise that you are playing a part in something really major.

At times the LPC may not seem very interesting, or it may be hard to grasp the applicability of what you are covering, but it is a mandatory step, and without it you would be lost as a trainee. You need to have covered the main areas that later become relatively simple tasks, like legal research, knowing the sources of law, doing company searches, finding the right forms and filling them in correctly, or knowing the structure of the court system. You learn some of these things at law degree level, and they come into more context on the LPC, but they become fundamental once you start training.

Qualifications offered by the Institute of Legal Executives

The Institute of Legal Executives (ILEX) system is made up of a combination of academic qualifications and legal work experience that lead to the qualification of legal executive lawyer. This is a professional qualification in its own right, alongside the qualifications of solicitor and barrister. ILEX lawyers can become partners in law firms, advocates and judges. With the appropriate ILEX qualifications and legal work experience, and subject to approval by the SRA, it is possible to use the ILEX route to qualify as a solicitor without having to complete a formal training contract in a law firm. However, many ILEX lawyers choose not to take the route to qualification as a solicitor, as their ILEX qualifications offer them everything they need, particularly given the vocational, practical aspects of the ILEX system. Most ILEX courses are taught part-time, and are designed for those already in work. You can choose to study at one of the 90 nationwide ILEX study centres, or by distance learning.

Academic requirements for ILEX

The recommended entry requirement for ILEX qualification is four GCSEs at grade C or above. If you hold no formal qualifications, these can be gained through introductory level ILEX courses. ILEX places emphasis on diversity, and broadening access to the legal profession – you do not need to have a degree to obtain ILEX qualifications, and indeed many ILEX members see the route as an alternative to university.

If you have no law degree or equivalent, there are two ILEX qualifications available instead. The two qualifications required to become a legal executive are the ILEX Level 3 Professional Diploma in Law and Practice, and the Level 6 Professional Higher Diploma in Law and Practice. The Professional Diploma is set at A level standard, while the Professional Higher Diploma is set at degree level. These can be studied part-time or full-time, and should each take two years to complete. These qualifications allow you to become a graduate member of ILEX.

If you have a law degree or equivalent (such as a GDL), the ILEX Graduate Fast-Track Diploma serves as the equivalent to the LPC or BPTC.

Completion of the relevant ILEX qualification, together with a prescribed five years of practical legal work experience, allows you to become a qualified legal executive.

ILEX offers a broad range of legal qualifications in addition to those mentioned above, from legal secretarial qualifications for administrators to advocacy and court work qualifications for qualified lawyers. Further details on ILEX courses are available at www.ilex.org.uk.

Profile: Institute of Legal Executives

Many people assume that getting a good law career is almost impossible. First you need a place at a good university, then take an expensive postgraduate qualification incurring massive student debt; and finally secure a very rare training contract

But, that's not the only way to be a lawyer.

Since 1963 the ILEX has enabled around 85,000 people to pursue a successful and rewarding career in law without incurring massive student debt.

Legal executives are recognised by the government as fully qualified lawyers and can be found working in 60% of the top law firms in the country. Many supervise solicitors or instruct barristers, and they are also eligible to become partners in law firms, judges or advocates.

But what is it like studying with ILEX? Meena Veja is currently a legal secretary at Taylor Vinters in Cambridge. She is also training to qualify as a legal executive lawyer.

Like many others, when Meena left school, she was only offered the standard advice and options by careers services so was unaware that she didn't have to go to university to become a lawyer. Meena started work in an office before being offered her first legal role in a small local law firm. It was here that she found out you could train to be a lawyer vocationally.

All her employers have been really supportive: 'My employer agreed to pay for my membership and exam fees, which has paved the way to a legal career for me.'

In fact, on average, 75% of employers pay for staff to study with ILEX which, Meena adds, works out perfectly for everyone: 'I have found most legal employers recognise and value ILEX qualifications and are always happy to pay for the membership and course fees. Once ILEX students get to a certain grade they become fee earners, which means their employer can charge their work out to clients and quickly recoup their investment.'

Of course, like any route into law, studying with ILEX is not easy. You have to juggle work and study, but you will be earning money at the same time as gaining practical legal work experience.

So what about the rest of your career? Well Meena was able to join one of the leading law firms in the region because she was studying through ILEX and her ambitions don't stop there. Once she qualifies as a legal executive lawyer, Meena will be eligible to become an advocate, a partner in a law firm, or even a judge.

If you want to know more about the best route into law, why not log on to the ILEX website – www.ilexcareers.org.uk – or call 01234 841 000.

Vocational Stage of training: for barristers

Objective

To complete the Barristers' Vocational Stage of training, you will need to have (in order):

- become a student member of an Inn of Court

- completed the Bar Professional Training Course (BPTC)

- been called to the Bar.

How and when to apply for student membership of an Inn of Court

- There are four Inns of Court – Gray's Inn, Lincoln's Inn, Inner Temple and Middle Temple (see Chapter 4 for more details). Applications for membership should be
  made direct to the Inn of your choice, through its online application form.

- Applications must be submitted by the end of May of the year in which you are due to start the BPTC.

BPTC entry requirements

- Completion of the Academic Stage of training. This is achieved either through obtaining a qualifying law degree or conversion at minimum 2.ii or equivalent (or confirmation from the Bar Standards Board (BSB) that an overseas equivalent qualification is acceptable).

- Membership of an Inn of Court: you are unable to start the BPTC without membership of an Inn (see above).

- Note that the BSB intends to introduce a pre-BPTC aptitude test in autumn 2012 to filter applicants for places on the BPTC (see box on p140 for details).

How to apply for the BPTC

All applications for BPTC courses (full-time and part-time) must be made online via the BSB's central applications system (www.barprofessionaltraining.org.uk). A fee is required for applications to be processed.

When to apply for the BPTC

- The BPTC usually starts in September of each year.

- You should aim to complete your application as early as possible. The system opens mid-October of the year before the BPTC start date.

- The deadline for applications for the first round of BPTC selections is mid-January of the year the BPTC is due to start, with offers made in early March.

- Applications received after mid-January of the BPTC year are processed in a second round of selections, closing at the end of August. First round offers must be accepted by early April, after which a clearing system operates to match candidates to potential places in time for the September start.

Eligibility for call to the Bar

- You need to have passed the BPTC before you can be called to the Bar (i.e. formal admission to the profession, through an Inn of Court).

- You need to attend 12 'qualifying sessions' at your Inn either during, or just after, your BPTC. These range from mooting and debating sessions to talks on legal subjects, and include dinners, drinks receptions and other social occasions.

- You need to submit a number of application forms to your Inn, known as 'call papers'. These are available from your Inn.

- All barristers are required to attend a formal call ceremony. These take place on four dates across the year.

Where to study the BPTC

The BSB has a list of validated BPTC course providers at www.barstandardsboard. org.uk/Educationandtraining/aboutthebvc. Contact details for each of these course providers is also available from the BSB. There are currently only 11 institutions validated to provide the BPTC around the country, all of which offer a very high standard of tuition. There are more BPTC course providers in London than elsewhere, which is perhaps not surprising given that the majority of practising barristers are based in London. There is, however, nothing to stop you choosing to study the BPTC at any of the other providers, based in Bristol, Manchester, Nottingham, Leeds and elsewhere.

When you have completed the barristers' Vocational Stage of training, you are eligible to start your professional training, as a barrister's pupil. Note that being called to the Bar is not the same as qualification as a practising barrister.

A note on the proposed BSB aptitude test

You should be aware that the BSB has piloted an aptitude test for prospective BPTC students, to assess whether applicants to the BPTC have the skills needed to successfully complete the BPTC and go on to a career at the Bar. This has come as a response to the fact there are many more Bar Vocation Course (BVC) or BPTC students than there are pupillage places available (see Chapter 1 for more details on this). The idea of a 'entry' test is to ensure that places on the BPTC are given to those students with the aptitude for a career as a practising barrister, to prevent students with no realistic prospect of getting pupillage from wasting their time and money. This is a controversial scheme – take a look at the BSB website for consultation responses, views and discussions.

The test is likely to be introduced in the autumn of 2012, for students wishing to start the BPTC in September 2013.

BPTC course content

The Bar Vocational Course, as it used to be called, has been revised, and is now the Bar Professional Training Course. The main changes are to the structure and style of some assessments, but generally the two courses are similar.

As we have seen, barristers are primarily engaged in litigation and dispute-related work, which shapes the nature of the BPTC course contents. The BPTC is intended to prepare law graduates for pupillage and for going on to work as a practising barrister. It is intensive and challenging, made up of many elements taught and tested throughout the course, and at least one formal assessment each month throughout the course.

Compulsory modules

Civil litigation

The module focuses on civil litigation procedure, civil evidence and remedies. Civil litigation cases are governed by the Civil Procedure Rules (the CPRs or *White Book*), which also govern court procedures and how evidence is managed and presented in trials. While rules of procedure are a fairly dry subject to teach and learn in absence of their practical application, they are of crucial importance in any civil dispute, at almost any stage of the dispute's development. Civil litigation teaching is usually through weekly classes, with assessment by multiple-choice style tests.

Criminal litigation

Criminal litigation and procedure in the magistrates' court, Crown Court and youth court are covered, from first arrest of the suspect, to trial, appeal and sentencing. Admissibility of evidence makes up a large part of the course, including hearsay evidence, and evidence obtained illegally. The main reference work for criminal law and procedure is *Blackstone's Criminal Practice*, which is referred to throughout the course, giving good exposure to one of the essential reference works used in criminal practice.

Opinion writing and drafting (two modules)

The barrister's spiritual home may be in court, but often, more time is spent giving written advice on the merits of a claim (from both sides' points of view) and how a case might best be conducted, usually on the instruction of a solicitor. Good drafting is therefore a crucial skill for a barrister. On the BPTC this is taught and assessed through drafting documents such as particulars of claim, defences to particulars of claim, responses to defences and preliminary injunctions. These are usually set in the context of contract- and tort-based problem scenarios.

Written exercises are set each week during the BPTC, with some providers allocating up to 20 sessions to opinion writing and drafting tuition throughout the course. Note that the opinion and drafting modules are now assessed through timed examinations at various points along the course, whereas on the BVC these were take-home papers.

Conference skills

'Conference' – the formal name given to a meeting between a barrister, his instructing solicitor and/or client – is the main opportunity for a barrister to discuss a case face to face, in advance of a court or tribunal hearing. On the BPTC, conference skills are taught through scenarios, which can be either based in civil or criminal law, and in which any number of issues might arise. The barrister must be able to deal with all issues appropriately, and advise accordingly. The course is taught through weekly classes, with a final oral examination based on a combination of pre-prepared materials, and materials added during the assessment itself, with an actor playing the part of the client.

Negotiation skills, and resolution of disputes out of court (two modules)

The cost, time and negative publicity often attached to court proceedings have together brought about an increase in alternative methods of dispute resolution (ADR). Barristers are increasingly being brought in to negotiate settlement with the opposing party. The negotiation module of the BPTC concentrates on good preparation and effective negotiation tactics, practised in the context of a civil claim where settlement can be achieved financially, through a sum of money being paid by one party to the other.

Mediation is another form of ADR and may be required in any number of legal contexts. A barrister may be required to represent a client in a mediation, or to advise on a form of dispute resolution that will be most effective to resolve a matter.

These modules are taught through weekly classes, and through practice negotiations with other BPTC students. As with the conference skills module, an actor plays the opposing barrister in the final assessment.

Advocacy

This is a key component of the BPTC, and covers applications to court, submissions in court, and handling witnesses. Applications to court may take the form of requesting a judge to grant a preliminary injunction, perhaps to prevent a neighbour from creating a nuisance. Witness handling usually takes the form of examination-in-chief and cross-examination of witnesses in court.

As with the negotiation skills module, advocacy is taught through a series of weekly interactive classes. Applications and witness handling are both assessed through oral examinations at the end of the term in which each module was taught, with actors playing the part of the judge, defendant or witness. Good advocacy skills are of such importance to barristers that some course providers allocate as much as 40 hours of tuition time to this part of the BPTC.

Professional ethics

This element of the BPTC looks at various professional ethical dilemmas that might be faced in practice, covering barristers' relationships with other members of the Bar, lay clients (i.e. those who are not professionally qualified), professional clients and the courts. There is no discrete assessment in professional ethics. Instead, ethical issues are placed within other course module assessments (oral or written), with students being expected to identify ethical and conduct issues as they crop up, and to deal with them appropriately.

Professional and ethical conduct of the barristers' profession is set out in the Code of Conduct of the Bar of England and Wales (www.barstandardsboard.org.uk/standardsandguidance/codeofconduct/).

Legal research and case preparation

The starting point for most legal problems, particularly those encountered early on in a barrister's career, is properly to research current case law and statutes relating to the problem. Legal research on the BPTC is structured to resemble the kinds of research tasks that might be encountered during pupillage. Problem questions are designed to require research using online resources (such as Westlaw and LexisNexis), and hardcopy resources (such as *Halsbury's Laws of England and Wales*). Research tasks are set on a weekly basis, culminating in a written exam, based around a pre-prepared problem scenario.

Optional modules

On completion of the compulsory modules, two further modules must be chosen to complete the BPTC. Most of these optional modules give insight into the legal and practical aspects of more specialised areas of practice, and serve as an introduction to the kinds of issues barristers may meet in the early stages of their career.

Some of the areas available as BPTC optional modules are:

- employment law

- company law

- family law

- international trade

- judicial review

- personal injury and clinical negligence

- property and chancery

- advanced criminal litigation.

These can be assessed in different ways, according to what is most appropriate for the subject matter. Some, such as company law and property, are assessed through written opinions on particular scenarios. Others might be assessed through practical oral exercises, such as an advocacy exercise for advanced criminal litigation, a conference with clients for family law, or a technical drafting exercise in the case of a judicial review scenario.

Advice on selecting optional modules on the BPTC, from a recent student

'Technically, it should not matter which optional modules you chose on the BPTC, as strictly you do not need to have studied these areas of law before doing the optional modules. My experience, however, was that if you were not familiar with the area of law covered in the optional module, then it was very difficult indeed to study. I would recommend only choosing *modules with which you are at least reasonably comfortable, and with which you have some familiarity before you start.'*

Modes of study

The BPTC can be taken as a one-year full-time course, with attendance required throughout the week, or a two-year part-time course with attendance at weekends. It is structured in two parts, with the compulsory modules taken first, followed by the two optional subjects.

Part-time or full-time?

Most course providers offer the BPTC as full-time or part-time courses. Full-time courses involve around 18 hours of formal teaching time, and as much private study time as is needed. Part-time BPTC courses usually consist of around 15 study weekends during the year, and require at least the equivalent of 30 hours of private study time.

Case study

Fredericka Argent is a non-practising barrister, and former BVC student. She has these views on how the BVC (now the BPTC) helped her in her later career

In terms of the work I do now, I have definitely found the procedural aspects of the law that I learned during the BVC very useful. For example, time spent learning the contents of the *White Book* has helped me apply the law in a much more practical way than I would have done had I only done an academic law degree without the extra year. My drafting skills are also much better following the BVC, which means I can be of more use to my employer when it comes to putting together the formal documentation that makes up a large part of our work.

Prior to the BVC, my writing experience was limited to essays, and I had never seen official court documents, forms and so on. I also learned important legal research skills on the BVC, including exactly where to look for specific information, and how to refine a search to make it as efficient as possible. These are apparently simple things, but they are crucial skills that the BVC has helped me develop. The main area that I have not had an opportunity to use since the BVC is advocacy, but all in all I feel that doing the BVC has definitely been beneficial to my career.

Summary

You now have a good idea of the kinds of subject areas and courses you will come across during the early stages of your legal career either as a solicitor or barrister. Each course provider gives detailed breakdowns of the various courses on their websites and in prospectus publications, so it's a good idea to look at a few different providers, to get an idea of how their teaching methods work, and to decide which one is likely to be best for you, before you sign up.

8

Extra-curricular opportunities while studying

While you are studying for your Graduate Diploma in Law (GDL), Legal Practice Course (LPC) or Bar Professional Training Course (BPTC), you have many opportunities to develop your CV, and to improve your career prospects by getting involved with extra-curricular groups and events. As the courses themselves are short (one-year each for full-time students), it is essential that you research what is on offer right at the start of the first term, and sign up to as many groups and activities that you think you will have time for, and which will directly benefit your CV. If a group does not exist in an area you are interested in, then start one. This demonstrates initiative and your commitment to building your experience.

Commercial awareness

If you are interested in commercial law, then all potential employers will expect you to demonstrate 'commercial awareness'. This is an elusive term, but it boils down to a few key points:

- understanding current commercial (i.e. non-legal) issues that affect both the wider economy, and any sectors you are interested in

- showing that you have thought these issues through, and have an opinion on them

- understanding how a legal adviser's role relates to these commercial points, in the context of a client's business.

Working on your commercial awareness helps you to demonstrate that you can analyse issues from a commercial and legal perspective, and that you have the potential and interest to understand clients operating in different sectors, and the factors that influence their businesses. This will signal to interviewers and people reading your applications that you have the potential to become a lawyer who can offer good quality, relevant legal services to clients. At the start of your legal career, just covering the course materials is not enough to convince an employer that you have what it takes. Future employers will be looking to see that you have taken the initiative, and will expect you to show evidence of broader skills that all good lawyers need.

Many students coming to law have not had a job before. If so, you may be wondering how to gain commercial awareness with only limited previous work experience. One answer is to get involved in commercial law groups, and other activities, as you do your law courses. Attending seminars and lectures outside of your courses is a good way of networking and keeping up to date on current developments – and it is even better if you can help organise these events. If you join an organising committee, you will benefit from the content of the seminars themselves and more importantly, you will be able to influence which speakers are invited, make contact with them directly, and impress them with your professionalism and organisational abilities. You can then add them to your network of relevant legal or commercial contacts. We will look at commercial awareness in the context of interviews in Chapter 9.

Another answer is to consider part-time work, while studying. This would of course need to be balanced with your studies, and you need to ensure you do not take on too much.

Advocacy experience: pro bono work and mooting

If you are interested in advocacy and court work, then it will be expected that you have some experience in doing this – getting involved in a pro bono group is the ideal opportunity for you to represent and help people with all manner of real-life legal issues.

Pro bono groups exist at most of the major course providers, with the purpose of offering free legal advice to those who need it, on all kinds of different legal issues, including family law, housing, criminal or employment law. Student volunteers are supervised by qualified practitioners, and may be required to interview clients, and to provide written or oral advice. Some pro bono units are affiliated to local councils. This creates a link with the local community, and offers an insight into the importance of advising the client on the legal issues that are relevant to them, while managing relationships with a number of interested parties.

Mooting

Most colleges and course providers offer the opportunity to get involved in mooting. This gives students the opportunity to develop their advocacy skills through arguing their case compellingly, on their feet. Mooting requires the ability to analyse a case, research related case law and legal principles, and to present a legal argument clearly and coherently. It is an adversarial process, requiring quick reactions to the opponent's arguments, to convince the presiding judge to decide in your favour. Mooting competitions are organised around the country, allowing you to test your advocacy against new opponents, and perhaps to raise your profile by winning prizes or awards. Mooting events are also an excellent opportunity to meet barristers and judges who often act as adjudicators, and who may become useful professional contacts in the future.

Other activities

All course providers and colleges have a number of other groups through which you can build additional experience for your CV. If you have not yet decided on a course provider or college, then make sure you take potential extra-curricular programmes on offer into account when you are looking into which one to choose. These do not all have to be law related, and can be used to demonstrate a range of skills that legal recruiters are looking for. For example, if you were on a social committee that organised an end-of-year ball, this will have required teamwork, organisation, time and budget management, negotiating with and managing people, and possibly even some commercial dispute resolution in a real-life context. However, do be aware that a lot of recruiters find this example very obvious and common, so be as creative as you can with your examples.

Acting, music and sport are other areas that involve interaction with others, project management, and a certain amount of work and discipline in order to achieve results. Make sure all this experience goes on your CV in a way that really sells the experience as something positive. And even if, in your opinion at least, something that you worked on was not the success you hoped it would be, there is always something positive to be said in terms of how you managed preparation and organisation, and what you learned from the experience.

Networking

A high proportion of jobs and training positions are offered to people who have made the effort to build a connection with an employer, be that a law firm, chambers or other organisation. This may seem on the surface to be evidence that perhaps the profession has not yet shaken off its elitist image, favouring people from familiar, connected backgrounds. If you do not yet have any contacts in law, then you may be asking yourself how you are going to be able to progress your career, if contacts are so important.

In fact, anyone can build up a network of useful contacts. Getting involved with college or university groups that interact with areas of the profession you are interested in is a very good way of making some initial contacts. In addition to joining groups, speak to your tutors, and make sure you use your careers service.

Tutors and careers advisers are on hand to give advice on who to approach and how, and are armed with up-to-date contact information. They also know former students who may be working in areas you are interested in, and who may be may be happy to meet informally over a coffee, to discuss what your options may be.

All law course providers are offering professional qualifications, and are aware that in today's competitive marketplace, their performance will be judged on the ultimate employability of their students. It is therefore in the colleges' interests to provide the best possible services to help students improve their chances of successfully progressing to the next level of qualification, and on into work: they will do all they can to help.

Making contacts and keeping them up

It may be appropriate in some situations to approach a potential contact 'cold', if they have published their contact details online, and to request politely if they might spare a moment to talk, as you would value their insight and advice. A carefully drafted email may well be all it takes to set up a meeting, and to give you the chance to gain an expert's view on whichever areas you find interesting, or may be seeking some guidance in. This may in turn lead to a chance to do some work shadowing, a mini-pupillage or placement, or perhaps, ultimately a job offer.

Ongoing contact with people you may have met in this way is quite an art, and there are no hard and fast rules that govern how you should keep in touch. When is a good time to get back in touch with a contact? The occasional email may be good, particularly if you have some good news to share, such as a good exam result. If your contact has recently had something published, or has been mentioned in the press, then this might create a good opportunity to re-establish contact. Use your initiative, be tactful, and you will find that there are a lot of people out there who are prepared to help you, and who will be impressed by your efforts. Who knows, one of these contacts may know of a vacancy or a role – either now, or years down the line – that you would not otherwise have known about, and which might be just what you are looking for.

Experience shows that generally, people working in law at all levels are prepared to help others on their way up through the profession. They all understand the challenges, as they have been through the same process themselves. If you approach people politely and professionally, the chances are that they won't mind sparing some time to talk to you and offer some advice, even if only by way of a quick email. Do your research, and see who is already doing what you want to do. A wealth of information is available on law firm websites, while social networking services such as LinkedIn, Twitter and Facebook are excellent sources of additional information, and potential contacts.

Social networking or career suicide?

Social networking services are being used increasingly to vet potential applicants in all professions, so be careful with photos and comments you put up on Facebook and other social networks. The chances are that your future employer is looking at your pages with as keen an interest as your friends — so don't say or publish anything that might later come back to haunt you!

9

Managing your studies

Balancing work and life outside of study

Work load and time management

It almost goes without saying that the best way to balance studying with other things in your life is to be highly organised, and to manage your time effectively. Everyone does this differently, and what works for some people will not work for others. The Academic and Vocational stage courses cover such a broad range of elements that inevitably some people will find some parts harder than others, even within the same class or study group. What matters is to make sure you keep on top of the courses as you go. The Graduate Diploma in Law (GDL), the Legal Practice Course (LPC) and the Bar Professional Training Course (BPTC) all cover a huge amount of ground in a short period of time, and the key to doing well in the assessments is to keep up with all the work as each course module progresses. Identify issues and difficulties as they arise, and deal with them as you go, rather than leaving them to the end: when it comes to revising for the exams and other assessments, you need to be sure you are relatively happy with everything covered before you start the revision. There will be plenty of questions and queries that you will need to go over before the exams, without having to use valuable revision time to tackle any missed modules, or areas you didn't cover properly the first time.

Below are some practical pointers, from successful GDL, LPC and BPTC students.

Treat studying like a job

If you are studying full-time, then treat all your courses as if they were a full-time job. If your classes are in the morning, stay in college and work in the afternoons to prepare for the following day. You may have other commitments, but if you do your best to put the hours in on an ongoing basis, this will help enormously in covering as much ground as possible at a sensible pace, without rushing to catch up.

Balance work and studying carefully

If you are studying part-time and working, then you do not have the luxury of being able to treat your studies like a full-time job – you probably already have one! There will be occasions when it will be hard to balance your career work with your academic work. Part-time courses are designed specifically with working people in mind, and your tutors will have seen students dealing with similar difficult situations to any you might face, and will know how to help. If you are having problems keeping up, then speak to your tutors as soon as you can. They can offer practical advice and guidance to help keep you on track, and can help you with any administrative issues, such as re-scheduling classes or assessments. You should also keep your employer updated with your progress, and give them regular updates on how you are getting on. The most appropriate way of doing this will depend on the employer, but by making sure that they are aware of positive progress as well as potential issues, they will be better able to help you if any problems do crop up.

Make time for your social life

Whether studying full-time or part-time, you will have family and other social commitments which are not related to your legal work. No matter how hard you work, and how focused you are on doing the very best you can, it is essential to make time for life outside of law. Family and friends are the best support network you have, and even if you feel fully engaged with your work, there is still a long way to go when you are still at law school. You'll be making a lot of friends and contacts, but be careful to pace yourself, and to make time for people who know you best. There is a lot to cover in the courses, and the temptation may be to spend every available moment studying, but you won't function well without contact from the outside world. Time spent with friends and family will help keep things in perspective, and keep your energy levels and morale up, even during more challenging times.

Spread out the workload

When studying, the temptation can sometimes be to put your head down and plough through as much material as you can in one sitting. It is well known that you can only concentrate fully for a couple of hours at a time, so make sure you take regular breaks as you work. If possible, go outside and stretch your legs for 10 minutes or so. Fresh air is a good cure for lapses in concentration, and it's important to give your eyes a rest from peering at books, or looking at your computer screen.

Get organised

When organising your time, set specific times aside for specific activities. If you have coursework to do as well as your training contract or pupillage applications, or contact emails to write or follow up on, make sure you have earmarked time slots for each thing you need to do. It's best to slightly overestimate how long each thing will take you, to allow time for breaks, and slippage if something takes longer than you think.

Use university holidays and consolidation weeks when there is no scheduled teaching to get on top of everything as the course progresses. This does not apply only to covering course content, but to your own admin as well. Organise your files, your revision notes, your tutorial and lecture notes, etc. while your timetable is free: it will save valuable time when revising.

Make the most of online resources

Some courses now offer online lectures and tutorials. Make use of the flexibility that these can offer – you can choose a time and place to suit you, which can be very useful to cut down on travel time to college, or having to wait until a lecture or class is scheduled.

Keep your notes, files and books

Make sure you keep all your notes and course materials, for every course you do, after you have completed them. You will find that you need to refer back to these throughout the early stages of your career. You may find some of your LPC or BPTC notes give a good overview of something that you are about to work on during your training contract or pupillage, and may serve as a convenient reminder. All the course materials link together and are designed to reflect real-life legal work, so don't lose them (or be tempted to throw them away) as you go from one stage to the next.

Prepare for exams from the start of each course

On any of the law courses, it is not possible to leave the work to the last minute, as the various course elements relate to each other, and join up as you go. On the GDL, you have seven courses to consolidate for exams, in a short period of time.

GDL results are 70% exam based, and your final grade will depend on your performance in the seven exams at the end of the course. Make sure you are prepared for these exams from the very start. Most course providers will offer mock exams at various stages of the courses, and while these are voluntary, they are the best way to assess your progress, to identify your weaker areas, and get you used to doing legal exams under timed conditions. You will do better in some areas than others, but an early 'wake up call' will give you the chance to focus on areas to work on while you still have time. Speak to your tutors about any particularly difficult areas as you go along, as they are there to help, and want you to succeed. There is more on exam strategy below.

The LPC and BPTC are both structured in two parts: the compulsory modules followed by optional modules. All the teaching and assessments for the first part are done in the first few months, after which you leave them behind. You then move on to the teaching and assessments for the second part. This gives very little time for consolidation, so you have to consolidate as you go. It is much harder to focus on the new course areas if you need to retake any exams or assessments at the same time.

Practise, practise, practise

The LPC and BPTC are very assessment heavy throughout the year, and there are exams and assessments at the end of both compulsory and elective/optional stages. This can be quite a shock for those coming from undergraduate law degrees, where more time was available to consolidate each course module during the three years. With these courses, it is not possible just to put your head in the books and rely on being good on paper: we saw earlier that the interviewing and advocacy assessments are oral, while others are practical research tasks, using online or library resources, to teach and test a range of skills. Again, take advantage of the opportunities offered to practise these in good time, before the assessments themselves.

Dealing with law exams

Everyone working in any qualified legal position has sat a huge number of exams along the way. There are no exceptions to this, so it's important to do your homework on exam strategy. Law exams generally test your ability to identify and apply specific legal concepts to factual scenarios. You have to know the law, you have to be able to work through the questions to identify the issues on the facts presented, and you are then required to formulate an accurate, coherent answer. Some aspects of the law are very closely prescribed, to the extent that there can be a 'right or wrong' answer. Other areas may have a little more capacity for your own interpretation, but generally you will be marked on fairly strict criteria, and there is no room for waffle.

Plan a proper revision schedule and stick to it

It is essential to work to a properly planned revision schedule. Allocating realistic timeslots (mornings, afternoons, whole days) to the elements of a course will give you a roadmap with which you can navigate your progress through to exam day. If exams are scheduled in a batch, then some people find it useful to arrange revision in reverse order, revising for the latest exams first, then working back to revise for the earliest exams at the end of the revision period. That way, it is a relatively straightforward job to go back over the revision for each subsequent exam, as they come along. You have already covered the material, and just need to go back over your notes before the exam.

Use summary cards

Condense your notes into summary cards containing the key information for each module or subject area, and test yourself on them as you go through the course.

Summaries are essential to revise from, and provide a quick overview of a course, in a format that is easily memorised, and which should not be too daunting to look over. This helps boost your confidence, when looking over the course material in the run up to exams.

Know the format of each exam paper

Law exams differ greatly from subject to subject, so it is really important to know exactly what the format of each paper will be. How many sections are there? What is in each section (essays, problem questions)? What choice of questions do you have? Do you need to answer two of three questions? One of four? Are they essays or problem questions? You also need to know how many marks are available for each section, and for each question, so you can plan exactly how long you need to allocate in the exam for each. This is easy to plan, but very hard to stick to under time pressure: in the exam room, put your watch on your desk, so you can check the time as you go.

Finish every paper

You need to make absolutely sure that you finish every exam you sit. You have to attempt all the required questions in any paper, in order to cover 100% of the available marks. You can't score marks in questions you haven't answered, and neither can you gain marks beyond the maximum available in those you have answered. The only way to guarantee the highest possible mark is to attempt every question, and that means planning your time, and answering every question.

Use your support network

Law exams can be a daunting prospect, but most people get through them without too many problems. Some people find that the best way to cope with the exams is to get a healthy balance between working alone, and following up with colleagues on specific areas that are unclear. One GDL class joked about having set up a 'revision hotline' before the exams: they would call each other at the end of each day's revision, to go over any points that were not clear. Almost every time, at least one person in the group would have understood a point that another had not, or had understood it in a slightly different way to the others. This made it easier to share difficult points with others who had not fully grasped them, in a clearer and more time efficient way than going over course notes or textbooks alone. By working in this way, gaps and grey areas are quickly closed off, while keeping up vital morale and team spirit as exams approach. Your course provider will organise revision sessions for all assessments, which you should always attend, even if they are voluntary.

Dealing with open-book exams

Some law courses include open-book exams, particularly for certain elements of the LPC. Open-book exams are a relatively recent development, and can seem strange and unfamiliar. The best way to approach an open-book exam is to consolidate your course materials well in advance, and to revise as if you could not take the materials into the exam. Taking reference materials into an exam may appear to make the exam easier. In fact, it sets a very easy trap to fall into, as you cannot rely on the materials you have, and risk wasting time looking things up. Marks are not awarded for copying sections from the books, and you need to focus on analysing the questions, applying the relevant law, and giving a properly considered and structured answer.

Your revision notes are the best reference material to take with you into the exam, as they will be accurate, concise and easy to navigate. Mark these up with specific page numbers and tabs for quick reference if needed in the exam, but use them only as a prompt, not as an initial point of reference.

Working with materials provided in advance of exams or assessments

You may be provided with pre-assessment materials, to review a few weeks before an exam. There will be certain restrictions on how you approach these, and you will probably not be permitted to discuss the materials in detail with tutors or colleagues. You will be able to do all the research you need in good time, to be able to answer the questions fully in the exam, so use the time you have as efficiently as possible. You may only be permitted to take a marked-up copy of the original pre-assessment document into the exam, so make notes on separate sheets first. Only add consolidated notes to the original after you know exactly what you need to have noted for the exam.

On the day of the exam

Last minute 'touching up' revision can make a big difference to your performance in an exam. Obviously, leaving anything other than overview revision to the last minute is a sure-fire way to failure, but going over your consolidated summaries the night before an exam, and for a couple of hours just before you take your seat on the day, can help boost your confidence. It can push the course content to the front of your mind, and ensure that any fiddly details, sequences or patterns of information can all be recalled as soon as they are needed. In the exam itself, there is nothing to stop you jotting down a few notes as soon as you are allowed to pick up your pen at the start – but don't get carried away!

Practical points

Law exams are often sat in conference centres or other large facilities to accommodate huge year groups, and these may be in locations away from your college that you do not know. Before all exams in unfamiliar locations, you must know where you are going well in advance. Use Streetmap or Google Earth to locate the venue, and to get an idea of what the area is like, so you don't get lost when you get there.

Work out your route, and how long the journey will take. Exams are important, and you don't want to risk any problems which might knock your concentration or leave you flustered. If you would usually take public transport or drive, then consider taking a taxi instead, booked to pick you up in good time. You can revise on the journey, and you will minimise the risk of getting lost or delayed. Finally, make sure you've eaten before the exam, and if you can, take some chocolate or an energy bar with you, as well as a bottle of water.

Summary

These are just a few of the tried and tested methods that have been proven to make a positive difference when coping with the pressure of GDL, LPC and BPTC exams. There is plenty more material available to help you manage your exam strategy; look online or in your college library, and make sure you talk to one of your course tutors if you have any questions or concerns. *Student Essentials: Revision and Exam Strategies* by Mark Wickham (Trotman, 2011) is another good resource, with useful information in a handy format.

10

The professional stage: training positions explained

Introduction

When you have successfully completed the Academic and Vocational stages of training, you will be eligible to go on to complete the professional stage of training: by completing a training contract for solicitors, or a barrister's pupillage. These are the final stages of training before you qualify.

As a trainee solicitor or pupil barrister, the first few months are spent assisting your supervisors with their practical, day-to-day work. This introduces you to aspects of life as a working lawyer, and while the precise nature of the work will vary by department or supervisor, and according to the kinds of matters being worked on at any particular time, you can expect to be working on a range of different matters relating to a number of different areas of law. You will receive appropriate supervision, but you will also get a good deal of responsibility for the work allocated to you.

Thoughts from a trainee in a city firm

'Securing a training contract can be very, very hard work, and quite soul destroying when rejections keep coming in, but this is the same in any profession where there is a lot of competition for places. It's only when you're doing your training contract that you realise how great an opportunity it really is. Unlike other professions like accountancy, you don't have continuous assessments and exams as you work. With a training contract or pupillage, you learn through the practical work you do, a bit like an apprenticeship. As long as you work hard, and satisfy the requirements set by the SRA or BSB, then by the time you're doing your professional legal training, you will have no more exams to do in order to qualify, which is great.'

Trainee solicitors may be given responsibility for managing their own clients and matters after a month or two in each 'seat' (see page 170), or they may find themselves working on larger matters that prevent them from taking on their own files. Trainees are usually expected to have direct supervision from a partner up to qualification, and often for some time later. Pupil barristers generally spend six months working with a pupil supervisor before going on to manage their own workload, with less direct supervision. The process for barristers is similar, but usually takes only one year, divided into two parts: six months under closer supervision from a suitably qualified barrister, and six months acting in a more independent capacity.

Before looking at how to get a training position, you need to know exactly what you are applying for. This is to make sure your applications are as good as they can be, and to show the employer that you have what they are looking for. There is quite a lot of information in this section, and you may think this might wait until you start your training. However, if you are to have a realistic chance of securing a place, you need to know what will be involved, so it is well worth familiarising yourself in some detail with what is usually covered in a training contract or pupillage. We will look at each one separately.

Solicitors' training contract

Objective

To complete your qualification as a solicitor, you will need to complete:

- a formal training contract with a supervising firm

- the Solicitors' Professional Skills Course (PSC; including optional Higher Rights of Audience qualification)

- a Criminal Records Bureau (CRB) check

- enrolment with the SRA as a solicitor.

Training contract eligibility

- Completion of the Academic Stage and solicitors' Vocational Stage of training (LPC).

- Enrolment with the SRA as a trainee solicitor.

ADDLESHAW GODDARD

EAGER

Help us grow as a team. We'll help you grow as an individual.

As a fast expanding and innovative law firm, a career with Addleshaw Goddard means more variety, earlier responsibility and greater future opportunities to develop with the firm. Training with us will mean working with top FTSE companies and other leading organisations.

With offices in London, Leeds and Manchester, we can offer quality training wherever you want to be based. If you are interested in a training contract with us or a Summer/Easter placement visit:

www.addleshawgoddard.com/graduates

Profile: Addleshaw Goddard   ADDLESHAW GODDARD

As a major force on the legal landscape, Addleshaw Goddard offers extensive and exciting opportunities to all its trainees across the entire spectrum of commercial law, from employment and banking to real estate, corporate finance, intellectual property, private finance initiative and litigation. As a trainee with this firm, you'll be a key member of the team from day one. Wherever you are based, you'll work closely with bluechip clients within a supportive yet challenging environment, and be part of a structured training programme designed to ensure your success – now and in the future.

Main areas of work

The firm has five main business divisions: finance and projects, litigation, commercial services, corporate and real estate. Within these divisions, as well as the main practice areas, it also has specialist areas such as intellectual property, employment and private client services such as trusts and tax.

Trainee profile

Graduates who are capable of achieving a 2.i and can demonstrate commercial awareness, motivation and enthusiasm. Applications from law and non-law graduates are welcomed, as are applications from students who may be considering a change of direction. We also have a diversity access programme for applicants on GDL or LPC with less conventional academic backgrounds. Further details can be found on our website.

Training environment

During each 6-month seat, there will be regular two-way performance reviews with the supervising partner or solicitor. Trainees have the opportunity to spend a seat in one of the firm's other offices and there are a number of secondments to clients available. Seated with a qualified solicitor or partner and working as part of a team enables trainees to develop the professional skills necessary to deal with the demanding and challenging work the firm carries out for its clients.

Sponsorship and benefits

GDL and LPC fees are paid, plus a maintenance grant of £7,000 (London) or £4,500 (elsewhere in the UK). Benefits include corporate gym membership, season ticket loan, subsidised restaurant, pension and private healthcare.

Vacation placements

Places for 2012 – 90
Duration – one or two weeks
Location – all offices
Apply by 31 January 2012

Locations

Milton Gate, 60 Chiswell Street, London EC1Y 4AG
Sovereign House, PO Box 8, Sovereign Street, Leeds LS1 1HQ
100 Barbirolli Square, Manchester M2 3AB

Website: www.addleshawgoddard.com/graduates

Key information

Partners – 160

Associates – 500+

Trainees – 89

Contact – grad@addleshawgoddard.com

Closing date for 2014 applications – 31 July 2012

Training contracts per year – 45–50

Applications per year – 2,000

Per cent interviewed – 8%

Required degree grade – 2.i

Case study

A day in the life of an Addleshaw Goddard trainee

Richard Line works in the litigation department as part of the reputation management team. He studied an LLB in Law at the University of Leicester (2004/07).

9.00a.m. I usually arrive at my desk by 9a.m., which gives me a chance to check my emails and voicemails. I normally have a couple of cases on the go, currently including a professional negligence case and a copyright infringement. I flag any important emails so that I can use my inbox as a 'to do' list (my top tip for aspiring trainees!) and then deal with the emails in order of urgency.

9.30a.m. I read relevant articles in the internal 'clients and markets' and 'daily legal update' emails. These are particularly useful to keep up to speed with business and legal developments.

10.00a.m. On Monday mornings my team has an informal catch-up, to discuss our current matters and any upcoming deadlines that we need to keep in mind. New cases are allocated to those with the most capacity and relevant experience, and we are kept up to speed on what the team is doing at all times.

10.30a.m. An urgent meeting has been scheduled with our client in the professional negligence matter, which I attend with my supervisor. We discuss any weaknesses in our case and how this affects the next steps which we will take.

11.30a.m. As a result of the meeting, I use the thorough note that I have taken to draft a letter to the other side's solicitors setting out our client's position. Once completed, I submit this to my supervisor for his comments.

12.30p.m. Lunch time! If there is training scheduled for 1p.m. (once or twice a week), I will take an early lunch break with the other trainees in the Milton Gate restaurant.

1.30p.m. I get back to my desk to see that I have received an email from a partner, asking me to research the extent to which correspondence with expert advisers is privileged. I immediately turn to the *White Book* (the litigation bible!) and other online research tools. I then draft a memo to the partner setting out my findings.

3.30p.m. I allocate 30 minutes each day to focus on non-work activities, such as our CSR [corporate social responsibility], graduate recruitment and international development programmes that I am involved in.

5.30p.m. I have a quick chat with my team to discuss any loose ends and outstanding matters that have come in throughout the day.

6.30p.m. There are usually a number of things going on after work. On Tuesday I volunteer at our pro bono clinic in Lambeth, and on Friday the trainees usually go out after work for a couple of drinks!

How to apply for a training contract

- Applications are usually made direct to solicitors' firms. Check the firm's website, or make contact with firms to check how they prefer applications to be made.

- Many of the larger firms have online forms with fixed deadlines, after which applications are closed.

- Some firms prefer a CV and covering letter. There may be some flexibility as to timing of applications with firms that do not use an online system. Again, check with the firm to find out their requirements.

See Chapter 11 for more information on training contract applications.

Advice from a partner in a City firm: Daniel Turnbull of Stewarts Law

'Nowadays, training contracts seem to be like gold dust. It is quite rare to secure one during your law degree, on the GDL or even on the LPC. The reality is that it's not unusual to see people start a training contract in their late twenties or even thirties. My advice is to get as much legal experience as you can, particularly through paralegalling. Often this opens doors in a firm; the firm sees how you work and gets to know you well. Many firms are recruiting from within like this.

'You should try to get as many strings to your bow as possible, including in non-legal areas like business development. This is important for any career, not just law, as you have to learn how to be confident with people, and build a network of contacts. An excellent way to get this experience is through working with charities, or volunteering. Working with other organisations like these gives you a range of experience, and can really give you the edge over another applicant. This looks good on your CV, and will greatly improve your chances of getting a training contract.'

When to apply for a training contract

- Training contracts usually start in September, while some of the larger firms take an additional intake the following March, allowing candidates time between the end of the LPC and start of the training contract. March starters will therefore qualify in March, six months after the September intake.

- For mid-sized and top tier law firms, applications are required to be submitted at the end of July, two years before the training contract is due to start. For example, applications for a training contract due to start in September 2014 would need to be submitted in July 2012. For undergraduates, this means submitting applications between the second and third years of their degree. For non-law graduates, applications will need to be submitted a few months **before** the GDL starts, in order to allow you to progress directly from the GDL to the LPC, and on to your training contract.

- Some firms have separate application processes for law graduates and for non-law graduates. Non-law graduates may be required to apply earlier than law graduates.

- Each firm has its own individual application process, so you should check carefully what is required and when, for each firm you intend to apply to.

- High-street and smaller firms may recruit much nearer to the start date of the training contract, and often recruit during the LPC year.

Deadlines and lead times

Note that training contract application procedures and deadlines vary from firm to firm, so you must ensure you know the deadlines and requirements well in advance for every application you make. Missing a deadline may mean you end up having to wait another year before you can apply again. As noted above, it is common for training contract applications and offers to be made two years before the training contract starts: this goes back to the days when most people came to law straight from undergraduate law degrees. The majority of training contract offers were made in the second year, to allow a year for finals, and a year for the LPC.

Today, more people come to training contracts from other routes, and for many, the two-year lead time can be a significant obstacle in the way of career progress. The lead time means that non-law graduates are required to apply for a training contract before they have studied any law. You need to bear this in mind when you are planning your career, as you may find yourself with at least a year's gap to fill, particularly for GDL students who are unable to secure a training contract during the GDL year. This can be turned to your advantage, however. Use the time to gain legal work experience, perhaps working as a paralegal. This experience may even count towards your training (see below). You need to be aware that you might need to be flexible in your planning, as it is not always possible to progress from the LPC directly to a training contract. The same goes for BPTC students looking for pupillage.

Relevant work experience

Relevant legal work experience may count towards your training contract, and may allow you to reduce the duration of your training contract from the usual two years. The SRA has further information on this, and you should discuss this with the firm with whom you are intending to train.

Preparing for qualification

In order to qualify as a solicitor, trainees are required to apply for full SRA membership. This includes arranging admission to the roll of solicitors, and your first practising certificate, upon payment of a fee. More details are available on the SRA website.

Trainees are also required to complete a Criminal Records Bureau (CRB) check. This is to check if any prospective solicitors have a criminal record, and if so, what the status of any penalties is. If you have a criminal record, this is likely to affect your eligibility to qualify. Detailed guidance is available from the CRB when you come to fill in the form. This is usually done about three months before the end of the training contract.

How training contracts work, and what is involved

Training contracts are usually two years long (unless qualifying through the Institute of Legal Executives (ILEX) route, see below), with time, spent in different departments of the firm. The objective is to achieve standards set by the SRA, through gaining practical experience in the following areas:

- advocacy and oral presentation

- case and transaction management

- client care and practice support

- communication skills

- dispute resolution

- drafting

- interviewing and advising

- legal research

- negotiation.

You will gain some experience in all these areas during your training, to varying levels, according to the work coming through the department in which you are sitting, or on which your supervisor is working.

Trainees are usually required to spend time in at least three different departments of the firm. Trainees working in firms with fewer departments may find themselves as a shared resource across the firm. Those working in larger firms will usually have their time divided into units of four or six months, known as 'seats', in specific departments. The six-month seat system gives more detailed exposure to the work of each department, and an opportunity to become well acquainted with the matters you are working on. Seats of four months offer the opportunity to experience a broader range of work in more departments, and then to go back to a department you were particularly interested in.

Secondments

Some firms send trainees on secondment to clients, which can be an excellent way of gaining hands-on working experience outside of the firm's working environment. Secondments are also a great way of putting yourself on the map as an ambassador to your firm, and a point of contact between the firm and the client. They look good on your CV, too.

Professional Skills Course

In addition to the day-to-day work covered during your training contract, all trainees must complete a compulsory Professional Skills Course (PSC) before they can be admitted as solicitors. The PSC is a practical course administered by the SRA, which covers many of the issues that are likely to come up in all areas of solicitors' practice. There are several modules to the PSC, the majority of which are often done in the first week of the training contract, before the first 'seat' starts. The other modules are taken as your training contract progresses. As with the LPC, the PSC is made up of core modules and electives, with the core modules usually being completed first. However, unlike the LPC, the PSC is covered mainly by attendance at seminars, with only one short written assessment (see below).

Core PSC modules

Advocacy and communication skills

This module covers case preparation, analysis and presentation. Criminal and/or civil court cases are used as case studies, with classroom-based mock trials used to demonstrate and discuss advocacy techniques at the various stages of a hearing (opening and closing speeches, examination-in-chief, cross-examination).

Client care and professional standards

The objective of this module is to further improve understanding of professional conduct, beyond what was covered on the LPC. This includes analysis of the Solicitors' Code of Conduct, ethical issues and risk management, and dealing with situations that are likely to crop up in practice, such as handing duties to third parties and the court, undertakings and implications of giving them, and project management.

Financial and business skills

This course deals with regulatory aspects of a solicitors' dealings with financial matters, and the rules governing when and how solicitors may give financial advice, by reference to the SRA Code of Conduct and regulatory regimes governing the provision of financial services, in particular the provisions of the Financial Services and Markets Act 2000 (FSMA). The PSC builds on the LPC in this area, and its importance is reflected in the fact that it is the only PSC module involving a written assessment. This is a multiple-choice exam of 1.5 hours, which tests the key areas covered in the course.

Elective PSC modules

You need to cover 24 further hours of PSC training through subjects appropriate to your areas of work, in order to complete the PSC. A minimum of 12 hours must be spent in face-to-face tuition, while the rest may be conducted by distance learning. PSC electives are usually taught classes or seminars, which are fitted around your other work as a trainee. Elective courses are available in all the main areas of a solicitor's work.

- Contentious electives include criminal, family and employment law, personal injury and dispute resolution.

- Non-contentious electives include corporate law, commercial property, commercial and intellectual property law, and private client law.

- Practice skills electives appropriate to all areas of practice include commercial law firm management, written and communication skills, negotiation and presentation skills.

For solicitor advocates, Higher Rights of Audience training counts towards the PSC requirements. This course can be done as either a trainee or a qualified solicitor, and is a qualification in its own right, aside from the other electives. More information on the qualification process for solicitor advocates is available from the Society of Solicitor Advocates (see www.solicitoradvocates.org).

Training record

The SRA requires all trainees to complete a record of the work they have done during their training contract to demonstrate that their work meets the SRA standards. The training record must include details of the work done, the particular skills covered (by reference to the SRA practice areas listed on page 170), observations on their own performance, and any professional conduct issues that might have come up. Further training or tuition received should also be noted, such as attendance at seminars or briefings, articles written or published, and so on.

The SRA is entitled to inspect law firms, to monitor their performance in how they train their trainee solicitors. You may be called upon at any time to produce your training record, so make sure you keep it updated as you go, to prevent you having to catch up later!

Contentious and non-contentious work

The SRA requires trainees to gain a balance of contentious and non-contentious experience as they cover off the practical areas above. If your firm (or employer, if you are training in-house) cannot offer you experience in a particular area, they can arrange for you to go on secondment to a firm that can offer this experience. If, for example, you are training in-house in a company, then it is possible that you will not gain experience in litigation or dispute resolution. In this case, a secondment to a law firm's litigation department for a few months will give you the experience the SRA requires.

Profile: Allen & Overy

ALLEN & OVERY

About Allen & Overy

Allen & Overy LLP is an international legal practice working in 39 major centres worldwide. Our clients include many of the world's top businesses, financial institutions and governments.

Start at the top

Starting your career with Allen & Overy means starting at the very top of international commercial law. We are renowned for the high quality of our banking, corporate and international capital markets advice, but also have major strengths in areas such as litigation and dispute resolution, employment and benefits, tax and real estate.

Training

We offer a truly flexible training contract and the most interesting work in a unique culture of support and mutual respect. The seat structure ensures that you get to see as many parts of the practice as possible and that your learning is hands-on, guided closely by an associate or partner. Most seats are for 6 months, with some three-month seats available. Given the strength of our international finance practice, we require our trainees to spend a minimum of 12 months in our core areas of banking, corporate and international capital markets. The firm offers its trainees the option of completing a litigation course. The course is run by Nottingham Law School and consists of five days' tuition and monthly visits to a legal advice centre for a year to gain practical contentious experience. In addition to the PSC there are numerous training courses available covering a broad range of legal and personal skills.

Trainees have told us that one of the things they value most about being at Allen & Overy is the excellent training they receive.

Who we are looking for

We expect to see a strong, consistent academic performance with at least a 2.i (or equivalent) predicted or achieved. At Allen & Overy you will be working in a team where you will use your initiative and manage your own time and workload, so we also look for evidence of teamwork, leadership, motivation and problem-solving.

Working environment

Life at Allen & Overy is about more than just the work we do – our team environment encourages professional and social relationships. The Trainees' Social Committee is responsible for planning a variety of events, from drinks and theatre trips, to the annual trainee summer ball. There are also sports teams, a fully equipped fitness centre, music rooms and multi-faith prayer rooms.

Application dates

Training contract – to apply for our March and September 2014 intakes, visit www.allenovery.com/careeruk.

Final year non-law undergraduates and graduates can apply from 1 November 2011 to 15 January 2012. Penultimate year law undergraduates and graduates can apply from 1 June 2012 to 31 July 2012.

'Allen & Overy LLP' refers to Allen & Overy LLP and/or its affiliated undertakings.

Case study

Victoria Gore – second seat trainee (studied history at Durham University)

I joined Allen & Overy in September 2010 and am now nearing the end of my second seat in the litigation department. When I began my training contract I knew I was joining a firm with an outstanding reputation throughout the legal profession and one which is also highly praised for its training programme. Not only have I found this to be the reality, but my expectations have been exceeded. The comprehensive nature of Allen & Overy's training contract has meant that I have developed both my professional and personal skills. The seminars organised by the firm during my LPC were an excellent way to gain an introduction to the firm's working life as well as adding value to the skills I was simultaneously gaining on the course. The Professional Skills Course run by Allen & Overy during your training contract, together with departmental breakfast briefings, lunchtime seminars and newsletters, provide easy access to a wealth of knowledge and skills and it is immensely satisfying when

you can see your knowledge having a positive impact on your daily work. The extensive support network, both in terms of the people and the services available, helped me settle in and the open door policy ensures continuing development. A further strength of life at Allen & Overy is the care given to your personal needs too, whether that's the ability to take an hour out to run up a sweat in the well-equipped gym or relax with your colleagues at the end of the day with a glass of wine and barbeque on the roof terraces.

My first six months were spent in the global loans sub-group of the banking department. General tasks included registering security taken over a loan, monitoring conditions precedent and having direct contact with solicitors across 23 jurisdictions. The work I have undertaken has been challenging but also highly rewarding. The wealth of opportunities to become involved in often high-profile, legally complex work is one of the core strengths of Allen & Overy's training contract. I am currently sitting in the banking, finance and regulatory group within the litigation department. From the excitement of filing claims at the Supreme Court and then attending the hearings, to the research of complex legal issues, the buzz of obtaining a judgment, and helping to draft a settlement agreement, my experiences in my second seat have been varied and have certainly not left me disappointed.

I am looking forward to further developing my legal skills and building upon business relationships during the rest of my training contract and hopefully beyond. When people ask where I am undertaking my training contract, I always say Allen & Overy's name with a smile!

Barristers' pupillage

As we mentioned earlier, barristers' pupillages last one year, and are divided into two six-month stages, known as 'sixes'. The first 'six' is referred to as the 'non-practising' six, since the pupil is not yet eligible to take on their own matters. Instead, they assist their pupil supervisor in case preparation, at hearings, conducting legal research, and observing the supervisor. In the second six, the pupil is eligible to take on his or her own matters, managing their own cases and clients. At this stage pupils start to develop their professional profile and reputation as practising barristers. When applying for pupillage, you need to bear this structure in mind, and demonstrate your capability to assist a pupil supervisor adequately for the first few months, before moving on very quickly to take on a good deal of work and responsibility yourself, in a relatively short period of time.

Objective

To complete your qualification as a barrister, you will need to complete:

- barristers' pupillage (one year spent training under a qualified barrister)

- compulsory training courses in advocacy, practice management and accounting.

Eligibility for obtaining pupillage

- Completion of the Academic Stage of training.

- Completion of the barristers' Vocational Stage of training (passing the BPTC or BVC) within the last five years.

- You will need to have been called to the Bar before you start pupillage.

How to apply for pupillage

The Pupillage Portal (www.pupillages.com – formerly the OLPAS system) allows candidates to submit applications to up to 12 chambers. The website also contains a list of all pupillages available, including those offered by chambers that are not part of the Pupillage Portal network.

See Chapter 1 for more information on how pupillage works.

When to apply for pupillage

- Pupillages usually start in September or October.

- The Pupillage Portal allows first applications for pupillages to be submitted only between the end of March and the end of April of each year, at which point the system closes to applicants.

- First round applications are considered between May and September, with first round offers being made from early August to early September.

- Applications may be made to the clearing system between March and September, with the clearing process taking place during October. The system closes altogether each year at the end of October, to reopen again for candidates the following March.

- The Pupillage Portal operates to a strict timetable, which is available at: www.pupillages.com/help/PreLogon/olpas/timetable.asp

- Chambers that are not part of the Pupillage Portal network may be approached direct – check with each one for application requirements and deadlines.

- You must register your pupillage with your Inn and with the BSB before you start, in order for all of your pupillage time to count towards qualification.

Preparing for qualification

You will need to obtain formal Certification of Pupillage on completion of the first six months of pupillage (the non-practising element of professional training), and a second Certification of Pupillage after the second, practising, six months.

When you have completed all the necessary stages of pupillage, you will be issued with a Full Qualification Certificate. Note that this is not the same as a Practising Certificate, which must be obtained separately from the Bar Council.

There are four core areas in which the BSB sets requirements for experience and competence in all pupils:

- conduct and etiquette

- advocacy

- conferences and negotiations

- drafting, paperwork and legal research.

The BSB issues checklists for use by pupils and supervisors, which set out details of these core areas, and the skills that need to be covered during both first and second sixes. These can be adapted by individual chambers to reflect the precise nature of the work carried out, and chambers or supervisors will ensure that pupils gain the required experience as their pupillage progresses. For full details of the BSB requirements, consult the current version of the BSB's *Pupillage Handbook,* available at www.barstandardsboard.org.uk.

In addition to the core skills and checklists above, the Bar Council requires all barristers to have completed three formal training courses before a practising certificate will be issued:

- advocacy training

- practice management training

- forensic accounting.

These courses are organised by a pupil's Inn, rather than by chambers, and course elements vary from Inn to Inn. You can expect the courses to go well beyond the minimum requirements, often being covered in weekend residential courses. These courses are outlined below.

Advocacy training

A minimum of 12 hours of advocacy training is required during pupillage, and must be completed within the first six months. Advocacy training is mainly conducted through exercises in legal argument and speeches, and making or opposing applications to court, such as injunctions. Witness handling, case analysis, examination of witnesses and cross-examination are also covered. Advocacy is often tested through practical exercises in court, with a judge presiding over the exercise as if it were a true hearing.

Practice management training

This is made up of several elements, and is usually covered in the second six months of pupillage. Subjects included in the practice management course include:

- managing the transition from Bar student to independent practitioner

- professional ethics

- managing tenancy as a practising barrister

- court etiquette

- accounts and book-keeping

- working with Legal Aid

You can also expect to receive training in specialist areas of the Bar, in which you may either wish to practise, or already be practising. These include the areas of barristers' practice that we looked at in Chapter 4, as well as additional areas such as local government and planning law, technology and construction law, commercial and admiralty law, immigration law or revenue law.

Forensic accounting

The forensic accounting course is an introduction to financial accounting information, as it applies to a barrister's work. The course covers the main principles of accounting, and financial documents that are likely to be encountered in the context of litigation, and to enhance awareness of accounting systems in order to improve individual barristers' own practice.

Profile: CMS Cameron McKenna LLP

The firm

CMS is the leading organisation of European law firms, which includes CMS Cameron McKenna. We advise on a wide range of transactions and issues, meaning that our clients benefit from working with teams that really understand their needs and concerns. To ensure this we've launched one of the legal sector's most comprehensive client feedback programmes to measure just how focused we are. This approach helps us get an honest opinion on our performance and has been recognised in a number of prestigious awards.

Acting on this feedback we have adopted a sector approach to provide clients with an industry-specific service and deep sector expertise. Working alongside our traditional practice group structure, industry focus groups enable us to build teams taking an industry, rather than a purely legal, perspective – something that we know our clients value highly. Our industry focus groups are: consumer products; energy and utilities; financial institutions and services; hotels and leisure; infrastructure and project finance; life sciences; real estate and construction; and technology, media and telecoms (TMT).

Types of work

Our practice groups are: energy, projects and construction; real estate; banking and international finance; corporate; commercial, regulatory and disputes; and human capital.

Who should apply

The firm welcomes applications from all backgrounds. Applicants must have 320 UCAS points (or equivalent) and be expected to achieve a 2.i degree or above (or equivalent).

Training programme

Training contracts last for two years. During this time you will have four six-month seats or placements. You will be awarded a priority seat and will undertake a compulsory seat in either banking or corporate, and a contentious seat. Additionally it is expected that graduates who join the firm will spend one seat outside of our London offices. This may include: time in the UK at other regional offices such as Aberdeen, Bristol or Edinburgh; a UK-based client secondment; or a secondment outside of the UK to one of our leading Central and Eastern European offices.

When and how to apply

Applications for training contracts must be received by 31 July 2012. The deadline for our summer and spring vacation schemes is 31 January 2012. All applications must be made online at www.cmstalklaw.com.

Work placements

The two-week scheme allows you to spend one week in two different practice areas, and undertake various presentations, workshops and social events. Our vacation schemes run over spring and summer, and are open to anyone who is interested in pursuing a legal career.

We also run schemes at our Bristol and Scottish offices so please refer to the website for further details.

Sponsorship

We cover fees for the GDL and LPC and provide you with a maintenance grant of up to £7,500. Please see our website for further details.

Case study

Lee Donovan studied ancient history at Durham University. He is now training at CMS Cameron McKenna

Why CMS Cameron McKenna?

It does not matter how much you prepared at university or law school, starting your first seat at one of the top European law firms is like being thrown in at the deep end of a very large pool. The thing that sets CMS Cameron McKenna (CMS) apart from other city firms is that you don't just have a single lifeline in the form of your supervisor; you are surrounded by them. This support proved invaluable when I was involved in completing one of the top UK PFI [private finance initiative] deals in just my second week in the Infrastructure and Project Finance team. Knowing that I had the support of the entire team gave me the confidence to present problems, and suggest solutions face to face to clients who were later surprised to learn that I was a first seat trainee.

CMS being a client-focused firm has a large effect on your training contract. The sector-based approach, involving teams created from different departments for individual clients and deals, means you get a real variety of work. Working with colleagues in projects, real estate and corporate as a single team allows us to understand each deal in full which in turn gives us a better understanding of the clients. Another huge advantage of training at CMS is that you are actively encouraged to spend your second seat away from the London office on secondment to either a client or another CMS office. This opportunity to take on more responsibility and experience the firm from either a client's point of view or that of another CMS office is one I look forward to greatly.

CMS prides itself on its people but it is not until you start at the firm that you realise why this is so important. The people in the office are not only intelligent, but more so they are balanced and diverse. The fact that after just a few months I have already been able to involve myself in a number of pro bono schemes and sport teams illustrates the work–life balance achievable but also shows that people actually want to do external activities with their colleagues; something I had not experienced in previous office jobs. CMS has in recent years tried to shake itself of the 'friendly' tag in a bid to show its serious side but it is exactly this 'friendly' atmosphere which sets it apart from other firms. The deals CMS has advised on and awards it has won speak for themselves, it is the people who ensure you get top level training in an environment you really enjoy.

11

Applying for a training position: how to approach employers

You now have an idea of what to expect during your training contract or pupillage. Armed with this knowledge, and after doing more of your own research into areas specific to your interests, you are ready to make a start on applying to firms or chambers, to obtain a training position. This is not an easy process, but with enough information, and good preparation, you will maximise your chances of success.

Where to start

As a starting point, for each application you make, whether you are a prospective solicitor or barrister, you need to demonstrate that:

- you have done your foundation research (see page 186)

- you know where you want to go in your career

- you understand the employer's areas of work, areas of law covered, and its client base

- you understand the role you're applying for

- you understand what the requirements and standards are for it

- you are confident that you can do a good job in that role

- you can give examples to back up what you say.

Here are some tips to help cover each of these areas, to help build your strategy to secure a place.

Foundation research, and knowing where you want to go

Before you make any applications, think carefully about who the right employers really are for you. You must be sure that by the time you start to make applications, you have a fairly clear idea of the areas of law you want to work in, and therefore who your target firms or chambers are. Don't worry if you are not sure exactly where you ultimately wish to specialise, or if you are unsure which department you might want to qualify into. You need to keep an open mind as your training progresses, as the more experience you gain, the better informed you will be to make this decision on qualification. All that matters at the application stage is that you know the general direction that you want your career to head in – are you looking to do commercial law, or more family- or high-street-oriented work? Criminal or civil?

With tough competition for places, the temptation is to think that it doesn't really matter where you end up, as long as you are offered something. You must, however, go for what is right for you. Ultimately, it's your training, and you need to be sure that at the end of it, you have gained experience and knowledge in areas that will be useful for the rest of your career. If you are confident that the role you are applying for will cover this, then you have a much better chance of convincing the employer of your suitability for that role.

Select a target group of employers to apply to, and focus on this group first. For solicitors this can be hard to do, for practical reasons. There are a lot of firms to choose from, and if there is a two-year lead time between applying for a training contract and starting it, this can make matters more complicated. However, with enough research and some work experience, you should have a good idea of which firms do the work you are interested in, and which ones are likely to be a good fit for you. Make a priority list, and apply to these first. You can go on to make further applications later, as necessary.

Understanding the employer's work

Law firm and chambers' websites are invaluable sources of information on the kinds of work they do. These sites are designed to give a positive and clear picture of areas that they specialise in, with information on recent successes and significant developments, and more general information. You should study in detail the websites of all employers you are particularly interested in. They will be regularly updated, and it is important for every applicant to know what the latest developments are within that organisation. Have they been working on any major cases, or commercial deals? Has one of their lawyers published something that relates to an area you are interested in?

It is often helpful to check the contacts sections, where lawyers mention their individual areas of expertise, and usually list a few recent matters they have worked on. When it comes to preparing for interviews, it can be very useful to put a face to the names of people you may meet, or who may interview you.

Go to law fairs, open days and other careers events. These give an excellent opportunity to speak with representatives of law firms or chambers, and to go over things face to face, rather than online. Trainees and pupils often attend law fairs on behalf of their employer, as well as human resources staff or more senior lawyers. They are happy to talk about what they do, and this is an ideal opportunity for you to get first-hand information on what to expect from any role you apply for.

It's important to make a good impression with all potential employers you meet, and particularly those you are keen on applying to. You can do this by showing you already have some understanding of what they do, and how the organisation is structured. This may be from articles on careers websites or publications, or just from a careful review of their own website. Being informed makes you stand out from the crowd. Use this as a basis from which to ask more detailed questions about areas of work, or the department of the particular person you are speaking to, and for any general advice or thoughts they may have for someone in your position.

You may find that it is possible to arrange a work placement or vacation scheme directly through contacts made at events like these. If not, you can at least find out in some detail what the application procedure is, and what they tend to look for in applicants for vacation placements and training positions.

Understanding the role

You can gain a good level of understanding of what to expect in any role you apply for from the employer's websites or from other publications, as mentioned above. However, you also need to have a good understanding of some of the more technical aspects of what is required at each stage of training, in order to make your applications as good as they possibly can be, and to ensure you are equipped with the knowledge you need for interviews. You will not be expected to know everything there is to know about law, but you should understand what your training will involve, and what the various stages and requirements are of a training contract or pupillage. Use the information earlier in this chapter as a starting point to research how the various training positions work at the places you are applying to. You will impress the recruiter if you show awareness of what is involved, and can use this as a basis to demonstrate how and why you are suitable.

To gain an understanding of what the role is like, try to speak to current trainees or pupils. Very often they will attend law fairs, as mentioned above, and they will certainly attend open days and other events hosted by the employer. They are happy to discuss their experiences, and are well versed in successfully navigating the application process as a whole. They will have personal experience of their employer's application and interview procedures, and are ideally placed to give you some really useful insight into what the employer is looking for, and what worked for them. You should always bear in mind that a good impression made when speaking with any representative from any organisation may well be fed back up, and serve as a mark in your favour.

You should also make sure you are in regular contact with your college careers service, updating them with progress you are making with applications, and in particular, letting them know which employers you have had contact with. Your careers advisers may know the firms or chambers you are applying to, and might be able to draw on the experience of past applicants, to help give you further information and advice on what to expect from the application process. Some careers services ask students to feed back on their experiences at interviews and assessments (whether they have gone well or not so well!). These are kept on file, and can be an invaluable source of insider information on what the structure of the interview or assessment was, what kinds of questions were asked, who the interviewers were, and other information based on their experiences. This information can be a great advantage when approaching an employer, or preparing for an interview.

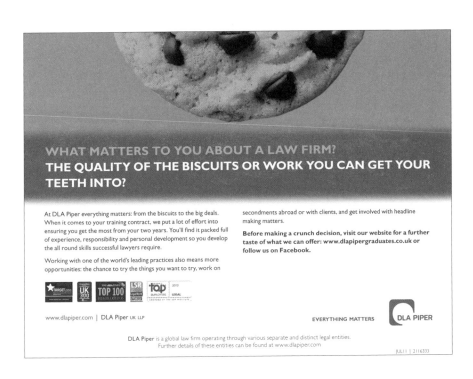

Profile: DLA Piper

DLA Piper is one of the world's largest global law firms, supporting businesses with their commercial legal needs. We now have 4,200 lawyers working in over 70 offices in Asia Pacific, Europe, the Middle East and the USA. In the UK we have a national presence with offices in Birmingham, Edinburgh, Glasgow, Leeds, Liverpool, London, Manchester and Sheffield.

Our vision is to be the leading global business law firm, delivering quality value-added services to our clients, who include some of the world's leading businesses, governments, banks and financial institutions. Our main areas of work include corporate; employment, pensions and benefits; finance and projects; intellectual property and technology; litigation and regulatory; real estate restructuring; and tax.

Our success depends on our most important asset – our people. We have been awarded a commendation for our diversity initiatives and policies, proving our commitment to recruiting and developing people from a wide variety of backgrounds. Our progressive approach to recruitment creates a mix of talents that contribute to our success, and our rankings in a number of national graduate employer surveys demonstrate our emphasis on providing trainees with the most well-rounded experience.

As a trainee you will complete four six-month seats after attending a comprehensive residential induction. You will have the opportunity to apply to do a seat abroad, or a client secondment. If you want responsibility, you will be given as much as you can handle and your progress will be monitored through regular performance reviews and feedback. The compulsory Professional Skills Course is run in-house and is tailored to meet the needs of the trainees. This, combined with on-the-job experience, will provide you with an excellent foundation on which to build your professional career.

At DLA Piper we have an extensive corporate responsibility programme to support local communities around each office and international charities and projects. This programme includes pro bono work, as well as educational and environmental projects, and our employees are actively encouraged to get involved!

There is no 'standard' DLA Piper trainee – we do not want clones and therefore consider every application on its own merits. We seek enthusiastic and committed individuals, whose strong communication and teamworking skills enable them to deal with the intellectual challenges of the job. A keen interest in the business world is essential – as is an appetite for life!

DLA Piper will have approximately 170 places on the summer scheme in 2012 and 90 vacancies for training contracts commencing in 2014. We welcome applications from students from all degree disciplines who have a minimum of ABB at A level (or equivalent) and expect, or have achieved, a 2.i degree classification. You can apply by completing the online application form, which can be accessed via our website (www.dlapipergraduates. co.uk).

Case study

James Duffy is a trainee solicitor at DLA Piper UK LLP, Leeds

I studied law at Newcastle University and then went on to the College of Law at York to complete my Legal Practice Course (LPC). After a year out travelling, during which time I visited South America and South Africa, I was ready to put the theory I had learnt from my degree and the skills I had learnt from the LPC into practice.

Life at DLA Piper started for me in September 2010. The firm put on a great induction week which was held in a luxury hotel in Reading. Trainees from all of the UK offices together with the new trainees in the Hong Kong office were in attendance and this was a great opportunity for me to meet my future colleagues in an informal and relaxed environment. The firm put on a number of social events together with practical seminars to ensure we were fully accustomed with the 'DLA Piper way'.

I would be lying if I said my first day in the office wasn't daunting, but I was soon made to feel very welcome by everyone in the team. You really get a lot of support as a trainee, and there are always people there to help out when you get stuck or if you make a mistake. My first seat was in IPT (intellectual property and technology) and I am currently sat in the banking department. To try to describe a day in the life of a trainee at DLA Piper in generic terms does not really do justice to the diversity, variety and unpredictability a training contract here can offer you. To be honest, this is one of the main attractions of working for a large corporate firm. Corresponding with colleagues and clients via email and phone makes up a big part of every day. I also spend a lot of time in training seminars that are specific to my particular department. I get a lot of client exposure and have had the opportunity to attend completion meetings for large headline matters. The tasks I do most often involve drafting legal documents, carrying out research into legal or commercial issues and preparing updates for clients and the rest of my department on legal developments relevant to their business or practice.

DLA Piper is a great firm to train with. It is a firm with a global presence and strong roots. The opportunities available to a trainee here are huge and if you approach your training contract with enthusiasm and ambition then DLA can be a very exciting place to work.

Understanding requirements and standards for entry

You need to satisfy the requirements of the role you are applying for. If you have a blip on your CV, or if you feel that further clarification is needed to explain your qualifications, you need to have a strategy in place to overcome this – see Chapter 6.

Being confident you can do a good job in the role

This is down to you as an individual. Once you have done all your foundation research, spoken with trainees or pupils, and you know where you are heading, it is likely that you have a good idea of what is involved in any particular training role, and that you are capable of doing it, and doing it well. Using clear, positive language is a good first step to demonstrating confidence in applications, and getting your suitability for the role across to the person reading your application. Backing up your statements with relevant examples adds further weight to showing yourself off as a capable individual, and a credible candidate – see below. Using a similar strategy in interviews will also show you in your best light.

Using examples to support what you are saying

We will look at some of the common application and interview questions in more detail later. Legal applications and interviews are designed to be challenging, to find out about your achievements, and, perhaps more tellingly, also to understand how you are as a person, testing your powers of reasoning and argument, how you react under pressure, and so on. The employer is looking for these skills, and the application form or interview is your chance to demonstrate them.

However, it is not enough simply to say you are good at something, or that you enjoy a particular area of law, and want to pursue it as a career. You must be able to back up what you say by drawing on relevant examples, preferably from your own experiences with the employer. If this is not possible, then you should set your answers in real life, preferably law-related, contexts. Think about your legal experience so far: the best answers will draw from practical experience, and link areas together, for example: 'I did a vacation scheme with your firm last summer, working in department B on matter C. I was responsible for tasks D and E, which involved using resources F and G, and skills H and I. I gained a good understanding of how areas of law J and K related to each other in the context of the matter, and what the commercial implications were for the client.' If you can back this up further with positive feedback from a supervisor, it will add weight to what you say.

Competition for places is tough, and you may need to think laterally as you progress with your applications. There will always be mainstream routes to qualification, via large law firms or the well-known barrister sets, but a wealth of alternative routes to qualification exist too. For example, some non-legal employers offer training schemes to staff working in-house. If a particular sector appeals to you more than the idea of working in legal practice, then you may be better off gaining some hands-on experience at graduate or paralegal level, before going on to train and qualify in-house. We will look at some alternative career plans in Chapter 12.

FRESHFIELDS

100 training contracts
plus
60 vacation places
18 international placements
4 open days and workshops
110 university visits
to help you decide
if a career in law with Freshfields
is for you.

Once you meet us you'll just know.
And we'll know too.

To find out more, go to:
www.freshfields.com/uktrainees

provider
Official
Olympic and
Paralympic Games

Freshfields Bruckhaus Deringer LLP

A CHANCE TO MAKE YOUR MARK
STRETCHED MINDS
LOYAL FRIENDS
FANTASTIC CLIENTS
YOUR DEAL IN THE NEWS
LIKE-MINDED COLLEAGUES
EXCEPTIONAL TRAINING
UNEXCEPTIONAL BISCUITS
OCCASIONAL GLORY
SHARED ACHIEVEMENTS
LATE FOR DINNER (AGAIN...)
STEEP LEARNING CURVES
GREAT SPORTS AND SOCIETIES
INTERNATIONAL TEAMS
BIG THINKERS
COMPLICATED PROBLEMS

Profile: Freshfields Bruckhaus Deringer

 **FRESHFIELDS**

Freshfields Bruckhaus Deringer is one of a handful of leading international law firms, with offices across the world

Our clients are mainly big commercial businesses whose names are well known. The type of work we do divides into helping clients achieve what they want through doing deals, advising them on real and potential problems, and helping them sort out their disputes. Our practice is very diverse, and constantly changing to meet our clients' evolving needs.

Clients look to the firm to be able to answer any legal or regulatory questions that confront them. Organisationally, the firm's lawyers work in one of eight departments: corporate; finance; dispute resolution; real estate; intellectual property/IT; tax; employment, pensions and benefits; and antitrust, competition and trade. But our practice is extremely broad and dynamic: we are constantly having to develop new areas of expertise as it becomes clear that we need to do so to serve our clients properly.

Who we are looking for

We are looking for around 100 trainees to start training with us in London in 2014, split between two intakes in February and August. Our training programme is vital to us, because today's trainees are where most of tomorrow's associates and partners will come from.

The firm wants its trainees to come from diverse backgrounds, and their choice of university or degree is immaterial. Current trainees studied at nearly 50 different universities. Many did a law degree, but others read subjects ranging from music to biochemistry. Whatever their background, trainees need some non-negotiable qualities. They need to be intellectually talented and have excellent English skills. They need to enjoy working on difficult problems, working alongside others, and never doing less than the best they can.

Training and development

Trainees who join our London training programme can move departments every 3 months, so they can see more of what's on offer. Many other firms are not so flexible. All departments provide formal training. But trainees learn most by working for clients alongside the firm's more experienced lawyers. They learn in London and in other offices in the USA, Europe and Asia. Some are also seconded to clients.

Training contract applications

To apply for a training contract to begin in February or August 2014, you will need to apply online between 1 November 2011 and 31 July 2012. Go to www.freshfields.com/uktrainees for details.

Work placements

We normally take students on vacation schemes who are in their penultimate year of their undergraduate degree. Some vacation students can spend time abroad as part of their placement. The application window for the 2012 schemes is from 1 October 2011 to 9 January 2012, but the sooner you apply the better.

Making written applications

Practical points on applications generally

We will look at the kinds of questions that may be asked in application forms and interviews later in the chapter. Meanwhile, wherever you are applying, and whatever method of application you need to use, a few foundation rules apply.

Do your research (again!)

Revisit your research on the organisation you are applying to. Understand their core areas and competencies, how big they are, who their main clients are, and so on. Try to relate your experiences to the type of work they do. This goes back to commercial awareness – you need to show that you understand the organisation, the sectors it operates in and its clients, to be able to demonstrate that you are a good fit. They will know if you've done your research or not.

What are you saying?

You need to think very carefully about the information you submit in each and every application. Everything you say has to be relevant to the position you are applying for. You should expect to be asked rigorous or difficult questions about what you have said, so you must make sure you are able to back up everything you submit in every application. Make sure the examples you give are relevant to the scenario in question, and if you can use an example relating to legal work, so much the better.

Timing

Start making applications for training positions as soon as you possibly can. For solicitors' training contracts, this may mean submitting some applications before you have started the Graduate Diploma in Law (GDL), or while you are still at undergraduate level. Timing is essential, particularly given the two-year lead time in place at some law firms. If you want to start your training contract as early as you can, and avoid having a year or more to fill, you have to apply in good time.

Be specific

Legal employers expect you to demonstrate why you are 100% committed to them, and them alone. In reality of course, you are desperate for a training contract, and you will be making a lot of applications! The way around this is to take each application on its own, and make sure you apply afresh to every one. Avoid generalisations in your answers: don't take a good example or phrase from one application and force it into another just because it sounded good. You need to go back to a blank sheet and draft each application from scratch. Recruiters will spot any re-hashed text, and will be on the look out for people who have taken the time to submit answers that could only apply to the questions they have asked.

Approach and tone

You are applying to professional organisations, so you must get the tone of your application right. This means using clear, professional language, and avoiding anything that is superfluous to getting your message across. Wait for a rapport to develop between you and the people you meet in the organisation before you take a less formal approach. This prevents hostages to fortune, and is an approach that will be expected of you throughout your legal career.

Open mindedness

Wherever you end up, you will be working with various areas of law, different colleagues and clients, and on different matters. It is essential to demonstrate flexibility, and open mindedness about the role, and the desire to learn, even if you have an idea of which areas appeal to you the most. Some questions in application forms and interviews are aimed at examining your commitment to a career in law, but you are only at the start of your career at this stage. All junior lawyers are expected to work on whatever matters need their input. You need to show willingness to experience a range of work, and make sure you do not come across as being set on one or two specific areas only.

Tips on writing well-structured, targeted law CVs and covering letters

You will often be required to fill in an online application form (see below), but many employers prefer a CV and covering letter, particularly when dealing with applicants for work experience or placements. These are not always easy, and while there is a lot of help available generally, here are some tips specific to legal CVs and covering letters.

CVs

Law CVs are hard to put together in some ways, but are relatively straightforward in others. They are hard because you need to get across important information that distinguishes you from other applicants. It may be difficult to judge what is a positive thing to mention to one firm or chambers, or what may not be relevant. On the other hand, they are quite straightforward in that they only need to contain two basic categories of information: your academic qualifications, and any other relevant information about you.

Structuring a good legal CV

A good, clear structure is essential. A few elements to be included in legal CVs are listed below; using this order will help structure your CV logically:

- personal statement (optional)
- contact addresses
- educational history
- legal work experience
- other work experience
- skills

- interests and activities

- references.

Profile or personal statement

This should be no longer than one line, written in the third person, to summarise who you are, and what you are looking for. This is optional: if you have more work history on your CV, one short statement may help focus the reader's attention on exactly what it is they are looking for. If you have less on your CV, it probably will not help to include a statement.

Contact address

Don't forget to put both a term-time address and a home address, as you may be to be contacted at any time.

Educational history, grades and dates

Put these in reverse chronological order, with the most recent first. Add every grade, and the dates of each exam or result you achieved. Add awards, prizes or other special points on a separate line, to give them prominence.

Legal work experience

You are applying for a job in law, so the first thing you need to show a potential employer is your awareness of working in the legal world. You then need to try to tie this to the position you are applying for. It's important to back up what you say here with examples, as we saw earlier in this chapter. Showing a range of experience is helpful, but even if you only have one or two examples to draw on, maximise these by summarising what you did, how you learned from them, and how this applies to what you are applying for.

Other work experience

You will most likely have some other work experience as you have progressed through school, university and beyond. This shows the reader of your CV that you are a good team worker, can apply yourself to a range of different tasks and responsibilities, have a good level of commercial awareness, and that you have been a valued employee in the past. This all counts in your favour, so don't be afraid to mention vacation jobs you may have had – this experience will show that you have some of the important non-legal skills a recruiter is looking for.

Skills

Any additional useful skills relevant to the role should be listed briefly. Languages are a definite plus, as are computer literacy (with qualifications if possible), a driving licence, and anything else you can offer that may either be useful to the role, or which demonstrates your abilities in other ways.

Interests and activities

The saying goes that 'all work and no play makes Jack a dull boy', and the last thing you want is for your application to look dull. Participation in anything from sports to acting, hobbies, travel, or anything else that you have an interest in is well worth adding. Very often a recruiter is looking for things that differentiate very high quality, but largely similar applications from each other. A particular extra-curricular achievement, or an unusual interest, may be just what they are looking for. This can also be very useful in interviews. If the interviewer is curious about something you are good at or enjoy, you will be able to answer questions on this with knowledge and authority, which will be very much to your advantage.

References

If you can, name two people who have specifically agreed to act as referees for you. If possible, one should be an academic contact who has known you and your work for at least a year or more. The other referee should be someone outside of your studies, perhaps a previous employer, or someone in a position of responsibility who has again known you for some time. Family members should not be used as referees. It is possible to state that 'references are available on request', but this may risk making your CV look incomplete, or suggest that you have not got round to asking anyone before you sent the CV in. It's better to get this organised well in advance of any submission deadlines.

Where will your talent take you?

Hogan Lovells is one of the world's top 10 legal practices. Our global reach and exceptional breadth of practice ensures a broad, enriching experience for graduate trainees. With a spectrum of practice areas to explore, a prestigious client list and a positive, open culture, our focus is to enable trainees to become lawyers, and lawyers to become leaders.

To see how we help graduates transform ambition and potential into a world-class career, visit our website at:

www.hoganlovells.com/graduates

 Join us on Facebook

THE TIMES
TOP 100
GRADUATE EMPLOYERS

Profile: Hogan Lovells

Who we are

Hogan Lovells is a leading global law firm, with 2,500 lawyers working in over 40 offices in Asia, Europe, Latin America, the Middle East, and the USA. Our scale and capability positions us among the global elite of law firms, and provides our trainees with an international stage on which to develop their legal career.

Types of work

Our international strength across a wide range of practice areas gives us a strong reputation for corporate, finance, dispute resolution, government regulatory and intellectual property. This provides good training opportunities for those joining us.

Training programme

Our recruitment and training philosophy is very simple: our continued success as a firm depends on our ability to attract and retain the brightest and most able people. We require every prospective trainee solicitor to undertake the accelerated LPC at BPP London. The course will prepare you for practice in the City.

Our two-year training contract is split into four six-month seats. As a trainee, you will move around four different practice areas during this time to gain as much experience as possible – one of your seats will be in either our corporate or finance group, and another in one of our litigation teams. You will also have the option of spending time in the second year of training on secondment to one of our international offices or to the in-house legal team of a major client.

As a trainee at Hogan Lovells, you will be offered as much responsibility as you can handle relating to client work as well as a comprehensive legal skills training programme, regular reviews and appraisals. After qualification continuous training and development remain a priority – we enable the brightest minds to deepen their professional and business expertise throughout their career, which enhances the quality of advice we provide to clients, our reputation and your ability to make the very best of your expertise.

When and how to apply

Law students should apply over the summer after completion of their penultimate year and when they have their exam results (if applicable). Non-law students and graduates should apply in their final year from January onwards. Please see our website (www.hoganlovells.com/graduates) for all deadline dates and to apply online.

What we look for

As a consequence of the high-profile, demanding work the firm does, applicants need to have achieved excellent academic results from GCSE onwards. A good 2.i (or equivalent) is the minimum standard of degree, applicants should have achieved consistently in their individual units and as their final degree classification.

Applicants also need to be happy working in a team yet capable of, and used to, independent action. You will need to demonstrate an ability and desire for lateral thinking, be capable of close attention to detail, and be ambitious to succeed in a top law firm.

Vacation schemes and open days

We offer up to 50 vacation placements over two summer schemes. Each scheme is carefully designed to offer students the opportunity to gain exposure to life and work in a global law firm. During the three-week programmes students gain a broad insight into the work of the firm, as their time is split between three of our business areas. Students get involved in real work with real clients in much the same way as our trainees. This includes drafting, attending meetings, doing legal research and, where possible, attending court. To complement this, there is a comprehensive programme of talks, workshops and social events.

Vacation scheme students are paid £300 per week. The closing date for applications for our 2012 schemes is 31 January 2012.

We also hold open days and programmes for first-year law students and events for final-year non-law students throughout the academic year. Information on the dates and application deadlines for these open events can be found on our website at www. hoganlovells.com/graduates.

Case study

David Denny is a trainee at Hogan Lovells International LLP, who studied law at Queen's Belfast University. Here he describes a day from his first seat in the Capital Markets group

8.00a.m. I arrive at work early to squeeze in a quick trip to the in-house gym. It's free to staff and having it in the office means there is really no excuse for me not to go!

9.10a.m. I get some breakfast from the staff canteen and head to my desk. The morning always begins with a quick read through emails and my to-do list. This morning I have a conference call with my supervisor Mike (partner and head of the trustee practice in

London). The call involves a complex, multi-jurisdictional bond repackaging programme worth in excess of $12 billion. We're acting on behalf of the corporate trustee.

9.30a.m. The conference call is with a committee of bondholders formed to give the trustee directions on the bonds they hold. It's an interesting dynamic because while the trustee represents the bondholders collectively, we must remain neutral, and are often required to reconcile and resolve the conflicting interests of the parties involved.

10.20a.m. It's an intense but productive call and thankfully Mike did all the talking! I draft an email providing a summary of the call, with a plan of action going forward.

10.30a.m. A senior associate asks me to comment on a draft transaction document. She's acting for a Russian client and we must advise the trustee for the transaction. I make a note to look at this after lunch. Receiving emails about extra work is very common. You learn to juggle different tasks and no two days are the same.

11.00a.m. I attend a department presentation. These are designed to help trainees decide where they'd like to work for the remainder of their training contract. Today it's a partner from banking litigation – a department I'm considering applying to next.

12.00p.m. Back at my desk, I read emails regarding this morning's call. One party has asked for financial data on their bonds. I send a quick reply and draft an appropriate email to my contact at the advisory firm.

12.45p.m. Lunchtime! Normally I'll eat with the other trainees in the staff canteen but today I'm at a lunch for the summer vacation students. Each student gets a mentor when they arrive at the firm and I've been helping one out for the past week.

1.30p.m. After lunch Mike tells me that we have another conference call at 3p.m. First, I read the documents for the Russian deal.

2.00p.m. I've helped Mike with these documents before so I'm happy to make suggestions. Drafting is a delicate process because the documents must protect the client's interests, but they also need to be clear and have the ability to work in practice. Attention to detail is crucial.

3.00p.m. I attend the conference call. It's on the same deal as this morning, but this time it's a meeting with our client and another law firm involved. I make notes and email them to Mike when we're finished.

4.30p.m. I finish reviewing the Russian deal's documents, making a copy for Mike to read. He only has minor changes so I make the amends and email the clean version.

5.30p.m. Mike asks me to draft a memo about the steps needed to move forward following this afternoon's call. I put this together and hand him a copy as he leaves.

6.30p.m. Information from the financial advisers arrives so I draft a reply to the bondholder's earlier email, asking them to contact me if there are further queries.

7.00p.m. I shut down my computer and head out. Tonight I'm meeting my old LPC class for drinks.

General tips

- Make the CV easy on the eye. Make sure information is well spaced out, and use a logical structure (perhaps the order suggested above).

- Remove anything that is not absolutely relevant, and don't try to squeeze more information in using smaller fonts or narrower margins.

- Focus on quality not quantity, and try to stick to two sides if possible. You will not be expected to have so much relevant experience early on in your legal career to justify anything longer. If you have particular experience then it's OK to run into the top of a third page, but anything more than a few lines may be off-putting. It is better to focus on the relevant areas and cover them briefly, than to have your entire life story set out. Properly presented summaries of good experience will invite the reader to want to find out more from you in interview. Anything irrelevant will not help the reader, or the chances of your application leading to an interview.

There is a lot of information available on writing CVs, so once again, take a look online, or in your college library or careers service. *You're Hired! CV* by Corinne Mills (Trotman, 2009) is a good place to start.

Covering letters

Similar rules apply to covering letters as to CVs: the contents should be clear, brief and logically structured. Elements that would be expected in a covering letter for a legal application are, in order:

- your address, date

- introduction

- why you are applying and what you have to offer

- practical points

- correct sign-off.

Address, date

Your address should be at the top of the letter, followed by the date. This is standard, and errors here do not look good. If you need more information on letter writing in general, there is a wealth of information online and elsewhere to help you.

Introduction

You should include one or two short sentences to introduce yourself. This may mention how you heard about the position, how you met a contact that put you in touch, or anything else that introduces you to the reader.

Why you are applying

Use only one or two paragraphs to show why you want the role, why you are the perfect candidate for it, and to point out specific experience, interests or other aspects of your CV that make you particularly suited to it. Try to go beyond mentioning academic results alone (although you should highlight any particular successes). It is impressive to show how your experience relates directly to the place you are applying to, and that you have done your research. Highlight what you have to offer to the employer, rather than the other way round. Show that you understand the role, and are very familiar with the organisation. Remember to tailor every application each time you send one off, specifying why you want to work for that particular firm or employer.

Practical points

Don't forget to mention that your CV is enclosed. It is also important to provide details of your availability for interview, or for an informal discussion. If there is anything else you feel the reader needs to know about you, add it here.

Correct sign-off

If you have used the addressee's name (which is always best), then sign off using 'Yours sincerely'. If you have been unable to find the names of the person to whom the letter is addressed, and have had to use 'Dear Sir or Madam', then you must sign off 'Yours faithfully'. This is a formality, but there is no flexibility with it. Finally, you will usually be enclosing something – your CV – so you should put the abbreviation 'Enc.' beneath your name, to indicate that there was an enclosure to the letter.

Practical tips

- Make absolutely sure that your grammar and spelling are correct. Proofreading letters and CVs two or three times is highly recommended, as is asking someone else to read them through as well.

- Always type your covering letter and CV, unless you have been specifically asked to write in longhand (some employers do request handwritten covering letters).

- Use good quality white letter writing paper for your letter, CV and envelope. These may be tricky to fit into your printer, but it makes a good impression. Laser printed documents look better than ink-jet.

- Print the recipient's address on the envelope if you can. Add your return address in smaller type on the front or rear.

- Don't staple anything together. If the recipient wants to do this, let them do it. This is better than requiring them to pull apart pages that are already stapled.

- Double check that you have the correct address and postcode, and use first class post!

Application forms

With online forms, some employers allow you simply to attach a CV and covering letter, and only require basic additional information to be submitted through a form. If you have followed the steps above, then this is a straightforward process.

Many other employers require applications to be made through a detailed online form. Online application forms are a particular favourite with the larger law firms, not least as they help with the administrative burden of processing several hundred applications, all of which are submitted around the same time. Online forms also allow the recruiting organisation to tailor questions specifically to their own requirements, increasing the likelihood that applicants' answers will be unique to that organisation.

This section of the chapter is therefore geared to those applying to these law firms, and we will use the term 'firm' here to mean any organisation that requires a form to be submitted as part of the application process for a training position. These forms can be daunting: in addition to requesting a lot of personal information from applicants, there may be five or more questions, each one requiring a few hundred words. The tips below will help you tackle them.

The golden rule is that no matter how many applications you make, they must all be unique, and tailored specifically to the firm you are approaching. It is a very time-consuming process, but poor applications or covering letters are very easy to identify, and the only progress that your application is likely to make will be into the bin.

Preparation

It will come as no surprise that preparation is key to completing a successful application form. In addition to areas where you will be required to provide your educational background, grades and dates, the most important sections are the free text questions. There will usually be four or five questions, each with a text box usually allowing you a maximum of perhaps 500 words to craft your answer. They look deceptively simple, but your application will stand or fall according to your responses!

Plan your time

Plan your time properly. Find out what the closing dates are for applications, and do not miss the deadline. You must always give yourself enough time to do a draft version of each application, and as many revisions as you need, well before it has to be submitted. Deadlines for online forms are automated, and missing the deadline by just a second or two will mean that your application will not be processed. Some firms frown on applications being sent in at the last minute. They may have made a start on collating responses already, and may look at last-minute submissions as hinting at poor time management. Other firms take a different approach, and will look at all submitted applications only after the closing date, as a single batch. In this case, submitting early may be a disadvantage, if you have gained something important to add to your application since submitting it. The best advice is to make sure you know exactly what the closing date is for every application, and make sure they are all submitted about a week before the closing date.

How long should you spend on an application?

Of course, this will vary from one employer to another, but it may take the equivalent of at least one–two full working days to put together the best responses possible. Most online forms have a 'save as you go' facility. Use this to buy yourself time, and to provide some breathing space between working on applications. Resist the temptation to draft and submit an application in one sitting. If you leave it a couple of days and come back to it, you will most likely see that improvements are needed. You may be surprised at how the application will benefit from some further improvement work, and how easy it is to spot where improvements are needed, when you look at it with fresh eyes.

Keep track

Keep a record of your progress. You will be approaching a number of different potential employers, as well as networking with many other people as you go through each stage of your application and training process. It can be hard to keep track of who you spoke to, when, and about what, as well as who you applied to, and when. If you keep a spreadsheet with a record of dates, contacts, and a note of what you did, this will be very useful to keep track of progress and help you remember who you have contacted and applied to over the months and years of training.

Reapply

Rejections are normal, and are part of the application process. It's reasonable, and sometimes necessary, to reapply after an initial rejection, particularly if you have subsequently gained additional experience or skills – or if you are now just better at making applications than the first time. Don't go overboard though. If you can't convince a firm or chambers after two or three applications, then you have probably done all you can. At this stage it is better use of your time to broaden your search for other opportunities and potential employers.

Be persistent

It's important to keep going, and to remember that one thing that is fully within your control is keeping up with your academic work, your applications, and your work experience, all of which help develop your CV. Everything you do to build your profile will be valuable, and each added piece of experience, or good grade you achieve, contributes directly to your employability.

Practical tips for online applications

- Check your spelling and grammar. Print out your form and read it on paper. It is easier to spot errors and inconsistencies on hard copy than on the screen.

- Stick to the word limit. Use concise, short sentences. Beware of conjunctions (words that join phrases together: 'and', 'but', 'with', etc.). These add to the word count, and make one long sentence, where two shorter ones may be clearer.

- Make sure you answer the question asked. This may seem obvious, but when you are keen to put across your achievements, you may be tempted to shape your answer around the question you wanted to be asked, rather than the one that actually was.

- Use different examples to illustrate different points. If you are asked about leadership in one question, and about teamwork in another, avoid using the same example in both. Recycling may suggest that you have limited experience to draw from.

- Make absolutely sure you have not put in any silly mistakes. The ultimate crime is to put the wrong firm name into an application. This is unforgiveable from the point of view of the reader, but it does happen, and occasionally errors creep in for all sorts of reasons. Before you send anything out, check and check again that nothing has slipped in that should not be there. This approach is exactly the same in legal practice, so it is a good habit to get into now.

Case study

James Evans is an Associate at Lewis Silkin LLP, and tells us about the application process

When it comes to training contract applications, you do have to manage your expectations, as it is a daunting process. Rejections will almost inevitably happen time and again, and you just have to learn not to take it personally, as it is part of the process. You have to find ways around any problem spots on your CV, and be realistic. For instance, I had glandular fever during my A levels and didn't feel this situation was dealt with well by my school. My grades were A, B and C, but I could have done better. I made up for this by gaining good results at law school, and am now an Associate at a City firm.

Case study

Ed Chivers is a solicitor working in a regional firm Buss Murton Law

I was one of the fortunate few who did not have to go through a huge number of interviews and flood the in-trays of HR departments with my CV in order to secure a training contract. I think this was because I was realistic in the firm that I applied to and ensured my application and CV were tailored specifically for that firm. Granted, the competition was less as I was applying to a regional firm, but there were still about 50 applicants for two training posts, so it was important to ensure that my application stood out.

It helped that I was historically from the area where the firm is based. When applying to a regional firm, this is vitally important – if you do not have links to the area then you must demonstrate a commitment to moving into the area. Regional firms do not like people who come down from London just because it's a job – they like to retain staff.

A recently qualified solicitor's opinion of the application process

'Getting a training contract or pupillage is a bit like organising a huge logistical operation, like planning D Day. You need to call in every available resource over a prolonged period of time to secure that training position. You almost need to be a bit obsessive about it, to try and find angles in everyday situations that might help you. Something you've read in the news or the legal press may crop up in an interview, or might make good material around which to shape an application response. Someone you meet may end up being a useful contact, or might know someone else who may be useful.

'And all the while, you're working away on your studies, and building your legal work experience. It's a lot to manage, but it really pays off when you finally get an offer. Plus, your suitability as a lawyer is closely related to your ability to manage all aspects of the qualification process: doing applications, studying, getting legal work experience, and all your extra-curricular stuff needed to get a really strong CV.'

In our own words
Challenging
Empowering
Inspiring

Rewarding

Just some of the words to describe the experience of working at Kirkland & Ellis.

As a trainee solicitor in our London office, you'll get hands-on experience of working on high profile deals with some of the world's leading companies, and be given the support to enable you to become the best lawyer you can be.

To learn more about training opportunities in our London office, go to kirkland.com/ukgraduate

KIRKLAND & ELLIS INTERNATIONAL LLP
Graduate careers in law

Profile: Kirkland & Ellis International LLP

KIRKLAND & ELLIS INTERNATIONAL LLP

Kirkland & Ellis International LLP is a 1,500-attorney law firm representing global clients in offices around the world; in Chicago, Hong Kong, London, Los Angeles, Munich, New York, Palo Alto, San Francisco, Shanghai, Washington, DC.

For over 100 years, major national and international clients have called upon Kirkland & Ellis to provide superior legal advice and client services. Our London office has been the hub of European operations since 1994. Here, approximately 120 lawyers offer detailed expertise to a wide range of UK and international clients.

In London we handle complex corporate, debt finance, restructuring, private funds, tax, intellectual property, antitrust and competition, litigation and arbitration work. We operate as a strategic network, committing the full resources of an international firm to any matter in any territory as appropriate.

Requirements

You'll have the initiative, the drive and the work ethic to thrive in our meritocratic culture. Crucially, you should already have decided that you aim to build your career in one of our practice areas, and so come to us with an understanding of the work undertaken in our London office.

Your academic record will be excellent, culminating in an expected or achieved 2.i. And while most of our applications come from penultimate-year law students and final-year non-law students, graduates and postgraduates are also eligible.

Training contracts

You can look forward to more personal attention and tailored career development at Kirkland & Ellis. Part of that is to do with our firm-wide approach to career planning. But it's also because we only take on a select number of trainees every year, meaning we can train and develop each one as an individual.

The programme is based around four, six-month seats, during which you'll learn about all of our core practice areas. As corporate law – specifically private equity and mergers and acquisitions – provides a key focus for our London office, this will be central to your training too.

Your on the job training will be actively supported by an extensive education programme, carefully tailored to meet your needs.

Vacation schemes

For two weeks over the summer, our vacation schemes provide the perfect introduction to life in our London office. Through a combination of real work, practice overview presentations and social events, you'll get a strong feel for our working culture.

Rewards

We think you'll find working at Kirkland & Ellis rewarding for all sorts of reasons. A package to attract and retain the very best is just one of them. We aim to encourage and incentivise strong performance throughout the firm, which is why we've created a cooperative, inclusive workplace in which initiative thrives and individual talent flourishes.

Visit www.kirkland.com/ukgraduate for more information.

Case study

Esther Scott qualified four years ago and is now a Funds Associate at Kirkland & Ellis International LLP

While law felt almost like the default choice of career for graduates when I left university, for me, it was something I had always set my sights on. Although in order to broaden my horizons and my skill set, I chose to study modern languages at St John's College, Oxford and convert to law afterwards.

Leaving Oxford for law school in London was a good transitional step. I found the GDL interesting; the LPC was slightly drier! It was also a great chance to meet all those friends who will understand when you have to cancel on them at the last minute because you have to work (the old adage about lawyers only having lawyer friends, is to a certain degree true!).

Post LPC, having studied for six years, it was about time to finally start work. I had accepted an offer for a training contract at SJ Berwin following a vacation scheme I undertook there. Vacation schemes enable you to see beyond the glossy brochure, and the patter at drinks receptions. Upon qualification I took up an offer to join Kirkland & Ellis, to be part of a team with whom I had worked previously and who had moved to Kirkland to grow and develop their Funds practice.

There are lot of rumours about US firms — some true, some not, and some just too stereotypical to take seriously. The welcoming, friendly US vibe is definitely true at Kirkland.

There is a real advantage to being part of a global team, enabling me to benefit from the expertise from other offices. It is also a great advantage for the clients I work for to be able to have US legal advice so easily accessible. And from a practical point of view, it's pretty useful having round the clock support too!

As to the myth about work–life balance (or lack of one), I think that is one of the best kept secrets of all. Although you do work hard as an associate here, it is no harder than at a magic circle or top City firm and while Kirkland does give you a lot of responsibility from day one, there is also lots of support. Kirkland gives you the responsibility to manage not only your workload, but how you work. As long as the work is done (and done well) then, to a certain extent, how you go about it is up to you.

The last couple of years have been interesting; the current climate enabling me to get involved with a variety of issues and work that I wouldn't have seen a few years ago – all good learning experience, and never a dull day.

How to shine at interview

Interviews are a vital part of the selection process, but it's natural to feel apprehensive about them. The role you are applying for is important, and it's a slightly artificial process to find yourself sitting in a room opposite people you have never met before, and being asked probing and often quite tricky questions. It's not an ideal way to get a dialogue going, but with good preparation, you can make interviews a genuinely two-way process, where you get to extract as much information from your potential future employer as they will from you.

Here are some hard earned tips from lawyers who have been through the process themselves and have survived to give their insight and advice. Some are lawyers who are involved in legal recruitment within their organisation, and are well placed to give some insight into what legal employers are looking for in their trainees or pupils.

Preparation before the interview

Once you hear that you have been asked in for interview, you should go back over your application, and make sure you are completely familiar with everything you said when you applied initially. Then, think about how you would question what you are now reading. Do you have examples, or more details to back up your statements? Is anything you said particularly likely to invite questions? Going over this again will help you prepare for some of the questions that are likely to come up. Do this well in advance of the interview, and a final time a day or two before the interview day, so it's fresh in your mind.

Take some time to research the organisation again, before the interview. You will have done a lot of research already, but you may benefit from a quick reminder of the firm's structure, or to get an update on what the firm has been doing recently. Are there any important new announcements or success stories on its website? Has it been mentioned in the legal press recently? Being up to speed on this will help you tackle many different kinds of questions in interview, and will give you material to draw from to back up what you say.

Make sure you know the interview process beforehand. You may have received some information on what the format of the interview will be, but if not, you should speak to HR, or the person who contacted you about the interview. They will be able to provide information on how many people will interview you, who they are, how many interviews there will be, how long they may take, and other general information, if this has not been communicated to you already.

Assessment days

Assessment days are becoming increasingly popular among many legal recruiters now. They are designed to test applicants' abilities not only in one-to-one interviews, but also in terms of how they interact with each other as a group. This may be done through assessing how candidates handle different assessments and tasks, as well as through less formal activities such as social gatherings over lunch, or over drinks at the end of the day. If your interview is structured more like an assessment day, it is even more important that you know the format.

In addition to getting details of how the interviews themselves may be structured, you should also ask about any other tasks or assessments you will be required to do, to give you a chance to prepare for them. Some common exercises that interviewees may be required to do are listed below.

- Making a presentation: Will you be given a topic, or can you choose one? How many people will you be presenting to? Who will they be? How long should your presentation be?

- Group activities: You will be set a task to complete as a group, with specific outcomes. You will be observed during the task, and assessed on how you participate and interact with others, as well as on your material contribution to the outcome. This is the ideal time to demonstrate that you really are a good team player, and can take the lead and/or work alone when needed. Think back to past episodes of

The Apprentice and you will be some way to seeing what works, and what doesn't!

- Written tests: This may take the form of a practical problem question, a legal case analysis, or writing a letter or memo based on a given scenario.

- 'Psychometric tests': These are designed to assess your suitability for the role. They can vary greatly: some are similar to personality tests, asking how you would react in certain situations. Others are reasoning exercises, which may involve reading and summarising a passage of text, or answering a number of discrete questions under strict timed conditions, to test the speed and accuracy with which you process information.

If you are unclear what will come up on the day, then ask. You need to know what to expect, if you are to be properly prepared. If you need more information or help in preparing for an interview, then speak to your careers advisers. They will be able to provide you with additional information based on experience, and can arrange invaluable practice interviews.

Interviews and assessments: dos and don'ts on the day

Do

- Dress appropriately. This means a suit and tie for men, and suit (skirt or trousers) for women. Make sure your hair is tidy and your shoes are clean. The same goes for open days and vacation schemes: don't get too comfortable and turn up in jeans on the last day, as this won't make a good impression. Let your charisma and personality shine through from what you say and do, not through what you wear.

- Bring a pen and paper. These will of course be provided for any assessments, but it may save a search or an awkward moment if you need to make a note of something such as a phone number or email address of someone you've met on the day.

- Aim to arrive about half an hour early. Don't arrive too early though, as you don't want to end up in any difficult situations, or having to wait in reception for ages. If you are very early, find somewhere round the corner to have a coffee, and go back over your application form, CV and/or covering letter.

- Ask where the interviewers want you to sit when you are called in to the interview. This is not only polite, but also shows you are happy to be positioned where they prefer. Note that with most law firms you will be interviewed in a meeting room or conference room, rather than in an individual's office.

- Be aware of any mannerisms you may have that may be off-putting or obvious to someone who doesn't know you. Be conscious of fidgeting, or other actions that might show you are nervous, and bear in mind that some mannerisms can be taken as signs of insecurity. As mentioned earlier, video-taped practice interviews with a careers adviser can help show you how you come across to others in interview situations, allowing you to make any adjustments in how you present yourself, well in advance of the real thing.

- Ask for a glass of water if you want one. This helps if you get a dry throat, and taking an occasional sip gives you time to think about an answer.

- Make sure you follow the format correctly, for any exercise you are asked to do. If you are writing a letter, make sure it is addressed and signed off correctly (for example see the information above for tips on structuring letters). If you are writing a memo, make sure you state who the memo is to, who it's from, with a date and a subject line. Use proper formatting, and bullet points for summaries.

- Expect to be pushed in an interview. Different interviewers will push you to different degrees. If you have a single interviewer, they may push a point until you can't answer it further. They are testing your ability to go to the very end of your thought process. Admitting that you just don't know the answer, or that you cannot take something any further may feel bad at the time, but if this is true, and you have shown how you have arrived at this end point, then you should not be afraid of saying it. There may be no further to go, and the interviewer will be interested in your thinking, and how you react to being right at the outer limits of your knowledge.

- Suggest possible answers that might be appropriate, if you are totally stuck as to what the correct answer might be to a question. This demonstrates that you can think around problems, and persist with tough points in a logical, well-structured way.

- Know how many people will be interviewing you. Typically it will be one or two, but you may be interviewed by a panel of three or more. Panel interviews are different to one-to-one interviews, but they are not necessarily worse. The more people you impress in the interview, the less of a sales job the interviewers have when reporting back to their colleagues to convince them to take you on. In a panel interview, there will inevitably be different levels of interaction with each interviewer. One interviewer may push you, while another may be disinterested. It is up to you to engage the attention of all the interviewers, whether they have asked you a question or not. If one is showing disinterest, get their attention with eye contact or subtle gesturing. Exactly how you do this will depend on the context of the interview, and you will need to assess the context, and react accordingly.

- Ask for clarification on anything you're stuck on. This gives you time to think, and increases your chances of giving a good answer. Some interviewers will push you outside your comfort zone, and ask questions which clearly do not have a right or wrong answer. Some questions will be based around dilemmas, and will not have an 'answer' at all. A good interviewer will push you with hard questions, to assess how you react under pressure. Focus on remaining calm and composed, and continuing to give good responses as the interview progresses.

- Recognise your strengths and weaknesses. You will very likely be asked about these, and because they appear to be quite personal questions, they may be unsettling unless you are prepared. If you are asked about weaknesses, be honest, and support your answers with examples. Turn the question around by also giving reasons why a particular weakness may have positive attributes, rather than being merely a negative characteristic. Understanding that a particular trait is a shortcoming, but that you have taken steps to address it, is a good way of demonstrating self-awareness, and your capacity for personal development.

- Make sure you expand on your answers, to add supporting information or additional context, to clarify your point. Very short, or one word answers are not likely to impress!

- Always bring a set of questions to ask. These must relate to the role, and should not be too basic or obvious. In particular, make sure you do not ask about anything that can easily be found from the website or from recruitment materials. The questions you ask will depend on who you are speaking to. It is fine to ask a human resources officer more practical questions, such as how many training places are available, or when you may hear from the firm with results. These questions might not be appropriate to a senior fee earner, who may be better asked about their area of practice, or their wider role in the firm.

- Visit the office a few days before the interview if you can, to get to know where it is, and how to plan your route on the day. If you need to drive, then make sure your car has plenty of petrol and is not likely to cause you problems, and plan a route that minimises the risk of getting stuck in traffic.

- Remember that you are choosing them to work for, as much as they are choosing you. Make sure you ask about some of the other things going on at the firm. These could be social events, sports clubs, community work or other activities that people in the firm take part in. Staff will always be involved with more than just the day job, so make sure you find out as much as you need about all areas of the organisation.

- Keep smiling (but not too much!), stay positive, and remain professional and attentive – you're on show, and you owe it to yourself to come across as well as you can.

Don't

- Lie, or try to bluff answers. If you do not know the answer to something specific, then you should not pretend that you do, or try to wing your way through. You are likely to be found out, and this could do damage to how you are perceived. Instead, try to draw from examples of things you have done that demonstrate that you are what they are looking for. This is where your involvement in extra-curricular activities, and work experience come in. However, if you are lacking experience in a particular area, and have little to draw on a particular point in the interview, then acknowledge this. Showing that you understand why the issue is important, and that you are willing to do something to address it, is far better than trying to talk your way around it.

- Waffle in your answers. Keep to the point, and if you notice you are drifting into vague territory, take a breath and regain focus.

- Be indignant, negative or aggressive, no matter how hard you are pushed, and no matter how frustrated you may be. It may be fine to be annoyed at yourself, but not at the interviewers!

- Come across as arrogant. Respect everyone you meet, be they qualified fee earners, support staff, fellow candidates, or anyone else.

- Ask questions on difficult or technical points of law, or for the interviewer's opinion on complex legal issues. This risks putting you on the spot, and exposing the limits of your legal knowledge. General questions about areas of practice are fine and are expected, but anything really technical or oblique may make you look as if you are trying to look smarter and more informed than you actually are. You will very likely be asked for your view on the same point, and if you can't put forward anything solid, this will not look good.

- Ask about the working hours, or how often you will be expected to work late. It may be fine to mention work–life balance, but only if this is something the employer makes a point of in their literature. You should already know quite a lot about the firm's culture, and if it has reputation for working its trainees particularly hard. Even if you don't, the interview is not the time to ask!

- Take risks with using slang, dressing casually, or being overly familiar. It takes time to get to know people, so treat the interview process with the respect it deserves. Some firms like to portray themselves as cool and forward thinking, but an interview is not the place to find out whether your definition of cool fits theirs.

- Finally – do not forget that being called for interview means that you have the potential to succeed. The organisation is not investing time and energy with you if you had not already shown them that you are worth meeting. This is a great achievement in itself, so build on this in the interview, and show them that you are who they are looking for.

Some of these things may seem obvious, but they are all important if you are to portray yourself as favourably as you can. There is a lot of crossover between preparing for an interview, and preparing for work in your future legal career. Both involve important skills for all lawyers, and you need to be able to demonstrate you understand the significance of good preparation and appropriate presentation, the very first time you meet your potential employer.

Want a career that's everything you expected?

Apply elsewhere

You'll have noticed, it's a changing world. Everywhere, new business models are emerging. Increasingly, size and reputation alone aren't enough – clients are more swayed by insight, flexibility and value. In ten years' time, the landscape for commercial law firms is going to look very different indeed.

Why not help shape it?

www.pinsentmasons.com/graduate

Pinsent Masons

Profile: Pinsent Masons LLP

Pinsent Masons is a full service international law firm with over 1,000 lawyers globally. We have offices in all the major UK business centres and more recently have been developing our overseas network of offices in the Asia Pacific and Gulf Region. Pinsent Masons provides legal services to a wide variety of clients including multi-national corporations, government departments and public sector institutions.

Pinsent Masons has an ambitious strategy for growth in the years ahead. Our London office will be stronger, our international reach will be greater, but our values will remain the same. Anyone looking to join the firm will need to buy into this vision.

To achieve the above we need exceptional individuals. This is not about the school or university you attended but your unique qualities as an individual. To be successful you will need to possess excellent analytical and problem-solving skills, have the ability to develop strong working relationships with both clients and colleagues, and finally you must have a genuine interest in our clients and the business world.

Vacation placement

A vacation placement is the ideal way to demonstrate you have the ability to be a successful commercial lawyer. By taking part you will get a 'real' appreciation of our firm, culture, people and the opportunities available. You can test drive a career with Pinsent Masons, experience the energy and dynamism of our teams and have a first-hand look at some of the work we do.

On the placement you will work alongside trainees and solicitors on real client matters, learn about the different practice areas within the firm and get to know as many of our people as possible. At the same time a vacation placement offers you the chance to demonstrate your suitability for a training contract through your appetite for work and responsibility, and your business sense. Indeed a majority of our trainee solicitors have completed a placement at the firm.

To find out more, visit our website (www.pinsentmasons.com/graduate), or alternatively you may like to read about the experience of former vacation placement students by visiting ratemyplacement.co.uk.

Training contract

Alternatively you can apply directly for a training contract outside of the vacation placement programme where you will be assessed at one of our assessment centres across the UK. This route can be more suitable for candidates who are either already in full-time employment or have previous legal work experience.

Either way we welcome applications from both law and non-law students and graduates. While numbers can fluctuate from year to year we typically recruit around 60 trainee solicitors each year across our UK offices.

Questions likely to come up in written applications and/or interviews

These are your opportunity to demonstrate that you have the skills and competencies the recruiter is looking for. There are limitless possible questions that might crop up. Here are some that have been known to be asked in training contract and pupillage interviews, to give you an idea of what you might expect.

Questions can usually be divided into five general areas.

1. Questions relating to how you view your career.

2. Questions relating to law.

3. Questions relating to your skills and competencies.

4. Questions relating to commercial awareness.

5. Questions designed to test your ability to deal with unexpected or tricky issues.

Questions relating to your career

- Why law? Why do you want to be a solicitor/barrister?

- Where do you see yourself in five years' time?

- Where else have you applied?

- What are you expecting to gain from a career in law?

- What qualities are needed to be a good solicitor/barrister? Do you have these?

- Explain how your (legal or other) experience applies to our work.

You should be prepared to answer questions on your career in some detail, and with conviction. You need to be able to show that your decisions are logical, and based on good information and experience.

Questions relating to law

- Why have you applied to this firm/set?

- What differentiates us from our competitors?

- What has been the most important development in an area of law we work in, and why?

- Give an example of a recent decision that you agree/disagree with, and explain your position.

These can often be fairly self-explanatory questions with no hidden traps. They are, however, central to your application. You are applying for a legal role, so you have to be strong on the legal aspects of the job. You won't be expected to be an expert, but you should be able to answer legally related questions convincingly, based on up-to-date information.

You need to be able to demonstrate why you chose the firm, chambers or organisation interviewing you, and why you are particularly suited to it. Go back over the 'Tips on successfully applying for a training position' earlier in this chapter. You need to demonstrate the same points at interview as you do in applications.

Expect questions on current developments in the commercial and legal world, and anything in the news that concerns the areas of law you are interested in, which relate to the position you are applying for. Think carefully about how areas of law may cross over. For example, if a news story breaks about financial wrongdoing, is this only a criminal investigation? Which other authorities might be involved? What about other aspects, such as directors' obligations, or how shareholders might be affected? What about reputation management, or any number of other issues that might come into place? Showing that you understand the relationship between the law and the commercial, everyday implications of its application will be looked on very favourably.

Questions relating to your skills and competencies

- Are you better working alone, or as part of a team?

- Give an example of a time you experienced conflict or disagreement. How did you resolve this?

- Give an example of your ability to negotiate and persuade. How did you go about this, and how successful were you?

- What is your greatest strength, and your greatest weakness? How do these help/hinder your work, and what are you doing about them?

- Give an example of a problem you solved. Explain your approach, and what you would do differently if faced with the same problem again.

- What achievement are you most proud of?

- What is the biggest mistake you have ever made?

- How do you deal with failure?

- How do your friends describe you?

- Why are you a good person to have on a team?

- What makes you the ideal candidate for the role?

You may be asked any number of standard questions about yourself, but you will not be expected to repeat what is on your CV or application form. There may be a particular point of interest in something you have mentioned, which may be explored in detail. Otherwise, be prepared to answer questions such as these clearly and positively.

Questions relating to commercial awareness

Commercial interview questions are intended to assess your ability to identify the key commercial considerations that a typical business will need to think about. From the answers you give, the interviewer will assess your suitability as a potential legal adviser to commercial clients. Your answers therefore need to demonstrate both commercial sense, and common sense. There will most likely not be a 'right or wrong' answer to these questions, but some points should usually be considered in most answers, such as:

- supply and demand

- competition

- pricing

- regulatory issues

- location, premises and leases

- branding and identity

- marketing and advertising

- company structure (independent company, partnership, franchise?)

- staff.

Further aspects that you can think of, which may be relevant to the question, include consideration of potential disputes or problems that might be faced, and how they may be resolved.

Some recent examples of commercially focused questions asked at interview are given below.

- Explain how the 2008 recession came about, and what you would expect its effects to have been on us as a firm/set. What might be done to minimise any negative effects? Might there have been any positive effects?

- You are about to set up a coffee shop next door. How would you go about doing this?

Commercial awareness can sometimes appear to be a concept that is shrouded in mystery. However, it is nothing more than having good practical knowledge of how businesses operate, coupled with a good understanding of current issues affecting the business world. Look back at 'Commercial awareness' in Chapter 8 for ideas on improving your general commercial awareness, if necessary.

Questions designed to test your ability to deal with unexpected or tricky issues

These can be very varied, ranging from 'dinner-party' style questions, to problems and dilemmas, or may just be questions designed to find out more about you as a person.

- With which three historical figures (living or dead) would you most like to have a dinner party, and why?

- How long is the London Tube network?

- What do you do in your spare time?

- You are in a client meeting with a supervisor, who is giving incorrect advice. What do you do?

- If you knew you were about to be stranded on a desert island for a year, which five things would you most want to have with you, and why?

These questions do not fit easily in the other categories, but your answers may be quite revealing about you as a person. They may be totally off the wall, or centred around a dilemma, to test clarity of thought, processes of reasoning and ability to present a coherent analysis of the problem.

Summary

The tips above should be helpful in getting you through the door, and securing that elusive training position. If all goes to plan, you still have some work ahead of you, to get to qualification and beyond, but by the time you have your training contract or pupillage in place, you're almost there. Congratulations!

PART 4
Alternative routes and career options

12

Alternative careers with a legal qualification

Many people come to law with the intention of progressing through each stage of qualification necessary to become a solicitor or barrister. For any number of reasons, however, not everyone makes it all the way to full qualification. There are many reasons for this, and it is a myth that not going all the way to full qualification is in some way a failure.

Regardless of the level of legal qualification you have, all are valuable and relevant to your professional life. Your legal studies and work experience may also have introduced you to areas of work, and possible career options that you might not have come across otherwise, and legal work experience will equip you with skills that apply to other areas as much as they do to law.

Very often there are forces at work beyond your control that influence how things work out, the most obvious being the ongoing effects of economic recession. Training opportunities have been significantly reduced, lawyers have been made redundant, and newly qualified solicitors and barristers are finding it hard going to secure a job at the end of their training. There has been no change to the calibre of candidates coming through the system, but the professional and economic environment has become more difficult, and many able candidates have found themselves in a position they could not have expected just a few years previously. Things are getting better however, and trainee solicitor retention rates are back on the increase, while recent figures from the Bar Council show the number of qualified barristers to have increased steadily between 2005 and 2010.

As with any competitive area, you will experience rejections as your career progresses. It can be almost impossible to react positively to a rejection, particularly when you know you have done all you can, but sometimes things happen which are out of your hands. The important thing is to accept a knock-back as part of the process, and keep going. Each rejection may be an opportunity to reconsider the direction you had planned for your career. Even if your route needs to be adjusted along the way, this doesn't mean you will end up with a career any less worthwhile than you initially intended.

Remember that experience is what sets you apart from your competitors. Continue to gain relevant experience, and this will make you increasingly employable. There is nothing to stop you working in a part-qualified role in a particular area of law, and gaining qualifications specific to that area. You can always go back to studying for the additional solicitors' or barristers' qualifications later, or you may feel this is no longer necessary if you have found an area that suits you.

In addition to technical legal knowledge, your legal qualifications provide you with a number of key skills, which all employers will be looking for.

- You are experienced in structuring reasoned arguments, and in making objective judgements and solving problems.

- You are well practised in identifying key issues in any given scenario, applying rules and other considerations, and forming conclusions and recommendations.

- You have proven ability in organising your time, managing a diverse workload, developing your own schedule and working to fixed deadlines.

- Your research skills can be applied to almost any situation requiring analysis of large amounts of written or other material.

- You have developed good communication skills, both orally and in writing.

- You have shown that you are self-motivated, with the various course elements demonstrating your ability to work independently, or as part of a group.

You may be yet to secure a training contract or pupillage, or you may have decided that going all the way to full qualification as a solicitor or barrister is not for you. If things haven't worked out at a particular stage of the qualification process, then you can always come back to law through another route later. Remember that the Academic Stage qualifications are valid for seven years, during which time you can go on to the Legal Practice Course (LPC) or Bar Professional Training Course (BPTC). Barristers must start their pupillage within five years of the Bar Vocational Course (BVC)/BPTC, while for future solicitors, the LPC is valid indefinitely.

Plenty of alternative careers options exist for people at all levels of legal qualification, and some suggestions are set out below.

Alternative careers where legal qualifications are seen as a distinct advantage

We looked at some of the different careers available to part-qualified lawyers or those looking for experience in specific areas of law in Chapter 5. There are many more options available too. Many recruiters will view a law degree or other legal qualification very positively: the law will always apply in various ways to any area you work in, although some are more closely regulated, or more focused on specific areas of law than others, and your legal skills will be especially useful.

Speak to your careers advisers for ideas, and keep up your research. Meanwhile, here are some alternative areas, in which legal qualifications are viewed favourably. These are arranged alphabetically.

Accountancy and tax consultancy

Chartered accountants advise on financial aspects of their clients' business, in order to improve performance and financial management, in accordance with law and regulation. They work in a wide variety of different areas, including commerce and industry, government, and the public sector. Areas of work include financial reporting, tax advice, carrying out or managing audits, corporate finance, insolvency, and management of accounting processes and systems.

There is considerable crossover between areas of accountancy and areas of law, given the extent to which tax and financial regulation are central to both professions. Any legal qualification is extremely useful to an accountant, indeed some of the professional accountants' qualifications include a legal element, and vice versa. Further, since many accountancy firms are structured in a similar way to law firms, skills picked up through work experience in a law firm will be applicable in an accountants' practice.

Useful experience relevant to this area:

- LPC and BPTC commercial, business and tax modules

- electives in any area of finance or commercial law.

Barristers' clerk

Barristers' clerks manage all administrative aspects of a barrister's practice, acting as practice managers. They take responsibility for liaising with instructing solicitors, selecting and booking out suitable barristers for the kinds of matters that are coming in, organising timetabling of court hearings, conferences and other work, and managing financial aspects of the practice, such as collecting fees and managing budgets. They need to be familiar with court procedures, and developments in areas of law relevant to the barristers they work with, and while clerks are not required to be legally qualified, legal experience is an advantage given the nature of the work.

Useful experience relevant to this area:

- any legal qualifications

- interest in litigation, court work and dispute resolution

- work experience in a barrister's chambers or litigation/contentious department of a solicitors' firm.

Business consultancy work

A solid grounding in the legal foundation subjects and practical knowledge of business and commercial law are useful in any commercial context. Consultancy work offers the opportunity to be involved in a wide variety of projects, in whichever areas interest you. You are your own boss – you can choose what you work on, how and when you work, and you can take on a lot of direct responsibility.

Useful experience relevant to this area:

- LPC and BPTC business law modules and commercially focused electives

- work experience in a law firm or barristers' chambers, operating in relevant commercial areas.

A warning on working freelance

If you decide to work freelance in areas that may make use of your legal knowledge, you need to be aware the types of work you are, and are not, eligible to do. Some legal work is 'reserved' for qualified solicitors only, requiring particular qualifications and professional indemnity insurance. These include certain kinds of court and litigation work, as well probate and notarial work (see Chapter 5 for more details on these). There are complex rules governing this, and you need to make absolutely sure you are operating within your levels of competence. You may not come across these areas in some commercial work, but it is essential that you understand what kinds of work you may or may not do. It is your responsibility to ensure that you know your limitations: check with the Solicitors Regulation Authority (SRA) or Bar Standards Board (BSB) for more information.

Chartered surveyor, chartered loss adjustor and insurance work

A huge amount of legal work is generated through the insurance industry, as claims are pursued following events that have resulted in loss or damage to insured parties. Familiarity with the legal foundation subjects of contract and tort, as well as any litigation experience, are distinct advantages to working in the insurance industry. The role of a chartered surveyor is to assess the value of an asset, to provide a report giving an objective assessment of its value, and any defects or points to note, for a prospective purchaser, insurer or lender. If loss or damage occurs to an asset and an insurance claim is made, then a chartered loss adjuster will investigate the circumstances and causes of the loss, and will inspect the damaged asset, if this is possible. They will provide a written report to the insurer as to the merits of any insurance claim made, and the value of reinstatement or payment that should be made.

Useful experience relevant to this area:

- **any legal qualifications**

- **interest or experience in litigation**

- **general commercial work experience.**

Citizens Advice Bureau and Law Centre work

These are free, impartial services offered to people to help with legal, financial or other problems. The Citizens Advice Bureau (CAB) offers free face-to-face advisory services, and services by phone and email to help people with their day-to-day legal problems. The CAB is also actively involved in shaping government policy and legislation. In addition to assisting with advisory work, opportunities exist within the CAB in areas such as lobbying, media relations, training and information management.

Law Centres assist individuals with access to legal support, as well as performing a number of more policy driven areas of work, such as taking on test cases, providing education and training services in specific areas of law, working with and providing legal services for public services and the community, and lobbying for changes in the law for the public benefit.

There are very few paid positions available, with solicitors, barristers and other staff usually offering their time voluntarily. CAB and Law Centre work is interesting and rewarding, giving excellent experience of advising clients in real-life situations. It also offers the opportunity to make a real difference to people's lives.

Useful experience relevant to this area:

- LPC and BPTC advocacy modules

- experience with litigation and advocacy in a law firm or with a barrister

- experience representing clients through pro bono or Law Centre work

- particular interest or experience in human rights, public and administrative law.

Civil Service

The Civil Service supports the government in providing advisory and other services, to assist the government in implementing its policies. Its main departments are the Department of Work and Pensions, the Ministry of Defence, HM Revenue and Customs, and the Ministry of Justice, which together span a vast range of activities. Lawyers are involved in all departments, and there are good career development prospects for graduates. The Civil Service Fast Stream programme exists to encourage talented graduates to apply to the service, and offers access to senior level experience (including legal experience) in a relatively short time frame, enabling rapid promotion for quality candidates. The 'streams' cover five areas: analysis and economics, human resources, technology in business, European institution work, and work in Northern Ireland. Legal experience is useful in almost any role within the Civil Service, not only within legal departments.

Useful experience relevant to this area:

- Graduate Diploma in Law (GDL), LPC or BVC/BPTC.

- particular interest or experience in human rights, public and administrative law, European and international law.

Company secretary

Company secretaries perform important administrative duties, such as ensuring documents and forms are filed at Companies House, signing off company accounts, chairing board meetings and drafting minutes. Company secretaries are mandatory for public companies, but it has not been a legal requirement for private limited companies to have a company secretary since April 2008. Many private limited companies have kept their company secretaries on however, as a dedicated staff member to keep on top of the company's corporate administrative work, and to be an important point of contact between management, shareholders, and other parties with an interest in the performance of the company.

Useful experience relevant to this area:

- LPC and BPTC business law modules

- work experience in a law firm's corporate or commercial departments

- work experience assisting senior management of a company or other organisation.

Foreign and Commonwealth Office work

The Foreign and Commonwealth Office (FCO), or Foreign Office, is the UK's international diplomatic service, supporting the British government and its citizens overseas. The FCO's objective is to maintain and advance Britain's influence in the international community, and to develop foreign policy in areas such as countering terrorism, preventing and resolving conflict, promoting economic growth, and developing effective international institutions. The FCO's work is dynamic and constantly adapting to international developments, and is interesting and rewarding. Work experience and placement schemes exist to give an insight into the work and culture of the service.

Useful experience relevant to this area:

- any legal qualifications or experience in the commercial or public sectors

- particular interest or experience in human rights, public and administrative law, European and international law.

HM Revenue and Customs

HM Revenue and Customs (HMRC) is the central authority managing tax and customs, and other central financial administration for the UK. Lawyers play a key role at HMRC in all areas of tax and finance matters, including advising government departments on policy, human rights, European and international law, as well as conducting litigation on HMRC's behalf to recover tax. Legal training opportunities exist within HMRC, and given the fundamental role and broad range of work, HMRC offers some of the best legal experience and training available in tax and related areas of law.

Useful experience relevant to this area:

- LPC and BPTC commercial, business and tax modules

- electives in any area of finance or commercial law

- interest or experience in contentious or non-contentious work

- interest in financial or tax-related work.

Human resources and recruitment

Effective management of staff within an organisation often requires a dedicated human resources manager or team. Working in human resources (HR) puts you at the heart of your employer's business, and will require good working knowledge of the business, its management, strategy and direction, as well as its people. Some of the main areas of HR work include recruiting and retaining staff, identifying and solving staff related problems, and managing staff procedures and training. Legally qualified HR staff are particularly valuable to some legal employers, as employment law is constantly updated, and an understanding of key legal principles is essential. The larger legal employers often look for legally qualified HR staff: working in HR in a law firm may be a good opportunity to build and develop your knowledge of employment law as well as your practical experience. Many of the larger legal recruitment consultancies look for legally qualified candidates when recruiting their own staff. This is a very popular route to take for those with legal qualifications.

Useful experience relevant to this area:

- employment law LPC or BPTC elective

- work experience in a law firm's employment, corporate or commercial departments

- other general commercial experience.

Investment banking, finance and insurance

Investment bankers are specialists in financial services, facilitating corporate mergers of companies, acquisitions of one or more companies by another, arranging loan facilities for large corporate or government clients, or dealing with the Stock Exchange on share issues.

Specific areas of work may include business analysis or trade and project finance, in the context of either commercial or private banking services. As with accountancy, the finance industry is subject to considerable regulation by law, and is regulated by the Financial Services Authority (FSA). Many of the FSA rules and regulations are familiar to lawyers, as the rules make up an important part of legal training and practice, particularly in areas such as prevention of money laundering. Since legal qualifications and banking are closely compatible, some employers in the banking sector will view legal qualifications as a very positive attribute on a CV.

Useful experience relevant to this area:

- LPC and BPTC commercial, business and tax modules

- electives in any area of finance, banking or commercial law.

Legal library work

If you are interested in the more academic or technical aspects of law, legal information and knowledge management, then library work may be an area to consider. Most of the larger law firms have extensive law libraries, as do barristers' chambers, universities, and some of the professional regulatory bodies. Librarians are not merely tasked with organising legal information and resources, but provide updates on developments in the law, put together training materials, respond to questions on specific points of law, and carry out general legal research. Law firm librarians work with colleagues across the firm, and interact with suppliers of law materials, IT and other information related services.

Useful experience relevant to this area:

- law degree or conversion, LPC or BPTC legal research modules

- any work experience involving legal research in a law firm or barristers' chambers.

Legal publishing and research, journalism and court reporting

There are a number of legal reference resources that are used across the profession, and which operate both online and in traditional print media. This is a growing area, as lawyers and commentators demand ever quicker and more flexible access to the latest available information. Qualified and part-qualified lawyers are often employed by legal publishers (e.g. Westlaw, LexisNexis, Practical Law Company) as staff writers and researchers to ensure that published material is relevant and accurate. Similarly, legal qualifications can be put to good use in journalism, either in the specialist legal press or elsewhere. Court reporting may also be an option: court reporters take a verbatim shorthand note of certain court proceedings, for publication as court reports.

Useful experience relevant to this area:

- all GDL, LPC and BPTC written modules and research tasks

- any experience writing articles, training materials or other documents

- any work experience involving legal research

- court and litigation experience.

Legal secretarial work

Legal secretaries play an important role assisting lawyers in all areas of legal practice, working in law firms and barristers' chambers, local authorities, and courts.

Legal secretarial work can be challenging and fast paced, perhaps assisting at court hearings, assisting with interviewing clients, researching points of law, and drafting legal documents, letters or forms. Salaries will vary according to location and experience, and employers frequently pay for legal secretaries to gain additional qualifications relevant to the legal work they do, adding to their skill set, and enhancing their career prospects.

Useful experience relevant to this area:

- LPC and BPTC business law modules

- work placements, vacation schemes or other experience in a law firm, chambers or court.

- non-legal work experience in a professional, office-based environment.

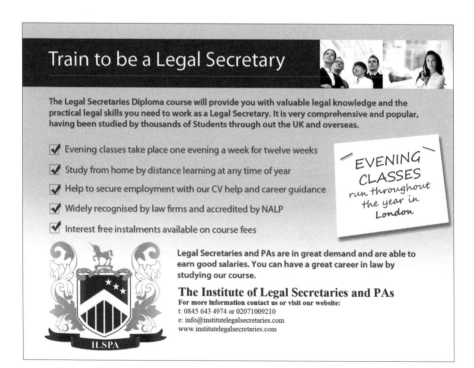

Case study: The Institute of Legal Secretaries and PAs

Have you considered a career as a legal secretary?

The role of a legal secretary is varied, challenging and interesting. It can be an excellent starting point for a career in law and there is great opportunity for career advancement. If you think it could be the career for you, there is an excellent course available to help you gain the valuable legal knowledge and practical skills you need to become a successful Legal Secretary.

Moushka Dickens, from London, took the Legal Secretaries Diploma course through The Institute of Legal Secretaries and PAs and she has only positive things to say about the Institute, her studies and her new job:

'I cannot praise the Institute enough for their help and advice, and Amanda Hamilton for being an amazing and inspirational tutor. She has a natural gift for teaching and for instilling in others the importance and precision of studying a very detailed and complex subject which spans many different topics in law. She managed to make lessons not only very interesting but also amusing. I have found The Institute of Legal Secretaries and PAs to be very helpful when I have either telephoned or emailed them with queries regarding the course. I would recommend both the Institute and Amanda Hamilton highly to any potential students, and indeed employers.'

Moushka achieved her goal and secured a position as a legal secretary/receptionist at a law firm in Wimbledon. Moushka tells us about her new career:

'I'm being trained on the job and the work is very varied and interesting – mostly probate, matrimonial, conveyancing and immigration. I must say that I felt really confident starting this role knowing that I had been fully trained by The Institute of Legal Secretaries and PAs and I have my file ready to refer to if need be. Everything I covered in my course is all here at my job. It's great to finally be able to put into practice what I've learned and the course folder and assignments have been invaluable to me in this respect. I have had feedback that my new employers and colleagues are very pleased and impressed with my work, which is nice to know. I am enjoying my new career so far and I hope to take it further in the future. I cannot recommend The Institute of Legal Secretaries and PAs and the course highly enough for anyone who is thinking of retraining.'

The Legal Secretaries Diploma course is widely recognised by law firms and it is accredited by the National Association of Licensed Paralegals, which is recognised as an awarding body by Ofqual, the regulator of qualifications in England. To find out more, visit www.institutelegalsecretaries.com.

Local government

Local government (county councils and district councils) employ around two million people in the UK, managing public services including healthcare, property and housing, education, and transport. Lawyers assist local government in a very wide range of areas, and opportunities exist for part-qualified lawyers as well as for qualified solicitors or barristers. Certain departments within councils may offer roles that are particularly well suited to those with legal experience or qualifications, such as building and planning departments, environmental services, dealing with issues in involving community officers and the police.

Useful experience relevant to this area:

- GDL, LPC or BVC/BPTC

- any work experience in legal practice

- particular interest or experience in public and administrative law, human rights including freedom of information, and community-focused work.

Management consultancy

Management consultants offer expert advice to assist organisations in optimising performance, helping to improve profitability, or assisting with specific projects that require specialist management input. The work can relate to any commercial sector, and tends to be project based, focused on strategy, general management and HR, or operational issues, such as supply chain management and information technology. The broad scope of potential areas of management consultancy work often means that several potential legal issues may apply to any given situation. A legal background is useful in identifying and understanding the implications of these issues, in order to manage them appropriately.

Useful experience relevant to this area:

- any legal qualification

- LPC or BPTC electives in business and commercial law

- work experience gained in a law firm, barristers' chambers or in-house.

Mediation and dispute resolution

Mediation is a form of alternative dispute resolution. It allows parties to a dispute to reach settlement confidentially, and under the parties' own terms, with no formal adjudication taking place. Mediation is voluntary, but is actively encouraged by the courts to run alongside formal litigation, as resolution can often be reached this way, without the time and expense of going all the way to court or tribunal. The role of the mediator is to act as an impartial go-between for both parties to the dispute, assisting with drafting terms to any mediated agreement or settlement, and coordinating logistical aspects of a mediation. More information is available from the Centre for Effective Dispute Resolution (CEDR; www.cedr.com).

Useful experience relevant to this area:

- any legal qualifications

- interest or experience in litigation and dispute resolution

- experience working with clients, perhaps through pro bono or Law Centre work.

Parliamentary work: parliamentary clerks

A parliamentary clerk is a skilled administrator working within the House of Commons (the 'House'), similar to a civil servant. They work in a central capacity, assisting all areas of the House, and are not affiliated to a political party. The work may involve assisting parliamentary committees with meetings and debates, preparing briefings, writing summaries and reports on positions and policies of parliamentary committees or drafting proposed amendments to parliamentary bills. Alternatively, a parliamentary clerk may be involved in procedural work within the House, which may include drafting summaries of the day's votes and other activities, or more specialist research on policy or procedure. Positions rotate every two years, giving parliamentary clerks insight into many aspects of the workings of government. The nature of the work means that many parliamentary clerks have undergraduate or higher degrees in law or other subjects, and many have previous legal experience.

Useful experience relevant to this area:

- GDL, LPC or BVC/BPTC

- particular interest or experience in politics, human rights, public and administrative law.

Police and criminal investigative work

Working for the police offers opportunities at different levels, including joining the force as a police officer, community support officer or in any number of different support roles, including analytical support. Certain forces, including the City of London, have specialist teams tackling criminal activity specific to their location, such as economic crime or counterterrorism activities. Experience gained through legal work or qualifications can be directly applicable in roles within many police departments.

Useful experience relevant to this area:

- GDL, LPC or BVC/BPTC modules in criminal law, public and administrative law, criminal litigation and advocacy

- particular interest in community work, helping others and combating crime.

Teaching and lecturing

Opportunities for teaching law are open to people at differing stages of qualification, with the expertise of qualified solicitors or barristers being particularly valued by colleges and universities. It is easy to envisage the kind of work this entails – take any course you have studied, and picture yourself being the person at the front of the room!

Useful experience relevant to this area:

- any legal qualifications

- any work experience in legal practice and/or teaching

- experience with advocacy, presenting and management.

Tribunal advocacy

Tribunals are similar to courts, in that cases are heard before a panel of adjudicators who decide on their outcome. They deal with specific areas of law, such as employment law, but are intended to be less formal than courts. They are intended to broaden access to dispute resolution, and to keep costs down through allowing people either to represent themselves more easily than in court, or to choose people other than barristers to represent them (although frequently barristers are instructed in tribunal cases).

A key point of difference between some tribunals and the courts is that you do not always need special qualifications, or 'rights of audience' to represent clients in tribunals (although clearly legal experience is a major advantage). Tribunal advocacy offers a combination of areas of work done by both solicitors and barristers, and is ideal for those with a keen interest in the sectors covered by the tribunal system, and who are looking for contentious work involving case and document preparation, and negotiation, as well as the advocacy itself.

Useful experience relevant to this area:

- LPC and BPTC advocacy modules

- experience with litigation and advocacy in a law firm or with a barrister

- experience representing clients through pro bono or Law Centre work.

13

What to do if things don't go to plan

What if . . .

. . . you don't get into law school?

Most course providers require applicants for the Graduate Diploma in Law (GDL) to have obtained at least a 2.i in their first degree. If you do not meet this requirement, and feel that your degree result does not fairly or accurately reflect your performance or potential, then discuss this with the course provider. They can give you feedback on your individual circumstances which will help you decide which direction to take.

If you do not manage to get a place, then a number of alternative routes to qualification are still available, and you will still be able to gain legal work experience that will count towards formal qualification, or to strengthen your legal CV. Options that will be open to you include training through the Institute of Legal Executives (ILEX), qualifying as a registered conveyancer or building your experience and contacts through paralegal work. See earlier chapters for more information on these.

. . . you don't get strong grades on the GDL, Legal Practice Course (LPC) or Bar Professional Training Course (BPTC)?

Strictly speaking, you are usually only required to gain a 'pass' on each of these courses, and there is no formal requirement to get a commendation or distinction in order to progress from one stage to the next, and on to your training contract or pupillage. The courses are not easy, and the number of assessments and exams involved means that sometimes things don't quite go to plan.

Most course providers allow you a number of retakes for certain exams or assessments, and you should check with your course provider for precise details. This will give you the opportunity to get back on track, but retakes may affect your ability to be awarded a commendation or distinction, even if you have achieved the required grades in other areas. If you are ill during exam time, then you should let your course provider know immediately, so you can plan how to progress. You may be able to sit the exams at a later time.

If you have a training contract, pupillage or other arrangement in place, you should be fully aware of any terms or conditions in the agreement with your employer which require you to achieve certain grades or standards. This is particularly important if your employer is covering any part of your course fees. Some solicitors firms will disqualify trainees if they do not achieve certain standards in all exams and assessments throughout the law degree or conversion. You should of course be aiming high anyway, but make sure you know exactly what is expected of you. If you are having difficulties during a course, make sure you discuss this with your employer, as well as with your tutors and/or careers advisers.

If your results are patchy, then make sure you highlight the positive results in applications and interviews. The chances are that you have performed well in areas that you find interesting, and in which you might want to work, so shape your applications around these successes. If you are asked in interview about areas where you did not perform quite so well, be honest – not everyone can be an expert in every area of such a broad range of subject matter. If you were involved in relevant activities or work experience outside of your studies, then this is a good thing. Highlight this, as time spent gaining broader, practical insight into areas of law that interest you might be fair justification for a 'blip' in your academic results.

. . . you don't get a training contract or pupillage?

The truth is that there are not enough places for all candidates, but this should not put you off applying. All employers are looking for good people, and the vacancies are out there. If you have the qualifications required, and show initiative and drive, this will separate you from the competition, and you are likely to succeed.

You may need to refine your search criteria as your search for a position continues, and you may need to broaden your scope, to include potential employers that you did not target first time round. You may have to look in a wider geographical area to the one you first had in mind. Revisit Chapter 11, speak to your tutors and contacts, and readjust where and how you are applying, in light of their feedback.

Sometimes you need to apply to the same employer a couple of times. You might not have had the right level of experience first time, or you may not have put in the best application, particularly if you have had to apply before starting your conversion degree. You won't be discriminated against for this, but it is much easier to show yourself off as a committed candidate if you have some legal experience, academic or practical, to draw from.

You may need to leave it a year or two to gain extra skills and experience before you continue with your applications. Firms and chambers do remember applicants, and it can make a very positive impression if you take any comments you received first time, build on them, and reapply later with exactly what they are looking for.

You will need to be flexible, and to use your common sense, but if you keep trying, you will find that persistence does pay. Concentrate on gaining skills and experience, and improving your applications. Applying year after year with nothing additional on your CV is not the way to go.

If it really is not working out, then look into the other career options covered in this chapter and Chapter 12. Continue to build your legal work experience, and stay on the look out for vacancies and new avenues to pursue. You will hear about opportunities as much by word of mouth as through your own research, so keep in touch with your contacts, and don't rely solely on internet searches and advertised vacancies.

. . . you decide at any point that after making the investment, law just isn't for you?

As with a lot of other things in life, there is no substitute for first-hand experience, and this is certainly the case with legal work. It is quite common for people to find that their expectations of what a legal career would entail are not matched by the reality of studying or working in law. Some law students find their law degree or GDL very interesting, only to find during the LPC or BPTC that they are not drawn to the practical realities of working in law. Others enjoy the academic side, but find that legal work in practice is perhaps not as interesting as a career somewhere else. Others find certain elements of law interesting, and do not want to spend the time and money getting qualifications in areas broader than those they need for their particular specialist areas. There may be fewer career possibilities available at a particular time in certain areas of law than you had hoped, which might force you to rethink where you are heading at any point in your legal career.

If after gaining any legal qualification you decide that a career in law isn't for you, this does not mean your experience is wasted. Everything you have learned can be applied to a huge number of other areas, and your skills will place you at a distinct advantage in the job market. The areas detailed above are just a start – tailor your research to your areas of interest, and you will find many more.

14

Overseas applicants

Overseas applicants are subject to complex immigration rules, which have a tendency to change frequently. If you are applying to study in the UK from overseas, you need to research the UK immigration authority rules as they apply to your country. Here is a basic overview of some of the issues you may face, but it is not possible to give more than a summary here. Use this as a starting point, and do your own research to find out what applies to you.

For complete and up-to-date information on the immigration rules that apply to overseas graduate students wishing to study in the UK, consult the Home Office UK Border Agency website section for adult students (www.ukba.homeoffice.gov.uk/studyingintheuk/adult-students).

Further useful information for overseas students on all aspects of studying in the UK is available from the UK Council for International Student Affairs (www.ukcisa.org.uk).

Are you eligible to study and/or work in the UK?

Immigration rules

The immigration rules for students currently fall under the Home Office Points Based Immigration System or PBS. The rules set out three key requirements for overseas students wishing to study in the UK.

- You are required to study at a college or university that has a PBS sponsor licence.

- The course you wish to study must be at a high enough academic level.

- You must be able to support yourself financially, by satisfying strict financial criteria.

Most of the major law course providers are licensed PBS sponsors. The postgraduate level of the law courses required for qualification in England and Wales are at a high enough academic level also to qualify. The first two requirements are therefore likely to be satisfied in most cases, for students looking to study the GDL, LPC or BPTC.

Financial points

For the third requirement, it is up to you to ensure that you satisfy the financial criteria set out in the Home Office rules. To give you an idea of the figures involved, the rules stated that in 2011, students studying in London for a course of 9 months or longer needed an absolute minimum of £7,200 per year of study, plus course fees. Students studying outside London needed £5,400 plus course fees.

Note that assistance with fees may be available to students domiciled in the UK, but may not be available to some overseas students. Many of the law course providers are private institutions, and external assistance with funding is limited. However, most of the colleges and universities offer bursaries and other schemes to assist talented candidates. You should check with your course provider to see if any options exist to assist with funding course fees.

There are also a number of important differences in the rules affecting European Union (EU) and non-EU students, including in relation to course fees and funding, and if you are from a non-EU country, you may be required to pay more than students from EU countries. You should look very carefully at how the immigration rules apply to you, and check with the course providers directly to ensure you have budgeted your fees and living expenses correctly.

Are your international qualifications recognised by the UK legal professional and regulatory bodies?

Earlier we mentioned the Solicitors Regulatory Authority (SRA) and Bar Standards Board (BSB) requirements to obtain a certificate of academic standing prior to studying the GDL, LPC and BPTC. It is essential that you check the current requirements, as set by the SRA or the BSB, in good time before you apply for any of the courses, to ensure that your home qualifications meet their eligibility criteria. You may be eligible to sign up to a course, but this in itself does not mean that your overseas academic qualifications will be recognised by the professional regulators. If they are not, then this will prevent you from going on to full qualification, even though you may have successfully completed one or some of the UK law courses.

Are the qualifications you intend to gain in the UK recognised as valid back home?

The qualifications for solicitors and barristers administered by the SRA and BSB are valid for practice in England and Wales. While English legal qualifications have a high perceived status internationally, you must ensure that any qualifications you receive as a result of your studies in English law are formally recognised by the relevant institutions and regulatory bodies in your home country. The courses are costly and time consuming: if you intend to make use of your English legal qualifications back home, then you need to know exactly how each qualification is recognised in your home country, well in advance of signing up to any courses, paying fees or making living or travel arrangements.

Language requirements

General language requirements for law

Excellent English is required at every stage of a career in law. Key elements of legal work include interpreting language, presenting and persuading others through verbal reasoning, understanding complex arguments, sifting through information, or researching cases, statutes and legal theory. Without a very solid grounding in English, it is not possible to perform well at the Academic or Vocational stages – and this is only the start. When it comes to working in legal practice, you will be stretched further, as your work gets more involved, and you go deeper into the detail, with legal issues often appearing in complex contexts. In addition to understanding the law, and the facts behind any particular matter or issue you are working on, you will always be required to communicate clearly and concisely to colleagues and clients, in writing and in person.

Formal language requirements

Some course providers will only make offers to applicants whose first language is not English subject to proof that the applicant has an adequate command of English. This is usually done by sitting an International English Language Testing System (IELTS) test, where a score of 7.5 or above is usually required. When it comes to applying for training positions, you will often be expected to do a written test, as well as face-to-face interviews. Your skills in written and oral English will be tested, so it's essential that you have the required fluency before you start.

Life outside of study

Moving to a new country to study is a big decision. It is exciting and challenging, and you need to make sure you are properly prepared. If you have never lived in the UK before, do you know what to expect? Will you be able to adjust to the pace of life, perhaps in London, Manchester, or one of the other big cities? It may take time to adjust to life in the UK, and you need to know where to go for support when you need it, as well as building up a good network of friends and colleagues. Your college or university will provide as much help as they can, and you will not find it difficult to meet a lot of like-minded people. Many will also be from overseas, and experiencing the same things as you, and will be perfectly placed to accompany you on your journey through the various stages of legal qualification.

Qualified overseas lawyers who wish to practise in the UK

Qualified Lawyers Transfer Scheme (QLTS)

Lawyers qualified outside of England and Wales, and some lawyers with English legal qualifications, may be entitled to have their qualifications recognised by the SRA, and to become qualified solicitors in England and Wales. A test is involved, covering the key areas of property law, litigation, professional conduct and accounts, and principles of common law. Lawyers qualified overseas who wish to become solicitors in England should check with the SRA as to the current eligibility criteria and procedures in place, as requirements change from year to year.

For more information, see www.sra.org.uk/solicitors/qltt.page.

Registered European lawyers (RELs)

Lawyers qualified in European countries are permitted to practise as solicitors in other European countries, provided certain criteria are met. In order to practise in another European country, lawyers must be nationals of, and qualified in, one of these countries. They must use the professional title of the country's profession (in the original language), and must be registered with the professional regulatory body in the country. After three years' uninterrupted work in the host country, a lawyer qualified in another European country is eligible to be registered with the host country's legal profession, without sitting any exams or other assessments. REL registration is a complex process, and you should check with the SRA for more information.

A separate system exists for registered foreign lawyers (RFLs) wishing to become partners in law firms, or to take on other senior management roles. This system is only available to qualified lawyers at senior level, and is outside the scope of this book.

Conclusion

opefully you now have a good idea of what is involved in the most popular areas of legal work, and what to expect when working in them. We've covered how the profession works and what some of the roles entail, the various qualifications required and how to get them, as well as some of the key issues you might face when approaching the professional legal world outside of your studies.

You will face challenges along the way, but with hard work, persistence and a good level of awareness of where you are headed and what is required to get there, there is nothing to stop you getting the job you want. Of course some areas are harder to get into than others, but the vacancies are there, and they are filled by the most appropriate, best skilled people – we've covered the basics here, so put this advice into practice, and get your name out there.

Good luck!

Glossary

ABS	Alternative Business Structures. Provisions of the Legal Services Act 2007 that came into force in October 2011 allow legal services to be provided in ways not previously permitted. ABS would allow shareholder investment in law firms, and for non-legal organisations to offer legal services.
Academic Stage	The requirement for both solicitors and barristers to have completed either an undergraduate law degree, or postgraduate conversion (*see* GDL).
ADR	Initialisation for alternative dispute resolution. A number of processes exist whereby parties to a dispute can seek resolution outside of the expensive and public forum of the court system. ADR includes mediation, arbitration and expert determination.

Arbitration	A method of resolving legal disputes without going through the courts. The parties to the dispute elect an independent adjudicator (an 'arbitrator'), and agree to be bound by the arbitrator's decision. *See also* ADR.
The Bar	The name given to the barristers' profession as a whole.
Bar Council	The approved regulator of the barristers' profession in England and Wales.
BPTC	Bar Professional Training Course. The current barrister's Vocational Stage qualification.
BSB	Bar Standards Board. Part of the Bar Council which takes on active regulatory functions of the barristers' profession.
BVC	Bar Vocational Course, the former barristers' Vocational Stage qualification. Now replaced by the BPTC (*see above*).
Bundle	Files of documents, generally used in the context of litigation or court procedures, containing statements, evidence and correspondence between the parties. Junior lawyers are often called upon to help with putting bundles together ('bundling'), which can offer detailed insight into the elements and structure of a case.
Call	Number of years since a barrister was called to the Bar. Similar to Post Qualification Experience for solicitors. *See* PQE.
Called to the Bar	The process by which a barrister formally enters the profession.
Chambers	A barrister's office, often shared with other barristers in a set. See set.
Clerk	A barrister's administrative assistant, responsible for all aspects of booking, scheduling and fee recovery for the barrister.

Contentious	A legal matter that is subject to a dispute, regardless of the formal legal process being taken.
Conversion	A postgraduate course allowing graduates with a degree in a subject other than law to 'convert' to the equivalent of a law degree, and thereby satisfy the Academic Stage of training. This is either the Graduate Diploma in Law, or Common Professional Examination.
Counsel	The formal word for a barrister, or the capacity of a barrister.
CPD	Continuous Professional Development. All solicitors and barristers are required to 'top up' their legal and professional knowledge after qualification.
CPE	Common Professional Examination. A qualification available to gain the Academic Stage qualification. *See also* GDL.
CPRs	The Civil Procedure Rules. The CPRs and Practice Directions are the authoritative directory for court and litigation procedure.
Cross-examination	In court proceedings, the questioning of a witness by the opponent's legal representative, usually a barrister.
Examination-in-chief	In court proceedings, the questioning of a witness by their own legal representative. *See* Cross-examination.
Firm	A group of solicitors, usually working in partnership as a private practice. Many firms are now limited liability partnerships, rather than traditional partnerships. *See* LLP.
Fee	Charges made by solicitors and barristers to their clients, in return for their legal services.
GDL	Graduate Diploma in Law. One of the conversion courses available to gain the Academic Stage qualification. *See also* CPE.

Higher Rights of Audience	A qualification available to solicitors, allowing them to conduct advocacy in the higher courts (House of Lords, Court of Appeal, High Court and Crown Court).
Junior	A practising barrister who is not yet a QC. *See* QC.
Law firm	Usually a partnership of solicitors. Note – if a firm is a partnership, then it is not a 'company', as it does not comply with the formal requirements of being a company. Referring to a solicitors' firm as a 'company' is, technically, incorrect.
Law Society	The organisation representing the interests of solicitors in England and Wales. *See also* SRA.
Litigation	The formal legal process taken to resolve a dispute, in either civil or criminal law contexts. This may include court proceedings, or ADR.
LLB	An undergraduate bachelor's degree in law. Comes from the Latin *Legum Baccalaureus.*
LLM	A postgraduate, master's degree in law. Comes from the Latin *Legum Magister.*
LLP	Limited Liability Partnership. Unlike traditional partnerships, where partners share unlimited liability for debts, negligence or misconduct, the LLP allows partners' liability to be limited, in a similar manner to limited companies. LLPs are still referred to as 'firms'. Many organisations, including law and accountancy firms, operate under this structure.
LPC	Legal Practice Course. The solicitors' Vocational Stage qualification.
Mediation	A form of ADR (*see above*) in which parties to a dispute elect an independent third party to assist them in negotiating a settlement to the dispute. The mediator does not act as an adjudicator, but as an intermediary.

PQE	Post Qualification Experience. The number of years' experience that a solicitor has since qualification. For barristers, *see* Call.
Pupil	A barrister in the final stage of training before obtaining a practising certificate.
Pupillage	The final stage of a barrister's training, after completing a law degree, the Bar Professional Training Course and being 'called to the Bar'.
QC	Queen's Counsel. The most senior lawyers in Commonwealth countries, selected from barristers or solicitors with Higher Rights of Audience (*see above*). After appointment, QCs wear a silk gown in court appearances, hence the process of appointment being known as 'taking silk', and QCs being referred to as 'silks'.
Qualifying law degree	A law degree taken at undergraduate level, from an institution recognised by the Joint Academic Stage Board of solicitors and barristers.
REL	Registered European Lawyer.
RFL	Registered Foreign Lawyer.
Seat	A period of time, usually between four and six months, where a trainee solicitor will sit with a more senior supervisor in a particular department.
Secondment	A placement undertaken by a trainee solicitor, pupil barrister or their qualified counterparts, where they join an organisation separate from their employer (perhaps a commercial client's offices, or government department), to work as a lawyer for that organisation. Secondments are often used to offer experience to lawyers in training that their own firm, chambers or employer is unable to offer.

Set	A group of barristers, often sharing premises. *See* Chambers.
Six	One of the two six-month stints that a pupil barrister will spend with a supervising junior.
SRA	Solicitors Regulation Authority. This is the independent regulatory arm of the Law Society of England and Wales, which is responsible for monitoring the training and qualification regulations of all solicitors in England and Wales.
Tenancy	The term used to describe a qualified, practising barrister's position within chambers.
Trainee	A future solicitor who has completed the Academic and Vocational stages, and who is in the process of completing their professional training, usually with a law firm.
Training contract	The final stage required for qualification as a solicitor, usually completed with a law firm, and lasting two years.
Undertaking	A legally binding agreement or promise, often required to be taken by solicitors and trainees in the context of property transactions.
Vocational Stage	The stage of training after the Academic Stage, satisfied by the BPTC and LPC, specific to barristers and solicitors, respectively.
White Book	A leading publication from legal publishers Sweet & Maxwell containing the Civil Procedure Rules and Practice Directions, commentary and other resources for lawyers acting on county court, high court or Court of Appeal matters.

Endnotes

1. Law Society (2010) Trends in the solicitors' profession: annual statistical report, p.6.
2. Ibid.
3. www.barcouncil.org.uk/CareersHome/TheStatistics/
4. ww2.prospects.ac.uk/p/types_of_job/barrister_salary.jsp
5. www.nus.org.uk/en/Student-Life/Money-And-Funding/Average-costs-of-living-and-study
6. juniorlawyers.lawsociety.org.uk/node/140
7. www.sra.org.uk/solicitors/handbook/code/content.page

Useful resources

The Law Society: www.lawsociety.org.uk
Represents solicitors in England and Wales. Offers training and advice, and lobbies on behalf of the solicitors' profession at government level.

The Solicitors Regulation Authority (SRA): www.sra.org.uk
Regulates solicitors and is an independent regulatory body of the Law Society. The SRA sets standards and guidelines for the profession, monitors training and professional development, and issues practicing certificates for qualified solicitors.

The General Council of the Bar, or Bar Council: www.barcouncil.org.uk
Regulates barristers in England and Wales, and operates its regulatory activities through a separate body, the Bar Standards Board.

For a full list of links to all resources and organisations mentioned in the book, visit www.charliephillips.info.

Index of advertisers

Index of advertisers

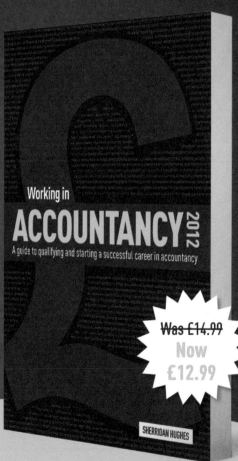

ACE YOUR INTERVIEW!

Find out how to:

- Prepare with confidence

- Make a good impression

- Handle tough questions

THE LEARNING CENTRE
HAMMERSMITH AND WEST
LONDON COLLEGE
GLIDDON ROAD
LONDON W14 9BL

LEADING
COLLABORATIVE
LEARNING

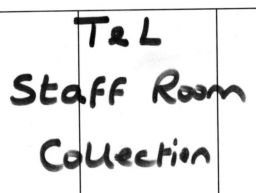

To

Ted and Peggy

Jim

Robert, Sarah, Robbie, Madeleine

Michelle, Bob, Jackson, Ryan

Stephanie, Chris, Aeson

Taylor, Karen

With love,

Lyn

To

Greg, Matthew, Michelle, and Melissa,

Erik and Austin

Wilf and Christine

My late parents, Erich and Ingeborg

With love,

Beate

What Your Colleagues Are Saying . . .

"Lyn Sharratt and Beate Planche have done us all a great favor by writing this book. This well-researched resource provides a useful vocabulary for talking about and understanding Collaborative Learning, describes an incredibly helpful set of tools so that anyone can use them to lead collaborative conversations, and clearly defines a Theory of Action to help us organize and ground our collaborative work."

Jim Knight, From the Foreword
President, Impact Research Lab, Lawrence,
Kansas, Director, Kansas Coaching Project at
The University of Kansas Center for Research on Learning

"Lyn Sharratt and Beate Planche not only highlight the power of collaboration, they go further to identify the key narratives to which this collective needs to attend. Their notion of Collaborative Learning involves systems and school leaders building collective capacity, energizing knowledge together, and moving schools from being places of 'plans and good intentions' to centers of 'purposeful practice' on the part of all teachers who then empower students to do the same. Who does not want to be a part of such a school?"

John Hattie, From the Introduction
Laureate Professor, Director, Melbourne Education
Research Institute at the University of Melbourne

"It is clear that Sharratt and Planche have themselves done everything that is in the book. What is even clearer is that they have helped scores of others engage in these actions suited to their own situations. . . . This is a book that has crystal clear concepts, co-learning galore, is guided by research and grounded in practice—all devoted to deep learning by students and adults alike."

Michael Fullan, From the Afterword
Professor Emeritus, University of Toronto, Canada

"The credibility of Sharratt and Planche, two of Ontario's most respected curriculum leaders, comes from the fact that they do not only write about what works, they have done the work! Their call for deeper learning as a result of collaboration or co-laboring takes this idea to a new level of much-needed inquiry. Their discussion of the research-informed elements for authentic learning and the related competencies further validate their assertions. I appreciate the holistic nature of their work with the focus on cognitive, interpersonal, and intrapersonal skills. The deconstruction of ideas related to innovation, creativity, and growth mindsets and the identification of the specific behaviors of classroom teachers that build strong learning cultures will contribute significantly to our knowledge base."

Avis Glaze, *Former Chief Student Achievement Officer of Ontario, Founding CEO, Literacy and Numeracy Secretariat*

"Good collaboration, collaborative skills, and behaviors increasingly are critical to our success in teaching and learning, and in the organization of education. *Leading Collaborative Learning* provides analysis and road maps for understanding, building and developing collaboration in the work of schools, and setting the stage for deeper learning. It builds on evidence from the field and points to actions we can take to strengthen collaboration. It is an important contribution, a good read with intriguing ideas for us each to reflect upon."

Gavin Dykes
Chair and Co-Founder, Education Fast Forward

"*Leading Collaborative Learning: Empowering Excellence* is a timely, important, and compelling call to collective action and professional agency. It reminds us that teachers working together on real issues of learning and teaching can be a powerful catalyst for change. This is a must-read book for anyone interested in securing and sustaining authentic school and system improvement."

Alma Harris, *Director, Institute of Educational Leadership University of Malaya, Malaysia Past President, ICSEI*

"This exceptional book is a rich and practical resource for leaders who realize the power of working together to improve schools. In a system where collaborative practices are the norm, student achievement and well-being become a shared responsibility. Deeper learning is maximized for everyone."

Joanne Robinson, *Director of Professional Learning*
Linda Massey, *Associate Director of Professional Learning Education Leadership Canada*

"Recent advances in digitized technology tend to isolate learners, but isolating teachers in their professional learning is dangerous. While collaborative inquiry may lead to deep and meaningful insights, this kind of work is easier to describe than practice. In this important book, the authors examine what it actually means to work together for a common purpose. They understand the complexity and analyze its components. It is essential reading for leaders and teachers committed to improvement in students' learning through authentic research in the classroom. Full of practical advice backed up by years of successful experience—the ultimate collaborative resource."

Alan Boyle, *Author, Researcher, Consultant Leannta Education Associates, United Kingdom*

"Finally, Lyn Sharratt and Beate Planche have delivered a bold definition, provocative insights, and a clear framework for Collaborative Learning. They compel us in *Leading Collaborative Learning* to recognize that collaboration is a focused learning while outlining outcomes of a quality collaborative process. Sharratt and Planche have created a vital challenge for improving systems, schools, and classroom practice. This book is a must-read for all who wish to make a difference for the future now."

Bill Hogarth, *Director of Education (retired)*
York Region District School Board, Ontario, Canada

"Sharratt and Planche understand that effective Collaborative Learning means co-laboring at all levels throughout the system. In this book, they help readers be better at co-laboring, be it at the school or systems level, and they offer extensive processes and resources to make Collaborative Learning be growth-producing for all involved."

Jennifer Abrams, *Consultant*
Author of Having Hard Conversations *and*
Hard Conversations Unpacked:
The Whos, the Whens, and the What-Ifs

"If we are to move forward with making learning the central focus of schools, then we need to understand how to get past adult issues and politics, and concentrate more on authentic collaboration, which when done well can improve learning among adults and students. In *Leading Collaborative Learning*, Lyn Sharratt and Beate Planche show us how to do that."

Peter DeWitt, EdD, *Author, Consultant*
Finding Common Ground blog (Education Week)

"Everyone knows that educators need to work better together—but the question of how to do so has rarely been addressed beyond the level of glittering generalities. In this breakthrough volume, Lyn Sharratt and Beate Planche provide busy professionals with precise action plans to build powerful and sustainable collaborative cultures in our schools. This is an indispensable contribution for all teachers, principals, and system-level leaders who are serious about uplifting learning for all students."

Dennis Shirley, *Professor, Lynch School of Education, Boston College*
Editor-in-Chief, Journal of Educational Change

"This valuable resource explains clearly and persuasively why Collaborative Learning really is a good idea. It challenges you to reflect deeply on your current collaborations, and it offers helpful definitions, examples, and tools, whatever your role in the system. A great read!"

Louise Stoll, *Professor of Professional Learning*
University College London Institute of Education

"I think the particular strength of this book is that it addresses something that is quite difficult to do, but easy to talk about—that is, establishing a collaborative culture of inquiry in a school. So many leaders talk about collaboration, but then lead by telling. This book helps leaders who may not have had the best leadership models themselves see what it looks like to 'co-labor' (a turn of the phrase that is particularly welcome and illustrative, in my opinion) in a school setting for the good of teachers and kids."

Jo Beth Jimerson, *Assistant Professor of Educational Leadership, Texas Christian University*

"*Leading Collaborative Learning: Empowering Excellence* is the definitive source for your comprehensive step-by-step implementation of Collaborative Learning. This book belongs on every educator's desk."

Mike Greenwood, *District Teacher Leader Windsor Public Schools, Connecticut*

"Is your school ready to learn to meet student needs as a team? If so, *Leading Collaborative Learning: Empowering Excellence* is the book to help your staff learn together in order to improve student learning."

Renee Peoples, *Teaching and Learning Coach West Elementary, North Carolina*

"The major strength of the text addresses two points: the opportunity to really connect the need to engage in collaborative processes as a way to improve schools, and the way in which that same learning assists teachers in developing similar processes in their classrooms with students."

Chad Ransom, *Director of Second Language Services Teton County School District, Wyoming*

"This is more than just another book on school leadership or school improvement. Collaborative Learning is essential for success, and educators working in any capacity can find information here about how their role contributes to the process. From system leaders to school leaders to teachers to students, this book clearly explains the necessity of everyone's participation in Collaborative Learning processes. As the authors state, participation in collaboration 'is a powerful way to deepen educator capacity, to increase the value of the professional capital in the school, and to harness the power of the collective.'"

Melanie Mares Sainz, *Instructional Coach Lowndes Middle School, Virginia*

LEADING COLLABORATIVE LEARNING

■ ■ ■

Empowering Excellence

■ ■ ■

LYN SHARRATT ▪ **BEATE PLANCHE**

Foreword by **JIM KNIGHT** ■ Introduction by **JOHN HATTIE** ■ Afterword by **MICHAEL FULLAN**

A JOINT
PUBLICATION

CORWIN
A SAGE Company

ONTARIO
PRINCIPALS'
COUNCIL
Exemplary Leadership in Public Education

FOR INFORMATION:

Corwin

A SAGE Company

2455 Teller Road

Thousand Oaks, California 91320

(800) 233-9936

www.corwin.com

SAGE Publications Ltd.

1 Oliver's Yard

55 City Road

London EC1Y 1SP

United Kingdom

SAGE Publications India Pvt. Ltd.

B 1/I 1 Mohan Cooperative Industrial Area

Mathura Road, New Delhi 110 044

India

SAGE Publications Asia-Pacific Pte. Ltd.

3 Church Street

#10-04 Samsung Hub

Singapore 049483

Executive Editor: Arnis Burvikovs

Senior Associate Editor: Desirée A. Bartlett

Editorial Assistant: Andrew Olson

Production Editor: Melanie Birdsall

Copy Editor: Terri Lee Paulsen

Typesetter: C&M Digitals (P) Ltd.

Proofreader: Theresa Kay

Indexer: Sheila Bodell

Cover Designer: Gail Buschman

Marketing Manager: Anna Mesick

Printed in the United States of America

Library of Congress Cataloging-in-Publication Data

Names: Sharratt, Lyn, author.

Title: Leading collaborative learning: empowering excellence/ Lyn Sharratt, Beate Planche.

Description: Thousand Oaks, California: Corwin, [2016] | Includes bibliographical references and index.

Identifiers: LCCN 2015040109 | ISBN 9781483368979 (pbk.: alk. paper)

Subjects: LCSH: Group work in education. | Team learning approach in education. | Learning, Psychology of.

Classification: LCC LB1032 .S458 2016 | DDC 371.39/5—dc23

LC record available at http://lccn.loc.gov/2015040109

This book is printed on acid-free paper.

Certified Chain of Custody

SUSTAINABLE FORESTRY INITIATIVE

Promoting Sustainable Forestry

www.sfiprogram.org

SFI-01268

SFI label applies to text stock

16 17 18 19 20 10 9 8 7 6 5 4 3 2

Contents

3. System Leaders Working Alongside School Leaders 52

6. Teachers and Students Working Alongside Each Other 169

List of Figures and Tables

Figures

Tables

Foreword

L yn Sharratt and Beate Planche have done us all a great favor by writing this book, *Leading Collaborative Learning: Empowering Excellence*. This well-researched resource provides a useful vocabulary for talking about and understanding Collaborative Learning, describes an incredibly helpful set of tools so that anyone can use them to lead collaborative conversations, and clearly defines a Theory of Action to help us organize and ground our collaborative work. They write what they truly believe and have experienced as researchers and practitioners: "together teachers and leaders who collaborate have positive impact on student outcomes."

For Sharratt and Planche, Collaborative Learning is goal-directed action that empowers teachers and leaders to construct new knowledge together, that builds and shares understanding about practice, and most importantly, that outlines specific strategies for improving the quality of students' lives. The authors stress that Collaborative Learning is a genuine way of interacting and learning together for the mutual benefit of students, teachers, and leaders. Therefore, finding the time to model Collaborative Learning is critically important for everyone in systems and schools. We construct knowledge, they say, by working on processes together, through conversation about co-work. Anyone who is learning in a school—and that should be everyone—needs this comprehensive guidebook!

This book is rich in examples of Collaborative Learning processes at the system, school, and classroom levels. Collaborative Learning takes place in facilitated conversations and emanates from structured inquiries. The most meaningful and productive Collaborative Learning will occur when people communicate effectively. Similarly, in my book, *Better Conversations: Coaching Ourselves and Each Other to Be More Credible, Caring, and Connected* (2015), I write about the same beliefs and habits that make effective communication possible as Sharratt and Planche describe in *Leading Collaborative Learning: Empowering Excellence.* I believe these shared beliefs and understandings are the lifeblood of Collaborative Learning. I identify six beliefs that are foundational for the kind of conversations that make deeper forms of collaboration possible:

1. I see conversation partners as equals.

2. I want to hear what others have to say.

3. People should have a lot of autonomy.

4. I don't judge others.

5. Conversation should be back and forth.

6. Conversation should be life-giving.

As Sharratt and Planche contend, learning conversations involve respectful listening and insightful presentation of one's own view regarding considered actions as well as learner challenges to the status quo because of the culture of safety and trust. Every teacher should believe that he or she can be more impactful when learning together with other colleagues and with their students.

The four elements of the Sharratt and Planche Theory of Action support deeper learning conversations by building an inquiry process on their bedrock of defined leader- or facilitator-led norms, protocols, vignettes, and case studies. A critical component of this book is the well-researched section in each chapter that makes the strong connection between the impact of Collaborative Learning and increasing all students' achievement. They show us the unique ways to build collective efficacy through planned Collaborative Learning processes.

In *Leading Collaborative Learning: Empowering Excellence*, Sharratt and Planche stress that capacity building is an essential part of system and school improvement that makes a difference. One capacity that must be developed to promote Collaborative Learning is co-learning through effective communication. Systems and schools where conversations leading to co-work are the norm and settings where the powerful tools, theories, and activities in this book can flourish. And when Collaborative Learning flourishes, growth and achievement will happen for all students, teachers, and leaders.

Jim Knight

President, Impact Research Lab, Lawrence, Kansas
Director, Kansas Coaching Project at The University of
Kansas Center for Research on Learning

Introduction

A major argument in Visible Learning is that the impact of educators is most powerful when principals lead schools to have debates and engage in critique about what "impact" means across the school, to help develop multiple ways to evaluate the magnitude of this impact, and to search for ways to ensure that all students gain the benefit of attaining this magnitude of impact. This highlights the "instructional" or "impact" power of school leaders but, most important, it also shows the power of the collective nature of our enterprise. Teachers can and should not engage in this debate alone—otherwise it becomes random each time a student meets a new teacher whether the student will make appropriate yearly gain or not.

Recently, Rachel Eells completed a dissertation on teacher collective efficacy (Eells, 2011). This concept relates to ways to empower teachers so that they can determine what changes can be made within their particular context by enhancing their confidence to overcome any limitations and truly make a difference to the learning outcomes of their students. This screams for leadership in the school to develop an organization climate, produce school norms, and create the time and direction to enhance all teachers in the school to share in this sense of confidence to make the difference.

Her work brings together two powerful disciplines. First, social-cognitive theory is based on Bandura's (1997, p. 3) notion that "perceived self-efficacy refers to beliefs in one's capabilities to organize and execute the courses of action required to produce given attainments," leading to a powerful sense of agency: "to be an agent is to intentionally make things happen by one's actions" (Bandura, 2001, p. 2). When teachers have efficacy expectations that they can positively influence the outcomes of student learning, then the likelihood of these outcomes increases (Rubie-Davis, 2015).

Second, she explores the notions of collective efficacy. This relates to "a group's shared belief in the conjoint capabilities to organize and execute the courses of action required producing given levels of attainment" (Bandura, 1997, p. 477). In schools this is less related to the addition or aggregation of individual beliefs about personal efficacies to accomplish group goals, but more to the aggregation of members' beliefs about the collective's ability to accomplish group goals (Bandura, 1997, 2000). Eells provides a powerful example: "If the collective activity consists of the sum of independent successes, as it does for a track and field team, then it is preferable to measure and aggregate the personal efficacies of the actors. When an entire group must interact, like a basketball team would, and collective activity is the product of cooperative work, then it makes more sense to meas- ure group members' beliefs about what the team can accomplish" (2011, p. 66). In schools, collective efficacy is influenced by school organizational features, such as responsiveness of administrators, teacher collaboration, encouragement of innovation, orderly student behavior leaders' attributes (Newmann, Rutter, & Smith, 1989), and the narrative developed by school leaders (in schools where teachers' conversations dwell on the insurmountable difficulties of educating students that are likely to undermine teachers' sense of efficacy but in schools where teachers work together to find ways to address the learning, motivation, and behavior problems of their students that are likely to enhance teachers' feelings of efficacy; Tschannen-Moran, Hoy, & Hoy, 1998).

Eells located 26 studies of the relation between teacher collective efficacy and student outcomes. The average correlation was 0.60, which translates to an effect size of 1.23—making it among the most powerful influences that we know on student achievement (Hattie, 2009, 2015a). This effect was high across all school subjects and at all levels of schooling (elementary, middle, and high). The message is clear: How teachers collectively think about their impact is most relevant to success for their students. But how to develop leaders to engender their group positive think—and then ensure it is operation- alized in the classrooms, is shared and esteemed in the staff room, and that lessons are learned in safe, high trust environments about what worked best and what did not—for whom and about what.

This collective efficacy flies in the face of the fundamental assumption that too many educators have about their profession—the right to teach and think as they want. Hence the importance of this book by Lyn Sharratt and Beate Planche. They not only highlight the power of collaboration, they go further to identify the key narratives to which this collective needs to attend. Their notion of Collaborative Learning involves systems and school leaders building collective capacity, energizing knowledge together, and moving schools from being places of "plans and good intentions" to centers of "purposeful practice" on the part of all teachers who then empower students to do the same. Who does not want to be a part of such a school? It is unfortunate that the answer too often is "many" who prefer to be left alone, supported to do it "their way." And this is not saying that "their way" is good or bad, but when it is good, what a powerful addition to the collective, what a wonderful role model, what a potentially excellent critique. We have to stop building models where we address one teacher, one school, and one system at a time; stop talking about my students, my class, my school, my system. It is time to learn from each other about what works best, to critique our notions of what impact and learning look like, to build a coalition of the successful to enable all to then make the difference, and to convince each other through evidence of student growth that it *is* possible to make major differences in the learning lives of students. There are so many examples of excellence in this happening throughout the world and so many identified in this book—if only we had greater courage to identify successful schools all around us. And from such success, scale it up to others. It is the collective and Collaborative Learning that needs capturing. This is the power of this book—to provide signposts to collaborative effectiveness, to provide many examples of this in action, and to indicate the underpinnings of Collaborative Learning.

It takes deliberate action by school leaders to build collective efficacy and work together. Sharratt and Planche see this as co-laboring—we are responsible to and accountable for our own learning while supporting the learning of other co-laborers (collaborators). Co-laboring fosters interdependence as we negotiate meaning and relevance together. This leads to a sense of joint-ownership of the success or not of what we do. They show examples of how they have implemented these notions in schools, and thence the powerful and consequential impact on student learning. They note the critical ways to build leaders who have the courage to create narratives about collective impact, how leaders can best work collaboratively with teachers, and teachers with other teachers, and teachers with students. It never loses the key focus of this collaboration (hint: it is a precise, focused daily devotion to learning linked to results).

What a wonderful contribution this book makes to the current debates about how to move the basic premise for most educators away from "my class/school is my kingdom" and away from "I need to be supported and left alone by my leaders"—to a basic premise that my major mission is to work collaboratively with other educators and students to collectively maximize our impact on students. As Jim Knight says in the Foreword, this book is rich in examples, it is timely, and the authors write what they truly believe and have experienced as researchers and practitioners. Michael Fullan in the Afterword notes that there are many crystal clear concepts, co-learning galore, guided by research, grounded in practice—all devoted to deep learning by students and adults alike. I endorse Michael's noting how this book complements his own recent book *Coherence: Putting the Right Drivers in Action* (Fullan & Quinn, 2015). Similarly, it provides the flesh, the examples, and the drivers of the major messages underlying the Visible Learning research— how educators can work together to understand and critique what they mean by impact, what acceptable levels of magnitude are, and how to ensure that *all* in the system gain acceptable levels of impact.

John Hattie

Laureate Professor, Director, Melbourne Education
Research Institute at the University of Melbourne

Preface

The definition of collaboration in education has evolved. Still today, some might say . . . *In our school, we all get along; we co-operate, discuss, and share resources; we work side by side, help each other out, and support each other. We work together on committees, sports teams, and special events. We're very collaborative . . . aren't we?*

While all of the activities listed above are important in creating a positive school climate, collaboration is not just about individuals cooperating or their sense of collegiality, is it? It is about them purposefully engaging; it is about them developing a culture of *learning together* to best serve students' needs—collaboratively learning. Our profession is charged with improving student achievement; therefore, school systems today require much more than collegial educators. School systems require educators who are willing to co-learn and co-labor in the service of students. **Collaborative Learning** is an approach in which system and school leaders build collective capacity; create new, energizing knowledge together; and move schools from being places of "plans and good intentions" to centers of "purposeful practice" on the part of all teachers who then empower students to do the same. To strengthen classroom practice, teachers' and leaders' learning must result in a greater understanding of how teaching impacts learning. To deliver that, authentic (close to real-life) Collaborative Learning opportunities need to take place in classroom settings as often as possible. And, to successfully grow practice and sustain potential impact on increasing student achievement, Collaborative Learning among teachers requires an atmosphere in which system and school leaders are intentional in demonstrating they are equally committed to continuous learning alongside teachers, students, and each other.

Similarly, skilled practitioners who also use a Collaborative Learning approach in the classroom develop significant academic and social benefits for students. Collaborative Learning promotes critical thinking, develops confidence, supports oral language and communication skills, and creates an environment of active and involved learning (Panitz, 1997). Teachers who are able to collaborate effectively with peers are more likely to see the value in partnering with students, parents, and the broader community.

We have reasonable clarity now on the characteristics of "good systems" and how lower-performing schools can be transformed through strategic leadership (Leithwood, Harris, & Strauss, 2010; Sharratt & Fullan, 2009, 2012). It has been suggested that change is a mirage to people unless they experience the reality of school improvement (Fullan, 2011). In *Realization: The Change Imperative for Deepening District-Wide Reform* (2009), Sharratt and Fullan report in depth on the learning from one very large district. Their conclusions were entirely consistent with the pursuit of district-wide reform that they reviewed (and have seen since) from across the globe. They researched and discovered 14 Parameters (see page 67) that lead to system, school, and student improvement that suggest an intentional, successful path for other districts seeking to establish a clear focus to build educator capacity (Sharratt & Fullan, 2009). Included in *Realization* was Parameter 1, the notion of shared beliefs and understandings that only comes from collaborative work at the system and school levels. *Putting FACES on the Data: What Great Leaders Do!* illuminated the many benefits of personalizing student data through assessment, instruction, ownership, and leadership practices (Sharratt & Fullan, 2012). We can't be satisfied with mere "Good" but must move forward from "Great to Innovate" to empower today's connected elementary and secondary students, K–12 and beyond, to move toward excellence (Sharratt & Harild, 2015).

Building on these foundational texts, we now write that in order to be effective **co-learners**, it is essential that educators at every level consider the issues of **Leading Collaborative Learning** and empowering excellence to strengthen moving forward together and learning from each other. There is much work to do.

Sustainable system-wide student achievement requires ongoing attention to supporting all staff members in setting their personal and their collective **Learning Goals**. Establishing Collaborative Learning as a process is a valuable goal at all levels of a learning organization. Today, improving schools hinges on growing and sustaining cultures for learning and embedding Collaborative Learning processes—in the classroom, in the staff room, and at tables where leaders make decisions.

> "FACES is not an acronym. FACES is capitalized for emphasis—that is, we all have responsibility to have cognitive insights about and make emotional connections to all learners to be able to put the FACES on our data and take action."
>
> Sharratt & Fullan, 2012, p. 3

Why is embedding this process so critical? While collaboration as a process has long been a part of the life of schools, societal work demands have brought the skills of collaboration and Collaborative Learning to the foreground. As is now commonly reported, workplaces seek employees with collaborative skills to work together to solve critical problems and to find innovative solutions to challenges. It is increasingly important that our educational systems graduate literate graduates who are ready for workplaces where collaboration and interdependence will be a prerequisite (Sharratt & Harild, 2015).

This book is intended for educators at all levels of school systems—in classrooms and in administrative positions—who are interested in learning more about the impact of leading and learning collaboratively. It addresses what is important about leadership as a key element of being able to mobilize and lead collaborative work and Collaborative Learning effectively—including how leaders deal with inhibiting conditions and how they enhance enabling conditions. This book is also for those who are preparing new educators for a changing workplace culture, one which increasingly requires collaborative learners and leaders.

The Foreword by Jim Knight reviews the landscape of collaboration. John Hattie's thoughtful Introduction reinforces the importance of building collective efficacy through focused collaborative work. Chapter 1 discusses "purpose"—the contextual calls for deeper learning that impacts student achievement as the primary outcome of Collaborative Learning. We offer key definitions and our research findings. In Chapter 2 we discuss our theory of action with its four elements:

- **Assessing to Plan** effectively,
- **Planning to Act** purposely,
- **Acting to Make Sense of Findings** thoughtfully, and
- **Making Sense of Our Impact** continually to **Refine** our practice and to **Learn** collaboratively.

In Chapter 3 we discuss the role that system leaders play in creating the conditions for Collaborative Learning in schools. Chapter 4 is focused on the key leadership behaviors needed at the school level to embed Collaborative Learning. In Chapter 5 we explore powerful forms of collaboration and co-learning for teachers working with their peers. Chapter 6 highlights aspects of collaborative inquiry as a key pedagogy for student engagement and empowerment, especially when students work with teachers and each other as collaborative partners. Throughout, we include observations and reflections about practices that support **Leading Collaborative Learning** in the form of vignettes, case studies, reflections, and personal stories. We include a matrix of expected practices using the Gradual Release Approach at the end of each chapter. Finally, Michael Fullan pulls together the

> *"Educators need time to think through the concepts related to global learning and leading themselves. . . . As well, educators need to self-assess to ensure they are engaging students in rich tasks that are relevant, authentic and realistic."*
>
> Sharratt & Harild, 2015, p. 196

threads of our discussion of collaborative leadership behaviors in a thought-provoking Afterword.

The Book Study following the Afterword summarizes reflective questions for each chapter that readers can use with staff members at meetings, in learning hubs, or with participants in Networked Learning Communities.

We believe this book will help you to collaboratively create a strategy to move your learning culture forward to benefit students across the globe.

Acknowledgments

Many people contributed to our understanding of what it means to purposefully lead Collaborative Learning. We wish to thank them for their gifts of professionalism and thoughtfulness as contributors to our personal learning. This is by no means an inclusive list as we have been influenced by, and learned from, many wonderful people to whom we are most grateful.

We must begin with an appreciation to Jim Coutts for his time, quality assistance, and ongoing support as an educator, businessman, a masterful writing critic, and the editor of our drafts and redrafts. We also thank Greg Planche, who was a great sounding board and very understanding of the long hours needed to push forward to finish this project. Thanks as well to our children and grandchildren for inspiring us to contribute to their future by writing this text to highlight the importance of Collaborative Learning within system and school learning environments.

A special thank you to Jim Knight for his thoughtful Foreword, to John Hattie for his reflective Introduction, and to Michael Fullan for his affirming Afterword. Jim, John, and Michael are highly regarded, outstanding researchers, writers, thought leaders, and good friends. We are honored to have their reflections.

Thank you to the more than 500 research survey participants and to those interviewees who offered stories about their personal experiences with Collaborative Learning. Their professional perceptions deepened our understanding of the impact of Collaborative Learning and the urgent need for more focused time for collaboration within systems and schools.

To the individuals, too many to list in this acknowledgment, who contributed quotes, personal stories, vignettes, and case studies in the text (and many which do not appear but were nevertheless influential), we are sincerely grateful for your interest and your contributions.

To the teachers, vice principals, principals, superintendents, and district leaders, at home and globally, who have been our colleagues, our teachers, and advisors over the years, thank you for your dedication to student success and for all your efforts to lead learning and to be lead learners.

To our Corwin advocates and friends, thank you for the opportunity to work with you to share our experience through this book. Sincere thanks to Arnis Burvikovs, executive editor at Corwin, who believes in our work and made it possible for us to publish our thinking. Arnis gave us the confidence to live up to his high expectations. Terri Lee Paulsen provided very real assistance to this project through her attention to detail—thank you, Terri! The entire Corwin team who cared about this book must be included in this thank you: Desirée Bartlett, Melanie Birdsall, Gail Buschman, Anna Mesick, and Andrew Olson.

Thank you sincerely to Mike Greenwood, Jo Beth Jimerson, Melanie Mares Sainz, Renee Peoples, and Chad Ransom, who reviewed our book and positively endorsed it. Many other colleagues and friends endorsed our work, and we are sincerely grateful to them: Jennifer Abrams, Alan Boyle, Peter DeWitt, Gavin Dykes, Avis Glaze, Alma Harris, Bill Hogarth, Linda Massey, Joanne Robinson, Dennis Shirley, and Louise Stoll. We appreciate the contributions of so many to capture our life's work.

Publisher's Acknowledgments

Corwin gratefully acknowledges the contributions of the following reviewers:

Mike Greenwood
District Teacher Leader, Pre-K–12
Windsor Public Schools
Windsor, CT

Jo Beth Jimerson
Assistant Professor of
    Educational Leadership
Texas Christian University
Fort Worth, TX

Melanie Mares Sainz
Instructional Coach
Lowndes Middle School
Valdosta, GA

Renee Peoples
Teaching and Learning Coach
West Elementary
Bryson City, NC

Chad Ransom
Director of Second
    Language Services
Teton County School District
Jackson, WY

About the Authors

 **Lyn Sharratt** coordinates the doctoral internship program in Educational Administration for the Department of Leadership, Higher and Adult Education at the Ontario Institute for Studies in Education at the University of Toronto. Lyn is the former superintendent of Curriculum & Instruction Services in the York Region District School Board, a large Canadian school district, where she and her curriculum team analyzed assessment data and developed a comprehensive literacy improvement program that they launched with the cooperation of senior leadership, principals in over 200 schools, and 9,000 teachers. The continuously improving 14 Parameter program resulted in increased achievement for a diverse, multicultural, and multilingual population of over 115,000 students, and the district became the top-performing district in Ontario. Lyn has been a curriculum consultant and administrator, and she has also taught all elementary grades and secondary-age students in inner-city and rural settings. Lyn has analyzed and commented on public policy for a provincial trustee organization, the Ontario Public School Boards' Association, has taught pre-service education at York University, and led in-service Professional Learning in a provincial teachers' union head office. She is lead author, with Michael Fullan, of *Realization: The Change Imperative for Increasing District-Wide Reform* (2009); *Putting FACES on the Data: What Great Leaders Do!* (2012), and with author/colleague Gale Harild, *Good to Great to Innovate: Recalculating the Route to Career Readiness* (2015). Currently, Lyn is on the Advisory Board of the International System and School Leadership Programs for the Ontario Principals' Council, is an Author Consultant for Corwin and consults internationally, working with states, systems, school districts, administrators, curriculum consultants, and teachers in Australia, Canada, Chile, the United States, the United Kingdom to systematically increase

all students' achievement by putting FACES on the data and taking intentional action to move from Good to Great to Innovate. Visit her website at www.lynsharratt.com; join her on Twitter @LynSharratt, and participate with tens of thousands in her Educational Leadership Group on LinkedIn.

 **Beate Planche** is an educational practitioner, consultant, and researcher. Beate is a sessional instructor in Graduate Education for the University of Western Ontario, Canada. Through her consulting work, Beate provides research, consulting, and coaching for educators in the areas of literacy programming, Collaborative Inquiry, and inquiry-based learning for students. Beate is a former superintendent of Curriculum and Instructional Services in the York Region District School Board as well as a former superintendent supervising schools, a principal, vice principal, and a co-director of a private school. During Beate's tenure as superintendent of Curriculum and Instructional Services, the department she led served over 200 schools and 9,000 teachers through their work with area superintendents, area learning networks and their work with new teachers, and teachers seeking individual support. In her 20 years in educational administration, Beate has led in-service Professional Learning and has supported and mentored many new administrators, as well as curriculum and teacher leaders. Beate taught elementary as well as secondary students, spending a large portion of her career in special education working with students identified with learning disabilities. Beate has been an adjunct professor supporting teacher candidates for York University, has worked on contract with Ontario's Literacy and Numeracy Secretariat, and is presently on the boards of Learning Forward Ontario and the Character Community Foundation of York Region. Beate is the author of over 20 published articles and reviewed papers. Visit Beate at LinkedIn, on Twitter @bmplanche, or on her website www.beateplanche.com.

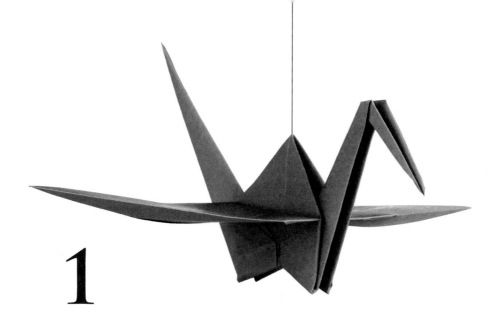

1

Leading
Collaborative Learning

"There are no miracles that happen, only hard work."

Helen Keller

Jan looked down at her students' broad range of results in mathematics and sighed. Here she was—in isolation again—planning her feedback to students and tomorrow's lesson. Even though she had 10 years' teaching experience, Jan was still very interested in learning—with and from her colleagues. A few had said they were interested in collaborative work and were open to discussing Collaborative Inquiry, but somehow the time was never available. Busy days seemed to fly by without any change in practice. Working with 30 teachers and 300 students shouldn't feel this lonely, Jan thought. And, Jan was convinced that not learning together with her colleagues wasn't good for their students. Her school's achievement results showed a very inconsistent pattern of improvement. Too many students were struggling despite remedial support. Something had to change. Could she be a catalyst for change? "How might we truly work together in ways that will deepen learning for everyone in the school?"—A question to consider and act upon.

Moving to Excellence

How educators work together in schools and what they work on together matters greatly. As highlighted in the opening vignette, no longer are traditional models where educators work in isolation from each other seen as effective ways to improve schools. Neither are the practice of placing students in sit-and-get style isolated classrooms nor having students study alone as individual learners seen to be effective ways to address the challenge of all students' learning. These models certainly provide no response to issues resulting from the rapid proliferation of technology-driven information that we face in schools every day. Nor do they produce graduates with the personal portfolio of skills employers and think-tanks across the globe see as important for today's new employees. No, educators need to develop a sense of collective agency and efficacy to make a significant difference in the way they respond to global changing needs. The work required in transforming education demands that teachers and system leaders be focused on expanded achievement in an array of students' skill levels in innovation, collaboration, curiosity, entrepreneurship, and creative problem solving (Sharratt & Harild, 2015). To accomplish this deepening of achievement outcomes, educators must become collaborative and employ **Collaborative Learning** approaches.

But what does that mean? Much has been written about Collaborative Learning using differing terms from differing contexts. Collaborative efforts and inquiry have deep roots, including work that many educators have undertaken in learning how to engage in action research (Calhoun, 2002). Inquiry is not a new concept, and several authors have discussed its important potential in the last few years (Dana, Tomas, & Boynton, 2011; Donohoo, 2013; Katz & Dack, 2013; Militello, Rallis, & Goldring, 2009; Nelson, Slavit, Perkins, & Hathorn, 2008).

Our purpose here is to simplify the discussion to enable more system leaders, principals, and teachers to understand and lead Collaborative Learning successfully. We build on previous thinking regarding effective **Collaborative Inquiry** by infusing purposeful assessment and specific action into every phase of our **Theory of Action**.

We believe a simple framework for collaboration (Figure 2.2, page 32) can help to focus educators' work together, and purposefully build strong learning relationships and positive outcomes for their students and themselves. Desired educational outcomes have shifted from the traditional model of memorizing knowledge that has been "poured in" to the new model of gaining skills and knowledge by learning how to learn and to work together. Again, the new model creates highly literate secondary school graduates, which includes the development of strong skills in critical thinking, communication, and collaboration to become interdependent, self-regulatory learners. While some call these skills **deeper learning**, we call them outcomes of quality collaborative processes. Yes, they are "deeper" concepts than learning curriculum details from a text or other stand-alone resources—but we think of them as critical skills within the toolkit for a successful graduate, teacher, or leader.

We want to state very clearly that adoption of the Collaborative Learning model for the sake of working together is, in itself, insufficient to make sustainable gains at the system or school level. There are four other vital elements to consider. First, as part of their collaboration, practitioners must themselves become very knowledgeable and comfortable with the curricular Learning Goals, expectations, and/or standards that their students need to acquire. Second, it is through engaged Collaborative Learning that educators can build a much stronger shared understanding of what

> "We need to build the awareness of all teachers and leaders about the importance of collaboration and their capacity to be collaborative. It must become second nature to all members of a school community—students, teachers, and leaders."
>
> Research survey participant

students need and how they are performing against standards and expectations. Third, collaborative efforts to better understand the impact of our instruction must begin with authentic data—ongoing evidence of what and how students are learning and are used to inform instructional starting points daily. Finally, while keeping the bar set high for students, teachers need to be purposeful in their approach to using collaboration in the classroom to enable students to own their learning as interdependent learners. For students, Collaborative Learning through inquiry approaches offers opportunities for **self-assessment**, reflection, challenge, and deep learning, which support needed skill development. For teachers and leaders, Collaborative Inquiry offers similar opportunities for learning, skill development, and improved educational practice. Our recent research allowed us to synthesize and deepen our understanding of Collaborative Learning as the vital underpinning of improving systems, schools, and classroom practice.

> We define collaboration as co-laboring to become responsible and accountable for our own work while supporting the work of other collaborators. Co-laboring fosters interdependence as we negotiate meaning and relevance together. True collaboration involves a sense of parity and reciprocity as we set clear goals, develop trust, and foster strong relationships, which drive and sustain our learning as a collective.

Guided by Research

Our research plan and details follow later in this chapter. Key findings for us, however, were the breadth of respondent experience, the consistency of their comments, and the confusion among many respondents concerning the many differing phrases in use to define **collaboration**. Further, the broad use of the term and related phrases such as Collaborative Learning and Collaborative Inquiry make the topic a vague mystery for many people. So it's easy to confuse **collegiality** for collaboration. With this confusion in mind we want to start with some definitions to set the context.

Definitions Set the Stage

The terms *collaboration, collaborative processes*, and *collaborative leadership* are used often in this text. There is no agreement in the research on a single definition for the term *collaboration*. However, it is defined in the sidebar with a specific context in mind, and that relates to work done together. Little's writing (1990) along with that from others (Pounder, 1998; Rubin, 2009; Slater, 2004) are foundational to our understanding and thinking about collaboration. Little's work highlighted that the content of collaboration among educators runs the gamut of weak to strong ties of professional engagement, dependent upon culture and relationships. This is, of course, still true. However, as school staff members experience moving from rather isolated practice to more collaborative practice with shared goals, they form stronger relationships and cultures, resulting in deeper learning for themselves and for their students. Success breeds success.

Values held within an organization's culture will have an impact too. Our values as professionals impact our understanding of collaborative work as well (Begley, 1999). Values may be debatable or taken for granted, but they are powerful because they are deeply entrenched in a school's culture. Values impact how we approach collaboration with others. School culture can be both a source of strength and inhibition as it acts as a form of normative glue (Schein, 1984).

> "Argyris (Argyris & Schön, 1974) argued that changes that are restricted to strategies and do not include the values that drive them are rarely effective. Therefore, we must include an examination of our values when making decisions. We must ask ourselves, 'What values guide my decisions?', and consider how these values differ from the ones espoused."
>
> Jenni Donohoo; personal communication, January 13, 2015

A working and learning culture is in constant interaction with both internal integration and external adaptation challenges (Schein, 1984). "Shared beliefs and understandings" is the fundamental first parameter from Realization (Sharratt & Fullan, 2009) required to create school and system reform. It is first as we must ensure that discussion about our values and beliefs about teaching and learning share the same common ground when we are moving forward together.

Defining Collaboration as Co-Laboring

We understand collaboration to be more complex than phrases like "working together." True collaboration is *purposeful*. We define collaboration as **co-laboring** as we are responsible to and accountable for our own (work of) learning while supporting the learning of other co-laborers (collaborators). Co-laboring fosters interdependence as we negotiate meaning and relevance together.

As collaboration involves a sense of parity and reciprocity as we set clear goals, develop trust, and foster strong relationships, it is critical to understand the notions of parity and reciprocity (Crow, 1998) to understand collaboration. **Parity** infers that all parties involved in the collaboration have some power—such as the ability to make decisions. If one party in a collaborative effort is in a position to coerce the other, it is difficult to achieve true collaboration. **Reciprocity** involves both leaders and followers believing they are receiving mutual benefit for their efforts. This requires leaders to be sensitive to existing power imbalances when participating in collaborative work.

> *Collaborative Learning is focused learning with a clear goal in mind. It is supported by group processes and further enabled, when needed, by facilitation. It is accountable learning—for "own" learning and that of co-learners. Collaborative Learning is grounded in trust, safety, and strong relationships.*

Collaborative Learning extends the notion of co-laboring to involve a group of learners working together to understand and improve teaching and learning challenges or dilemmas. It is situated within a social context and builds upon a framework of individual **prior knowledge** and evolving collective knowledge.

As collaborative learners, those involved benefit from the discourse and debate that evolves through integrating diverse views and perspectives. Learning is both an individual and a shared process. Collaborative Learning is an approach to learning and a way of doing things—a process (Panitz, 1997). A sense of joint-ownership through shared experience becomes part of the culture for groups able to employ recurrent and effective collaborative processes (Panitz, 1997).

Those seeking to mobilize Collaborative Learning in a school context must have a specific curricular focus and clear student Learning Goals/intentions and **Success Criteria** in their planning. In addition, educator work needs to be grounded in trust and respect for each other's capability. There are many collaborative processes that facilitate learning for individuals and groups—be they used in a class, school, or system work environment. Collaborative assessment of student work (see Chapter 5) through teacher and leader moderation is an example of a deeper form of collaboration because of the critical dialogue that results—dialogue that is a precursor to informed understanding and action. Deeper forms of collaboration develop more authentically through shared learning experiences combined with opportunities for personal and group reflection. This concept of deeper learning is precisely parallel to the notions of strong skills in critical thinking, communication, collaboration, and in becoming interdependent.

An **inquiry approach** within a Collaborative Learning process is an approach that sets the stage for deeper learning. It is rooted in the notion of inquiring about issues of teaching and learning as a process for problem solving and finding the most impactful assessment and instructional strategies for each learner. The Ontario Ministry of Education (2010, 2014b) suggests that collaborative teacher inquiry is a learning process in which shared understandings and further knowledge about student learning and effective instruction are constructed. We would add to this thinking that it is in the practicing, assessing, applying, and refining of the outcomes of Collaborative Inquiry processes that changes in student learning are best experienced and thus

> *"Moving to a more open-to-learning stance means teachers embrace a different truth: there may not always be a fixed right or wrong answer, there may not be an answer at all, and they most certainly do not know the answers to all problems posed. Taking this stance was essential to open their students to the possibility that there are many potential truths in the world. Teachers were poised and ready to take this next step with their colleagues to help students deal with complexity in a productive way, designing new and better solutions to difficult challenges and not merely repeating messaging that had been previously transmitted. The outcome has brought a sense of wonder and possibility for learning among students and teachers alike."*
>
> Audrey Hensen, MEd, Acting Principal, W. H. Ballard School, Ontario Canada; Dr. Kelly Rizzo, Principal, Guy B. Brown School, Ontario, Canada

most likely to be implemented. Building and applying new knowledge through informed **assessment-in-action** (see Chapter 2) is our particular lens on purposeful co-laboring or collaborative work.

Defining Deeper Learning

Deeper learning has become an over-used and under-defined term. Essentially the same as deeper forms of collaboration described above, its use by many authors has created a foggy view of Collaborative Learning in the classroom as it has been intertwined with notions about using ever-evolving technologies and applications in classrooms. The National Research Council (NRC) Report Brief (National Academies, 2012) *Education for Life and Work: Developing Transferable Knowledge and Skills in the 21st Century* defined deeper learning as "the process through which a person becomes capable of taking what was learned in one situation and applying it to new situations" (p. 1). Through the process of deeper learning, the report contends that students develop what are coined as 21st century competencies. These competencies include the cognitive, interpersonal, and intrapersonal domains as follow:

- **Cognitive skills** include areas such as critical thinking and analytic reasoning.
- **Interpersonal skills** include areas such as teamwork and complex communications.
- **Intrapersonal skills** include areas such as resiliency and conscientiousness.

These competencies delineate knowledge and skills that are applicable and transferable in different settings. Students today must be "taught" these skills in order to graduate as critical and creative thinkers, able to apply and transfer knowledge and be ready to work on collaborative teams. They will need to bring deeper learning through innovative thinking, creativity, and entrepreneurial dispositions to the workplace. The Ministry of Education has intentionally defined innovation, creativity, and entrepreneurship (ICE) in their revised vision for Ontario students as follows.

Innovation is defined as the generation and realization of new-to-the-world ideas that add value to people's lives. Innovation demands a positive mindset that values understanding the world from another person's perspective (Ontario Ministry of Education, 2014b).

Creativity is a process of generating ideas, making connections, and imagining what could be and demands a **growth mindset** that believes there are multiple possibilities that can be created (Ontario Ministry of Education, 2014b).

Entrepreneurship is defined as a set of activities for building and scaling an idea sustainably. The inspired mindset needed reflects the confidence to develop strategies to implement and sustain the idea; willingness to take smart risks and learn from them; belief in learning from ideas and strategies regardless of their success; and the ability to understand and consider the impact and consequences of innovations developed (Ontario Ministry of Education, 2014b).

To develop these competencies of innovation, creativity, and entrepreneurship needed for deeper learning in classrooms today requires educators to reframe how learning experiences are planned and implemented. In thinking about this, the National Academies report offers the following examples of research-based teaching for deeper learning:

- Using multiple and varied representations of concepts;
- Encouraging elaboration, questioning, and explanation;
- Engaging learners in challenging tasks;
- Teaching with examples and case studies;
- Connecting topics to the personal lives and interests of students; and
- Using assessments to continually monitor student progress with frequent feedback (National Academies, 2012, p. 3).

The un-asked question is how to engage students in deeper learning using the six elements above. Our answer is through Collaborative Learning when used as a teaching technique in a classroom culture of safety, trust, and support. The term *deeper learning* then really is the product of a quality process of those who have engaged in an inquiry approach or problem-solving experiences, versus those who have not.

Today, many authors write that deep learning aligns with notions of authentic learning and real-world connections. For years, we have read about the need for authentic learning that includes opportunities for students to express preferences for *doing* rather than *listening* (emphasis from Lombardi, 2007). When using new technologies, students build connections to create new forms of *doing*—often called **authentic learning**. Using real-world, complex, compelling problems as the fuel for student inquiry and learning, it is very possible to employ a multidisciplinary approach to program planning, and yet this kind of integration is not seen consistently implemented across all schools in a system.

Fullan and Langworthy (2013) have expressed their notions of deep learning as it specifically refers to the use of technologies. They suggest that deep learning is learning that extends beyond the mastery of existing knowledge to creating and using new knowledge, integrating digital technologies to extend the reach of learning opportunities.

Research continues on assessment of deep learning, examining the learning conditions in relation to deep learning processes and the changing role of the teacher as the designer of impactful learning experiences. As Peter Hill and Michael Barber outline compellingly, "Assessment is the lagging factor in providing quality information about learning and teaching and in reflecting the educational needs of students living in the modern world" (Hill & Barber, 2014, p. 40).

An American perspective is offered by the William & Flora Hewlett Foundation (2015), where the term *deeper learning* is used as an umbrella term for the skills and knowledge students need. It refers to six important competencies for deeper learning, including the ability to

1. master core academic content,
2. think critically and solve complex problems,
3. work collaboratively,
4. communicate effectively,
5. learn how to learn, and
6. develop academic mindsets.

These align with the powerful, evolving Literate Graduate Profile (Sharratt & Harild, 2015, pp. 131–135), which defines Literate Graduates who

- write with purpose and clarity;
- communicate effectively using a variety of text forms;
- read for purpose and pleasure;
- think critically;
- locate and access information from a variety of sources;
- use oral communication appropriate to purpose and audience;
- read and interpret multiple text forms;
- articulate a point of view;
- have innovation mindsets; and
- are creative, collaborative, and curious.

The graduate competencies listed above are seen as foundational and essential within individual disciplines and across interdisciplinary studies. We believe that *these competencies must be embedded in a cognitively demanding curriculum inquiry that requires students to seek out, research, and acquire new knowledge, apply their learning, and build on existing knowledge to create new knowledge—in collaboration with teachers, peers, and the broader community.* To us, this defines deep and deeper learning.

The emphasis we would add is that the integration of efforts to deepen learning must develop within a very important social context—*the third teacher*—or the classroom and the school learning environment (Sharratt & Harild, 2015). The first teacher is, of course, a student's parent(s), and the second teacher is the classroom practitioner. The "third teacher," the learning environment, is enhanced by teachers who are able to use a repertoire of strong teaching methodologies in open-to-learning spaces. In school and out-of-school settings, such as experiential learning programs, educators must consider a balance of individual, small group, and whole group work; shared and personal responsibilities; **personalization**; differentiation; and ongoing **Descriptive Feedback** to help students move forward. Teaching is complex work. Embedding a competency approach or specific learning expectations requires strategic planning, cooperation among educators, and collaborative leadership to serve *all* students in a school system.

> "A lot of people have gone further than they thought they could because someone else thought they could."
>
> Zig Ziglar, American author and motivational speaker

Success for all students must be our constant vision. The goal of a strong education system is to produce highly accomplished literate graduates who are able to reach their full potential and become contributing citizens ready to participate in an increasingly complex world.

So are we there yet? The short answer is no, deep learning is not everywhere, not all the time. The other critical question then is, how does a system "get there"? We must consider strategic leadership as the key to "getting there."

How We Lead Matters

Those who can lead Collaborative Learning effectively are better positioned to revitalize and transform school programming, for example, by ensuring there are multiple, clearly marked pathways to success, which will engage more students and activate deeper learning processes (Sharratt & Harild, 2015). Using learning processes that employ an inquiry approach assists learners in understanding the power of intentional integration across subject areas (Planche, 2013a).

Collaborative Learning adds social and cultural dimensions to the construction of individual meaning. Our responsibility as teachers and leaders is to ensure that opportunities for Collaborative Learning are powerful and meaningful to individuals and teams of learners—be they students or staff members. Why? Because Collaborative Learning makes a difference to increasing all students' achievement.

Leading Collaborative Learning requires leaders to pay attention to cultural, structural, and organizational issues as well as the instructional processes they employ to model expected practice. In the next chapter, we discuss five principles of collaborative leadership that leaders must cultivate to lead Collaborative Learning.

Trying to build learning capacity without needed structural changes, such as designated time for co-learners to talk, reflect, and act on changed practice, is an exercise in frustration. And changing structures without

> Leading Collaborative Learning adds the complexity of how individuals within a learning community take on the responsibility of and accountability for facilitation, resource management, mitigating challenges, and supporting the learning of others while being engaged and modeling learning themselves. We often use the phrase "learning is the work" to describe the cycle of learning, teaching, and leading. In that sense, formal or informal leaders of Collaborative Learning are co-learners and co-workers or co-laborers—hence collaborators within the cycle of learning and, as such, have powerful, positive influence. When they are open to learning themselves, leaders can produce powerful personal learning opportunities too.

specific efforts to build learners' collective capacity leads to little change at the end of the day. Building capacity doesn't just happen by itself. Leading Collaborative Learning is dependent upon the development of important systemic values and specific norms for operating, such as mutual respect, tolerance, and empathy. At its core, it is an exercise in building trust and solid learning relationships. With so much at stake in terms of developing strong cultures and structures where Collaborative Learning can thrive, we sought to better understand, through research, how collaboratively led learning builds educator capacity in order to improve achievement for all **FACES**.

Our Research

As a part of our study, we collected educator perceptions regarding the potential for and impact of Collaborative Learning. Our preparations included

- scanning and studying current research regarding collaborative practices that underpin school improvement efforts and the leadership behaviors that support the growth of collaborative cultures;

> "Collaborative leading is at the heart of building relational trust with staff and relational trust is foundational to a school that is genuinely focused on student-centered leadership."
>
> Research survey participant

- executing a research survey with questions that probed the complexities of developing and sustaining Collaborative Learning cultures. The survey had questions that offered choices for response as well as opportunities for additional open-ended anecdotal responses (see Appendix A);
- conducting interviews and informal conversations with teacher leaders and school and district leaders who promote Collaborative Learning; and
- collecting vignettes, case studies, and reflections from the field, highlighting the challenges and impact of Leading Collaborative Learning.

Our specific research questions included:

1. What are the leadership behaviors that build readiness for deeper forms of Collaborative Learning?
2. What are some tangible steps that foster a culture of co-learning about powerful practice?
3. What are collaborative processes that you feel have had an impact on student achievement? What is the evidence of impact?
4. How do educators sustain a culture of collaboration and inquiry that increases student achievement?

The use of social media and professional and personal networking tools (e.g., Twitter, LinkedIn) made it possible to consider the views of an international group of survey participants from New Zealand, Australia, Chile, European countries, the United States, and Canada. The survey was written and translated into Spanish by S. Rodriguez and S. Galdames. Impressively, more than 470 people participated in the research survey. Many participants added personal comments and anecdotes about their own experiences with Collaborative Learning endeavors. Table 1.1 shows that our participants represented individuals who were working across many levels.

TABLE 1.1

Levels Within Educational Systems Represented by Respondents

Primary Grades (K–3)	36%
Junior Grades (4–6)	37%
Intermediate Grades (7–8)	26%
High School	43%
Post-Secondary	8%

Authors' Note: The percentages total more than 100% as participants worked in more than one area within a system.

The research information from surveys and interviews gave us an overview of perceptions held by many. We were mindful of the very personal, subjective nature of perceptual data and that there were multiple realities inherent in the data; however, the fact is, experience with a process does shape perception and opinion. There was consensus among respondents about what leaders *should* be doing or what leadership actions *should* involve regarding collaboration but less evidence that *should bes* were actually embedded in educational practice.

The results were encouraging in that many participants indicated that the amount of collaboration they experienced was growing in their work settings. It was also apparent through the open-ended, anecdotal comments that many participants felt cultural, structural, and/or relationship issues limited opportunities for Collaborative Learning. Some participants offered suggestions as to how limiting factors could be improved to foster collaborative work. Improved student achievement for many of our research participants is the result of multiple collaborative and individual efforts and certainly involves sustained time and focus as important variables. Respondent comments corroborate other research. Collaboration and Collaborative Learning are certainly the answer to improvement when they are added to individual educator effort, persistence, and hard work. Improvement work is both an individual and a team responsibility (Fullan & Sharratt, 2007).

Broad Themes Emerging From the Research

Emerging from analysis of the data from the four research questions were 10 key themes that are pertinent to the discussion of Leading Collaborative Learning. These 10 themes include the following:

1. Shared beliefs and understandings can solidify purpose and sustain motivation.
2. Collaborative Learning is best understood as an evolving journey.
3. Some collaborative processes allow for deeper learning than others.

4. Practicing together using an inquiry approach can accelerate educator learning and improve outcomes for students.

5. Leadership behaviors and organizational structures impact relationships and the depth of work collaborators can do together.

6. Strong collaboration usually includes impactful leadership and facilitation.

7. Strong relationships are foundational in building a positive learning culture.

8. Creative solutions are needed to mitigate the problem of time to work together.

9. A focus on student work as data and learning helps to keep collaborative efforts on track.

10. Deeper forms of Collaborative Learning for both students and educators are built on foundations of trust and safety.

Inquiring Minds Seek to Understand

This research reinforced our previously held positions by adding the weight of many collective perceptions. First among these positions is that a lack of clearly articulated focus and alignment at all levels in a system limits learning and moving forward. Second, Collaborative Learning delivers deeper learning outcomes when we stay focused on the FACES of student data as in Parameter 1 (Sharratt & Fullan, 2009, 2012). Finally, leaders and teachers must use an inquiry approach to learning (Planche, 2012a; Sharratt & Harild, 2015) in order to address the perplexing and complex challenges of system and school improvement. We believe that Collaborative Inquiry is possible at all levels of a system as a mechanism for engaging in productive dialogue and informed decision making. There are many effective collaborative processes to consider. However, integrating an inquiry approach into any collaborative process sparks opportunities for reflection, critical thinking, and commitment to action.

Our research speaks to the necessary structures and conditions that will be "the work" outlined in this book. Our work is purposeful and as Hattie contends, it is important that we know our impact. In a school setting, Hattie (2012, p. 171) suggests

We need to collaborate to build a team working together to solve the dilemmas in learning; to collectively share and critique the nature and quantity of evidence that shows our impact on student learning; and to cooperate in planning and critiquing lessons, learning intentions and success criteria on a regular basis.

While agreeing with John Hattie, our research is very clear that critiquing and challenging understandings about teaching and learning fall far from the mark of finding optimal solutions unless a collaborative culture is developed through modeling strong leadership and skillful facilitation. The good news is that we can learn how to critique and challenge understandings effectively by doing the work together. It is clear that we must use the lowercase "L" that is "l," when we speak about leadership. Many staff members (informal leaders) in school districts, not just formal leaders, are capable of leading the learning given the right opportunity, time, and support through coaching, mentoring, and ongoing learning experiences within a culture of learning.

As the case studies examined in the Mitchell Report (Bentley & Cazaly, 2015) demonstrate, collaboration can be used in practice to achieve sustained improvement in student outcomes. Similarly, our research concludes that teachers and leaders as co-learners, who focus on the causal learning pathways, impact on increasing all students' achievement and well-being. In this text, we will explain how that looks at all leadership levels.

Collaborative Learning Cultivates Leadership

Leadership knowledge, skills, and dispositions are no longer solely the domain of those with titles or leadership positions. Leadership is as possible in the classroom as it is in the principal's office or at the board table. Leaders are culture-builders whether they hold formal or informal leadership positions. When they build positive cultures of learning, their impact on improvement is immense. Leaders are vital to the development of what Thomas Sergiovanni (2007) described as learner-centered schools. Such schools become "communities of relationships, of place, of mind, of memory, practice and action"

(Sergiovanni, 2007, p. 98). Today's schools must be learner-centered and educational leaders at all levels, with or without titles, must ensure that opportunities for Collaborative Learning are powerful and meaningful. For schools where professional learning communities (Dufour & Eaker, 1998) have been well established, the groundwork has been laid for deeper forms of collaboration such as Collaborative Inquiry.

Creating the conditions so that deeper learning is possible is vital leadership work and it is encouraging that the time for deeper Collaborative Learning is clearly now. As Linda Darling-Hammond reported in research presented at the National Center for Literacy Education (NCLE), educators in every subject area and role are eager to work together to deepen literacy learning (Strauss, 2013). In systems that move forward successfully, literacy is chosen as the driver for deep learning and as such becomes the impetus or Theory of Action. It is chosen because everyone can see themselves involved in literacy as critical work at every level. For example, in moving systems forward, literacy achievement can generate deeper learning for all simply because it becomes the clear focus that is articulated and reinforced by putting Collaborative Learning supports in place that ensure the focus can be actualized (Sharratt & Fullan, 2009).

The Power of a Positive Learning Stance

In conclusion, we must define the overall approach to Leading Collaborative Learning as modeling a **learning stance**. It is *not taking* a knowing stance. Simply, it means being willing to become a collaborator and a co-laborer as well as a co-learner. Learning is the work. This means both participating in making a decision to undertake an inquiry and enabling the collective capacity of the inquiry teams by providing positive, supportive cultures to deliberate on the impact of the inquiry findings.

We believe that a learning stance is having an openness to learning driven by a sense of curiosity and responsibility, as aptly expressed in the quote from teacher consultant Kelly Winney.

It is apparent that there is strong agreement that the three strategies—collaboration, an inquiry approach, and a learning stance—are

> "In the past few years I have seen again and again how administrators, coaches, consultants, and teacher leaders create the conditions for Collaborative Inquiry by working from a learning stance instead of a knowing stance. A leader's learning stance builds trust and responsibility. When leaders are invested in learning, their team members feel that their experiences, successes, and failures are points of learning for the whole team. They will share their insights and reflections because they trust that their insights will not be judged, but will be used to better understand the challenge of the practice at hand. This type of sharing is not merely acceptable, it is an expectation. Team members feel a sense of responsibility as co-learners to experience, to reflect and to share in the service of Collaborative Inquiry. What is the essential ingredient for leading this type of Collaborative Inquiry?—A learning stance!"
>
> Kelly Winney, EdD, Greater Essex District School Board, Ontario, Canada; personal communication, August 19, 2014

increasingly being deployed together in the most effective system and school improvement efforts. So how do we use these strategies and translate all of the *"we shoulds"* from the research into a viable Theory of Action? Chapter 2 offers a detailed view of how our Theory of Action, using assessment "for" and "as" learning, and assessment-in-action can be the right drivers for Leading Collaborative Learning.

> "Leaders who position themselves as co-learners communicate to all members of a learning community that they value learning and are willing to take risks. They acknowledge all ideas are improvable, maintain an open mind to different pedagogies that may meet the needs of all students, and welcome diversity in thinking. From this position of trust, leaders are able to create environments in which Collaborative Learning and shared leadership can occur."
>
> Audrey Hensen, MEd, Acting Principal, W. H. Ballard School, & Kelly Rizzo, PhD, Principal, Guy Brown School, Hamilton-Wentworth District School Board, Ontario, Canada

The Impact of Collaboration on Student Learning

"Most great learning happens in groups. Collaboration is the stuff of growth."

Sir Ken Robinson

Although we wholeheartedly agree with Sir Ken Robinson, in these sections throughout our book we will use hard data to draw that same conclusion and make the case for spending time during the school day to collaborate—co-labor—at every level of the system to increase all students' achievement.

With about 5,000 schools in 72 school districts, the highest population in Canada and the highest proportion of immigrant students, the Province (State) of Ontario has jumped the improvement curve. For example, in PISA 2014, Canadian 15-year-olds ranked fifth among 44 countries—beaten only by Singapore, Japan, Korea, and four regions of China (considered one country)—on the new PISA assessment of "creative problem-solving skills." In the Pan Canadian Assessment Program 2010, Ontario was the only province above the Canadian average in reading, math, and science. High school graduation rates have increased from 68% to 82%; low-performing schools are down by 75%; 95% of students are at "competence" and students in Levels 3 and 4—the Literacy/Numeracy Top 2 Bands—increased from 54% to 70% (Dr. Mary Jean Gallagher, Assistant Deputy Minister, Ontario Government; personal communication, June 2015).

These inspiring results didn't happen by good luck or by hoping for improvement. Instead, a collaboratively planned, comprehensive approach to improvement was carefully thought out, implemented, and monitored across the province. Interdisciplinary approaches, systems thinking, and Collaborative Inquiry into issues of practice are increasingly the norm in Ontario schools, strongly supported by the work of the Literacy and Numeracy Secretariat, the Student Success/Learning to 18 team, and other units in the government all aligned to the core work supported by a nonpunitive, collaborative approach. Among the enabling conditions embedded was a consistent vigilance to establishing *collaborative professionalism*, not seen anywhere across the globe in similar diverse and large

(Continued)

(Continued)

educational communities. This improvement allows us, as practitioners in Ontario and authors of this text, to summarize the impact of collaboration on student learning in the following ways:

1. Enacting authentic collaboration at every level achieves sustained improvement in student outcomes (Hargreaves & Fullan, 2013).
2. Developing a sense of collective agency and efficacy, described as co-laboring, increases students' achievement.
3. Embedding thinking critically, communicating clearly, and learning to collaborate will directly and powerfully impact on students' achievement.
4. Modeling collaboration impacts teaching practices and in turn increases student achievement.
5. Planning for collaborative inquiries enables students to own their own improvement to become interdependent stewards of everyone's learning.

A Pause for Reflection

Sharratt and Fullan (2009, 2012) created a high-impact learning progression using the Gradual Release of Responsibility Model (adapted from Vygotsky, 1978) in their 14 Parameter research. They show how to move Professional Learning in systems and schools from modeling to sharing to guiding, and finally to creating interdependent practitioners in 14 areas. It takes vision and the experience that comes from practice to know when to encourage systems, leaders, teachers, or students to fly confidently on their own and to continue to learn and to work interdependently.

Matrix Themes 1–2

Learning how to release leadership authority is the essence of Leading Collaborative Learning. In our matrix resulting from the ten key research themes, we emphasize that interdependent practice (our right-hand column in Table 1.2) ultimately *is* and also *deepens* Collaborative Learning. Sharing and building upon one's learning with other educators is an essential part of the journey, just as it is for students. In the matrix, Table 1.2, we begin with the first two themes originating in our research. We use the term *non-negotiables* to indicate the importance of each practice. The first two key themes form the foundation of the learning progression: Key Theme 1 (shared beliefs and understandings) underpins effective collaborative work, and is essential to sustaining Key Theme 2 (a powerful learning journey).

TABLE 1.2

Implementation Matrix of the First and Second of the 10 Non-Negotiables of Evidence-Proven Collaborative Learning Practices

Evidence-Proven Practice	Modeled Collaborative Learning	Shared Collaborative Learning	Guided Collaborative Learning	Interdependent Collaborative Learning	Beneficial Professional Learning for Those Who Lead Collaborative Learning
Key Theme 1	Includes	Includes	Includes	Includes	Includes
Shared beliefs and understandings solidify purpose and sustain motivation	• articulating a vision of improvement • maintaining a vision of improvement • modeling response to student data	• distributing the work and the responsibility of leading • co-constructing a vision of success • identifying improved achievement goals together	• maintaining high expectations for all • differentiating human and material resource support as needed	• reinforcing shared beliefs and understandings through co-learning • determining strategies for delivering Collaborative Learning to raise achievement for all • using research and inquiry as a vehicle to learn about deeper learning for students	• understanding the complexities of change processes • learning how to design an implementation plan • sharing leadership opportunities to deeply engage others • using student evidence of learning as a driver for co-work and co-learning

Evidence-Proven Practice	Modeled Collaborative Learning	Shared Collaborative Learning	Guided Collaborative Learning	Interdependent Collaborative Learning	Beneficial Professional Learning for Those Who Lead Collaborative Learning
Key Theme 2	Includes	Includes	Includes	Includes	Includes
Collaborative Learning is best understood as an evolving journey	• leading with purpose, passion, patience, and persistence	• rolling up sleeves and working alongside teachers and other leaders • solving teaching and learning issues together • showing a passion for learning with others	• steering others toward more support as needed • scaffolding learning to meet learners where they are	• celebrating small and large wins • hosting an annual institute or symposium (Learning Fair, for example, to have educators share learning and success as well as outline areas of growth in the coming year • learning from FAIL FAST, or how to learn from failures and recover quickly • sharing learning from classroom inquiries within and across schools during the school year	• learning how to build and sustain all learners' personal resiliency • experiencing and facilitating ongoing Collaborative Inquiry approaches • learning the lessons of personnel management and knowing how to take those who will not get "on the implementation train" off the track completely and headed toward other employment options

25

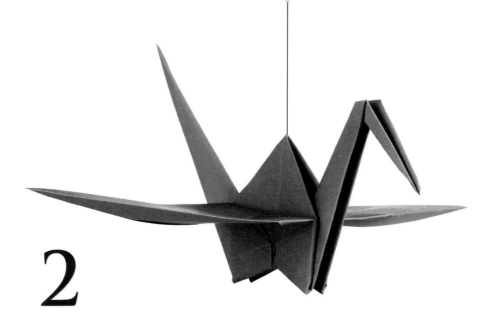

2

From Theory Into Action

"Formal leaders are important but the informal leaders and staff are critical to the process. It does no good to lead if no one follows. That's just a lonely walk to nowhere."

Research survey participant

Conditions for System Success

The day-to-day work in classrooms and schools ultimately determines success for all system stakeholders—students, staff, parents, and other community partners. The level of success possible is directly influenced by the organizational structures, cultures, and systemic processes that are put in place and modeled daily.

Conditions that senior team members create, control, and influence are the "givens" of *how* people are meant to work together. Therefore, any Theory of Action for developing Collaborative Learning is academic until, as a first step, a team moves from good intentions to working through existing systemic realities to remove corrosive elements of structure and culture. And only then will a focused action plan (or Theory of Action) begin to drive and support success across the system.

The research participants in our study corroborate the conclusion above. Many participants shared that they often felt like collaboration was being "done to them." Clearly, the notion of involvement in Collaborative Learning becomes untenable if people feel coerced into participation. System leaders must be inclusive of all stakeholders by offering them authentic voice and choice. Further, system leaders need to be aware of current individual role responsibilities that already demand a great deal of time and the new responsibilities of collective work that may be equally demanding. Collaborative work, including cultural and structural changes, must be perceived to be very valuable in order to be fully implemented and to be sustainable.

Constructivism Frames Our Approach to Inquiry

It is very relevant to examine the relationship between principles of **Constructivism** and elements of Leading Collaborative Learning. Deborah Walker (2002) outlined several important principles involved in constructivism that strongly align with our research findings in Leading Collaborative Learning. Walker (2002) suggests that knowledge and beliefs are formed within each of us

> "We need to have a deep purpose, a real desire to improve student learning . . . that is . . . have a real purpose for collaboration."
>
> Research survey participant

as learners and that our experiences influence the meaning that we attach to the learning. Social activity through shared inquiry offers rich opportunities to develop shared meaning. *Constructivist learning* involves the learner constructing personal meaning that integrates one's values, beliefs, and experiences while *constructivist leading* involves a reciprocal process among the adults in a school as they shape the culture together and work to articulate a joint vision of improvement (Walker, 2002). Clearly, there is a strong relationship between Constructivism and Leading Collaborative Learning.

Collaborative Learning Is Our Approach to Leading

The concept of learning together (about your system, school, or class) with a common purpose through an inquiry process produces authentic collaboration. Strategic planning ensures that the outcomes of collaboration are purposeful, which deepens and validates trust among collaborators. Trust takes time to build, and processes to build trust need practice to become effective. This is not an overnight process, but the investment in time to plan and practice is overwhelmingly positive.

Why Use the Collaborative Inquiry Approach?

A strong culture of powerful Collaborative Learning can be a dominant factor in increasing student achievement, staff satisfaction, and overall system success. At the system level, leaders can enhance the culture of Collaborative Learning by embracing inquiry as a way of mobilizing and monitoring ongoing improvement efforts. At the school level, leaders may consider an inquiry approach to know and ensure the success of all FACES in the school, classroom by classroom. At the classroom level, Collaborative Inquiry is a learning approach we endorse to ensure that instruction is learner-centered and allows for collaborative endeavors involving students and teachers as co-learners. Considering each FACE at the classroom level involves teachers knowing the learning strengths and needs of each learner in their charge in order to motivate, differentiate, and empower students.

We know collaboration makes a difference! Our research results align strongly with a recently reported study that surveyed over 9,000 teachers in Miami and Dade County schools in Florida, USA, where the researchers reported that over 90% of teachers agreed that collaborative work resulted in better outcomes for students (Hart, 2015). Collaborative Inquiry begins with wonderings about specific areas of improvement for students, which become focused as inquirers ask questions about teaching and learning practices while studying classroom and school data. Figure 2.1 shows how Collaborative Inquiry is applicable at every level of a school system. The system may use the approach to identify and solve problems across its breadth. A network or cluster of schools working together may identify a common learning challenge to problem-solve together through Collaborative Inquiry. A school may identify specific student learning issues from data such as daily, ongoing **assessment "for" and "as" learning**. In classrooms, teachers can facilitate student inquiries, resulting in teachers and students co-learning and students working together to innovate and create dynamic learning experiences. What is fascinating and exciting about this view is that while networks, schools, or classes within a system may have different inquiries underway, *they all begin with data*. Thus, there is a vast crossover of issues being studied for which sharing of the findings has enormous significance across the system. We call this knowledge mobilization or systems' thinking. Figure 2.1 displays our "system-ness," which aligns the work into a coherent picture of improvement at every level.

The systemic view of improvement shown in Figure 2.1 provides focus throughout a system and results in cohesion and alignment. Each inquiry brings added strength to a shared purpose so that

FIGURE 2.1

A Systemic View of Collaboration Through Inquiry

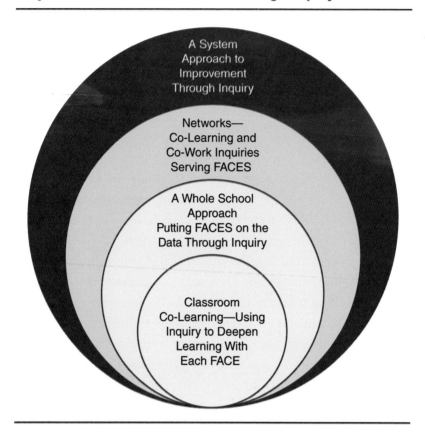

A System Approach to Improvement Through Inquiry

Networks—Co-Learning and Co-Work Inquiries Serving FACES

A Whole School Approach Putting FACES on the Data Through Inquiry

Classroom Co-Learning—Using Inquiry to Deepen Learning With Each FACE

stakeholders become integral to a learning organization with a common focus. There is evidence that a cyclical process that keeps the focus on continual knowledge building can improve outcomes (Bruce & Flynn, 2013). This becomes our Theory of Action: uncovering an iterative process to stimulate continuous knowledge creation about student and staff learning. It is the action and commitment to continuous assessment and reflection at all phases of an inquiry process that we believe moves collaborative work from good intentions to transformed practice.

Translating Our Theory of Action Into Four Practical Elements

Our Theory of Action is practical at all levels for leaders and their teams. The Theory of Action for Collaborative Learning has four elements that integrate assessment literacy at all stages of inquiry, as collaborative assessment is the driver that keeps purpose front and center at each stage. Our Theory of Action ultimately leads to informed instruction for students. The four elements are:

1. **Assessing to Plan.** Developing a clear focus for learning and inquiry through analyzing evidence of student learning.
2. **Planning to Act.** Informing system and school decisions based on evidence-proven strategies.
3. **Acting to Make Sense of Findings.** Collaborating by using ongoing assessment, and monitoring of Learning Goals to evaluate or make sense of our impact.
4. **Making Sense of Impact to Refine and Learn.** Refining the way forward by reflecting on the learning, sharing practice, and giving and getting feedback.

Note: The four segments of the inquiry process are meant to strengthen working and learning relationships, so it is important that a protocol for the norms of engagement be developed before an inquiry process actually begins (see Appendix B).

In our Theory of Action (Figure 2.2), we intentionally use action words to illustrate the dynamic quality of inquiring together. The arrows demonstrate the flow of constructing and refining individual and shared knowledge between and among the elements as meaning is negotiated together. The assessment links are purposeful in each of the four elements to reinforce the relationship between assessment and reflective planning, and action and sense making in order to learn.

FIGURE 2.2

Theory of Action for Leading Collaborative Learning

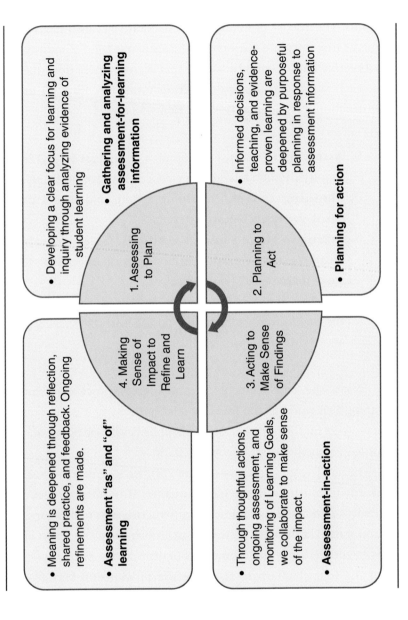

- Developing a clear focus for learning and inquiry through analyzing evidence of student learning
- **Gathering and analyzing assessment-for-learning information**

1. Assessing to Plan

- Informed decisions, teaching, and evidence-proven learning are deepened by purposeful planning in response to assessment information
- **Planning for action**

2. Planning to Act

- Meaning is deepened through reflection, shared practice, and feedback. Ongoing refinements are made.
- **Assessment "as" and "of" learning**

4. Making Sense of Impact to Refine and Learn

- Through thoughtful actions, ongoing assessment, and monitoring of Learning Goals, we collaborate to make sense of the impact.
- **Assessment-in-action**

3. Acting to Make Sense of Findings

The four elements above, while cyclical, can be considered in a reciprocal and iterative way as well. What is constant and central is the role of *assessment as the driving force* for this Collaborative Learning model. We follow with a detailed discussion of each element.

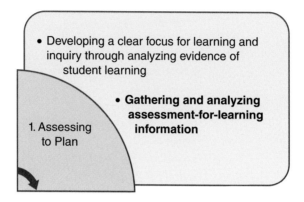

Element 1: Assessing to Plan

Inquiry at every level, be it system, school, or classroom, must begin with **assessment**. We use the word *assessment* to mean considered and informed decisions, using data about learning, and using an inquiry framework so assessment has a "for" and "as" learning meaning. The assessment context involves a process of co-learning, which helps educators understand where they are, how they are doing, and where they are going. The process begins with gathering the right data for planning purposes. To assess productively, we begin the learning process with direction-setting questions, such as:

- What do the data sources say? What area is of concern? Why is this area worthy of our collaborative work? How many FACES will it support compared to another area of work?
- Do we have the right information in front of us to make an informed assessment?

Table 2.1 offers concrete steps and further questions that guide the Assessing to Plan stage for Leading Collaborative Learning.

TABLE 2.1

A Guide for Element 1: Assessing to Plan

Assessing to Plan	Questions for the Assessment Phase
1. Have the right information	• What do we note or question as we analyze the data? • What trends do we see? • How are the data pieces related to class and student profiles and student learning? • How are the data pieces related to issues of assessment and instruction? • How are the data pieces related to issues of learning skills? • Are we looking at a learning process issue or an issue of pedagogy or both? • Is this a trend we see across classrooms and/or schools? • What further information do we think we need, and how can we access it?
2. Check assumptions regarding interpretation	• What assumptions were made about the data? • Do we need to gather further information before planning begins? • Do we have a balance of qualitative and quantitative data? • Are we confident that our interpretation is valid and reliable? • What limitations about the data do we have to keep in mind?
3. Articulate learning concerns as questions	• How will the assessment information in front of us help define a clear question of learning?
4. Refine to have one question for learning at a time	• Do we have a compelling question or do we need to reframe it, perhaps break it down to several questions and choose one from those?
5. Create a S.M.A.R.T. goal regarding our question of inquiry (Specific, Measurable, Ambitious, Relevant, Time-bound)	• Focusing on our data, what Success Criteria will we co-construct to tell us if we have been successful? • What will short- and long-term success look like?

Assessing to Plan	Questions for the Assessment Phase
6. Determine what format will be used for Collaborative Learning (e.g., using a teaching-learning cycle, a 4 Cs experience, moderating student work, coaching, a Case Management Approach, Learning Walks and Talks, or establishing a "Learning Collaborative" of system and school leaders)	• Who needs to be involved in the co-planning process? • How can the goals be shared widely and commitment be galvanized?

Element 1, the assessing-to-plan process, and each succeeding element needs to be recorded to ensure faithfulness to and reflection on the journey, and to guard against what otherwise would make detours inevitable. That is, teams need to focus their work on each phase, align their resources, and continuously give and get feedback on their progress. This first phase of Collaborative Learning in the Theory of Action is crucial to ensuring that each system team, group of principals, school leadership team, divisional team in a school, or grade partners are *satisfied that they are going to engage in valuable work*. Ultimately, the precious time spent together as collaborators needs to make a difference to increasing all students' achievement. Facilitating the assessment phase includes asking probing questions that may

"Assessing to Plan" Actions

- Assessing system, school, and class data as learning evidence;
- Checking assumptions about interpretations;
- Articulating concerns from the data as questions;
- Refining concerns to one question of inquiry;
- Developing a S.M.A.R.T. goal aligned to the question and co-constructing Success Criteria; and
- Determining a Collaborative Inquiry process to use.

> *"I like the distinction between information and knowledge in our information age. We are surrounded by information and we can access vast amounts of data very easily through the internet. Knowledge is something else. We continuously create and adapt our own knowledge through some kind of interaction with information. It is particularly effective when that interaction is social and face-to-face but it can also be online, or in our own heads through our thought processes."*
>
> Alan Boyle, Director of Leannta;
> personal communication, September 16, 2014

challenge some participants. Agreeing to disagree respectfully is an important norm to embed. However, teams must probe beliefs and understandings to truly know each other and not "think they understand each other" to move beyond the status quo.

At the end of the assessing-to-plan element, each team needs to have developed a clear and focused question for learning that ultimately impacts student achievement while building and mobilizing practitioner knowledge. That means paring down information to some crucial and manageable key pieces. If they are looking at system data, they should be looking for trends and patterns over time to craft relevant Professional Learning (PL) needed for staff. If they are looking at classroom data, the questions must relate to the learning profiles of individual students to put FACES on the data and differentiate instruction. If they are looking at grade data, the questions relate to the trends seen across groups of students or schools at the district level to determine and differentiate additional supports and resources needed. Table 2.2 highlights possible data sources that support the assessment phase. There are many other sources to add and consider.

In facilitating the assessing-to-plan element and knowing when to move to the next element, system or school leaders must ask: Do we have a clear and reasonable question for Collaborative Learning and

TABLE 2.2

System and School Data Sources to Use in Element 1: Assessing to Plan

System Data That Provide Strategic Direction-Setting	Classroom, School, and Student Data to Inform Instruction and Interventions
Information from Data Walls that documents growth *and* achievement for the system over several years and documents progress of student cohorts	Individual student profiles and class profiles
Assessment results for all schools over several years	Moderated samples of student work
Summaries of year-end report card data for all schools	Class achievement summaries
Summaries from all schools of early intervention data such as Observation Survey data (Clay, 2013), Running Records, Reading Recovery® data, PM Benchmarks, DRA (Diagnostic Reading Assessment)	Early intervention data such as early screening data, Observation Survey, Running Records, Reading Recovery® data, PM Benchmarks
Perception data, interviews, and focus groups from public sector groups, community partners	Perception data: surveys, observations, and feedback Digital pictures and anecdotal records
Demographic information	Individual educational plans
Data Walls in all of the above areas begin every system conversation and Learning Walks and Talks (see Chapter 3)	Data Walls co-constructed at every level showing student growth needs *and* achievement

inquiry? Leaders need to be able to recall and enact *Guiding Leadership Principle 1: We can't inquire about everything at once and while assessment is important, it is equally important to keep our data and Learning Goal in mind.*

Element 2: Planning to Act

Assessment for planning purposes now moves into Element 2: Planning to Act.

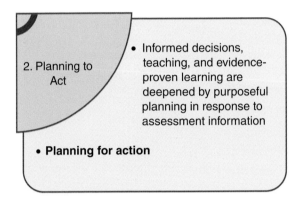

The amount of time, energy, and thought that goes into system and school planning can be enormous and frustrating if discussion is not focused on and aligned with the data sources that reveal system and school needs, and if analysis does not reveal the FACES in the data (Sharratt & Fullan, 2012). It is a different experience when a focusing question has been determined and the facilitator holds participants to a conversation about that area of need. For example, collaborators who have determined a question of focus by looking at student work samples together (discussed in Chapter 5) are better able to plan for instruction with clear purpose. The outcome of planning should involve key actions that can be implemented and monitored.

Less is more in most cases. What is the learning question—at the system, school, or classroom level? How can a S.M.A.R.T goal be reworked into an inquiry question and a process be researched that leads to reasoned action? In trying to answer the learning question, what decisions will be recorded to implement key actions? *Guiding Leadership Principle 2: The process of Collaborative Learning through inquiry can be modified, reduced, or added to at any point as the actions unfold through collaborative decision making.* This sounds easy, but it is not easy work! To narrow down many possibilities to a few measurable actions, teams need to co-construct Success Criteria. What will success look like, feel like, and sound like? Teams will want to ensure their inquiry and resulting learning will be of value to the system, staff, and students. Planning needs to be specific and to indicate a clear path for addressing the question at hand. Specific steps and questions for planning to act are found in Table 2.3 on the next page.

A thoughtful Collaborative Learning experience involves planning wisely to ensure action will result. The planning-to-act phase must be carefully

"Planning to Act" Actions

- Determining collaborative actions to address a question of inquiry;
- Using the S.M.A.R.T. goal to plan actions—Specific, Measurable, Ambitious, Relevant, and Time-bound;
- Ensuring that planning actions respond to the Theory of Action and are based on research (e.g., "*If* we respond to this issue of student learning in this way . . . *then* we expect the result to be . . . ");
- Determining resources required to support the work;
- Articulating and aligning the Success Criteria—that is, the evidence of impact that improves student learning; and
- Planning the steps to implement and monitor.

considered and also needs to be time-bound. It is important to begin putting words into action; it is in the Acting to Make Sense of Findings phase—Element 3—where collaborative planning is tested.

Element 3: Acting to Make Sense of Findings

Acting to make sense includes the importance of having critical reflection as assessment-in-action during the implementation processes. It is not only the *doing* that is important but it is also vital that leaders embrace *Guiding Leadership Principle 3: Build in time to reflect together using a facilitated process.* Learning begins to take root in moving from an academic exercise to putting learning into action. Reflection is built into both the *acting to make sense* stage as well as *the making sense of findings* stage conversations to refine our actions in Element 4. Acting to make sense of findings involves assessment-in-action.

TABLE 2.3

A Guide for Element 2: Planning to Act

Steps in Planning to Act: Keeping Purpose in Mind	Questions to Consider in Leading Collaborative Learning Through a Planning Phase
1. Establish a S.M.A.R.T. goal and subsequent Theory of Action (i.e., if we do "x," then we expect "y" to happen).	• Is the goal **S**pecific, **M**easurable, **A**mbitious, **R**elevant, and **T**ime-bound? • What about the goal makes it seem ambitious to us?
2. Express the S.M.A.R.T. goal as an inquiry question including a goal and a process to determine the goal (e.g., "If we intentionally engage our students in meaningful daily writing with specific Descriptive Feedback, then we will see improvement in writing achievement by 100% of students in Grade 3 by the end of term one.").	• What evidenced-proven research influences our Theory of Action? • Have all involved in the collaboration had a chance to review the research evidence? • Have we reached consensus on the inquiry question?
3. Articulate the beginning point of action.	• What steps do we envision to this "beginning" action? • Who will take ownership of and champion the progress?
4. Determine the resources needed.	• What are the Success Criteria to assess resources needed? • What information will we gather to determine differentiated resource needs? • Who will be responsible for ensuring they are in place?
5. Set timelines for our first few steps.	• Will our steps involve being in classrooms and schools, and how will we organize this time? • What resource will be dedicated to this, and how will that be funded? What will not be funded?

Steps in Planning to Act: Keeping Purpose in Mind	Questions to Consider in Leading Collaborative Learning Through a Planning Phase
6. Articulate and align the Success Criteria with the high-impact actions to be taken.	• What are the "look-fors" regarding each of the Success Criteria? • How can they be expressed in observable, measurable terms?
7. Take responsibility for writing up the plan and sharing it with each member of the inquiry group.	• Who is acting as the note taker? • Who is acting as the synthesizer? • Who is facilitating our discussions to make decisions? • Who is acting as communicator? How are we going to share our work?
8. Follow up on the implementation and monitoring actions planned.	• Who will be responsible for implementation? • Who will be involved in monitoring? • How will information be shared? • How will the learning be celebrated?

As teams act, they must seek to make sense. Table 2.4 demonstrates the steps in the Collaborative Learning process at the Acting to Make Sense stage and suggests sample questions a leader would ask to enhance knowledge building with a group of collaborative learners.

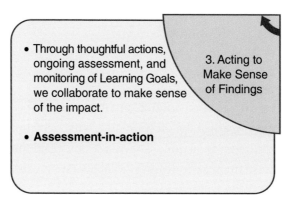

• Through thoughtful actions, ongoing assessment, and monitoring of Learning Goals, we collaborate to make sense of the impact.

• **Assessment-in-action**

3. Acting to Make Sense of Findings

TABLE 2.4

A Guide for Element 3: Acting to Make Sense of Findings

Steps in Acting to Make Sense	Questions to Consider in Leading Collaborative Learning Through Defined Actions
1. Co-learners as collaborators monitor their actions regarding their S.M.A.R.T. goal and check in with each other formally and informally to share their learning.	• What are those we are impacting with our actions saying and doing? • How will feedback be gathered? • How often will we check in to see if our actions impact the learning? • How will we make sense of our work as co-learners? • What are the Success Criteria for knowing we have made sense? • What do we commit to documenting and reporting back?
2. Co-learners as collaborators are keen observers.	• What are key, relevant observations about the learning experience? • What stands out? • What do we need to analyze for further learning and reflection? • What can we do differently?
3. Co-learners as collaborators adjust their plans as needed.	• Have we planned enough time for implementation? • Are there some things we can tweak or shift right away?
4. Co-learners reflect and assess their actions together.	• How do our observations align with our assumptions? • What surprises us? • What is reinforced for us? • What assumptions are changed? • How will we capture our learning?

Acting to make sense of findings involves data that causes reflective action accompanied by Accountable Talk, which is our definition of assessment-in-action. The questions team members ask themselves cause them as co-learners to deliberately pause and make mid-course corrections, if necessary. In this phase, teams listen to feedback because they can often refine the acting-to-make-sense element to become more precise about the work as they move through it. As *Guiding Leadership Principle 4 highlights: It is not a question of being right or wrong but one of being open to learning.* It is critical that as part of an inquiry process, making sense together must be non-judgmental, non-accusatory, and non-evaluative. Engaging in inquiry with others is a learning process. Engaging with others as co-learners must be a highly respectful, intentional process.

"Acting to Make Sense" Involves Collaborators as Co-Learners

- Acting with responsibility and accountability—supporting "my own" learning and the learning of others;
- Acting to observe, give and get Descriptive Feedback as the process of improving practice;
- Acting alongside to monitor S.M.A.R.T. goals;
- Acting and reflecting—attending to reflections and experiences to make sense and develop collective capacity; and
- Acting to orchestrate Accountable Talk is part of collaborative assessment-in-action.

Element 3 in our Theory of Action is interchangeable in an iterative way with Element 4. Making Sense of Impact to Refine and Learn reminds us to keep in mind the purpose of continual, collective capacity building.

- Meaning is deepened through reflection, shared practice, and feedback. Ongoing refinements are made.

- **Assessment "as" and "of" learning**

4. Making Sense of Impact to Refine and Learn

"Making Sense of Impact to Refine and Learn": Collaborators as Co-Learners

- Making time for reflection and discussion;
- Sharing observations and unpacking assumptions together;
- Co-assessing progress, impact, and areas of challenge;
- Naming the learning;
- Determining next steps; and
- Continuing to refine, practice, and to build understanding and ongoing learning.

Element 4: Making Sense of Impact to Refine and Learn

Making sense of impact of the work being done together is an ongoing Learning Goal for co-learners, and it is made more powerful when experienced collaboratively. We use the words *refine* and *learn* intentionally because it is about improving practice. If the process has been followed rigorously, the work will seldom be completely off-base. Seeking improvement is a constant goal; it is the cyclical and iterative nature of collaborative work that moves teams forward. Too many times, we have seen system or school implementation planning teams (or leaders who may not be as collaborative as they believe they are) speed through to decisions about actions without thoughtful mechanisms for collaborative assessment, analysis, and refinement. Without intentional refinement and reflection, great ideas lose their luster and are replaced by new ideas. This results in a system losing the focused priority before the original goal has been implemented or solidified. Often school systems have moved from one initiative to another while pieces of the work have simply faded away. Sometimes, the course of action required is simply to slow down and take time for reflection, refinement, and possibly finding further evidence for "the initiative" to become an approach that is more intentional, embedded, and thus sustained. Constantly changing priorities, often called "initiatives," erode the power of collaborative processes to sustain and empower improvement teams.

Thus, a well-conducted Collaborative Inquiry process sets the stage for embedded Collaborative Learning. One inquiry leads naturally to another, uncovering new layers of complexity in the search for system and school improvement on behalf of all students. Collaborative

Learning through inquiry does not end but rather completes phases of inquiring. Informal and formal leaders facilitating inquiry processes are bridge builders in effect—building important connections between what is already known and what is becoming clearer. In Table 2.5 on the next page, we offer questions to consider when working to make sense of the findings and learn.

Working through this element, Making Sense of Impact to Refine and Learn, contributes real value for those who experience the learning process together. Meaning becomes collectively co-constructed through assessment, dialogue, planning, implementation, debriefing, and reflecting. System leaders need to ensure that all staff have the opportunity to experience Collaborative Inquiry processes. Although leaders can share information as a result of Professional Learning, they deepen learning by offering all colleagues a chance to actively co-learn and by planning for the mobilization of the new knowledge created.

The skills of productive and enriching collaboration are learned in practicing rather than through theorizing. This leads us to *Guiding Leadership Principle 5: Include all staff systematically in the work of inquiry.* Formal leaders, especially system leaders, must schedule time and opportunity for staff learning teams to collaborate in inquiry processes.

The list below summarizes the five guiding principles for leaders at every level that underpin efforts to Lead Collaborative Learning using an inquiry approach.

Five Guiding Principles for Leading Collaborative Learning

1. We can't inquire about everything at once.
2. A Collaborative Inquiry process can be modified, reduced, or added to, at any point as the actions unfold through collaborative decision making.
3. Build in time to reflect together using a facilitated process.
4. It is not a question of being right or wrong but of being open to learning.
5. Include all staff systematically in the work of inquiry.

TABLE 2.5

A Guide for Element 4:
Making Sense of Impact to Refine and Learn

Steps in Making Sense of Impact to Refine and Learn	Questions to Consider in Leading This Process
1. Time for reflection and dialogue	• When will time be found for the inquiry? • Who will facilitate the conversation? • How do we capture the valuable reflections discussed?
2. Share observations	• What did we see and hear in student/staff work and thinking?
3. Unpack assumptions	• How does our evidence of learning align with our assumptions for learning? • What was noteworthy? • What was surprising? • What was concerning?
4. Assess progress	• What has gone well? • What factors led to success?
5. Assess areas of challenge	• What was more difficult to implement? • What Success Criteria were difficult to achieve? • What were the factors that made it challenging? • How and why were our assumptions different from our findings?
6. Name the learning shift or positive change in thinking about practice	• What have we learned? • How might we apply what we have learned quickly? In the longer term?
7. Determine next steps	• What will we do differently next time? • What do we need to refine and practice again? • Who needs to know about our learning?

Steps in Making Sense of Impact to Refine and Learn	Questions to Consider in Leading This Process
7. Determine next steps (continued)	• How will we share it across the system? • How will we celebrate our smaller and larger wins? • Who else can we involve in taking these findings forward while we take a new inquiry forward?
8. Continue to practice to learn and refine	• What do we commit to continuing to practice? • When will we reflect on our practice to ensure changed practices are increasing students' achievement? • What data will guide our continuing inquiry?

A Theory of Action and Guiding Principles to strategic leadership are seldom useful unless they translate into practical work that impacts student learning.

The Impact of Collaboration on Student Learning

Stoll, Bolam, McMahon, Wallace, and Thomas (2006) write, "International evidence suggests that educational reform's progress depends on teachers' individual and collective capacity and its link with school-wide capacity for promoting pupils' learning. Building capacity is therefore critical. Capacity is a complex blend of motivation, skill, positive learning, organisational conditions and culture, and infrastructure of support. Put together, it gives individuals, groups, whole school communities and school systems the power to get involved in and sustain learning over time."

Similar beliefs about the power of teacher and leader capacity building have been foundational in the York Region District School Board (YRDSB). With school board leaders, we worked

(Continued)

(Continued)

on establishing a community focused on learning across the 200 schools in York Region from 2002 to 2012 as superintendents of curriculum and instruction. This was a collaborative effort within the whole system. As well, the district established partnerships with researchers from the Ontario Institute for Studies in Education (OISE), with leadership and change expert Dr. Michael Fullan, and with school teams from across neighboring school districts. Our belief was, and still is, that the focus on learning together in teams, with a common purpose, increases all teachers' capacity for quality assessment and instruction. When leaders and teachers learn alongside one another like this, students benefit.

This sustained emphasis on supportive collaboration in the YRDSB has steadily improved literacy results in EQAO. Student achievement in Ontario is assessed through standards-based assessments for all children in Grades 3, 6, and 9 conducted by an independent agency, the Education and Quality Accountability Office (EQAO). For example, over 10 years from 2003 to 2014, the number of Grade 3 students in expected levels 3 and 4 (the top 2 bands) has increased in Reading 14%, and in Writing 18%. Similarly, the number of students in expected levels 3 and 4 (the top 2 bands) in Grade 6 Reading has increased 19% and in Writing 22%. Likewise, results of the Ontario Secondary School Literacy Test (OSSLT), a diploma-bearing assessment, indicate that since its inception in 2002, the number of students passing has increased 19%, from 71% to an outstanding 90% in YRDSB. The work of teachers and leaders in this district has been both intentional and collaborative; it points to the importance of creating system- and school-wide cultures of Collaborative Learning that positively impact students' learning. We know that impact is tangible; for example:

1. If collaboration is seen as purposeful, relevant, and a valuable use of time, then practice is transformed and students learn.
2. An investment in time to collaborate connects the causal pathways for teachers that increase students' achievement.
3. Collaborative work results in better learning outcomes for students (Hart, 2015; Ronfeldt et al., 2015).
4. Questioning issues of practice, as co-learners, cause teachers' to reflect on changing practice and result in increased student achievement (Sharratt, 1996).

A Pause for Reflection

The work of Leading Collaborative Learning by using an inquiry approach requires a growth mindset (learning stance) and an openness to working together. Collaborative approaches that integrate questions for improvement offer opportunities for deep analysis of current evidence, application of collective planning and action, and reflection on the findings. The goal is learning and improving system, school, and student achievement; it is not to have a perfect process. Informal and formal leaders benefit from support in the development of impactful questions and in understanding how to move groups from one stage of an inquiry to another and when to go back a step as the process is iterative. Leading Collaborative Learning requires insightful leadership, facilitation skills, perseverance, and resilience.

Matrix Themes 3–4

In Table 2.6, we continue to build the implementation list of non-negotiable Collaborative Learning practices. Themes 3 and 4 show how our thinking in this chapter fits into the Gradual Release of Responsibility Model.

Looking Ahead

In Chapter 3, we discuss how the four elements of our Theory of Action align with the work that system leaders do collaboratively with school leaders to co-construct shared meaning, thereby embedding Collaborative Learning as an expectation at every level.

TABLE 2.6

**Implementation Matrix of the Third and Fourth of the
10 Non-Negotiables of Evidence-Proven Collaborative Learning Practices**

Evidence-Proven Practice	Modeled Collaborative Learning	Shared Collaborative Learning	Guided Collaborative Learning	Interdependent Collaborative Learning	Beneficial Professional Learning for Those Who Lead Collaborative Learning
Key Theme 3	Includes	Includes	Includes	Includes	Includes
Some collaborative processes allow for deeper learning than others	• utilizing a growth mindset or co-learning stance • actively participating as a co-learner • integrating an inquiry approach to learning	• distributing leadership and learning opportunities among others	• ensuring collaborative processes include clear Learning Goals and co-constructed Success Criteria	• using high-impact learning strategies that meet the needs of all students	• co-learning strategies such as co-teaching, moderating, and assessing student work • embedding co-learning into classroom practice • establishing a growth mindset

Evidence-Proven Practice	Modeled Collaborative Learning	Shared Collaborative Learning	Guided Collaborative Learning	Interdependent Collaborative Learning	Beneficial Professional Learning for Those Who Lead Collaborative Learning
Key Theme 4	**Includes**	**Includes**	**Includes**	**Includes**	**Includes**
Practicing together using an inquiry stance can accelerate educator learning and improve outcomes for students	• embedding inquiry as a Collaborative Learning approach • posing thoughtful questions to begin learning dialogues • determining S.M.A.R.T. goals that are Specific, Measurable, Ambitious, Relevant, and Time-bound • demonstrating how to determine priorities	• having strong listening skills to hear others • paraphrasing and summarizing key points made in discussions • encouraging other opinions, questions, and reflections	• refocusing the discussion of key learning questions • helping others reach decisions about actions to be taken by building consensus	• garnering the commitment of collaborators to specific actions • determining a timeline for practice • encouraging the use of technology to assist with clear, ongoing, and collaborative communication approaches	• learning through collaborative experiences such as action research, inquiry, and moderating student work • using new technologies to accelerate learning and improve communications • learning how to use data analysis for inquiry and planning purposes

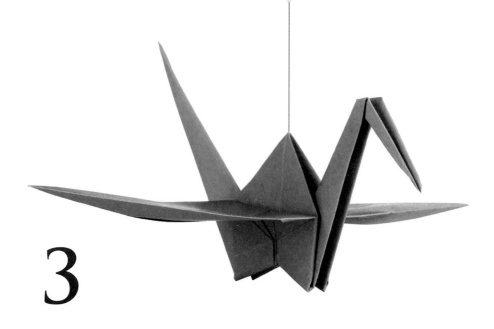

3

System Leaders Working Alongside School Leaders

"Leaders become great, not because of their power, but because of their ability to empower others."

John C. Maxwell

The Importance of System Leadership

J. K. looked over the latest results for the schools that she super-vised. Finding a solution to low student achievement was her big challenge as a superintendent new to her region. All the questions she asked in one-on-one follow-up conversations with each princi-pal appeared to have made no difference to student achievement. Her schools were stuck. Even with the best of intentions, her "open to learning" conversations were leading to little change. If it was frustrating for her, "how must the principals feel?" she asked herself. She took her supervisory position seriously, and finally realized this was not a supervision issue but was a leadership problem she needed to resolve.

As she thought it through she noted that her schools worked in isolation and exhibited cultures of limited and uncoordinated effort, resulting in minimal improvement. It was "show and tell" when she visited. Things sounded good but the data said something much different. There was no evidence of learning clearly evident in classrooms nor was it a focus during her school meetings. With a moment of insight, J. K. admitted to herself that the change must begin with her. She committed to putting the need to be "the superintendent" aside and learning how to become a co-learner, co-laborer, and collaborator with those whose leadership she wanted to develop. At her next administrator's meeting, J. K. immediately changed her approach by modeling being a lead-learner and inviting the principals and assistant principals to begin to inquire with her about potential solutions as a first step to creating improvement in their schools.

This vignette speaks to the changing role of system leadership. System leaders continue to have responsibilities as supervisors, stewards, and managers of human and program resources in education. However, their most pressing role as leaders is to become involved in creating strong learning cultures focused on observable, high-impact assessment and instructional practices in every classroom. They must lead by modeling their own passion for teaching and learning, their commitment to co-learning, and their impact on supporting the learning of others.

> "Without strong motivated leadership the idea of moving Collaborative Learning forward will not happen."
>
> Research survey participant

As we consider our research data about the leadership needed for *Leading Collaborative Learning: empowering excellent learning environments*, our understanding is built upon the leadership attributes discussed in *Realization* (Sharratt & Fullan, 2009), *Putting FACES on the Data*

(Sharratt & Fullan, 2012), and *Good to Great to Innovate* (Sharratt & Harild, 2015). Those system and school leadership attributes include

- being knowledgeable about teaching and learning (Knowledge-ability),
- being able to mobilize and focus others (Mobilize-ability),
- being able to sustain efforts to improve by developing many other leaders (Sustain-ability), and
- being open to imagining new ideas and innovation (Imagine-ability).

Together these are vital leadership dimensions to improving education systems and schools. From our new research we find a strong collaborative leader is able to grasp and exhibit all four leadership dimensions as a learner and a culture builder. And, this leader empowers others to co-learn and co-labor to do the challenging work of "closing the gap to raise the bar" in order to improve student outcomes. This fifth and newest dimension, Collabor-ability, is discussed further on page 57.

While today's improvement processes are well-served by both informal and formal leaders, system leaders, such as education directors, supervisory officers like J. K., directors of teaching and learning, coordinators, and consultants, are in critical positions to champion the work of schools and school leaders while strategically modeling the role of lead learners. As our colleague Dr. John Malloy writes thoughtfully:

Educators improve student learning by engaging in their own learning. Educators bring their expertise and experience to the table and together with their colleagues focus on using effective instructional strategies for each student. The power of this Collaborative Learning is that together, educators meet the needs of each student. Together, educators ask critical questions, gather evidence about student learning, try different strategies, observe results and reflect on impact. This learning process leads to effective instructional practices which in turn lead to more students achieving. This learning community of educators does not simply speak theoretically about teaching and learning; rather these educators learn deeply by focusing on how individual students are actually learning.

Collaborative Learning insists that all educators are leaders in this process. Having said this, those who have positions of leadership, such as principals, play a very important role to create the conditions necessary for inquiry to lead to changed practice. When conditions exist for teachers and administrators to co-learn with each other, always focused on instruction and student learning, improvement will happen. (John Malloy, EdD, Assistant Deputy Minister, Leadership and Learning Environment Division, Ontario Ministry of Education, Canada; personal communication, May 11, 2015)

As Hattie (2015b) suggests, for collaboration to make a difference it must focus on evidence of student learning and on understanding what impact the teaching had or did not have. Ultimately, we need to understand how to best change classroom practice so that all students can achieve expected levels of growth each school year.

Let us repeat: Dr. Malloy signals that specific conditions must be evident to all participants in order to lead Collaborative Learning, and that is the first "environmental situation" J. K., as system superintendent, should address.

Building Readiness for Collaborative Learning

Our research inquired about the perceptions of leader behaviors that build *readiness* for deeper forms of Collaborative Learning. There was significant agreement on the following leadership behaviors, which while they can certainly be ascribed to formal and informal leaders, in Table 3.1 they are presented as important system and school leader behaviors. While the list is not inclusive of all factors, it is important to note that those included are strategic and vital.

TABLE 3.1

Leadership Behaviors That Build Readiness for Collaborative Learning

Leadership Behaviors That Build Readiness for Collaborative Learning	% of Survey Participants Who Agreed or Very Much Agreed
Building strong relationships	99%
Articulating why collaboration is important—particularly by formal leaders	98%
Modeling a positive growth mindset	98%
Maintaining student learning as the driver for collaboration	97%
Ensuring that participation in collaborative endeavors is inclusive	97%
Partnering with staff to establish clear Learning Goals for collaboration	96%

TABLE 3.2

Steps to Building a Culture of Co-Learning

Specific Steps That Build a Culture of Co-Learning	% of Survey Participants Who Agree or Very Much Agree
Leaders find ways to support staff efforts to co-learn and collaborate	98%
Formal and informal leaders have skills in facilitative processes	97%
Formal and informal leaders are skilled in mediating conflict	97%
Leaders model being co-learners	97%
Those interested in facilitating collaborative processes are mentored or coached by leaders	93%
Leaders offer feedback to staff on efforts to establish co-learning	92%

In the research survey and follow up interviews, participants were asked to consider specific and concrete steps that leaders take to foster *a culture of co-learning* about powerful practice. Again, there was strong consensus regarding perceptions as seen in Table 3.2.

A Vision of "Should-Bes"

Many research participants added anecdotal comments about the leadership actions that they felt *should be* a part of building and fostering a Collaborative Learning culture. Samples of these comments are found in Table 3.3 on the next page.

Many research participants added that while they could articulate their vision of the ideal Collaborative Learning culture, in practice collaboration was more likely to happen in pockets of their working environment, rather than being widespread and embedded. In interviews, we probed these perceptions further and not surprisingly conclude that in cultures where time is not made for reflective conversations, deeper forms of collaboration are difficult to sustain.

Leadership decisions about the use of time make a difference. There is no more time in the school day, so it is critical that leaders reconstruct the time they have to make time available for teachers, leaders, and themselves to focus on creating rich Collaborative Learning experiences.

Anecdotal comments made by our survey and interview participants about building readiness for deeper forms of collaboration included key insights into the knowledge, skills, and dispositions leaders *should* demonstrate through their actions. As well, there were repeated comments that emphasized the importance of safety and trust versus judgment and evaluation in collaborative work.

Impactful Leadership Behaviors: Collabor-ability

The following overview, on page 59, of recurrent leadership behaviors that appear to deepen learning experiences comes from the research and our experience. The verbs that describe the behaviors are italicized for emphasis.

TABLE 3.3

Participant Views on How to Build a Collaborative Learning Culture

Understanding the Issues of Safety

"A culture of safety and risk-taking has been developed."

"Mutual trust and respect are evident."

"Individual contributions are valued and encouraged."

"Staff are consulted as to what would assist them with collaborative work."

"Leaders must be the motivating force to aid resistant teachers to incorporate Collaborative Learning in the classroom."

Understanding the Importance of Focus

"We need to ensure collaborative work has a clear focus and purpose."

"We should have goals and a long-term plan."

"We need goal setting with a deep understanding of Success Criteria."

Understanding Co-Learning and Empowerment

"Demonstrate and model co-learning."

"Learn the work by doing the work."

"You have to be at the table with your teams to make a difference, to ask the tough questions, and to share the work of learning."

"Give and share constructive feedback."

"Demonstrate the ability to influence others."

"Collaborators are involved in the decision-making about the work to be done."

"Principals, vice principals, and superintendents are actively involved in learning."

"Students and parents are involved as partners."

"Encourage peer sharing."

Understanding the Power of Facilitation

"Facilitators demonstrate strong communication skills including active listening."

"Formal leaders have to facilitate collaboration, not direct it."

"Leaders need to understand the processes for deep collaboration and believe in their importance to improve student outcomes."

Collaborative Learning with staff is deepened when system and school leaders possess Collabor-ability and can:

- clearly *articulate* the purpose for the work;
- *organize* time periods and schedules so that members of a school staff can work together;
- *reinforce* shared beliefs and understandings that underpin student and teacher success;
- *build* consensus on areas for Collaborative Learning through analyses of student data;
- *research* high-impact practices to consider with colleagues;
- *determine* clear Learning Goals and *co-construct* the Success Criteria for learning through collaborative discourse and analysis;
- *solidify* commitment to an inquiry approach to the work;
- *establish* and *implement* norms and protocols for engagement and safety with colleagues;
- *support* goals with ongoing scheduled time, learning resources, and reflective group processes;
- *project* a growth mindset and a belief in the capacity of others;
- *model* responsibility and accountability for their own learning and the learning of others;
- *facilitate* the working/learning process (use a **learning protocol** to help facilitate);
- *engage* many stakeholder voices in the work;
- *foster* a culture of trust and strong working relationships; and
- *reinforce* the development of a vibrant community of learners by keeping purpose front and center in their work.

Moral and social purpose has never been clearer for all leaders. The challenges may seem daunting but can be overcome by leaders acting on the urgent need to model how to work together for students and teachers. Deeper learning for students involves having opportunities to build social as well as academic skills—vital as students learn to negotiate the complexities of working together. The application of learning through *active, relevant inquiry seen as purposeful work* is at the heart of deeper learning for students *and* for staff, including system leaders, principals, and vice principals.

Compelling Challenges for Systems and Schools

It is vital to understand the factors that can inhibit or enable Collaborative Learning environments to thrive (see Appendix C). Impacting learning cultures, especially toxic cultures, is a challenging leadership exercise, as A. Muhammad articulates:

> School culture is a complex web of history, psychology, sociology, economics and political science. To effectively diagnose and eliminate toxic school culture, we must take an honest look at the internal and external factors that create the conditions that make cultural transformation difficult. (Muhammad, 2009, p. 17)

System cultures are also very complex webs. Resistance to change is a natural force. System leaders who wish to lead collaboratively must acknowledge and wrestle with the issues of readiness in moving learning forward. Leadership behaviors that support deeper forms of collaborative work must be tangible and visible in the system and schools as they are pivotal in moving individuals from low states of readiness to greater readiness for sustainable change. Skilled leaders help to connect all involved in collaborative work to the specific mission, vision, and values of an organization. System leaders, in particular, require a clear understanding of desired outcomes, and how to support and assess the readiness of schools to delve more deeply into their improvement processes. System and school data collection and analysis processes offer rich opportunities to create compelling purpose for collaborative efforts. Embarking on a system review can be a strategic time for system leaders to examine issues like established relationships for learning, readiness for change, and the impact of system and school culture on student and staff learning. If relationships are not evident, the work needs to begin with sensitivity but begin it must, nevertheless. Readiness must not stall improvement efforts. Readiness can be developed through collaborative work if leaders are prepared to take on the challenge of building Collaborative Learning cultures.

Leadership With Attitude: From Collegiality to Co-Learning

Leaders in most school systems speak about a good level of collegiality in their day-to-day working lives. Not as clear, but as vital, are the relationships built between unions and school systems, systems and community partners, and systems and elected officials as they influence what kind of cultures are built, what kind of structures are possible, and what collaborative processes can be enabled.

In all these relationships, collegiality is a necessary aspect of culture but in itself is insufficient to fuel and sustain system and school improvement. Building *a culture of co-learning* is critical for deeper forms of learning to thrive. Learning growth for system and school leaders is influenced by systemically embedded learning structures. New leaders require orientation and coaching while experienced leaders benefit from mentoring and renewal. System leaders must address the need for an ongoing continuum of learning opportunities over a professional career to sustain high levels of motivation. It matters greatly when system leaders offer their experience as learning facilitators, provide personal support, and engage completely.

What we are discussing is not unique to education. We note the critical convergence of leadership characteristics required in business, industry, government sectors, and post-secondary partners (Sharratt & Harild, 2015). It is clear that the ability to work interdependently and collaboratively is a necessity in all environments and is now a career-long leadership reality.

How can all leaders model leadership that propels systems and schools forward? In the following vignette, Assistant Superintendent Karen Steffensen describes her leadership with positive attitude. She sees the roles of curiosity, observation, robust questions, and co-learning as pivotal to creating a co-learning community of school administrators.

I have found the greatest impact on learning for everyone (students as well as educators) has been when student work, as data, is at the center of the dialogue and principals are integrally engaged in the inquiry along with staff. Another key to supporting change in school cultures and communities of practice is when senior leaders are prepared to roll up their sleeves and try an aspect of teaching being discussed. They do this not as the expert, but as someone who sincerely wants to risk exploring something new, to try out a particular strategy or to see the impact of implementing a technological device. They are willing to become learners among learners.

My work has focused on turning school growth plans into "living documents," encouraging principals to be constantly wondering where things are bubbling up in classrooms, and actively gathering artifacts of learning in a process of pedagogical documentation. I began to model this process for them by capturing my reflections from my school walks through photographs, video clips, and in notes that I share with the principals, creating an e-portfolio for each school. I will start our first area meeting next year by sharing a video montage of some school visit "noticings." We will dialogue about, "What do you notice? What do you wonder?" From there, we can begin to identify significant practices that are supporting student learning and ask ourselves, "How do we know how all students are learning? What practices do we have in common? Where are they different? Why might they be different? What changes to our practice might we consider and why?" Then we can co-construct Professional Learning Goals and Success Criteria based on the "evidence" of our collective work. This will make our Professional Learning more personalized and intentionally supportive.

Karen Steffensen, Assistant Superintendent, West Area Schools,
Surrey District School Board, #36, British Columbia

Steffensen's reflections echo our findings about the importance of evidence documentation as the work of system leaders. Carefully formed critical questions based on the evidence, posed in a non-threatening manner, promote reflection on practice. These questions must result in answers that themselves should lead to actions taken by system leaders. Where do we start? With the FACES of all involved, of course.

Begin With Shared Beliefs

We begin with Parameter 1, and having conversations to unpack shared beliefs and understandings to develop a common language of improvement. Personal learning, networking, and reflection will remain important throughout a professional career. However, as members of system and school teams, it is vital to embrace strategic and powerful shared beliefs and understandings. If system mission statements are to have any value and result in actual implemen-

Parameter 1

Shared Beliefs and Understandings

- All students can achieve high standards given sufficient time and the right support.
- High expectations and early and ongoing intervention are essential.
- All teachers can teach to high standards given the right assistance.
- Teachers and leaders can clearly articulate what they do and why they teach and lead the way they do—and students and parents can articulate what improvement looks like (Sharratt & Fullan, 2009, 2012, adapted from Hill & Crevola, 1999).

tation, we must begin by articulating a singular, clear, measurable goal for student success: The success of all students and its corollary, the improvement of all schools.

System leaders also need to have a clear vision of the evidence that the goal has been achieved. De-constructed Learning Goals and co-constructed Success Criteria have proven to be highly effective (Hattie, 2012; Sharratt & Fullan, 2012; Sharratt & Harild, 2015) in terms of focusing classroom instruction around what will be learned (clear Learning Goals) derived from the curriculum, as well as including students as partners in articulating what good work looks like (Success Criteria). In the same way, it is a valuable process for system leaders and school leaders to co-construct Learning Goals and Success Criteria for implementing learning strategies, and analyzing effective assessment practices where specific aspects of the school data have identified improvement is required. Co-learning through co-laboring like this—intentionally seeking to learn ourselves and to support the learning of those who labor with us—will lead to developing shared beliefs and understandings and to noticing them appearing in changed practice. For system leaders, co-learning through co-laboring can involve co-analysis and assessment, co-planning, decisions made collaboratively about actions and implementation, co-monitoring effectiveness, co-debriefing and co-reflection on progress made (see Chapters 4 and 5). By doing the work, we develop shared understandings, bring more meaning to our collective efforts, and generate significant new levels of trust.

> "We define capacity building as the collective investment in the development of the knowledge, skills and competencies of individuals and groups to focus on assessment literacy and instructional effectiveness that leads to school improvement."
>
> Sharratt & Fullan, 2009

Building Capacity for Co-Learning

Developing collaborative cultures where co-learning is valued as the format for collective capacity building requires both technical (first-order) and cultural (second-order) change (Planche, Sharratt, & Belchetz, 2008). Technical changes are those that affect the mechanisms or tools we use to do our jobs (Muhammad, 2009). For example, school schedules may change from five days to six days to create larger blocks of instructional time. Another example would be changes in school timetables so staff members have common planning time. These first-order changes are foundational but do not represent silver bullets for change or solutions in themselves unless second order or adaptive changes are evident to implement and embed a culture of learning (Planche et al., 2008). Examples of second-order change include putting FACES on the data and taking action, addressing the gender and diversity gaps, achieving equity and excellence for all, and supporting educators in becoming confident collaborators.

There are always challenges and opportunities for system leaders working to empower school leaders to deepen their learning. Second-order challenges include dealing with resistance to change, with the complexities of collective agreements, with finding time to co-labor, and with timetables that seem to revolve around staff contractual realities more than student learning. Pressures emanating from standards and learning expectations abound as parents and trustees/board members struggle to translate a criterion-referenced educational delivery system with their own past experiences of percentages and class standings and current political realities.

Second-order opportunities engage students and teachers in finding meaningful solu-

A System Leader as a Co-Learner

- Reflects on data analysis and participates in discussions regarding follow-up actions.
- Collaborates with others to ask challenging questions about teaching and learning.
- Considers the reallocation of resources when needed.
- Engages in problem solving for each student and school in need.
- Monitors implementation plans while supporting efforts to move learning forward (Sharratt & Harild, 2015, p. 53).

tions to complex, wicked problems that add value to another's life, and pave the way for school leaders and staff to take informed risks to experiment with experiential programming that engages and interests students in real-world, collaborative problem solving (Sharratt & Harild, 2015).

While much of the work of system leaders is interdependent with the work of school leaders, the responsibility for direction-setting and developing policy and procedures lies in the hands of the organization's senior leaders. Their work will impact both first-order and second-order aspects of the system's operation. Research participants in our study reinforced that healthy system and school cultures are dependent upon strong relationships, a second-order change, that impacts on student learning. It is especially important for system leaders to monitor learning relationships in schools where student achievement is a particular concern and to consider what leadership actions can move schools in difficulty forward (Leithwood, Harris, & Strauss, 2010).

Equity of outcomes for students requires a collective and systemic understanding of effective assessment, instruction, and intervention approaches for struggling students, which system leaders must

Core leadership skills that facilitate Collaborative Learning include the ability to demonstrate

- maintaining neutrality during discussions,
- being an active listener,
- using a variety of question types to move discussion forward,
- skillful paraphrasing,
- summarizing discussion points,
- testing assumptions made by a group, and
- synthesizing points made during the discussion so the group will move to accountable action (adapted from Planche, 2004, 2008a; Bens, 2012).

build through co-learning and co-laboring processes found in this text. Learning is the work.

Greater Systemic Coherence: A Worthy Goal

One of the most impactful actions system leaders can pursue is engaging in Collaborative Learning and co-laboring to strive for greater systemic coherence in instruction, assessment, and the ownership of student achievement and educator growth. Indeed, developing a common language across a system, between schools, and within schools is one of the most difficult and important tasks senior leaders who co-labor can undertake. Leaders who know how to teach and lead, mobilize others, and sustain the improvement work will do more to create a sense of "we" rather than "me" (Sharratt & Fullan, 2012). The greater the level of "we-ness," the greater the level of system-ness and coherence.

We have spoken above about how co-laboring, using the parameters as a reflective tool for improvement, enhances system coherence-building. For example, Parameter 13 (Sharratt & Fullan, 2009, 2012) suggests that cross-curricular literacy connections are powerful and generate collaborative and strategic conversations across disciplines as well as develop an appreciation that several curricula can be integrated in program delivery. System leaders must lead the conversation about coherent learning environments. Rather than viewing an education system as a compartmentalized institution, collaboration across schools and departments can develop shared understandings about powerful learning processes while sustaining the centrality of any particular discipline.

The 14 Parameters to Align, Focus, and Increase System, School, and Student Achievement

1. Shared Beliefs and Understandings
2. Embedded Instructional Coaches
3. Large Blocks of Time Focused on High-Impact Assessment and Instruction
4. Principal as Lead Learner
5. Early and Ongoing Intervention
6. Case Management Approach
7. Focused Professional Learning at Staff Meetings
8. In-School Grade/Subject Meetings to Moderate Student Work
9. Book Rooms of Leveled Texts, Varied Media, and Resources
10. Allocation of System and School Budgets for Literacy Instruction and Resources
11. Collaborative Inquiry Focused on Data to Make Intentional Decisions
12. Parental and Community Involvement
13. Cross-Curricular Literacy Connections
14. Shared Responsibility and Accountability (Sharratt & Harild, 2015, based on Sharratt & Fullan, 2009, 2012)

The following e-mail letter (page 68) to system leaders describes how one principal and leadership team collaboratively and enthusiastically involved all staff in understanding the 14 Parameters as a lens for system and school improvement—then looked at their data and selected one or two areas (besides 1 and 14) in need of immediate attention to improve their students' achievement.

> *If the meeting agendas of the most senior leaders and learners in a school system leave little space for learning or problem solving about student progress, it is very difficult to shift it toward a more reflective, cohesive, and collaborative culture of learning.*

Structure Drives Behavior

System leaders define, sanction, and oversee the supports for learning structures in schools. System leaders who model a **co-learning stance** build credibility and commitment. As

April 30, 2015
Good morning, Dave and Mary Anne.

Had a fantastic staff meeting here yesterday where the staff all taught each other the 14 Parameters from Lyn Sharratt's work with all of us in our system. Criteria was to learn one parameter in pairs in the week and then come to the staff meeting and present to others . . . the twist—there had to be a creative element to the presentation!

Creativity and learning abounded, some examples being:

- The literacy scarf dance (Parameter 1);
- The in-school subject meeting blues—a highlight! (Parameter 8);
- Spoken choir on Data Walls (Parameter 6);
- Raps about guided literacy instruction and other things in "da hood" (Parameter 3);
- Frozen frames drama on parent and community involvement (Parameter 12), and of course,
- The obligatory ditty about principal leadership (to the tune of *Cars!*).
- Lots of laugh and lots of arts :)

We then identified and investigated Parameter 6 as our area of need, beginning with Data Walls. . . . replete with roller blinds to ensure privacy. We are struggling with measuring progression using the PAT-R and will put that to teachers regarding how to show continual progress as well as achievement. It is exciting to see the FACES and to hear the teachers asking reflective questions about the FACES on the Data Wall and how we can make genuine representations of student progress or "stuckness" to motivate the Case Management process. It *is* happening! This was the best staff meeting I have ever been at—the learning was tangible! Thank you for your leadership. Our focus on the 14 Parameters *will* make a difference! The work is inspiring and world changing.

Anthony Lucey, Principal, CEO Brisbane,
Australia, St. William's School Grovely

experienced system superintendents, we know first-hand how difficult it is to find the time for productive conversations about teaching and learning dilemmas with other colleagues at the system level. However, if meeting agendas of system leaders and other senior leaders/lead learners in a system leave little space for learning, inquiry, or problem solving about student progress, it will be very difficult to shift the system toward a more reflective, cohesive, and collaborative way of doing business. System leaders must start every meeting with data that illuminate one student's FACE, one teacher's FACE, or the collective FACE of one school. Prioritizing one key area, using an inquiry approach, would model for a whole system that the quest for deeper understanding and learning applies to every system and school stakeholder.

Preparing Leaders to Lead Learning

For leaders to engage colleagues in reflective, iterative, and deeper forms of Collaborative Learning, strategic preparation processes need to be systemically embedded within the Professional Learning time, and it must include time for practice and feedback. For example, it is clear that system leaders and school leaders benefit from skill development in

1. facilitating group dynamics;
2. learning how to determine a focus and build consensus;
3. using key Collaborative Learning processes, including learning protocols (see Appendices G and H);
4. analyzing both formal and informal school and system data; and
5. reviewing and monitoring the use of high-impact practices for implementation.

> "You will not get schools to collaborate with each other unless there is a genuine collaborative culture within the school. Evidence from research across England bears this out."
>
> Alan Boyle, Director of Leannta; personal communication, September 16, 2014

Other authors agree that collaborative skill development is best situated within systemic leadership development and coaching/ mentoring processes. The area of facilitation is clearly important to moving learning forward at all levels. There are overlapping skills sets with coaching concepts that are worth noting (Knight, 2007, 2011). Conversation **scaffolds** or learning protocols (see Appendices D, G, and H) have been proven to be very worthwhile in engaging educators at all levels (Donohoo, 2013; Easton, 2009). Facilitation practices such as active listening, asking probing questions, paraphrasing frequently, summarizing key points, and recording ideas move group processes forward (Bens, 2012; Knight, 2007, 2011; Planche, 2004, 2008a). Coaching and being open to learning conversations move the establishment of collaborative cultures forward if those involved see relevance of and purpose for the conversations.

Beware of Pitfalls

Caution is needed when encouraging Collaborative Learning between diverse employee groups if an imbalance of power exists. Some leadership cautions include the following:

- Considering the impact of an issue through the eyes of those who will be impacted by it.
- Persisting in shaping and adapting a problem-solving environment while being sensitive to the needs of learners.
- Using diplomacy and strategic leadership to advocate for a specific position or course of action within collaborative endeavors.
- "Going toward the danger" by acknowledging resistors and meeting with each to understand the issues.
- Using a protocol for discussion (see Appendix D) that encourages an inquiry approach to problem solving and keeps conversations focused and moving forward.

> "From a leadership perspective, it is important to have personal involvement in any collaborative process. Lead by example, walk the walk, not just talk the talk. Outwardly demonstrate being intentional through changed habits, new routines and by publicly role modeling what you seek."
>
> Mark W. Carbone, Chief Information Officer, Waterloo District School Board, Ontario

Ultimately, collaborative processes are tools for leaders as problem solvers when goals for collaboration are clear, purposeful, and time is seen as well spent. A skilled collaborator understands the flow, the need for parity, and the importance of reciprocity between acting as a partner and acting as a leader.

Structures That Drive Learning

Many structures systems have used are proven to help leaders focus their learning. We discuss four: (1) networked learning communities, (2) a Case Management Approach, (3) Learning Walks and Talks, and (4) systemic inquiry.

1. Networked Learning Communities

The application of good ideas and their transfer into changed practice often remains at the good-intention level unless collective responsibility and accountability are involved. As Dufour, Eaker, and Dufour point out, professional learning communities face three important challenges: developing and applying shared knowledge, sustaining the hard work of change, and transforming school cultures (2005, p. 9). The concept of networking across schools to share learning is gaining ground as another venue to grow professional knowledge and practice. However, learning communities whose work only remains at the conversation or research level may simply open the door to more respectful relationships between members and reflective conversation. In contrast, by adding an important question of inquiry with a commitment to act, a learning community has the power to change practice dramatically. A networked learning community usually consists of individuals working together within or across schools to use data to consider a common area of focus as a collective. Monthly or bimonthly meetings for those attending result in a "homework commitment" to put into practice what is being learned about the area of focus. In our experience, learning communities can be highly impactful or rather unfocused. The difference is often due to the lack of short and sharp conversations, led by "knowledgeable others" (Sharratt, Ostinelli, & Cattaneo, 2010) who use evidence as data, for example, student work samples and video clips to focus the groups' Accountable Talk on cutting-edge classroom practices and measurable outcomes.

> "Collaboration must become an ordinary part of learning."
>
> Research survey participant

System leaders who take the time to be co-learners with school leadership teams make a significant difference in moving the work of networked learning communities forward. Those who just "drop by" to visit may be cheerleading, but they are not modeling collaborative leadership. The value of professional learning networks is dependent upon how focused the work becomes and how deep the conversations prove to be. Most importantly, a Collaborative Learning process needs to outline how collaborators will be accountable to each other in the actions that follow.

Three enablers to networked professional learning communities are

- being clear on the focus (*the what*),
- challenging thinking through inquiry (*the how*), and
- facilitating instructional leadership (*the who*).

Determining a focus for a network is challenging work and is facilitated through an inquiry process (Donohoo, 2013). When an impactful Collaborative Inquiry process is in play, titles are left at the door and ego-free leaders consider themselves as co-learners. The work of the "knowledgeable other" (Planche, 2010a; Sharratt et al., 2010), such as the literacy or instructional coach, is challenging but invaluable in moving people from identifying an issue to researching strong practice and deciding on purposeful action. The issues for the many staff members who are not members of a networked learning community are feeling the lack of inclusion in the process and not learning the why and how of the mobilization of the key learnings. As it is impossible to release everyone to attend network meetings, finding ways for all to "belong" and engage in learning—including the learning emanating from the network inquiry—is a clear and vital leadership challenge. Learning as a part of the everyday work in systems and schools *is* the leadership imperative. The benefits and challenges of networked learning communities are further described in Appendix E. The vignette below describes the power of learning from and with each other when researchers as "knowledgeable others" keep the network participants focused on the data, essential questions, and taking action.

The Power of Forming Clusters and Networks to Learn Together

The Eastern Learning Network (ELN) was established in Auckland, New Zealand, in 2013 within a cluster of 10 schools and colleges with students ranging from K–13. An initiative independent of the Ministry of Education arose from self-managing schools realizing like-needs in the area of Professional Learning and an appreciation for the value of working within a collaborative network.

The New Zealand Government's recent Investing in Educational Success (Ministry of Education, 2014) initiative to increase student achievement further raises the importance of sustainability across a network of schools. Schools are expected to maintain change, not only within themselves but also across the system, by forming networks. At the time of this writing, the ELN schools participate in a contracted Professional Learning program facilitated by Senior Consultant Maggie Ogram and three Auckland University of Technology academic staff, Dr. Howard Youngs, Dr. Leon Benade, and Dr. Patricia Stringer, who are researching the impact of this learning network on building teacher-leader instructional capacity and increasing student achievement.

The collaborative Professional Learning program is developed through regular sessions that provide support for those in school leadership roles and for classroom teachers as they meet together to:

- grow their expertise in understanding collaborative, critical **reflective practice**;
- consider how, through supporting each other schools, they might share expertise in teaching and learning to raise student achievement; and
- better understand strategic leadership processes and school systems in sustaining both Professional Learning and critical inquiry.

(Continued)

(Continued)

Figure 3.1, on the facing page, outlines the contextual levels of the ELN in accomplishing collaborative, critical reflective practice that relates to each school's inquiry focus that is driven by data. The 10 schools are shown as School A, School B, to School J in the figure.

Another networked community is currently happening in Ontario, where some system leaders are involved in the Leading From the Middle (LFTM) project, funded by the Ministry of Education (MoE) and the Council of Directors of Education (CODE), Ontario, with researchers Drs. Andy Hargreaves and Dennis Shirley from Boston College, USA. It is a *purposeful network* of 10 large and small school districts that have come together to define LFTM and take action. Thus far, LFTM is defined by where your location is within an organization with the bottom line being that, through engagement, collaboration, and innovation, every educator can influence system and school direction and coherence—upwards, downwards, and sideways—building on each other's capacity for improvement through knowledge creation and dissemination. The core focus is on applying what we learn in increasing all students' achievement and well-being across the globe. This network or cluster has developed a purposeful design and a robust theory of action to examine impact of LFTM. Stay tuned!

Another system and school structure and strategy to engage leaders of learning at all levels is having a system Case Management approach (Parameter 6).

2. The Case Management Approach

The Case Management approach has two elements: Data Walls and Case Management Meetings. System-level Data Walls and Case Management Meetings are as important to compiling and acting on evidence as are those at the school level. Living these strategies at the system level models them as critically important to school leaders and demonstrates the power in gathering data and taking action at every level.

FIGURE 3.1

A Very Successful Networked Learning Community in New Zealand

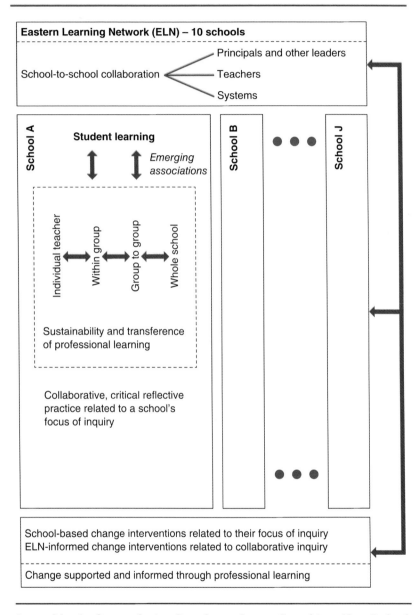

Source: Maggie Ogram, Senior Consultant, Osprey Consulting, New Zealand; personal communication, May 18, 2015

Data Walls

At the system level, Data Walls provide leaders with an overview of how all schools are doing against specific targets or expectations. All Data Walls must provide two views: achievement and growth and, importantly, move from being static displays (wallpaper) to becoming active documentation (evidence). When leaders stand in front of Data Walls together, rich conversations result, leading to system-initiated action. In Figure 3.2, the system Circle of Practice Data Wall developed in North Queensland Region has generated reflective dialogue about which expected practices are in their Circle of Practice and which others still need focused attention from system and school leaders to bring them into the Circle of Practice.

Circle of Practice Data Wall

A focus on a Circle of Practice has helped us to keep our focus sharp and narrow. We had to stop talking in generalisations, we had to stop thinking about the end goal and bring our thinking to observable actions that leadership teams could take right now.

By thinking big (where did we want to be in three years) we were able to start small (what's one step we could take today that would bring us closer to that big picture). Around our Circle of Practice we placed our look-fors (see page 80). These are seven evidence-proven, high-impact practices, deeply rooted in the research on improvement about which Lyn Sharratt works with us. These are practical, observable, and phrased in ways that we can all conduct Learning Walks and Talks in our schools and look for agreed-upon evidence that they are embedded. These are achievable in the short term, but keep our eyes on the big picture. One small step toward our three-year vision.

Each week we are able to stand in front of our Circle of Practice and discuss particular schools in depth. We talk about the evidence that we see that indicates that the look-for is being implemented. We talk about the next steps in support for that school and who will need to be involved in delivering that support.

> Tracey Petersen, Curriculum Consultant, Townsville,
> North Queensland Region (NQR), Australia;
> personal communication, June 14, 2015

FIGURE 3.2

System Circle of Practice Data Wall, North Queensland Region, Australia

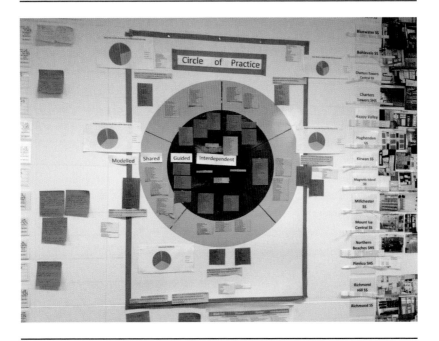

Source: Photo by Tracey Petersen, Curriculum Consultant, North Queensland Region, April 2015.

Gradual Release/Acceptance of Responsibility Explained

Modeled Practice: Leaders at every level model learning, not just teaching. Learning is the common thread critical for students, teachers, principals, support staff, system leaders, and parents to model. District and school leaders model actions that build capacity across schools and systems. Teachers model actions that build school and individual learning capacity. Lead learners, whether they be principals, teachers, or divisional, department, or curriculum leads, know how to manage a broad range of good ideas and model how to turn them into focused instructional practices that increase students' learning.

(Continued)

(Continued)

Shared Practice: Scaffolding learning from leader-led modeled practice to shared practice means moving to engage learners as active participants. As with modeled practice, shared practice occurs outside the school itself, usually in a central location (like a network) to enable system, school, and classroom leaders to come together to share the learning in a safe and supportive environment that permits learners to take risks confidently. It takes thoughtful, structured planning to scaffold this new learning onto modeled practice. In-service sessions and networked learning communities are established to share learning with school leadership teams with the expectation that they plan how to transfer knowledge and skills, and create cultures of learning back at their schools. At these networked learning sessions, school superintendents and district program staff as "knowledgeable others" share beliefs and related experiences about how to increase students' literacy achievement (for example). Beginning each session with student assessment data, they build understanding of how assessment must inform instruction. In return for this shared practice support, school superintendents expect to see evidence of initial improvement of student learning in every school for all students within a defined time period. In other words, when teachers feel that they are not alone but working together with a common purpose and shared practice, a cultural shift occurs. This is the essence of moving beyond modeled practice to embrace shared practice at every level. Finding time to walk in classrooms and creating opportunities to discuss what was seen are invaluable administrator pursuits (see Learning Walks and Talks discussion below). When there is a commitment at the school and system levels to sharing practice, leaders find the time to support such mutual learning.

Guided Practice: Modeling and sharing are not sufficient. Everyone in the system needs to get better and better at instructional practice, and in the process take more and more ownership over increasingly precise capacity-building activities. We call this process guided practice.

Guided practice is a change in the learning and leading balance. Learners step forward, taking greater control of their learning, and leaders step back—releasing the leadership reins—somewhat hard for some, necessary for all. Now we move beyond the initial modeling of capacity building and beyond "pull-out" shared practice learning sessions, to a deeper experience with teachers and administrators, embedding assessment and instructional literacy in classrooms for each student. The work in this stage requires much more precision, focus, and alignment than we or others previously thought.

In our earlier research, we found that it is not the surface beliefs and understandings that make a difference but rather the deep understanding and commitment, staying the course and the detailed know-how that comes from learning by doing and reflecting on practice that allow leaders and learners to graduate to this stage (Sharratt & Fullan, 2006). In guided practice, we get learners doing more. This stage is a more fine-grained analysis of what has to happen in every school, in every class, in order that differentiation of instruction occurs at all levels. Strategies are developed through guided practice that enable teachers and leaders to learn more about how to precisely engage in continuous improvement of classroom practice. Leaders are able to conceptualize and carry out their roles with ever-increasing knowledge, commitment, and precision. The gradual release/acceptance of responsibility from system to schools, from schools to classrooms, and from teachers to students has been planned and becomes observable at this stage. At every level—system, school, and classroom—everyone is "walking the talk" and "talking the walk" about how to increase students' achievement. This guided practice starts with the disaggregation of the data to determine the lowest-performing or "stuck" schools in order to differentiate support. The system not only identifies these schools but differentiates the support to them in terms of instructional Professional Learning support to all teachers and leaders. Our experience tells us that if system, school, and teacher-leaders embrace our definition of equity, then they are ready to embrace the notion of all schools and all students being supported differently in increasing student achievement. One size does not fit all. This is "walking the talk" of guided practice. Thus, guided practice signals a shift in thinking from what teachers and administrators need to do to what students can do, independently and consistently, across all grades, schools, and disciplines.

Interdependent Practice: New capacities to implement high-quality assessment and instruction are continually developed through modeling, sharing, and guiding practice in a joint learning proposition within and across schools, and between schools and the system. But this is not sufficient for sustainable improvement. For the latter you need co-equal, co-determined, interdependent practice. The fourth and final stage of our Gradual Release of Responsibility (GRR) model to accomplish systematic, system-wide reform is interdependent practice or what we are calling "realization." Realization is a much more sophisticated, systematic approach to deepening educational reform. It requires the elements and conditions provided by successful transition through the first three stages: (a) "on the ground" expertise in every school that is precisely matched by the same expertise at the system level; (b) authentic leaders in schools and systems who understand not only successful instructional practices but also strategic timing; and (c) a collective commitment to knowing when to do "the right thing" and how to "do the right things right" to move a system and its schools forward. It is a focused mobilization against inertia.

(Continued)

(Continued)

Will, perseverance, and trust building are necessary inputs as well as positive outcomes of interdependent practice or realization. Figuring out what the "right things" are, finding out how to do them, and doing them everywhere—for all students—continuously assessing and adding new strategies is realization. This vision of increased student achievement is clearly evident not only in the vertical alignment throughout the system (district, schools, and classrooms), but also in the horizontal coherence created across the system (among leaders in schools and classroom relating the same message).

Besides being an excellent teaching model, the GRR approach provides a Professional Learning model that highlights the importance of scaffolding the learning to ultimately reach interdependence. In NRQ, system leaders walk in their schools, with the seven look-fors (below) in mind, and then collaborate to determine where schools are in their Circle of Practice using the GRR model as an assessment tool to differentiate the scaffolded support needed.

The Seven Look-Fors in NQR

1. Leaders can articulate how student data informs the provision of Professional Learning;
2. Leaders can discuss how they are planning for the four stages of the Gradual Release of Responsibility approach (modeled, shared, guided, interdependent) to be represented in school documentation;
3. Teachers can articulate what students need to know and be able to do to be successful in the assessment task before they start teaching (Learning Goals/Intentions and Success Criteria are evident in every classroom);
4. Classroom artifacts and displays are aligned to the curriculum being taught and make learning visible;
5. Students can answer the question, "What do you have to know and be able to do to be successful in the assessment task?" in a way that aligns to the Guide to Making Judgments or Success Criteria visible in classrooms;
6. Data Walls are being used to track the growth and achievement of students below benchmark; and
7. Teacher aides are working to support the work of teachers and are not delivering instruction.

As Consultant Tracey Petersen says,

We'll move these seven practices into the centre of the Circle of Practice Data Wall based on the evidence collected during our system leaders' weekly Learning Walks and Talks in schools.

Our system leadership team will need to see them in 90% of our schools, 90% of the time before they can be considered inside the Circle of Practice. Otherwise they stay outside the Circle and we continue to work on them. Yellow cards will show how we indicate whether a school needs modelled, shared or guided support or if they are working interdependently on these seven high-impact practices. (Tracey Petersen, NQR; personal communication, April 15 and May 26, 2015)

Figures 3.3 and 3.4 show different ways of displaying data at the system level. All Data Walls are very specific and promote rich conversations, sometimes heated discussions, note-taking, and taking action to improve practice—always.

FIGURE 3.3

Putting FACES on the Data at the System Level in Metro Region Queensland, Australia

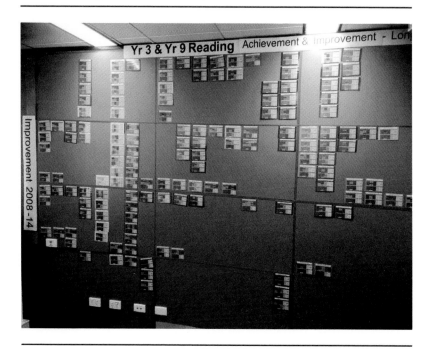

Source: Photo by Mark Campling, Regional Director, Metro Region, Queensland, Australia, June 4, 2015.

FIGURE 3.4

Leanne Nixon Discussing the Attributes of Data Walls at the State Level to Promote Collaborative Conversations

Source: Photo by Lyn Sharratt, Australia, June 5, 2015.

In Metro Region, Queensland, weekly system leader meetings begin at their system Data Wall (Figure 3.3), which displays both improvement and achievement—in Year 3 and 9 Reading. Regional Director Mark Campling leads system leaders in rich discussion focused on system and school improvement. Sometimes academic controversy ensues—a bonus! Plans are made and actions taken to differentiate support as a result of this ever-evolving system Data Wall.

Figure 3.4 shows a Data Wall being used at a state level rather than system, region, or school level.

Our state Data Wall has acted in the same way as we would use it in a school or system. It has provided a line of sight from the centre to schools that need support. It has shown us patterns that on paper weren't visible to us. The high visibility of the Data Wall meant that when anyone came into my office they talked with me about the right work. People, whether from audit, human resources, finance or policy, couldn't help but ask and engage with the real work of a central agency, student outcomes. It allowed us to create common understandings, as different people saw different patterns and asked different and challenging questions that deepened our thinking about how to support schools from a state level. (Leanne Nixon, Assistant Director General State Schools–Performance, Department of Education and Training, Queensland Government, Australia; personal communication, June 5, 2015)

Case Management Meetings

System leader Sue Walsh, deputy executive director, Parramatta Diocese, Australia, and the entire leadership team work closely with Sharratt. Walsh and the senior team have led the implementation of a Case Management approach in every primary and secondary school in Parramatta Diocese and attribute their rapidly growing success to school leaders fully implementing the approach across their system with differentiated system support.

As well, directors of education lead using a Case Management approach to focus and align the work to achieve system coherence. In Figure 3.5, Sharon Schimming, regional director, NQR, Australia, starts each meeting with a focused discussion at the system Data Wall followed by leading a weekly Case Management Meeting with staff to determine steps forward for each school in challenging circumstances in the region. Principals and leadership teams from each school are invited to participate, one at a time. Decisions, such as what are

- the next levels of work necessary,
- Professional Learning topics needed, or
- the resources and supports that need to be differentiated

are made collaboratively in this forum—beginning with scrutinizing the school's data to validate the decisions made.

The Case Management Approach

There is no greater capacity builder for teachers and leaders than a Case Management Approach to improve teaching practice and know every student's FACE (also see Chapter 4). Teachers and leaders work collaboratively to problem solve next steps to enhance a student's learning . . . one student at a time. The result over time is teachers' "trying on" and adopting high-impact instructional strategies that are necessary for that one student, but will be good for all students in the class.

The Case Management approach is two-pronged: Data Walls and Case Management Meetings.

1. Data Walls build commitment and understanding for teachers and leaders together. The FACES of the students are there for all to see and own; those FACES demand response and attention. Data Walls are a call to action.
2. Case Management Meetings build teachers' confidence and strengthen their trust in each other when they know that they are not alone in finding the pathways to instruction for all students.

This powerful approach (Parameter 6; Sharratt & Fullan, 2009, 2012) builds the collective responsibility of all school staff members in the school: the students belong to all!

Sue Walsh, Deputy Executive Director, Parramatta Diocese,
NSW, Australia; personal communication, May 14, 2015

3. Learning Walks and Talks

Learning Walks and Talks (Sharratt, 2008–2015) are known as a systematic, non-evaluative approach to knowing what is happening in every classroom, in every school. To know "what" is happening, and "why" it is happening, is our core business. Walks and Talks are meant to be a growth-promoting, collaborative process that focuses on students' thinking through the rich performance tasks they are given, which then give the "walkers" insights into what teachers are teaching and students are learning. Often we learn by knowing what an approach is not; thus, Figure 3.6 (page 86) demonstrates what the Walks and Talks process is and is not.

FIGURE 3.5

A Sample System Case Management Meeting in Support of All Schools Achieving in NQR, Australia

Source: Photo by Lyn Sharratt, Australia, March 2015.

A Collaborative Approach to Differentiating System and School Improvement

In our region we take a differentiated approach to supporting leadership teams in our schools. We know that context demands this of us. Leadership teams of schools in challenging circumstances need particular attention to support them to contextualise the Professional Learning that we deliver.

We begin by using our system Data Walls. These indicate to us where our energies need to be directed. We look for a finer grain of data where our data doesn't tell us how to offer support. We sit with leadership teams, holding Case Management Meetings, to listen to their journeys and consider the ways that we

(Continued)

(Continued)

can best support the work that they are doing to deliver Professional Learning which will improve that data. We make plans together to deliver that Professional Learning. We co-plan/**co-teach**, co-plan/co-lead and co-reflect together.

This work is just beginning, but is already showing promising signs. We are developing shared language about our work, we are developing shared under-standings about the necessity to have clarity about what is being taught and how students need to be clear about what they need to know and be able to do to be successful in planned assessment tasks. We are seeing changes in professional knowledge which is being evidenced in changed professional practice.

With Lyn's guidance, we are developing a culture of quality teaching and learning one school at a time through a careful Case Management approach. It's an exciting time to be in our region.

Tracey Petersen, Consultant, NQR, Queensland, Australia;
personal communication, June 14, 2015

FIGURE 3.6

Clarifying the Purpose of Learning Walks and Talks

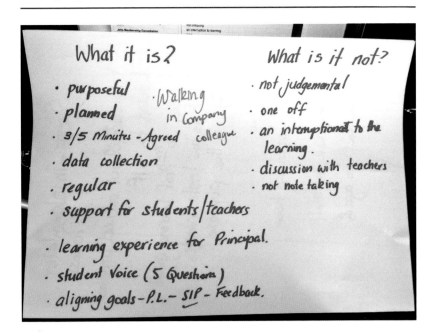

Source: Lyn Sharratt, Parramatta Diocese, NSW, Australia, March 2014.

Walks and Talks Guidelines

We know the impact of having protocols to direct our collaborative work in order to stay focused.

- The protocol for Learning Walks and Talks includes:
  - Leaders (teachers and students, too, if appropriate) walk in classrooms to listen and observe;
  - Leaders do not interrupt the lesson; and
  - Walks are 3–5 minutes in length in each classroom.

- They focus on
  - what the students are learning;
  - the challenge of the tasks in which students are engaged;
  - evidence of deconstructed curriculum Learning Goals/ Intentions, co-constructed Success Criteria, and Descriptive Feedback based only on the Success Criteria; and
  - evidence of staff Professional Learning and/or the School Improvement Plan.

- If it does not interfere with the learning, Walkers may ask individual students the five key questions below.
- Walkers exit quietly and later may ask the teacher a question or two directly related to observations they made and an authentic question they may have.

The Five Key Questions

The answers to the five key questions tell all. Asking students the five key questions during each Walk and Talk unlocks the mystery of knowing what learning is occurring without ever having to interrupt the teaching. If whole-group instruction is not happening, then Walkers quietly ask a student:

a. What are you learning?
b. How are you doing?
c. How do you know?

d. How can you improve?

e. Where do you go for help? (Sharratt & Fullan 2012; Sharratt & Harild, 2015)

The answers will reveal if teachers have made the learning explicit and clearly understood by deconstructing curriculum expectations (Learning Goal/Intention) in student-friendly language and co-constructing the Success Criteria with students as lessons and units develop. Students have a right to know how to be successful—there must be no mystery about what, why, and how students are learning to apply curriculum content.

In Figure 3.7, Sue Walsh is asking students the five key questions at R. L. Graham Public School while visiting Principal Jill Maar, York Region District School Board, Ontario, Canada.

FIGURE 3.7

Asking the Five Questions

Source: Photo by Lyn Sharratt, R. L. Graham Public School, Ontario, Canada.

What the "Talks" Are All About

Conversations with teachers do not happen during or after each Learning Walk and Talk. It is critical that Walks and Talks remain non-evaluative. When there is an opportunity to talk to teachers without interrupting the learning, the conversation may follow this pattern:

- sharing an observation;
- following up with a reflective question; and
- coaching—including attentive listening, paraphrasing, and pausing.

Collaborative conversations with teachers offer administrators opportunities to become even better instructional leaders. These reflective conversations

- have no "right" answer or even an "answer" in the traditional sense;
- provide openings for learning-focused conversations;
- encourage teacher voice that honors the view of the teacher as a *decision maker* who is capable and willing to alter teaching practice based on a variety of forms of Descriptive Feedback from students, themselves, colleagues, and administrators; and
- can be a catalyst for reflective practice that influences teacher practice not just today but over a lifetime.

When Learning Walks and Talks are implemented with regularity and integrity to the above protocols, leaders create a responsive culture of learning. Regularity means on a daily basis in a classroom or a few classrooms. One principal recently changed her practice from walking once per month to walking into a sample of her 27 classrooms daily. It has changed her outlook and relationship with her staff team—not because it is evaluative but because they feel she cares enough to come into the classes to see what is happening and ask the five questions of students. One superintendent recently reported proudly that he walked into schools every November. After some time training in Learning Walks and Talks, he realized how much he was missing and vowed to make weekly Learning Walks and Talks a priority. Note: We believe from experience that weekly is not sufficient either, and we believe this superintendent will increase his time commitment after he notices the impact that Learning Walks and Talks are having in his jurisdiction.

4. Systemic Inquiry

A systemic inquiry process regarding a single focus like literacy acquisition has proven to be very worthwhile, especially in jurisdictions that want to focus an entire system on a clear direction (Sharratt & Fullan, 2009). Presently, Ontario's education system has a clear focus on Mathematics as is outlined in the box below. Our point is not to suggest there is a "right way" to collaborate. There are many impactful ways to work together, but all are deepened if a question of inquiry driven by data is the clear driver of the work.

An inquiry approach can be added to any form of Collaborative Learning. Critical to its success is the productive dialogue that the work sparks between, within, and across schools. However, the dialogue is only productive if it helps to crystalize the leadership knowledge, skills, and dispositions that advance improvement work in schools; if informed action follows to impact student learning; and if that impact can be measured.

Ontario Ministry of Education's Collaborative Inquiry for Learning–Mathematics (CIL–M) involves a co-planning, **Co-Teaching Cycle** often facilitated by a "knowledgeable other" in Mathematics (*someone with skills in both Mathematics and facilitation*). This form of Collaborative Inquiry and practice is an integral part of Professional Learning in Mathematics in the Province of Ontario and has been formally researched by the Ministry of Education as a part of the province's strategy to move forward progress in Mathematics.

For further information, visit www.edu.gov.on.ca/eng/research/CILM.html.

System and school leaders must wrestle with very important decisions about which structures and processes support or impede learning if they are to positively impact student achievement within schools.

There are many topics of conversation that directly impact schools and would be vital for *system leaders* in their work *with school leaders*. A Collaborative Inquiry approach can be used to address our core business. Some examples are provided in Table 3.4.

The reality of positive system change represents many years of collaborative work with intentional planning, assessment, implementation, and monitoring. When system leaders engage school leaders in open, honest learning conversations, it leads to collaborative inquiries that

TABLE 3.4

Sample Topics and Rationale for Inquiry Among System and School Leaders

Topic	Rationale
Assessment sources for learning	• System data and school data sources need to be analyzed to determine system/school goals for improvement.
Focus for Collaborative Learning	• Decisions are made as to which data stand out as areas for system and/or school improvement and Professional Learning and why the need for a specific focus.
School learning strategies	• Decisions are made on school-specific Learning Goals and Success Criteria in employing specific system strategies. • System and school leaders decide which key factors should be included in planning for improvement.
Seamless integration of technology	• The use of technology is analyzed from an equity perspective and intentionally integrated into curricular planning and seamlessly in the school day. • System and school leaders probe how the use of technology can support students and staff learning in areas of particular focus (e.g., how technology can assist gathering assessment data or how technology can advance students' problem-solving skills).

(Continued)

TABLE 3.4 (Continued)

Topic	Rationale
Examination of school processes and structures and what adjustments are needed to facilitate Collaborative Learning	• System and school leaders need to consider and remove the barriers involved in collaborative processes.
Issues of inclusion	• System leaders probe with school leaders how learning processes for staff are inclusive, relevant, and fairly distributed.
Equity issues for students with learning challenges	• System and school leaders assess evidence of personalized learning, integrated special education planning, and differentiated programming and instruction.
Alignment and mobilization of the outcomes of a particular improvement strategy	• System and school leaders probe how knowledge building will be mobilized and how outcomes of learning will be shared, implemented, and monitored.
Planning	• Key milestones are determined in the planning phases for strategy implementation.
Implementation	• Decisions are made as to who will be involved in the implementation process of a learning strategy and how resources will be considered and deployed as supports.
Reflection and review	• Analysis of the actions taken in monitoring progress is part of ongoing reflection and review.
Adjustment of strategy as needed	• Mid-course corrections in strategies and key time frames are made as needed.

benefit *not only individual schools but several schools* through the development of a systemic culture of learning.

From these results, as one strong example among many, it is safe for us to say that collaboration at the system level has the following impact on student learning:

1. The impact of collaboration on student learning that creates a culture of change and learning begins with a common sense of "shared beliefs and understandings" (Parameter 1, Sharratt & Fullan, 2012).

2. System leaders know that when teachers change practice together, students learn (Sharratt, 1996).

3. When system leaders create compelling purposes and space for leader, teacher, student, and community partner collaboration, students' learning is positively impacted.

4. When system leaders model learning together (collaboration), school leaders and teachers impact student learning.

5. Tangible, visible collaboration by system leaders impacts the organizational culture of learning that indirectly increases all students' achievement.

6. Using data, system leaders as co-learners use systematic evidence of student growth *and* achievement to propel collaboration forward to have coherent impact across and within schools as learning organizations (Sharratt, 1996).

7. System leaders who co-labor develop a common "expected practices" language that is foundational to increasing leader, teacher, student, community learning and creates the system as a learning organization (Sharratt, 1996).

8. System leaders can articulate examples that structure drives behavior—for example, having time for a Case Management approach, Collaborative Inquiry, and Learning Walks and Talks at every level—to positively impact stakeholders' learning.

Applying Our Theory of Action

Figure 3.8 applies our Theory of Action and its four elements to highlight the process that system leaders use with school leaders in establishing a focus for co-learning. Ideally, system leaders would engage school leaders and their teams in a reflective, iterative inquiry cycle aimed at problem solving to move all schools forward. In Chapter 1 we noted a list of questions that system and school leaders can ask themselves as they assess to plan and plan to act. Inquiry questions will vary as they only work well if they are contextually relevant.

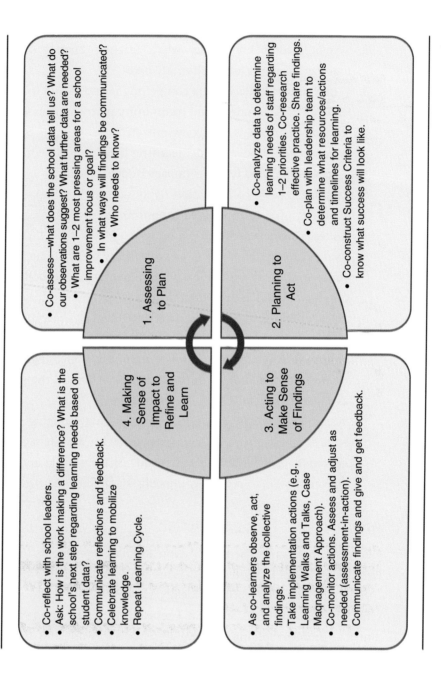

FIGURE 3.8

Theory of Action for System Leaders Working Alongside School Leaders

1. Assessing to Plan

- Co-assess—what does the school data tell us? What do our observations suggest? What further data are needed?
  - What are 1–2 most pressing areas for a school improvement focus or goal?
    - In what ways will findings be communicated?
      - Who needs to know?

2. Planning to Act

- Co-analyze data to determine learning needs of staff regarding 1–2 priorities. Co-research effective practice. Share findings.
  - Co-plan with leadership team to determine what resources/actions and timelines for learning.
  - Co-construct Success Criteria to know what success will look like.

3. Acting to Make Sense of Findings

- As co-learners observe, act, and analyze the collective findings.
  - Take implementation actions (e.g., Learning Walks and Talks, Case Maqnagement Approach).
  - Co-monitor actions. Assess and adjust as needed (assessment-in-action).
  - Communicate findings and give and get feedback.

4. Making Sense of Impact to Refine and Learn

- Co-reflect with school leaders.
- Ask: How is the work making a difference? What is the school's next step regarding learning needs based on student data?
- Communicate reflections and feedback.
- Celebrate learning to mobilize knowledge.
- Repeat Learning Cycle.

The Impact of Collaboration on Student Learning

Parramatta Diocese is the perfect example of how system leaders influence students' achievement by being results oriented, paying attention to detail, modeling collaboration, and being "present" in the work—every day and in every way. Its three high-impact strategies for collaborative improvement are co-constructing Data Walls, leading Case Management Meetings, and conducting Learning Walks and Talks. Its results show that the work of creating a culture of learning over three years with Sharratt and Fullan has caused a steady rise in achievement. The system focus has been on Literacy and Numeracy, K–2, in every school, and their results have been impressive. For example, shown in Table 3.5, on the next page, in Kindergarten, students have more than doubled their progress in Reading Comprehension in four months during 2015; in Year 1, the percentage of students at the expected levels in Aspects of Writing has more than doubled during the same four months of 2015; and in Year 2, Text Reading has improved with 10% more students reading at the expected text levels by June 2015. This has occurred because of the clear direction-setting, articulated expectations, support, and collaborative structures put into place across this diocese.

A Pause for Reflection

As we said, ultimately on a day-to-day basis it is what happens in the classroom that counts. It is the actual and the observed work of system leaders that models, encourages, and enables the interdependent learning that goes on in schools and across schools. System leaders have the big picture and must strive to bring great clarity, relevance, coherence, and authentic motivation to all stakeholders. Because everything they do is visible and influences perceptions, leaders must be intentional in what they choose to model. They shape their systems' culture by what they share, pay attention to, what they guide, how they offer and receive feedback, what they support, what they recognize, and what they reward. In other words, system leaders must be extraordinarily vigilant in "walking the talk" as interdependent practitioners.

TABLE 3.5

Improvements in Literacy Performance in Parramatta Diocese, 2015

Year Level	% of Students at Expected Level in Feb. 2015	% of Students at Expected Level in June 2015	Description of Expected Practices to Which Support Was Given
Comprehension–K	40.89	87.4	All classes have implemented a daily two-hour balanced Literacy program that includes Shared Book, Guided Reading, Independent Reading, and Reading to Students for Pleasure. Students also have the opportunities to respond to texts.
Aspects of Writing–Year 1	22.67	46.10	All classes have implemented a daily two-hour balanced Literacy program that includes Modeled Writing, Guided Writing, and Independent Writing.
Reading Texts–Year 2	76.28	87.99	All classes have implemented a daily two-hour balanced Literacy program that includes Shared Book, Guided Reading, Independent Reading, and Reading to Students for Pleasure.

Matrix Themes 5–6

We continue our discussion here of the 10 non-negotiable themes that are a result of our research about Leading Collaborative Learning. Displayed in Table 3.6 are Themes 5 and 6.

Looking Ahead

How would having a clear vision, articulating expected practices, embedding collaborative structures, and adding a Collaborative Inquiry approach to the work that system leaders do with school leaders help to develop a culture of deeper learning and collaboration in your setting? In Chapter 4, we discuss the important work that school leaders do with teacher-leaders and how learning conversations can be deepened through utilizing an inquiry approach.

TABLE 3.6

Implementation Matrix of the Fifth and Sixth of the 10 Non-Negotiables of Evidence-Proven Collaborative Learning Practices

Evidence-Proven Practice	Modeled Collaborative Learning	Shared Collaborative Learning	Guided Collaborative Learning	Interdependent Collaborative Learning	Beneficial Professional Learning for Those Who Lead Collaborative Learning
Key Theme 5	Includes	Includes	Includes	Includes	Includes
Leadership behaviors and organizational structures impact relationships and the depth of work collaborators can do together	• demonstrating how to work through difficulties • showing flexibility and creativity	• seeking purposeful solutions with others • addressing constraints caused by structures • applying policy and procedures in ways that move the work of schools forward	• using proactive measures to establish reasonable solutions • building consensus so decisions can be made	• including many voices in seeking the best solutions	• developing political skills in building consensus • working inclusively with diverse stakeholders
Key Theme 6	Includes	Includes	Includes	Includes	Includes
Strong collaboration includes impactful leadership and facilitation skills	• using intentional facilitation strategies to lead diverse groups	• facilitating group work with other emerging leaders	• using intuition in recognizing when to intervene to move work forward	• integrating diverse views and inviting engagement	• engaging in leadership coaching • using facilitation skills authentically

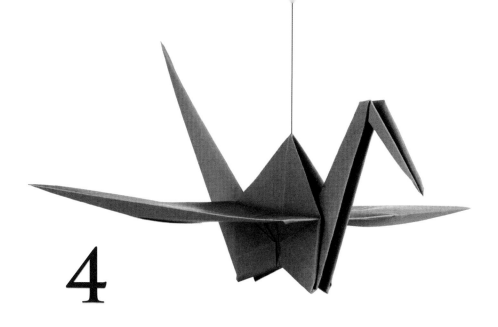

4

School Leaders Working Alongside Teacher-Leaders

"There has to be a shared understanding and shared purpose at the core of collaborative practice. It has to be a reciprocal learning process that leads to collective action and meaningful change."

Leithwood et al., 2010, p. 248

Leadership for Student Achievement and Collaborative Learning

A report issued by the National Association of Secondary School Principals (NASSP) on the Correlations of Collaborative School Cultures with School Achievement (Gruenert, 2005) was very clear on the impact of the school leader. The survey of 2,750 participants, which correlated language and math achievement with the level of collaborative school culture, reported that schools with a greater collaborative culture tended to have higher student achievement (p. 46). One conclusion particularly stuck with us. Rather than looking at student achievement and school culture as opposite ends of a continuum that goes from seeking optimum student achievement to seeking optimum Collaborative Learning, the survey reported that it is important for leaders to see the two goals as "complementary, reciprocal and convergent in nature" (p. 50), as both take intentional time to build. As this seminal research report highlighted, the school improvement process resulting in increased student achievement can be accelerated when leaders establish a culture of Collaborative Learning using an inquiry approach as a key strategy. Figure 4.1 illustrates our belief that as the level of collaborative cultures spreads so does the level of

FIGURE 4.1

The Correlation Between Collaborative Cultures and Increased Student Achievement

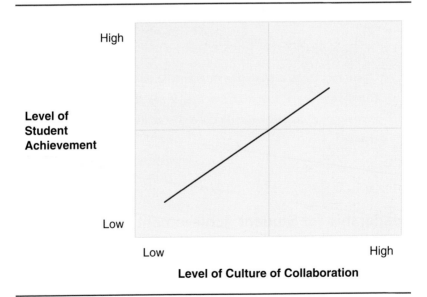

student achievement increase as reported in the NASSP study. Again, the role of the principal in building the collaborative culture *and* having high expectations is paramount in bringing about the convergence of these two constructs in schools.

Others have studied and written about the relationship among collaborative culture, intentional practice, and increasing all students' achievement (Dana et al., 2011; Militello et al., 2009). In *Realization* (Sharratt & Fullan, 2009), the authors write about the impact of the 14 Parameters on increasing student achievement at the system and school levels. Parameter 1, the notion of shared beliefs and understandings, sets the stage for system- and school-wide shared beliefs and understandings, that begin to create a positive cultural base and common foundation. Parameter 11 specifically addresses the importance of undertaking Collaborative Inquiry—using student data to ask system- and school-level questions. And Parameter 2, embedding experienced master teachers as Instructional Coaches or "knowledgeable others," brings us to where we are in this chapter: discussing the necessary leadership dimensions of (1) the principal, who can lead the development of a culture of collaboration and have high expectations for all students' success, and (2) the teacher-leader, who has professional knowledge of teaching and learning. Both need strong interpersonal skills in working alongside others.

> "Issues and questions that surface during inquiry are not so much problems to be resolved, as they are tensions to be negotiated, a means to gain deeper insights and to explore alternative perspectives. This kind of nuanced and differentiated interaction calls for understanding of an authentic experience with learning 'on the ground.'"
>
> Research survey participant

Further agreement with the NASSP study findings comes from states and systems that understand the need for leadership development to be a system responsibility and a school-based one. For example, Ontario, which has one of the highest education performance records on the Program for International Student Assessment (PISA) and other markers, has developed a detailed leadership framework that is used as a self-assessment tool for school leaders (http://www.education-leadership-ontario.ca/storage/6/1380680840/OLF_User_Guide_FINAL.pdf). The Institute for Education Leadership (IEL) (https://www.education-leadership-ontario.ca/content/home) has developed the Ontario Leadership Framework (OLF), which describes what good leadership looks like based on evidence of what makes the most difference to student achievement and well-being. It identifies the practices of successful school and system leaders, as well as the organizational practices of successful schools and districts. The OLF includes a small but critical number of personal leadership resources (leadership traits and dispositions) that have been found to increase the effectiveness of leadership practices, many of which mesh with those we present below. As well, the IEL has developed self-assessment tools for school and system leaders.

Five Dimensions of Leadership

The five dimensions of leadership we discuss here are (1) Knowledge-ability, (2) Mobilize-ability, (3) Sustain-ability, (4) Imagine-ability, and (5) Collabor-ability. Sharratt and Fullan (2012) investigated what leadership skills are needed to put FACES on the data to improve student achievement in schools. They determined there were three key areas of leadership:

1. **"Knowledge-ability."** Leaders need to model an understanding of strong classroom practice (e.g., assessment that differentiates use of high-impact instructional strategies).

2. **"Mobilize-ability."** The ability of leaders to inspire and focus self and others by communicating clearly (e.g., Data Walls to transparently track student progress); knowing all the FACES and

Reflections on Learning Through Collaborative Inquiry

Figures 4.2 and 4.3 demonstrate our presentation at our Learning Fair where we presented our growth in using the Collaborative Inquiry model. Our thinking is explained here:

Overseeing our Collaborative Inquiry process was carefully cultivated by developing a safe environment based on developing mutual respect, building rapport, and promoting empowerment. Leading through example required a leadership balancing act by promoting transparent communication via discussion, debate, and examination. Steering Collaborative Inquiry was possible by motivating, inspiring teamwork, and mentoring all along the way. As a leader, establishing trusting relationships meant being present in the moment to listen to ongoing conversations, where an atmosphere of trust made it possible for vulnerability to lean into the discomfort to make purposeful connections. Listening without judgment or interruption was necessary to propel forward the cycle of Collaborative Inquiry. In so doing, misperceptions were challenged while new insights were elongated. Our professional reflections at round table conversations progressed to changed classroom practice. We noticed improved student achievement by moving away from maintaining static teaching positions.

Anna Garito Cassar, Vice Principal,
Holy Spirit Catholic School, Dufferin-Peel
Catholic District School Board, Ontario, Canada

taking action (e.g., Case Management Meetings); and celebrating and intentionally sharing learning (e.g., the Learning Fair as featured in Figures 4.2 and 4.3 in Dufferin-Peel Catholic District School Board [DPCDSB], Ontario, Canada).

3. **"Sustain-ability."** Leaders who make a difference measure their impact by the number of leaders they leave behind to continue the student improvement work when they have gone on to other responsibilities. These leaders establish a lasting collaborative culture of shared responsibility and accountability in their schools. For example, they Walk and Talk daily in their schools looking for evidence of

expected practices and the impact of Professional Learning, and they have authentic conversations with teachers to share learning about strong practice and to provide individualized support.

FIGURE 4.2

DPCDSB's Learning Fair Promotes Collaborative Thinking About Practice by Teachers and Leaders

Source: Photo by Lyn Sharratt, May 1, 2014. The Journey of Collaborative Inquiry. Left to right, educational leaders Sue Steer, Gina Sideroff, and Anna Garito Cassar.

When these leadership abilities, which in themselves are components of collaboration, are all in play, the result is increased student achievement (Sharratt & Fullan, 2012, p. 49). These three leadership dimensions align directly with the work of Louise Stoll. Stoll highlighted six areas of leadership learning that are pertinent to the development of collaborative leadership strengths (Stoll, 2015; Stoll & IARTV, 2004):

- **Leading learning and teaching**—the core work of schools (Knowledge-ability)
- **Creating the future**—developing a shared vision driven by moral purpose (Sustain-ability)
- **Developing self and others**—relationships underpin the work and help to motivate (Sustain-ability)

FIGURE 4.3

Knowledge Circulation Through Collaboration at the Learning Fair, DPCDSB

Source: Photo by Lyn Sharratt, May 1, 2014. "How do we engage all learners?" Teaching and Learning Conversations at The Learning Fair, DPCDSB. Left to right: Principal Sandra Res, Consultant Lyn Sharratt, and Superintendent Sue Steer.

- **Strengthening community through collaboration**—developing intellectual and social capital (Mobilize-ability)
- **Managing the organization**—it is both managing and leading effectively and efficiently (Mobilize-ability)
- **Deepening professional accountability and developing "an inquiry habit of mind"** (Earl & Katz, 2002; Knowledge-ability, Mobilize-ability, and Sustain-ability adapted from Stoll, 2015; Stoll & IARTV, 2004).

We agree with Stoll (2015) that research and inquiry are key elements of a learning-centered approach to leadership and would add "integrating giving and getting feedback" as a critical part of Collaborative Learning.

Questions for Leaders (Informal and Formal) Who Wish to Lead Collaborative Learning

- Am I able to articulate a clear vision?
- Do I have a sense of a path forward?
- Can I facilitate a team approach?
- How will I assist in breaking down our goals into reasonable, doable actions?
- How will I lead reflections on our determined actions?
- How will we, as a team, ensure that we refine and adjust actions as needed?
- How will our school leadership team monitor progress?
- How will I support the efforts of staff and teacher-leaders?
- How will I model encouragement and persistence?
- How do I model an inquiry learning stance and an interest in continuous learning?
- How will we structure time for collaboration during the school day?

4. **"Imagine-ability."** In *Good to Great to Innovate* (Sharratt & Harild, 2015, pp. 44–62), the authors add the fourth element—Imagine-ability—that implies open and inclusive learning environments; a structured, collaboratively planned approach; the ability to think ahead to what is possible; and a collective responsibility

for all learning and all learners. Innovation leadership skills, including an up-shift in attitude that cause Imagine-ability to occur, are related to

- imagining the possibilities of offering multiple opportunities for success for *all* students;
- having an open mind to new ideas focused on the FACES of all learners;
- understanding the student growth and achievement data;
- understanding the experiential learning needs of students who face changing economic and employment conditions;
- taking informed risks;
- having strong interpersonal skills;
- developing a broad base of community partners with whom leaders are willing to share decision making; and
- understanding the current reality and complexity of social, economic, and academic learning (SEAL).

While there are small, progressive steps along the imagine-ability journey toward becoming an innovation leader, one of the early stages is to see the benefits of, and to take action to establish a Collaborative Learning culture (Sharratt & Harild, 2015).

5. **"Collabor-ability."** As a result of research for this book, we offer a fifth vital element of leadership that we call "Collabor-ability"—the ability to collaborate and work with others as authentic partners doing purposeful work. Almost universally, our respondents connected the willingness to collaborate to improved schools and increased student achievement. As we have defined in Chapter 1, we see deeper forms of collaboration as co-laboring in that we are responsible to, and accountable for, working alongside each other and supporting the learning of other collaborators. As we co-labor, we build trust and negotiate meaning and relevance together. Co-laboring also strengthens our interdependence. Collabor-ability at the leadership level integrates Knowledge-ability, Mobilize-ability, Sustain-ability,

and Imagine-ability and demonstrates the ability to optimize a co-learning approach to co-work.

Leaders have influence through what they model. Table 4.1 summarizes our five leadership dimensions. These skills and attributes apply to formal and informal leaders working and learning together.

Table 4.1 is a useful self-assessment tool for principals and teacher-leaders in rating their efforts to embed leading in a culture of collaboration to increase all students' success.

Contextual Factors That Build Collaboration

To understand more about Leading Collaborative Learning we asked survey respondents to consider the following:

1. What are the contextual factors that build collaboration?
2. Rank the leadership behaviors that enable collaboration.
3. Describe the leadership behaviors that build cultures for Collaborative Learning.

Participants ranked contextual factors that influenced the establishment of collaboration in a school setting from most important to least important. The most important, Positive School Culture, earned a score of 6.0 and least important, Volunteerism, earned a score of 1.8. Table 4.2 depicts the top four factors with their average ranking—6.0 being the highest. It is no surprise to us that establishing a positive school culture was ranked highest and yet is often a challenge to find the time to achieve and sustain. The other factors listed underpin positive school culture and impact sustainability as well.

Noteworthy is that having time to collaborate—which is usually thought to be the most challenging issue—is listed by respondents as the fourth factor, but even at that ranking, it is still a looming issue for all school leaders. Without trust built through communication and establishing authentic relationships that lead to building a base

TABLE 4.1

Leadership Knowledge, Skills, and Dispositions

The credibility of collaborative leaders includes "Knowledge-ability": Deep understanding of high-impact classroom practices by	The authenticity of collaborative leaders includes "Mobilize-ability": Focused coherence in and energy for the work by	The integrity of collaborative leaders is demonstrated in "Sustain-ability": Advocating for relationship building, trust, and learning by	The creativity of collaborative leaders is demonstrated in "Imagine-ability": Structured Collaboration + Imagination = Innovation and an openness to possibilities by	The influence of collaborative leaders and team members is demonstrated in "Collabor-ability": Optimizing a co-learning approach to co-work by
• believing every student and teacher can and will learn with the right support and time • understanding change processes and not using context as an excuse • facilitating collaboration when learning about strong assessment and instructional practices	• believing every student and teacher can and will learn with the right support and time • articulating a vision • using "systems thinking"	• believing every student and teacher can and will learn with the right support and time • articulating collective purpose and developing processes to achieve shared understanding	• believing every student and teacher can and will learn with the right support and time • engaging a broad base of parental and community partners at decision-making tables • being learner-centered	• believing every student and teacher can and will learn with the right support and time • integrating the four previous dimensions to act as an "umbrella dimension" • modeling a "partners in learning" approach to co-work

(Continued)

TABLE 4.1 (Continued)

The credibility of collaborative leaders includes "Knowledge-ability": Deep understanding of high-impact classroom practices by	The authenticity of collaborative leaders includes "Mobilize-ability": Focused coherence in and energy for the work by	The integrity of collaborative leaders is demonstrated in "Sustain-ability": Advocating for relationship building, trust, and learning by	The creativity of collaborative leaders is demonstrated in "Imagine-ability": Structured Collaboration + Imagination = Innovation and an openness to possibilities by	The influence of collaborative leaders and team members is demonstrated in "Collabor-ability": Optimizing a co-learning approach to co-work by
• using relevant data for analysis and action through Data Walls and Case Management Meetings • modeling the development of Learning Goals, Success Criteria, and Descriptive Feedback to be evident in every classroom • involving key stakeholders as resources	• demonstrating emotional intelligence in interpersonal interactions • translating data analysis into planning actions • asking open-ended questions	• taking every opportunity to develop other leaders • valuing the contribution of others • using an ethic of service to and care to know every FACE • demonstrating an attitude of optimism	• ensuring each student has experienced multiple pathways to success before graduation • seeing solutions to problems where no one else sees the problem • moving theory into practice out into communities through an experiential learning approach	• building trust while negotiating meaning and relevance together • distributing or taking part in leadership actions to work alongside staff and other leaders across a district or region • reinforcing the team's interdependence as co-learners and co-leaders

The credibility of collaborative leaders includes "Knowledge-ability": Deep understanding of high-impact classroom practices by	The authenticity of collaborative leaders includes "Mobilize-ability": Focused coherence in and energy for the work by	The integrity of collaborative leaders is demonstrated in "Sustain-ability": Advocating for relationship building, trust, and learning by	The creativity of collaborative leaders is demonstrated in "Imagine-ability": Structured Collaboration + Imagination = Innovation and an openness to possibilities by	The influence of collaborative leaders and team members is demonstrated in "Collabor-ability": Optimizing a co-learning approach to co-work by
<ul><li>setting clear, measurable learning priorities and monitoring progress toward expected goals</li><li>expecting the use of high-impact assessment and instructional practices in every classroom</li><li>facilitating inquiry as a learning vehicle</li><li>recognizing and videoing signs of a "learning" classroom</li><li>being a "lead learner"</li><li>giving teachers intentional support to learn together about best practices</li></ul>	<ul><li>gaining the commitment of others to co-learn</li><li>accomplishing action plan tasks</li><li>finding resources to enable inquiries including common learning time in time-tables</li></ul>	<ul><li>sustaining ongoing support, modeling courage to proceed, and encouraging small wins</li><li>believing in own ability and the competence of colleagues</li><li>ensuring the improvement plan is not leader-dependent but owned by everyone so that leader replacements can keep the plan in place</li></ul>	<ul><li>personalizing leadership so that every student has a pathway plan that captures student's interests and abilities</li><li>embracing the global community and going out to it or bringing it into classrooms</li><li>focusing on learning for life versus learning for school</li><li>being open to innovative approaches that center around improving the life chances of each student</li></ul>	<ul><li>asking the tough questions by having high expectations that lead to multiple collaboratively built solutions</li><li>knowing that many ideas are better than one, so is open to listening for a groups' creative ideas and informed risk taking, always focused on student data</li><li>using protocols to develop collaborative processes to bring same-grade and cross-grade teachers together to learn (e.g., using Collaborative Assessment of Student Work as the catalyst)</li></ul>

(Continued)

TABLE 4.1 (Continued)

The credibility of collaborative leaders includes "Knowledge-ability": Deep understanding of high-impact classroom practices by	The authenticity of collaborative leaders includes "Mobilize-ability": Focused coherence in and energy for the work by	The integrity of collaborative leaders is demonstrated in "Sustain-ability": Advocating for relationship building, trust, and learning by	The creativity of collaborative leaders is demonstrated in "Imagine-ability": Structured Collaboration + Imagination = Innovation and an openness to possibilities by	The influence of collaborative leaders and team members is demonstrated in "Collabor-ability": Optimizing a co-learning approach to co-work by
• taking teachers to see successful practice in other schools and classrooms, and following up with co-developed action plans • catching successful practice on video and sharing the results in small groups to learn and try together	• sourcing whatever will aid teachers in their classroom work	• advocating for all students' learning, ensuring collective responsibility and accountability to own all the FACES	• viewing student work as formative data (ongoing) versus summative data (finished) • growing the work organically • celebrating diversity • hearing students' voice and choice so they try multiple pathways before graduation	• finding time in the school day for teachers and leaders to learn together through a collaborative 4 Cs approach

Sources: Adapted from Sharratt & Fullan, 2012; Sharratt & Harild, 2015.

TABLE 4.2

Contextual Factors That Build Collaboration

Factors	Average Ranking Out of 10
Positive school culture	6.00
Strong relationships	5.93
Shared beliefs and understandings	5.27
Time to collaborate	5.20

of shared beliefs and understandings, there is no need to have time to collaborate. If time to collaborate is a critical factor in school improvement, we must reconstruct the time we have—there is no more time in the school day. Note that this issue with time for Professional Learning regarding Collaborative Learning is precisely parallel to the time considerations we have discussed previously at the system level.

Comments in the box below represent concerns as expressed by our research participants. They speak to issues of time, structure, relationships, and culture. Most of all, the comments speak to the need for leadership that is committed to building a dynamic culture of professionals learning together, and we would add, the comments seem to reinforce the notion that leadership that sustains progress is interdependent and uplifting (Hargreaves, Boyle, & Harris, 2015).

Sample Research Participant Perceptions and Concerns Regarding the Work of Collaborative Inquiry

- "Give us time during the instructional day to collaborate with our colleagues. Time is the issue."
- "There are pockets of collaboration that are separate from each other."
- "It is important to create an environment that is safe to learn and make mistakes. This has to be modeled by leaders in order for teachers to believe in it and feel safe to risk take."

(Continued)

(Continued)

- "Giving the why is important—not to critique current practices but to improve student learning."
- "Groundwork must be done with unions so that barriers are not created."
- "We must deal with the ego of participants and build an environment of equity and trust."
- "I have no experience with the inquiry model . . . never been invited to an in-service. Should I be going online to research this model? How am I being included in my teaching profession?"
- "There is no collaboration in my work environment . . . only fear."

Using Leadership Influence

There are challenges to "getting to" collaborative work, which principals and teacher-leaders need to address. Table 4.3 displays our participants' ranking of school leadership behaviors and conditions that enable collaborative work. The results support our view that being

TABLE 4.3

Ranking of Leadership Behaviors That Enable Getting to Collaborative Work

Leadership Behavior	Respondents' Ranking of Behavior as Perceived as Very Important or Important
Informal and formal leaders are able to build strong relationships	99%
Student learning evidence is used as the driver for staff Learning Goals	98%
Informal and formal leaders model inclusiveness regarding participation in collaborative work	98%
Formal leaders partner with staff to establish Learning Goals for collaboration	97%
Informal and formal leaders model an approach that is open to risk taking	97%

able to build relationships that create a culture of collaboration, which is focused on evidence of teacher and student learning, are the first steps in "getting to" collaborative work.

School leader actions in finding or re-organizing resources to support teachers (Mobilize-ability) and in working and learning together (Knowledge-ability) speak louder than their words. These actions that are marks of their leadership authenticity are foundational to culture-building and to getting to learning together. Table 4.4 summarizes research participants' comments concerning the leadership behaviors (actions) that build and support cultures for Collaborative Learning.

TABLE 4.4

Leadership Behaviors (Actions) That Support Collaborative Learning

Leaders build cultures that support Collaborative Learning by

- modeling a non-judgmental approach as an operating norm—separating evaluation processes from learning and co-learning;
- scheduling time to practice new skills with skilled colleagues as mentoring and coaching are important for staff at all stages of their career;
- putting organizational structures in place to support collaborative work (e.g., coordinating timetables to facilitate co-planning and co-working time);
- scaffolding individualized support for staff who are struggling—understanding that not all staff will engage in co-work at the same rate or time;
- valuing all ideas that teachers bring forward and trusting their professional judgment;
- sharing decision making on key issues of teaching and learning;
- modeling being co-learners by leaving titles at the door;
- co-facilitating learning processes with teacher-leaders;
- supporting risk taking by co-constructing meaning with teachers;
- knowing and dealing individually with resistors to understand why and support with a clear message to move forward if approaches are "good for all kids";
- protecting instructional time and valuing Professional Learning time; and
- being visible in classrooms, asking students questions about their learning, and seeking authentic conversations about practice with teachers (Sharratt, 2013a).

We interpret what the participants were beginning to say as being vital to the relationship between engagement and commitment and how that affects group accomplishments. With positive leadership actions taken, with the fostering of positive collaborative cultures and environments, and with intentional determination on the leader's part, the improvement work begins and is sustained. To portray these important findings in another way, the top right quadrant in Figure 4.4 demonstrates the power of focused work on establishing collaborative time and spaces to increase all students' learning and being an active participant in that work.

Operating norms are critical to embedding the behaviors noted above in systems and schools. Figure 4.5 displays examples of these positive norms of engagement that must be consistently reinforced as the way of doing daily business, in order to weather the personality storms that can gain momentum when adults exchange ideas about which they feel strongly.

FIGURE 4.4

The Relationship Between Commitment and Engagement in Leading Collaborative Learning

Engagement Level		
High	Barriers, roadblocks, some early, unsustainable success, unlikely to try again, unfocused	Infectious enthusiasm, team interaction, hard work ensuring success, sustainable focus on the process and improvement
Low	Process breakdowns, inertia, blame game	Contagious verbal support, social interaction, little actual "doing the work"
	Low	High

Commitment Level

FIGURE 4.5

Sample Staff Norms of Engagement and Empowerment

Everyone's voice is important. We listen respectfully. We reflect on our work as we learn with and from each other.

- Being respectful in our engagement builds strong working relationships that led to empowerment.

In collaborating, we empower our own learning and the learning of our colleagues. We build learning capacity together.

- Collaborating authentically builds confidence and success.

We persevere. We believe all students can learn and all teachers can teach with impact given the right time and support. We believe in our interdependence to achieve student Learning Goals.

- Having shared beliefs and understandings about student achievement guides our work.

It is critical that the principal and teacher-leaders model these operating norms of engagement because doing so, using Collaborative Learning strategies, leads to empowerment of all participants. A leader's integrity, transparency in intention, action, and communication are vital to building trust and strong working relationships to make a difference for all students.

The takeaway from the notion of having operating norms in place is the importance of the leader's personal attitude. Every single behavior noted by team members will be under microscopic scrutiny by even the most ardent supporters. Co-created group norms to which everyone subscribes and is responsible to maintain are critical elements to ensure school teams can learn together bringing creative, multifaceted solutions to Collaborative Inquiry questions that lead to their own sense of empowerment. This thinking is expertly captured by our colleague Theresa Meikle.

Practical First Steps
Enabling Collaborative Inquiry

The following vignette offers a few very practical first steps in embedding an inquiry stance, as Meikle so eloquently points out above.

In our school, the principal (P) and vice principal (VP) provide ongoing structures to support collaboration. Working with the literacy teacher-leader to set a vision that is aligned with the School Improvement Plan (SIP), the leadership team is

- creating connections and goals that relate to school data in easy-to-understand terms;
- "massaging" the timetable to provide grade-level teams with weekly job-embedded co-planning time;
- having the literacy lead teacher cycle through a Collaborative Inquiry model, which means checking in every six weeks on each team's progress and sharing strategies being tried by other teams;
- gathering an inventory of Professional Learning (PL) needs that emerge from the meetings to plan for resources or guest speakers to be brought in (when budget is available) to build the collective capacity of the teaching faculty;
- attending the inquiry sessions as observers and supporters as teachers guide the work and direction;
- encouraging the notion of FAIL FAST, where teams learn quickly from mistakes or where observations do not support original hypotheses and then just as quickly move to the next iteration of the action plan design;
- celebrating early successes with the teams;
- reporting progress toward goals at full staff meetings as data and evidence are gathered;
- leading the whole-school celebrations of all accomplishments; and
- ensuring documents, templates, and resources are made accessible to all through a shared network drive.

Tania Sterling, EdD, 2014

We especially endorse FAIL FAST thinking in the above Collaborative Inquiry process. It relates to our assessment-in-action and highlights the importance of mid-course corrections in any process. Nothing is so debilitating as spinning wheels and building bridges to nowhere. The role of the teacher-leader in this vignette is that of a bridge-builder who is a key learning partner across the entire staff team.

The Strong Case for Accomplished Teacher-Leaders in Every School

Depending on the jurisdiction, school leadership teams have added a critical player—the teacher-leader—who may be called a literacy leader, an instructional coach, a master teacher, or by some other term. In addition to having recognized teaching expertise, adding this role to the leadership team offers the principal opportunities to learn alongside the teacher-leader about high-impact assessment and instructional strategies that work in all classrooms. We know that teacher-leaders must be knowledgeable about teaching and learning and must be seen to be "partners in learning" alongside other teachers (Planche, 2010a). Appendix F lists guiding questions to help leaders and teacher-leaders develop leadership teams with all members operating from the same reference points.

Skills-Based Selection of Teacher-Leaders Matters

Teacher-leaders must be carefully selected. Teacher-leaders are highly influential members of school leadership teams because they are recognized by their peers as

- exhibiting skill in instruction and assessment,
- being valuable to them as professionals,
- being passionate about ongoing learning,
- having strong interpersonal skills,
- being good listeners,
- having strong communication skills,
- having high energy and being enthusiastic about being part of collaborative teams,
- being open to learning, and
- being committed to taking action with others.

It is clear then that selecting the "right" teacher-leaders from the beginning makes a difference. For teacher-leaders to become truly influential stakeholders, they need support in their development to understand and to model for others by

- examining their own and the practice of others reflectively;
- honing their own assessment and instructional skills while supporting and modeling for their peers; and

- working with teachers as co-teachers using self-, peer, and teacher assessment processes with learning partners as this improves both student achievement and teacher efficacy (Hattie, 2009).

Becoming knowledgeable about the impact of various collaborative approaches is important information for school leaders with or without positional power.

Knowledge of Collaborative Strategies Matters

Table 4.5, on the next page, displays our survey participants' ranking of the perceived impact of a selected sample of Collaborative Learning strategies.

Table 4.5 shows that our respondents have strong perceptions regarding the impact of these high-yield strategies used by leaders in schools. Some of these strategies more than others will deliver forms of "data" that will be beneficial in promoting rich dialogue about practice to increase all students' achievement. "Which ones" and "how do you know" would be rich conversation starters.

Data That Matter

We believe that the most important artifact on the table for Collaborative Learning with staff is knowing the impact through agreed upon evidence of student learning. Data Walls, student work samples, video clips, observations, anecdotal notes, Running Records®, purchased assessment tools, and teacher-prepared assessments are all valid documentation of student learning that can be catalysts for rich, often controversial, conversations. They are vital to deepening our learning and in moving the work from theory about learning to informed actions that improve learning in every classroom.

There are many Collaborative Learning processes a principal and the leadership team may use to mobilize learning. Leaders who are skilled in facilitation approaches and in using learning protocols (see Appendices G and H) are better positioned to move purposeful

TABLE 4.5

Perceived Impact of Collaborative Strategies

Collaborative Strategy	Percentage Reporting Very Impactful or Impactful (rounded)	Percentage Reporting No Experience With Strategy as Yet
Co-planning, co-teaching, co-debriefing, and co-reflection cycle (Inquiry Process)	86%	8%
Professional Learning community with a clear learning focus	86%	5%
Professional Learning network with a clear learning focus	81%	8%
Team teaching (planning/co-teaching among grade partners)	80%	9%
Collaborative assessment or moderating student work	76%	12%
Staff Coaching	75%	9%
Learning Walks & Talks	60%	28%
Critical Friends Study Group	51%	30%
Instructional Rounds	49%	34%
Japanese Lesson Study	44%	39%
Online Professional Learning community	46%	18%

conversation to informed action. We highlight four high-impact strategies that promote rich conversations in schools about teaching and learning: (1) Case Management Approach, (2) Learning Walks and Talks, (3) Instructional Coaching, and (4) Collaborative Co-Teaching. And yes, the first two are parallel to system leadership learning structures discussed in Chapter 3, because these high-impact strategies work at every level to put the FACES of students on the data.

1. The Case Management Approach

The Case Management approach is two-pronged: Data Walls and Case Management Meetings. You can't say you are strategically putting FACES on your data if you are only doing one of the two prongs.

The School Data Wall

Data Walls have existed as far back as there have been walls with blackboards in staff rooms. For us, the modern-day explosion of Data Walls began in Ontario and continues as we write (Sharratt & Fullan, 2012, p. 80). Every school leader and every classroom teacher must be able to define the data that represent their students' growth and achievement in multiple ways. Data Walls are most optimal when they are paper-based, concrete, visual, and tangible as shown in Figure 4.6 on the next page. An evidence-proven discussion that permits knowing and moving each FACE to explain growth and discuss next steps for instruction is invaluable. Data Walls need to be documentation, not decorative wall paper. The precise purpose is to create a space for dialogue among all teachers and leaders. It is a physical and inescapably visible space in which to know each student of concern or in need of extension so that no student is ever missed. Students of concern who are struggling, stuck, or needing extension are brought, one at a time, to a Case Management Meeting.

An Integrated Case Management Approach

This a regularly time-tabled 15–20 minute opportunity for any classroom teacher to bring forward any student either from observations resulting from the Data Wall conversations or from classroom assistance sought in a supportive forum. At the table, additional professional experience may be provided by the teacher-leader, specialist teacher(s), and the principal. Attendance at the table will vary depending on the student brought forward and the supportive colleagues available. Bringing the student's work as evidence of the instructional issue that the teacher is having ensures the meeting is only about instruction. The collaborators offer one instructional approach; the teacher agrees to try it (for at least three weeks to give it an honest

FIGURE 4.6

The School Data Wall Provides the Content for Rich, Collaborative Discussion About Each Student's Instructional Need

Source: Photo by Lyn Sharratt, March 31, 2015. John Paul II Catholic College, Parramatta Diocese, NSW, Australia.

opportunity to work) and to report back in a defined period. We use a secondary school Case Study example here to make our point about the clarity and power of the Case Management Approach in knowing and instructing all the FACES.

Nagle College is a systemic Catholic all-girls secondary college located in the Western Suburbs of Sydney, Diocese of Parramatta, Australia. The community is diverse. It is a school with students from over 70 different cultural backgrounds, a wide range of socioeconomic situations, and highly varied learning needs. It is this diversity of learning needs that highlights the requirement of teachers to know each individual student as a learner. It is this knowledge that is key to the development of successful instructional strategies to assist in the promotion of learning progression and success for every student.

Case Management at Nagle College is building collective teacher capacity and improving student learning outcomes in their secondary school context. At Nagle College, Case Management has provided a collaborative forum that has reinvigorated and reshaped the way teachers reflect on and develop instructional strategies. It is through the development of the capacity for instructional intelligence that teachers are better able to meet the learning needs of *all* the FACES in their classrooms.

The first step in Case Management should be described more as a "leap." Not because it is impossible, rather because it often feels overwhelming for classroom teachers, that is, knowing and owning all the FACES in a classroom. With class sizes between 15 and 30 students (Key Stages 4 and 5) and 20 to 25 students (Key Stage 6), this may feel like an unachievable challenge for many teachers. However, *through the implementation of student Data Walls, developing a "picture" of each student as a learner, and using selected literacy and numeracy data, this task becomes much more realistic for a classroom teacher. There is now a concrete link for teachers between data and individual student development as a learner.* Within the context of Nagle College, the "unpacking" of relevant literacy and numeracy data has been essential in identifying students who are plummeting or stuck in their learning within a specific area. It is from these data sources that the instructional coach engages in consultation with past and current teachers of the student to gather additional information and data on their learning progress in the classroom. *It is through this two-way process of data collection and consultation that classroom teachers are able to experience the significance of knowing each and every student as a "learner."* Building on this knowledge and understanding, the Case Management process can now shift its focus to working collaboratively with teachers to develop specific instructional strategies to meet the needs of the identified learners. The success of encouraging teachers to own all of the FACES in their classrooms is highlighted by the number of teachers now approaching the instructional coach with concerns about specific students who are underperforming or not making progress in an area of literacy and/or numeracy.

At this stage of the Case Management process, the focus has shifted from investigating the student's learning progress and needs, to critically examining how those needs can be met through specific instructional strategies. *Through a series of three 20-minute fortnightly meetings, up to four classroom teachers work collaboratively to critically reflect upon student learning progress (in the*

(Continued)

(Continued)

identified area of need), current instructional strategies used, and the develop-
ment of specific instructional strategies to assist in progressing student learn-
ing in the identified area. The Case Management model has reinvigorated and
refocused many teachers by giving them a common language and structure to
deconstruct and evaluate their practice.

Specifically, the Case Management model has required teachers to clearly articulate the learning context, Learning Goal/Intention, Success Criteria, and Descriptive Feedback given to students during learning activities. This is essential in ensuring that there is clear, skill-focused learning taking place in each and every classroom, and for every student. In addition, using the Gradual Release of Responsibility Model (Vygotsky, 1978) provides teachers with the structure and language to construct and implement specific instructional strategies for each and every student in their classrooms. At Nagle College, the implementation of the Gradual Release of Responsibility Model within the context of Case Management is supporting the creation of a more open and student-centred dialogue amongst teachers about *how* different instructional strategies can be implemented to support learning successes for all our students. As a result of the collaborative and targeted instructional strategies, we have seen learning improvement and success within the targeted area for various individual students. *An unanticipated impact of the implementation of the Case Management Approach has been its capacity to impact more widely on school-wide teacher practice.* That is, as more and more teachers engage in the Case Management process they are exposed to a model that encourages them to critically reflect on the relationship between every student's learning and their instructional practice. *It is in this reflective and collaborative environment that teachers continue to develop a broader knowledge and understanding of high-impact instructional strategies that can be modified and implemented across all learning contexts.* At Nagle College, Case Management is beginning to have a broader impact on first-wave teaching and instructional practice through the development of teacher instructional intelligence in a collaborative, yet individualized learning context.

Amanda Newell, Instructional Coach, supported by Delma Horan,
Principal of Nagle College, Diocese of Parramatta, NSW, Australia

2. Learning Walks and Talks

In Chapter 3 we described the power of Learning Walks and Talks as a strategy for system leaders. It is as powerful in all schools as school-based Walks and Talks allow all staff at a school to

- know and observe their learners,
- note places where expected practices are occurring,
- buddy-up teachers who need more support,
- plan for ongoing Professional Learning, and
- see patterns and trends over time.

Sharratt has been working on whole system improvement with system and school leaders, consultants, and teachers in the Diocese of Parramatta for nearly three years. The diocese has adopted these three high-impact strategies: Data Walls, Case Management Meetings, and Learning Walks and Talks. She has trained every system leader and every school principal, and, as a result, the strategies are evident in every school. Their data have shown improvement that has never been seen before. As Executive Director Greg Whitby and Deputy Executive Director Sue Walsh say, "These three strategies are the learning center of our work and have become the knowledge engine that drives continuous improvement in teaching and learning to new heights for all our teachers' and students' benefit."

The expressed energy and enthusiasm says it all. There is time to make room for collaboration when staff, parents, and students are actively involved in clearly articulating and owning their learning—together.

3. Instructional Coaching

System leaders look to their cadre of specifically skilled collaborators, such as literacy coaches, curriculum consultants, and specialist teachers, when planning to embed improvement actions. An instructional coach is a valuable asset; those who can approach colleagues with sensitivity and inviting dispositions are soon welcomed into teacher-leader learning conversations. Collaborative Learning with a "knowledgeable other" has its advantages and its cautions. Dr. Jim Knight's insightful book, *Unmistakable Impact: A Partnership Approach for Dramatically Improving Instruction* (2011), clearly outlines the elements of impactful instructional coaching. Working from what he calls "partnership principles" (Knight, 2011, p. 28), effective coaches become partners with administrators and teachers to support change processes. Instructional coaches have expertise in quality teaching practices, such as assessment that improves instruction, and often in particular subject areas. They are highly sought-after to share that knowledge. Instructional coaches model practices in the classroom, work alongside teachers, and engage in supportive learning conversations. One of the important takeaways from reflecting on instructional coaching is that good coaches have learned to

- resist rushing in to solve the problems of others,
- help others to solve their own problems,
- listen actively,
- respond reflectively, then
- support and partner (adapted from Knight, 2007, 2011).

When voice, choice, and respectful listening are evident while working with an instructional coach, teachers are more likely to feel a sense of partnership as professional equals, which helps to keep an important sense of efficacy intact (Knight, 2007, 2011). Effective coaches listen as much as speak or suggest. They focus on assessment that gives teachers information to differentiate instruction the very next day for all learners. Partners discuss learning, dialogue together to make good decisions, and give each other feedback that increases learning for all involved—including learning for the instructional coaches. Principals and coaches must realize the time commitment needed and what a partnership approach entails. They have to balance that investment of time against the return in higher student achievement and the increased depth of teaching capacity.

4. Collaborative Co-Teaching

We have moved well beyond traditional notions of **team teaching** that included the work a special education teacher might have done with a classroom teacher in the service of individual students (Scruggs, Mastropieri, & McDuffie, 2007). Today, however, we emphasize level playing fields for all collaborators involved in co-work and co-teaching. Co-teaching can take many forms, including what is further described as 4 Cs co-work in Chapter 5. The goal of a partnership approach to co-teaching is to become focused on the collective impact that teaching has on student learning and thinking. The important factor to remember in implementing a Co-Teaching Cycle is to find release time to support staff in this kind of learning together. Time to plan, teach, debrief, and reflect together is critical to having successful experiences.

In essence, co-teaching works as follows:

- pairs of teachers working as co-teachers first assess their student data together;
- as co-teachers, they would co-plan a lesson and determine what aspect of his or her teaching practice each would like to improve through constructive feedback from the partner;
- co-teach the lesson using video to observe that part of their practice each wants to improve and to look for evidence of student thinking;
- co-debrief after the lesson; and
- co-reflect on the learning of students and their own learning from the experience in order to plan for next steps.

The inquiry process within the Co-Teaching Cycle allows for deeper conversations about student understanding of concepts and weaves in assessment as a core component of the learning. Before the lesson, participants question their assumptions of what prior knowledge they think students have. During the lesson, the teachers observe students' thinking. After the lesson, they debrief their own assumptions from the observed evidence and reflect on their inquiry question about an aspect of improving practice in order to inform their next steps. As our vignette describes below, co-teachers learn to

- value colleagues and their contributions,
- listen respectfully to others,
- refrain from judgment,

- reflect on improving their practices,
- become intentional in trying to understand student thinking and learning, and
- share learning across the system.

In their Co-Teaching Inquiry Cycle that follows in the vignette below, two Australian middle school mathematics teachers have discovered that

Teaching Collaboratively + 46 Students +
a Problem-Solving Challenge = A Great Results Guarantee.

Co-Teaching Inquiry in a Mathematics Classroom

After teaching Year/Grade 6 Mathematics for a number of years, we were keen to reverse a trend where our students generally underperform on an external test, the International Competitions and Assessments for Schools (ICAS) assessment, involving nonroutine problems. We had exposed students to many different types of routine and nonroutine problems but had never provided a structured program before. We planned a more explicit model of delivery and a team approach for planning, teaching, and evaluating. Then we started: with two teachers, 46 students, an open classroom, and a desire to improve our students' problem-solving skills.

The first obstacle was to effectively organize our students. At our school, Ballarat Clarendon College (BCC), mathematics classes are usually grouped for instruction. Our classes were from the upper and lower ability sets; the middle group was not involved. When Dr. Lyn Sharratt first mooted the idea of co-teaching the Year 6 classes, our reaction was hesitant because of the disparate ability levels and approaches to learning in our classes. As we discussed the possibilities, though, we saw there could be some advantages in bringing the two classes together.

Our goal was to improve our students' problem-solving efficacy. Major stumbling blocks for the more capable students were careless errors and overconfidence; while, for the less capable students, the difficulties lay in getting started on problems and then choosing an effective and efficient strategy for each problem type. We believed that by pairing students—one from each end of the cohort—we would expose less-capable students to a broader range of problem-solving skills and allow them to see a more competent problem-solver in action. More-capable students were then forced to slow down, to explain their processes, and to justify their choice of strategy. All students needed to be more reflective in their thinking processes. We promoted the use of checking strategies and developed a greater respect for the questions—particularly as the easier items were sometimes rushed and completed incorrectly.

Our Problem-Solving Co-Teaching Project operated Friday mornings for two terms. We started in separate classrooms then moved into the open classroom for an hour session, which began with a warm-up, minds-on question. Our 18-week inquiry was divided into four stages:

STAGE 1–Weeks 1–4: Compelling Problems

- We set up clear expectations (Learning Goals/Intensions) and protocols, and worked through a selection of compelling problems in pairs.
- One teacher led the discussion, drawing out the main concepts from the student pairs, sharing their solution process; the other teacher documented the main skills and understandings on an anchor chart.
- Individual reflection of progress was made by each student at the end of each session.

STAGE 2–Weeks 5–7: Number Review Modeling

- We looked at selected problems from the number strand, in a similar format to our first stage.
- Number was chosen because it is fundamental to all other strands; number is a key indicator of performance at the Year 6 level.
- In the final week, the whole cohort completed similar problems. We analyzed the results, comparing them to the 2012 Year 6 cohort as a benchmark. It also provided data about students' relative strengths in the other strands.

STAGE 3–Weeks 8–12: A Measurement, Number, Algebra/Pattern Focus

- We started with a Measurement focus, as data indicated that this was our students' weakest strand so the focus area in our parallel classes.
- In groups of three, students reworked their errors on each question.

(Continued)

(Continued)

- A similar process was followed using the number and then the algebra/pattern tasks.
- We expected students to follow our modeling from Stages 1 and 2 by reading the questions carefully, planning their response process, using checking strategies, and estimating to test the reasonableness of their solutions.
- Throughout this stage, as teachers, we operated clinics (guided, **differentiated instruction**) on specific skills—"just in time" teaching. Students were invited and in some cases co-opted to participate in groups limited to 10 students each time. We addressed a wide range of specific skills, such as transferring 3D shapes to a 2D elevation, moving between time zones, and so on.

STAGE 4—Weeks 13–18: Problem-Solving Status and Differentiation

- We introduced the idea of a problem-solving continua and discussed what a student's status may look like, at various places along the continua—a formative self-assessment process.
- Students solved a diagnostic problem set that was corrected as a whole class. We then prompted students to self-assess their position on the continua.
- We developed some broad headings of beginning, developing, competent, and expert, and co-constructed with the students the specific Success Criteria that could then be mapped along the continua.
- We sorted the students into four distinct groups according to their performance levels and their perceived status.
- Students were placed in groups of three, according to their needs and position on the continua.
- They were given appropriate tasks and level of scaffolding based on their recent performance, always knowing what their next steps to improvement were.

Key Lessons Learned From the Co-Teaching Inquiry Process

- Misreading the question is a significant issue for most students. Misreading is highly prevalent among the more confident mathematicians because of lack of care, and the less-capable students because of lower comprehension and vocabulary skills.
- Problem solving needs a context. It's more effective to discuss the strategies using well-chosen, compelling problems.

- Start with individual and independent problem-solving opportunities first. It's easier to work through questions after the students have already made their own attempt.
- Ensure students document their thinking during the problem-solving process and provide modeling about what the documentation could look like. Emphasize that diagrams and tables are particularly useful.
- Problem-solving strategies need to be explicitly taught. Students need to have a list of strategies that link to core mathematics skills and understandings, and be allowed to transfer their skills between routine and non-routine problems.
- Students need to have both the problem-solving skills and the basic mathematics skills to solve multistep problems. To develop these skills, students need explicit teaching, and opportunities for guided and independent practice.

In conclusion, we have been amazed by the benefits of our co-teaching experience. By working together we have shared a common language and developed what we feel has been a best-practice approach to the explicit teaching of problem solving. It has also been useful to have a third person to observe our teaching and to provide useful input during the class and feedback afterwards.

The third member of our team, Deputy Principal Jan McClure, was always available to answer our questions and extend our thinking toward the idea of a continua. Over time, with Jan's encouragement, our problem-solving sessions have evolved to include more teachers and students within our middle school setting.

We were very excited to celebrate our improved mathematics results with our students at the end of the first year of problem-solving sessions. After consistently achieving "At Below" State Level from 2006–2012, we have now achieved "At Above" State Level for Year 6 in ICAS for two consecutive years. Our Problem-Solving Co-Teaching Project is now in its third year and has been expanded to involve both Year 5 and Year 6 students.

Table 4.6 displays the Year 6 ICAS Results at BCC, showing a comparison between the number of correct questions achieved by Year 6 students and the state cohort in a similar time period.

We all attribute our success to the time we took to implement the Co-Teaching Cycle, staying true to each component (Sharratt & Fullan, 2012).

(Continued)

(Continued)

TABLE 4.6

Positive Results of Co-Teaching at Ballarat Clarendon College

ICAS Assessment	BCC Average	National Average	BCC-State differential
2012	19.4	21.9	−1.5
2013	21.2	18.8	+2.4
2014	22.3	21.2	+1.1

Hayley Graham and Caitlin Pohl, Teachers of Mathematics, and Jan McClure, Deputy Principal, Ballarat Clarendon College, Victoria, Australia; personal communication, May 29, 2015

Caitlin and Haley had common planning time during the school day to co-plan, then co-teach, and afterwards co-debrief and co-reflect together. Fortunately, they were and continue to be encouraged and empowered by Deputy Principal Jan McClure to embed the Co-Teaching Cycle to learn from each other. In many Leading Collaborative Learning situations, it is not that easy as time is an issue.

When Time Is an Issue, a System Leader or Principal Might...

Enabling time to collaborate is one of the most important considerations for principals and teacher-leaders in order to improve classroom practice together. Time management is both a school and a system responsibility as we have discussed previously in this text. Many systems have carved out useful collaborative working time from staff timetables by

- having early or late start days on a biweekly or monthly basis;
- time-tabling Professional Learning community (PLC) time;

- time-tabling common planning time for same-grade/subject teachers;
- hosting Professional Learning days, system-wide, that translate into site-based learning;
- using specialist teachers to provide time;
- providing occasional teacher-release days during the school year; and
- organizing flexible teacher-release time on a rotating basis.

It is clear that if systems leaders value capacity building through Professional Learning, they must find ways to support their principals so staff can learn to work together more collaboratively. As has been noted by many principals, another powerful and often under-utilized support for Professional Learning is a well-informed parent community. Leaders who keep their parent communities well-informed will support Professional Learning that is in the best interests of their children. We must clearly articulate the purpose of Collaborative Learning as a part of sharing our school improvement plans.

Finding ways of "making space" for embedded Professional Learning through teacher collaboration is the basis of an insightful report by the Rennie Center on Educational Research & Policy and Edvestors (2012). The report focuses on "Schools on the Move—Best Practice Research" highlighting five successful elementary schools in Boston, Massachusetts, USA.

Their effective practices included organizing time for teachers to work together, setting professional norms, and using learning protocols. Structural changes were not seen as sufficiently powerful in themselves to build strong collaborative cultures. Leaders in this study who could articulate a vision for a school culture that valued increased teacher voice and teacher leadership were especially influential (p. 9).

Teacher teamwork became a teacher-owned enterprise and was the key to improving student learning. While principals may share influence with teacher-leaders, school principals have the means to mobilize learning through resources such as time and facilitation assistance (Mobilize-ability).

In their meta-analysis, V. Robinson, Hohepa, and Lloyd (2009) analyzed international studies that made links between leadership and increased student outcomes. They stated that when school leaders promote or participate in effective teacher professional learning and development they have impact across a whole school, not just in one class (2009, p. 39). Their findings certainly reinforce the concept of the school leader needing to prioritize time to be the lead learner among many learners on staff.

Voices From the Field: A Case Study

The following case study is a good example of the impact of Collaborative Inquiry on changing school culture in a situation where the principal merged staff from two schools, building a new team to move learning forward in unison.

Leading Collaborative Learning at Fred C. Cook Public School, Simcoe District School Board, Ontario, Canada

Fred C. Cook Public School, in Bradford, Ontario, has a population of just over 400 as a result of a merger of two schools. The merger brought together 16 regular classroom teachers and 15 support staff, approximately 200 primary students, and 200 junior/intermediate students.

To build a collective understanding of student needs, three data sources (classroom observations, teacher voice, and assessment achievement data) were analyzed by the whole merged school staff. As a team, we began to note patterns and trends in all three data sets, and developed collective "wonderings" to promote inquiry as our mode of teacher learning.

Our Navigation Team further analyzed these results as well as teacher feedback from our whole school session. The larger, whole school inquiry or Theory of Action was then connected with this input and with the school board improvement plan. Our school inquiry question/school Theory of Action was "*if* we further develop our students' ability to monitor comprehension of texts in all subject areas with a special focus in mathematics, *then* students will be able to decipher important information and provide responses that directly relate to our question."

As a team, we identified the key strategies or essential practices that would need to be areas of focus for our teachers in order to address this inquiry question. These three strategies were

- diagnostic assessment to inform instruction and differentiation;
- "think aloud" strategies; and
- use of Learning Goals/Intentions and Success Criteria to identify purpose and support assessment "for," "as," and "of" learning.

Staff needed to consider these three strategies in developing their own inquiry statements. Overall evidence of impact would be determined through pre-, mid-, and post-assessments; teacher observation (by collecting artifacts of learning); and improvement in larger system and provincial assessments.

A Collaborative Inquiry process was implemented to

- validate teachers' own wonderings in the focus area,
- provide for cross-grade and division learning,
- model differentiation, and
- continue to build collegial relations in our newly merged setting.

It was believed that a Collaborative Inquiry structure would more fully engage teachers in the process as they owned the question and would therefore be more actively engaged in an inquiry process as they sought solutions/answers.

The Navigation Team shared with the staff our overall "if, then" statement and together we developed essential practices that were most relevant to addressing this goal. Teachers completed a survey and based on the survey results, "formative feedback to support assessment 'for,' 'as,' and 'of' learning" became the school-wide Professional Learning area of focus for teachers to develop their related inquiry question. The other key essential practices (Learning Goals/Intentions and Success Criteria, modeling through "think alouds" and differentiated instruction) continued to be addressed/supported through our monthly staff meetings.

Once teachers created their inquiry questions, cross-grade and division groupings based on commonalities in the questions were formed. Three collaborative groupings were created: (1) Feedback through consolidation; (2) Documenting and using Descriptive Feedback for assessment "for" and "as" learning; and (3) Descriptive Feedback through problem solving.

(Continued)

(Continued)

In the initial inquiry learning sessions, teachers shared their question with the group, identified the reasoning for their question, and determined the Professional Learning (PL) needed to help them in their inquiry. Together teachers planned a lesson and a teacher from each group modeled the lesson in his/her classroom while the team observed student learning. During the debrief, observations and questions were identified to further address the focus area and to reconstruct the lesson. During PL sessions, teachers worked through the artifacts collected by moderating work, and by listening, observing, and dialoguing about what was working and what the challenges were. Each artifact was to represent the evidence of impact along each teacher's learning journey. The final PL session for the school year was used to

- reflect on the learning process,
- further assess needs based on the focus area, and
- plan the sharing of the work with teaching colleagues at our final staff meeting.

Through this whole group sharing session, new imperatives were identified for building coherence and consistency in our building. Teachers self-assessed their needs in these areas to identify next steps for their learning and to support learning in their classrooms, which enabled us to move forward with our school improvement plans for the following school year. Throughout the inquiry process, the ongoing monitoring of our actions occurred through this shared process.

By developing a shared responsibility for student learning, our school staff members were able to move forward with their own learning needs while working collaboratively. Success enabled us to further build consistency and coherence in our building in support of student learning. The biggest challenge to this process was and is sustainability. Staff involvement and ownership of the process were key to its success and sustainability. It helped to re-assure teachers that the work could and would continue with or without the same administrator providing direction.

In this case, I did move on from this school. The practices were well established and built on effective collaborative processes that could be continued because our staff members shared leadership accountability. As with all learning, time is another factor. Time is needed to work together, to implement, and to see the overall impact of the process on student growth and achievement.

As a current principal supporting several schools through the collaborative process, I draw on this learning experience daily. The key lessons that I reflect on are

- assessing where staff members are in terms of a Collaborative Learning culture,
- modeling curiosity and inquiry as a co-learner,
- valuing and honoring student and teacher voice while developing a shared responsibility for student learning,
- providing opportunity for varied teacher inquiries within a larger focus area, and
- establishing cross-grade/division learning groups.

These collaborative actions helped us as a school move from good to better and to continue to work toward best.

Tina Delaire, School Effectiveness Principal,
Simcoe District School Board, Ontario

Applying Our Theory of Action

The most important step in collaboration is to move from assessment data and planning to informed (or considered) actions with strategic reflections and adjustments built into the work. What really matters is the intentionality of both the considered actions and the follow-through actions resulting from the reflections and adjustments.

If we apply our Theory of Action for Collaborative Learning with its four elements to a whole school approach, a school leader working with teacher-leaders would consider the following process: assessment focused on planning; planning focused on responsive action; action focused on negotiating meaning; and consolidating meaning and assessing impact to refine or revise, and to learn.

Figure 4.7 is a look at our Theory of Action through a lens of integrating Co-Planning, Co-Teaching, Co-Debriefing, and Co-Reflecting.

FIGURE 4.7

Theory of Action for School Leaders Working Alongside Teacher-Leaders

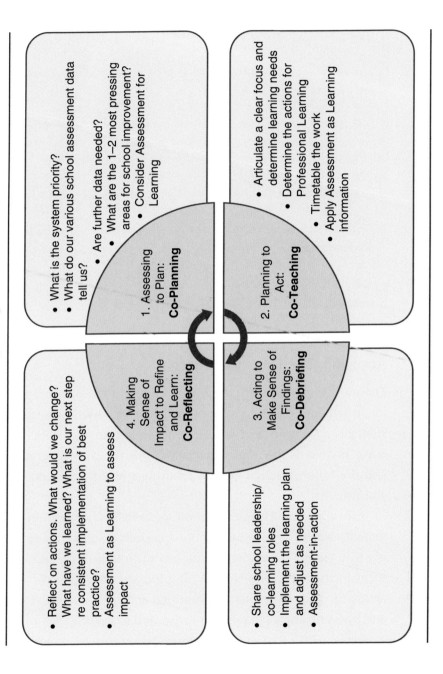

1. Assessing to Plan: Co-Planning
- What is the system priority?
- What do our various school assessment data tell us?
  - Are further data needed?
  - What are the 1–2 most pressing areas for school improvement?
    - Consider Assessment for Learning

2. Planning to Act: Co-Teaching
- Articulate a clear focus and determine learning needs
  - Determine the actions for Professional Learning
  - Timetable the work
  - Apply Assessment as Learning information

3. Acting to Make Sense of Findings: Co-Debriefing
- Share school leadership/co-learning roles
- Implement the learning plan and adjust as needed
- Assessment-in-action

4. Making Sense of Impact to Refine and Learn: Co-Reflecting
- Reflect on actions. What would we change? What have we learned? What is our next step re consistent implementation of best practice?
- Assessment as Learning to assess impact

The Impact of Collaboration on Student Learning

The impact that school leaders working alongside teacher-leaders can have is profound. Collaborative Inquiry leads to different kinds of conversations and actions (M. Robinson et al., 2010). Both teaching practice and student outcomes improve when Collaborative Inquiry is aligned with individual student achievement results that become school improvement goals.

For example, Sharratt has been working in Diocese of Parramatta for three years directly with secondary English coordinators, principals and assistant principals, superintendents, and central office staff in a collaborative project that focuses on improving practice together. Specifically, they learn what is needed to embed high-impact assessment that drives instruction in reading, writing, and critical thinking skills across all content areas (Parameter 13). Impressively, the following learning gains have been experienced in Grade 9 when leaders and teacher-leaders share practice and collaborative inquiries together. Writing gains in Grade/Year 9 have exceeded the New South Wales' results by +11.60; Year/Grade 9 Literacy scores have exceeded the NSW's results with a gain of +6.70; and Year/Grade 9 Reading results have gained +4.90 over NSWs.

As a summary, in this chapter we believe:

1. Schools where teachers are encouraged to work across curriculum departments, with a focus on critical thinking and problem solving, have increased student achievement.
2. Student achievement is accelerated in a culture of Collaborative Learning.
3. The work of the leader and teacher-leader is to build collaborative processes centered on student work as evidence that will open conversations, change practice, and increase students' achievement.
4. School leaders working alongside teacher-leaders understand and bring together collaboration and increased student achievement efforts as being a reciprocal process that demands implementation together.
5. Leader and teacher collaboration regarding assessment practice is predictive of achievement gains in both reading and mathematics (Ronfeldt, Farmer, McQueen, & Grissom, 2015, p. 506).

A Pause for Reflection

Trust is a dichotomy within any school Collaborative Inquiry team. It is both a critical by-product of generating Collaborative Inquiry and an integral foundation to generating thoughtful action. Building and sustaining trust is a leader's key to initiating and continuing the life of the Collaborative Inquiry community, and to applying the findings that will enhance individual classroom practice enabling higher student achievement. Why? Because trust allows team members to believe that they can be themselves, can "think out loud" without fear of recrimination, and can trial the findings of inquiry in their classrooms with support from their colleagues. The level of trust translates into the amount and level of interaction in the group. Social trust is one level, contractual trust another, but relational trust is the most important as a catalyst for Collaborative Learning (Bryk & Schneider, 2002). Without trust, people lose focus easily and attention is diverted away from learning (Mitchell & Sackney, 2000).

> "You must be willing to listen and learn together. No losers in this process. We learn by doing and supporting actions that are built on trust."
>
> Research survey participant

Matrix Themes 7–8

Table 4.7 highlights the next two non-negotiables. They speak to strong relationships as foundational to Collaborative Learning and solutions to the issue of finding time to work together.

Looking Ahead

School leaders create and influence the conditions for teacher-leaders to work effectively with their peers. In Chapter 5 we discuss the importance of Leading Collaborative Learning as it applies to teachers working alongside teachers to improve student learning.

TABLE 4.7

Implementation Matrix of the Seventh and Eighth of the 10 Non-Negotiables of Evidence-Proven Collaborative Learning Practices

Evidence-Proven Practice	Modeled Collaborative Learning	Shared Collaborative Learning	Guided Collaborative Learning	Interdependent Collaborative Learning	Beneficial Professional Learning for Those Who Lead Collaborative Learning
Key Theme 7	Includes	Includes	Includes	Includes	Includes
Strong relationships are foundational in building a positive learning culture	• being approachable and inclusive • demonstrating a positive, growth mindset	• intentionally distributing leadership opportunities	• negotiating, navigating, and influencing when needed	• investing in his or her own learning and the learning of others	• developing emotional intelligence • being culturally responsive

(Continued)

TABLE 4.7 (Continued)

Key Theme 8	Modeled Collaborative Learning: Includes	Shared Collaborative Learning: Includes	Guided Collaborative Learning: Includes	Interdependent Collaborative Learning: Includes	Beneficial Professional Learning for Those Who Lead Collaborative Learning: Includes
Evidence-Proven Practice					
Creative solutions are needed to mitigate the problem of time together	• modeling optimism that solutions can be found • mobilizing resources to support learning	• sharing the resource of time equitably • encouraging others to share ideas and work together	• influencing and guiding opportunities to work together through strategic time-tabling	• being intentional in terms of whole school, cross divisional, and grade approaches to collaboration • developing a school ethos of co-learning • writing and sharing a thought-provoking Case Study about school improvement, so that others can learn from it	• coaching and mentoring regarding creative time-tabling • developing strong organizational skills • using new technologies to enable new, powerful, and collaborative approaches for learning (Sharratt, 1996)

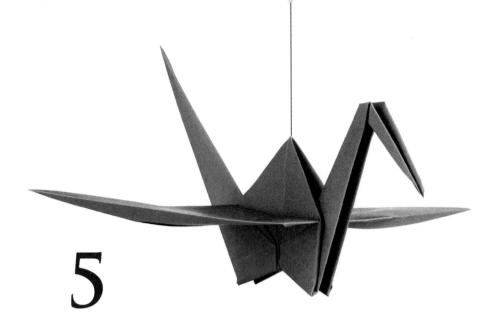

5

Teachers Working Alongside Teachers

"He who dares to teach must never cease to learn."

Richard Henry Dann

Unstructured and Structured Collaboration

Essential to developing a cohesive and coherent learning culture is paying attention to the distinctive characteristics of, and differences between, informal, collegial peer interaction and the planned, measured activities within Collaborative Learning structures. It is common practice for teachers to informally share ideas about resources, to share unit plans, to discuss how to solve student management issues, and how to better communicate with parents. For generations, school hallways and staff rooms have been places where teachers have shared experiences and good ideas—before, between, and after classes.

Informal contacts build relationships and can help to solve problems. These outcomes are positive in so many ways but together are a haphazard and undependable, and at best, only a partial solution to system improvement. Without losing the personal contacts and informality, more strategic and systematic opportunities to learn together are required to move a system or school beyond the comfortable status quo to make impactful, sustainable changes in teaching practice and learner outcomes.

> "Collaborative meetings with peers are, in my opinion, the missing piece in educational reform efforts. Schools with strong collaboration processes in place tend to be the most successful and have high teacher efficacy rates."
>
> Research survey participant

The purpose of an intentional learning structure is to provide a safe venue for co-constructing new knowledge, deepening shared understandings, making adjustments, and otherwise refining practice to improve the quality of teaching decisions and their impact on student learning. Our research participants had thoughtful insights about the value of inquiry as one form of structured collaboration (or learning structure) including that the work itself involves negotiating the subtle nuances of understanding and meaning. Observing students working together and understanding what to look for in student work samples or portfolios that are reflections of students' thinking are crucial drivers for staff learning together. Teachers become thought-leaders through the interpretation of classroom observations and student work samples by

- inquiring into practice as peers,
- sharing knowledge as reflective colleagues, and
- mentoring or coaching each other.

In previous chapters we have spoken about distributed leadership in Collaborative Inquiry processes saying that distribution of leadership must go beyond the principal, vice principal, and teacher-leaders.

All teachers can become leaders in their own classrooms, and many become informal leaders within their schools via participation in collaboration. It is a catalyst for the emergence of many new teacher-leaders who, as team members, are thinking about improved outcomes for all students. Collaboration is a powerful way to deepen educator capacity, to increase the total value of the professional capital in the school, and to harness the power of the collective.

As Hargreaves and Fullan (2013) suggest, an optimal way to support and motivate teachers to build professional capital is to create the conditions where they can be successful day after day—involved in structured collaborative work in schools as well as across and beyond school systems. When the right conditions are in place, teacher leadership emerges. Those conditions include

- focusing on the FACES of individual students (Sharratt & Fullan, 2012),
- building a culture of trust,
- being open to dialogue,
- supporting professional relationships, and
- putting structures in place to allow teachers to work together.

Shared ownership of the outcomes (a positive culture) and the infusion of skilled collaborators ("home grown" via intentional learning structures) are factors that develop strong team work. One of our research participants noted that teachers change their practice when they are supported to take risks to try more effective teaching strategies. They become better teachers and step-up as grounded leaders with their peers. A double win.

> *"A co-learner approach is key. We are learning together to better meet our students' strengths and needs."*
>
> Research survey participant

The complexity of classroom teaching speaks to genuine skill domains that need to be developed (Yates & Hattie, 2013). When leaders make site-based Collaborative Inquiry possible, teachers are engaged deeply if observations, assessment, and analysis are purposeful and guided. As teachers work together with a clear student learning focus in mind, skillful instructional knowledge can be brought to the surface and refined (Ontario Ministry of Education, 2010, 2014b).

Changing the "What" in Learning Conversations

Collaborative Learning through inquiry also changes the nature of learning conversations. A report by M. Robinson et al. (2010) for the Consortium for Policy Research in Education highlighted school perspectives on Collaborative Inquiry in 13 New York City schools. The three-year study of both elementary and secondary schools summarized that principals who promoted shared decision making enhanced teacher participation in Collaborative Inquiry (M. Robinson et al., 2010, p. ii). Most importantly, the process of inquiry resulted in qualitatively different kinds of conversations between and among teachers—conversations that indicated an intention to take action to address student learning needs. Robinson found that when the work of inquiry was aligned with school improvement goals, it became more focused and productive (p. ii) through rich conversation. Crucial to this work was the leadership that provided the conditions for success, such as protected time to work together, a classic example of providing the structure mentioned above, and Mobilize-ability, as described by Sharratt and Fullan (2012).

We discuss four strategies below that we know teachers working with teachers and leaders use to produce collaborative conversations that lead to changed classroom practice and all students' learning: (1) Case Management Approach, (2) the 4 Cs Model, (3) Observation Inquiry, and (4) Collaborative Assessment of Student Work.

1. The Case Management Approach

The growth of teachers as leaders through structured Collaborative Inquiry is essentially what has been defined as one form of "site-based" teacher leadership development. Danielson (2007) acknowledges that the development of site-based teacher leadership generates a renewed interest in Professional Learning and this interest sets the stage for deeper forms of collaboration. In previous chapters, we have discussed many forms of job-embedded (or site-based) co-learning that promote learning conversations: Data Walls, Case Management Meetings, Learning Walks and Talks, and the Co-Teaching Cycle. In the following, administrators Mike Sutton and Kylie Morris have used the Case Management Approach (Sharratt & Fullan, 2009, 2012) as a strategy to create a collaborative culture. They not only put FACES on their data, but through that also develop a focused culture of collaborative conversations that leads teachers to action through empowerment, and leads teams of teachers to ownership of all students' growth and achievement.

Our FACES boards have been levers of change in strengthening a Collaborative Learning community at Rototuna Primary School, transforming learning conversations across the school.

Our school is organized in year-level teams with four or five classrooms at each year level, from Year 1 to Year 6. Each week, teams meet to discuss the teaching and learning of focus students—those students who are not achieving at the expected levels. The FACES boards shape the team's discussion of the progress and learning of their focus students. The FACES boards are the team's action plan, outlining specific Learning Goals for each student with the commitment to accelerating learning for focus students.

Each teacher shares evidence of how their focus students are progressing. Explicit teaching strategies and ideas are discussed and shared collaboratively among the team. This contributes to the acceleration of learning for students, as well as to growing the knowledge and pedagogy of teachers. All teachers in the team become instructional coaches, sharing what has worked, what hasn't, and suggesting what to try next.

The team leaders bring their FACES boards to the senior leadership meetings each fortnight, where evidence of progress and achievement of focus students across the school is shared with colleagues on the senior leadership team. This is another forum where we talk openly and honestly about instruction—what works and what doesn't. Colleagues often take successful instructional strategies that have been shared in this forum back to their teams and discuss whether these could support all students—necessary for some, good for all.

(Continued)

The Case Management Approach to FACES boards and rich conversations that follow in meetings is embedded at teacher, team, and senior leadership levels across the school, creating a Collaborative Learning environment focused on individual student learning, progress, and achievement.

Mike Sutton, Principal, and Kylie Morris, Deputy Principal,
Rototuna Primary School, Hamilton, New Zealand;
personal communication, May 18, 2015

> "Create the conditions: (1) time for the learning, (2) the needed resources (print and human) to support the learning, (3) clear expectations regarding classroom follow-up, and (4) at least four learning opportunities to build a habit of mind."
>
> Research survey participant

This powerful example of Leading Collaborative Learning and Empowering Excellence by teachers, with teachers, and alongside leaders sets the gold standard for co-laboring as inquiry. This collaboratively planned inquiry process at Rototuna Primary School results in greater precision in selecting the instruction that is needed for each FACE in the school, as shown in Figure 5.1.

In addition to the Case Management Approach, there are three additional inquiry processes that inspire learning conversations. The 4 Cs Model, Observation Inquiry, and Collaborative Assessment of Student Work are excellent examples of Professional Learning that give opportunities to lead Collaborative Learning.

2. The 4 Cs Model

A "4 Cs day" is an intensive Professional Learning day (Planche, 2012a). The process is called 4 Cs because it involves teacher-leader participants from across several schools gathering at one school to work together to co-plan, co-teach, co-debrief, and co-reflect. The purpose of the 4 Cs model is to

FIGURE 5.1

Data Boards Inspire Collaborative Conversations About the FACES

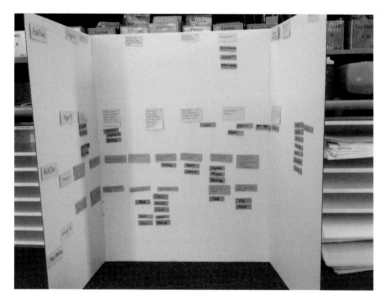

Source: Mike Sutton, Principal, and Kylie Morris, Deputy Principal, Rototuna Primary School, Hamilton, New Zealand.

- build collective capacity in instruction at the school level,
- build teacher leadership to continue to lead this work at the school level, and
- build equity and excellence through system-wide sharing of expertise among teachers.

A 4 Cs day is Professional Learning for teacher-leaders who then replicate the process with teachers in their own schools. Although the headers are the same and the outcome is similar in focusing on changing classroom practice, it is different than the Co-Teaching Cycle described in Chapter 4. In that case, two teachers co-investigate an instructional concern through the Co-Teaching inquiry cycle. *The focus here in the 4 Cs day is building collective capacity of small groups of teacher-leaders who then lead the process in their own schools.* The key difference is that there is not necessarily a specific issue to resolve at the school; the program is designed to assist participating teachers to become more effective practitioners and to foster the building of a positive culture within each school. Both processes ultimately aim to increase all students' learning through building teachers' collective capacity to teach all students.

The following describes a 4 Cs process.

A Typical 4 Cs Model

This is not a one-day program, but ideally is repeated four times per year with a group of four to six teachers participating, with the host site rotating among their schools. The following vignette describes a typical 4 Cs co-work day, specifically focusing on Mathematics. The process involves a "knowledgeable other" assisting with facilitation, and principals and vice principals are invited to participate as co-learners—not as observers. Their involvement and modeling as co-learners sends a message that making time available to find and share the most powerful ways to teach all learners is important work that makes a difference!

Phase 1: Co-Planning

This is a joint planning process in which all participants plan and "own" the lesson planned. This builds confidence in the plan and removes any basis for judgment.

("See, I told you it wouldn't work!" suddenly becomes a nonviable response within the group.) Teachers will take risks and move out of their comfort zones if they feel they will not be judged but instead will be supported by colleagues.

Phase 2: Co-Teaching

The teacher from the host school is the lead teacher in the classroom with a co-teacher from the group while one or two other co-teachers assist. One takes on an "insider view" to watch individual students and gather evidence of student thinking during the learning experience; another has an "outsider view" to watch the dynamic flow and cognitive demands of the lesson plan across the whole class. Ideally, the whole lesson is recorded digitally for viewing and discussion together later.

Phase 3: Co-Debriefing

Debriefing time includes collective discussion regarding participants' hypotheses and assumptions about what would happen in the teaching experience. After reviewing student work samples from the lesson, questions might include: (1) Were we successful in establishing clear Learning Goals from the curriculum expectations; co-constructing Success Criteria with students; giving Descriptive Feedback; anticipating where students might struggle? and (2) What did we observe that surprised us? For example, extra pairs of adult eyes in the classroom observing how students were processing a big idea in Mathematics might offer valuable feedback for the teachers and ignite insightful professional dialogue about the necessary next steps for instruction.

A typical 4 Cs day would have participants co-plan and then co-teach for about 50 minutes in the morning. After lunch, they would co-debrief and then for 30 to 40 minutes plan again, incorporating adjustments to the lesson based on the analysis of the first round of teaching. Finally, they would return to teach the lesson again to a new group of students with roles as before.

Phase 4: Co-Reflecting

After the second round of teaching, time is set aside to process and consider what has been learned as a group, and what participants can take back to their own schools from their learning to share with their colleagues there.

Commitments are made to repeat the 4 Cs process at the home school with local teacher colleagues. Another date is set for the collective 4 Cs day learning "hub" with each school acting as host during the year. Because it is iterative, the 4 Cs Model offers a "comfortable" and safe Professional Learning environment that can deliver very real gains in changed teacher practice through deep learning conversations (Planche, 2012a).

The benefit to Professional Learning from the 4 Cs day is that leaders and teachers "practice the practice" together. A key discovery is that there may be significant areas of Mathematics content knowledge, for example, that need to be clarified for staff as well as for students. *One critical learning from observing 4 Cs days is to never underestimate the role of a skilled "knowledgeable other."* That role must be flexible as it changes from that of coach to consultant, to collaborator, to facilitator, and to participant depending on what is required in the moment. And it is so that they can become "knowledgeable other" facilitators at their own schools, that it is important to invest in sending some teachers to learn the 4 Cs process together as shown in the vignette.

> "The 4 Cs pedagogy involved a true reflection of the Assessment 'for' Learning process as we mucked about a lot with Success Criteria and when they should be developed. Oral feedback to students was frequent and ongoing during our 'mind-on activities' and helped develop the teachers' understanding of its effectiveness. The student was really empowered through this process by the use of peer feedback."
>
> Principal, York Region District School Board, Survey Participant, in Planche, 2012a

At the school level, teacher-leaders who have experienced the 4 Cs hub days can work with logical groupings of classroom teachers or subject specialists on school-based 4 Cs days. Release time becomes less of an issue if classes are managed together, but it is still an issue to be handled. Teachers have reported that this process creates a team atmosphere where taking risks, engaging in meaningful reflections, and setting personal as well as team-wide professional goals becomes common practice.

One principal, whose teacher was involved in the 4 Cs program, reported that once trust was established, the process was incredibly powerful among the teachers from the four schools involved. It allowed teacher-leaders to take the learning back and tailor it to their own context. The lesson plan model developed in co-planning was helpful to shift thinking and practice to a Collaborative Inquiry approach. Teachers' co-teaching encouraged risk taking as everyone was viewed as an equal contributing member because they had planned together and all owned the outcomes. The use of student evidence of work resulting from the lesson in the co-debriefing was a powerful objective review of lesson impact on students' thinking that informed next teaching steps.

The following reflection demonstrates the use of the 4 Cs approach in an Early Years project and shows how easily it transfers to other grades and subject areas.

We asked our research participants to consider the importance of supports for teachers working through an inquiry process with peers. Table 5.1, on the next page, reinforces the importance of a non-judgmental approach, and time to work together and practice.

"The most effective learning experience I have had in 20 years of teaching. It pushes teachers to the proximal zone of learning, slightly out of comfort level, and you re-evaluate your teaching practices in a safe and supportive environment. . . . teaching in pairs or triads provides scaffolding and safety."

Teacher, York Region District School Board, Survey Participant, in Planche, 2012a

One teacher-leader commented on the impact that observing a Kindergarten (K) class learning experience had had on a Grade 2 teacher. Until that point, the teacher had been hesitant to give up her old ways of teaching. After one lesson as observer in the K classroom, she commented on the joyful, engaged learning that had prompted students' meaningful talk. The team co-planned another lesson, this time with the Grade 2 teacher as host. The invitational learning stance of the 4 Cs framework led to new insights regarding how students learn best across the K–2 continuum. The Grade 2 teachers agreed that watching a lesson that they had collaboratively planned allowed them to see student learning through a different lens. "At first we were nervous to allow others into our classroom but once we had gone through the process, we quickly realized it's not so much about the teacher as it is about seeing and hearing how learning is or isn't occurring with students."

Deborah Sinyard, Former Curriculum Coordinator, York Region District School Board, Ontario, Canada

TABLE 5.1

Considering Learning Supports for Teachers

Supports for Teachers	Percentage of Respondents Who Strongly Agreed or Agreed Regarding the Importance of Supports
A non-judgmental approach to learning	97%
Time to work with peers during the day	96%
Opportunities to practice	95%
Being a participant in inquiry	94%
Having an inquiry approach modeled	91%
Seeing exemplary practice	88%
Watching a video of a Collaborative Inquiry process in action	64%

Table 5.2 displays many collaborative processes that can provide rich conversations and focus on students' FACES through co-work. Any of them could be the focus of a 4 Cs day.

TABLE 5.2

Examples of Collaborative Learning Processes

1. Co-analyze the interpretation of learning expectations or curriculum content standards.
2. Co-moderate student work to apply and understand learning expectations or curriculum content standards (see #4 below).
3. Co-plan assessment strategies.
4. Co-plan teaching responses to student data.
5. Co-observe students doing a rich performance task to observe/determine students' thinking.
6. Co-analyze evidence of student understanding.
7. Co-plan and discuss Descriptive Feedback to students on a piece of work.
8. Co-design modifications to program for exceptional students.
9. Co-research appropriate technology to integrate into program planning.
10. Co-learn using an online environment and a variety of digital tools.

3. Observational Inquiry

Tonya Ward Singer shares her reflections about the impact of another collaborative process known as **Observational Inquiry** below. While contexts differ, the goals are similar to those of the 4 Cs process, and the positive impact of creating trust is the same.

The fourth process that creates valuable learning conversations is the collaborative assessment of student work.

Observational Inquiry (OI) is a powerful process that engages teachers in collaborating to test and refine strategies by observing multiple lessons in a year in each other's classrooms (Singer, 2015). It may sound like a simple process to launch; however, *building trust for peer observation* is an essential first step. Observing a lesson together is a big step for many teams, as teachers in most schools only collaborate after school hours and rarely watch one another teach. Build trust and buy-in for teams to step into classrooms together using the following tips. (Note: This is essentially the protocol for OI as practiced by Singer.)

- **Be sincere about fear.** Brainstorm together the worst-possible outcomes of observing together and notice the universal fears that emerge. Create norms together that honor those fears and create safety for team observations.
- **Choose a focus that matters.** Engage teachers in identifying a challenge in their practice that they especially want to solve, and use that as the reason for observation inquiry.
- **Use a non-evaluative protocol.** Observers watch to gather descriptive evidence of student learning, not to evaluate the teacher. Use a protocol to keep conversations centered on impact, and ask each other: "what can we as a team do to refine our approach?"
- **Model risk taking.** The host teacher teaches the first lesson the team plans and observes.
- **Honor imperfection.** When a lesson doesn't go as planned, teams have the richest conversations. Don't rob yourself of this experience by structuring or rehearsing lesson elements to the point of predictability. Invite imperfection so that together you can dare to push the edge of what is possible for students—and yourselves.

(Continued)

(Continued)

Impact on Student Learning

Shifting teacher practice and personal professional expectations are important and ultimately only matter when the end result is elevation of student learning. [Note: This is italicized as we appreciate Singer's statement because it highlights the intent of this book.] Every observation inquiry team tracks student achievement using local measures specific to their problem of practice and team goals. Two specific examples of impact follow:

At one K–6 school, teacher teams engaged in Observational Inquiry with a focus on elevating academic conversations among linguistically diverse learners. For pre- and post-data, teachers tracked students' discourse skills and expression of academic ideas. Across the six months that teachers engaged in the OI process, students gained on average 1.5 points on the 4-point **rubric**. This reflects a shift from many students being silent in classrooms, to all students engaging in academic dialogue with peers every day. This reflects also a shift from a heavy reliance on teacher scaffolds to increased student independence with more sophisticated conversation tasks.

That same year, administrators and teacher-leaders who engaged in Instructional Rounds (City, Elmore, Fiarman, & Teitel, 2009) at the same school also noticed a significant increase in students' active participation in academic conversations across all grades.

At another school, where a second-grade team focused on elevating student achievement with tasks about multiple-meaning words, specific to a state literacy assessment, teachers used pre- and post-assessments to measure the impact of their OI work on student learning. Few students could do the pre-assessment even with the teacher reading the task aloud; the majority passed the post-assessment independently. The second graders across all three classrooms also scored higher that year on the state assessment than any second-grade class in the history of the school.

Teachers also reported that as a result of their shared focus on student engagement during their OI lessons, their students who had initially struggled with simple pair-share processes were all engaged in ongoing dialogue during daily lessons to make claims, justify thinking, and agree and disagree agreeably.

Tonya Ward Singer,
Author and Consultant, California

4. Collaborative Assessment of Student Work

Moderation of learning through collaborative assessment of student work helps teachers to develop deeper and shared understandings of curriculum expectations or achievement standards as they apply to instruction. Potential collaborators include grade partners, literacy and/or numeracy leads, special education teachers, and classroom teachers across subject areas and grades. The teacher-leader's or principal's role in this process is to facilitate the moderation to ensure that, during the process, participating teachers learn how assessment informs differentiated instruction when all have a common understanding of **leveled work**.

The principal's role includes finding resource time to work together, then listening, questioning, observing, and participating as a co-learner. A guiding question for this work is, "What feedback about our teaching does the work sample give us as teachers, and what Descriptive Feedback can we give this student to help with the next steps in learning?" As Hattie (2012) outlines, the most effective teachers gauge the success of their teaching on how well their students are learning and take this as powerful feedback about the effectiveness of their teaching. We add that effective leaders gauge the success of their leading by how well their teachers are teaching and their students are learning and take that as powerful feedback about their leading. Given constructively, Descriptive Feedback can change not only learning conversations but also classroom practice. Hattie (2015b) strongly maintains that for collaboration to make a difference it must focus on evidence of student learning and on understanding what impact the teaching has or not had. Ultimately, teachers and leaders need to

> "An inquiry 'habit of mind' or inquiry stance is cultivated when educator learning is evidence based. It must be an active process anchored in problem-based situations that emerge daily within classroom settings."
>
> Research survey participant

understand how to best change classroom practice so that all students can achieve expected levels of growth each school year.

If collaborative assessment of student work takes place on a regular basis and several teachers share samples of student work at each session, program coherence is strengthened and consistency of practice across classrooms is more likely (Sharratt, 2014).

Collaborative assessment of student work leads quite naturally to opportunities to plan formative assessment and consequent instructional strategies together. The key to developing the culture of trust to support this kind of co-learning is to keep the focus on the student work samples and not permit teachers to begin to feel that assessing the student work is critiquing their work. Establishing and referring back to group norms when necessary keeps conversations on track. Sample norms for collaborative assessment of student work include

- beginning and ending on time,
- listening respectfully,
- seeking to understand and to have clarity first—withholding judgment,
- challenging ideas not individuals, and
- keeping the focus on student learning.

(See Appendix B for a suggested process to establish collaborative norms.)

At times, challenging questions will arise, especially if moderated student work reflects variations in teacher understandings or interpretations of specific curriculum expectations or achievement standards. The process of collaborative analysis of student work not only reduces these potential variations mentioned, but it also works to establish assessment literacy, cultivate a culture for inquiry, provide excellent examples of Descriptive Feedback to students, and foster a sense of collective responsibility and accountability, which leads to a desire to repeat the process or engage in similar collaborative and sharing processes.

Learning Protocols as Scaffolds to Successful Collaborative Inquiry

Meaningful changes in schools are contingent on the discussion and co-work that evolves through learning processes such as Collaborative Inquiry (Donohoo, 2013). As important as facilitators are to engaging team members in discussion, protocols can be important frameworks for those discussions. Easton describes protocols as "processes which help groups achieve deep understanding through dialogue" (2009, p. 1). Protocols integrate guidelines for conversations based on agreed-upon norms of engagement, provide a series of steps or structures that facilitate the dialogue, and ensure that the process advances in a timely way. As protocols often specify roles that different participants will play, they are very useful as new learning groups are formed, especially when participants do not yet know each other well. The protocol defines the parameters of engagement, meaning participant behavior is controlled for negativity, which should encourage authentic participation by everyone. There are many protocols available in print that can serve different kinds of collaborative endeavors. See Appendix G for a sample protocol for developing a Collaborative Learning experience.

Challenges to Overcome

There are four major challenges to the Collaborative Learning processes that we have discussed.

1. **Time.** A 4 Cs co-work day, for example, involves following a process while practicing together. One practice round does not make for sustainable change. Ideally, participants in the leader training sessions or in their own schools would benefit from at least four opportunities per year for intensive 4 Cs work with time between sessions to practice areas of assessment, instruction, and integrating technology. Balancing the need for training with time concerns, the full-day 4 Cs experience has been modified successfully to be both a half-day experience and a multiday experience. In some schools, team members are

motivated so they find time to complete reflective conversations after school or during shared preparation time. Participants find ways to circumvent the time management difficulties to make Collaborative Inquiry processes work when they have learned to value them.

2. **Facilitation.** A good facilitator moves conversation along, especially if there is a learning protocol to support the discussion (see Appendix D). If the facilitator is also knowledgeable in the subject area under study, her impact can be considerably multiplied. Most would agree that learning experiences are enhanced by skillful facilitators; however, they are not always available or affordable. Investing in training for teacher-leaders to facilitate co-work and co-learning processes is time and money well-spent as teacher-leaders being on-site resources are likely to want to use their learning to the benefit of their own school, colleagues, and students in their schools.

3. **Absence.** Over time, leader absence from Professional Learning or from involvement in collaborative processes clearly indicates the work being done by teachers and teacher-leaders is not valued. If administrators are present as co-learners, their involvement is a very tangible measure of support and an indicator of being valued. Participating in co-learning as a lead learner moves the learning forward by focusing attention on the importance of the work and its results and in this way, it strengthens the learning culture.

4. **Fear.** In the coaching work Planche and Sharratt are doing with teachers using Collaborative Inquiry and **inquiry-based learning**, one theme recurs regularly. It seems that any change including those to professional practice releases anxieties, or causes some to feel fear. Rather than simply acknowledging these as givens, there is another option for leaders or facilitators. Fullan (in personal communication, January 2013) says to go toward the danger and investigate the reasons for fear of change. They often surface as fear of failure. Empathy, perseverance, and patience are needed but, at times, courageous conversations are in order (Abrams, 2009). For many, this is best unpacked by keeping the focus on what data reveal about student growth and achievement, not the quality of the anxious teachers' work.

Employing a collaborative approach to the moderation of student work defuses the fear and focuses the conversations on what instructional practices are recommended to bring each student along (Knight, 2013). For those in fear of failure or of making changes to undifferentiated teaching practices, for example, the resulting discussions of specific pedagogical change are easier when they are perceived to be supportive of co-learning and when leaders use a coaching stance within a school culture that authentically supports changing practice.

Creating safe environments for "practicing our practice" together is beneficial for all concerned. Negotiating meaning together and working to align our actions with our espoused values is a powerful, positive experience that underpins sustainable change. Consider the four elements in our Theory of Action to ensure that co-learning experiences move from a Collaborative Inquiry process to being applied in practice.

Applying Our Theory of Action

Figure 5.2 shows how to *integrate* a co-learning stance into each element of our Theory of Action.

A Pause for Reflection

Co-learning requires a growth mindset and a confidence that by working together we learn more than we learn on our own. A culture of open doors and collegial sharing underpins co-learning and is a good starting point for all schools. Co-learning, when teachers work with teachers, is collaboration at its best because they are charged with responsibility for their own learning and that of their peers such that they can improve their practice to ultimately improve student achievement and well-being. City and colleagues state that students are not likely to take risks, collaborate, learn together, and experience higher-order tasks unless their teachers are doing so (City et al., 2009, p. 174).

FIGURE 5.2

Theory of Action for Teachers Working Alongside Teachers

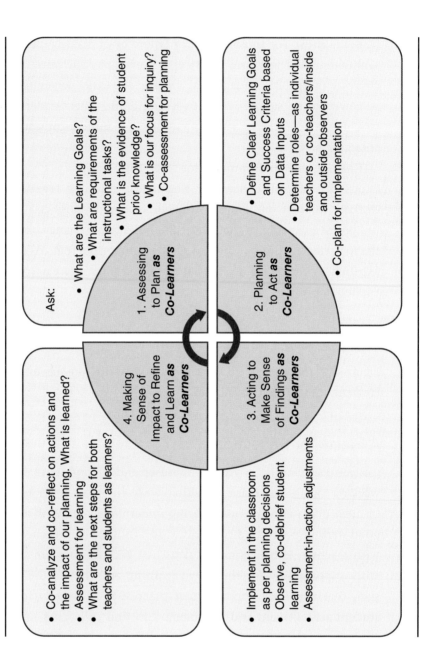

Ask:

- What are the Learning Goals?
  - What are requirements of the instructional tasks?
    - What is the evidence of student prior knowledge?
      - What is our focus for inquiry?
        - Co-assessment for planning

1. Assessing to Plan *as Co-Learners*

2. Planning to Act *as Co-Learners*

- Define Clear Learning Goals and Success Criteria based on Data Inputs
  - Determine roles—as individual teachers or co-teachers/inside and outside observers
    - Co-plan for implementation

4. Making Sense of Impact to Refine and Learn *as Co-Learners*

- Co-analyze and co-reflect on actions and the impact of our planning. What is learned?
  - Assessment for learning
  - What are the next steps for both teachers and students as learners?

3. Acting to Make Sense of Findings *as Co-Learners*

- Implement in the classroom as per planning decisions
- Observe, co-debrief student learning
- Assessment-in-action adjustments

The Impact of Collaboration on Student Learning

Analyses of survey and interview data from teacher-leaders provides further evidence that "collaboration among teachers paves the way for the spread of effective teaching practices, improved outcomes for the students they teach, and the retention of the most accomplished teachers in high-needs schools" (Berry, Daughtrey, & Wieder, 2009). Sixty-four percent of the respondents to the Teachers' Network survey said that they joined their local collaborative networks primarily because they "wanted a professional community" of other teachers with whom to exchange ideas and best practices for their classrooms.

This is certainly reflected in the work we do with systems and schools. For example, North Queensland Region (NQR), Australia, has focused on all students' learning by bringing teachers and leaders together to work collaboratively with system leaders on intentional capacity-building in assessment and instruction. Their laser-like focus on increasing all students' achievement through collaborative structures has paid off. They collect data regularly as feedback on how they are progressing. In comparing results from 2014 and 2015, the number of students achieving level 8 (expected level) or better by the end of kindergarten/Prep has increased by an additional 862 students; the number of students achieving level 16 (expected level) or better at the end of Grade/Year 1 increased by 774 students; and the number of students in Year/Grade 2 achieving level 20 (expected level) or better increased by 470 students. NQR leaders and teachers know that increased collaboration ensures that teachers support each other to change practice and students learn as a result. Thus we believe that the following can be stated:

1. When teachers set Learning Goals and Success Criteria when co-learning, they model their own classroom contexts and consciously improve student learning.

2. Collaborative Learning for teachers builds a sense of collective efficacy and the shared belief that students can and will be successful (Klassen & Durksen, 2012).

(Continued)

(Continued)

3. Increased trust and professionalism among teachers is an outcome of building professional and social capital through collaborative work (Hargreaves & Fullan, 2013).

4. When collaborative forms of deep learning, such as Collaborative Inquiry, are developed with other teachers and evidenced in every classroom, students learn.

5. When teachers learn alongside other teachers by solving dilemmas in teaching and learning, students' increase in achievement is measurable (Planche, 2012b).

6. When teachers change practice together, students learn (Sharratt, 1996).

7. Teachers who work in collaborative cultures improve their confidence and well-being by having their voices heard and valued, by setting focused and achievable goals, and by engaging in dialogue around both content and process (adapted from Fink & Markholt, 2011).

Matrix Themes 9–10

Table 5.3 outlines the final two non-negotiables, which address the importance of focus and foundations of trust and safety.

Looking Ahead

In our final chapter, we consider the new frontier and focus on teachers working with students, teachers learning from students, and students working with each other.

TABLE 5.3

**Implementation Matrix of the Ninth and Tenth of the
10 Non-Negotiables of Evidence-Proven Collaborative Learning Practices**

Evidence-Proven Practice	Modeled Collaborative Learning	Shared Collaborative Learning	Guided Collaborative Learning	Interdependent Collaborative Learning	Beneficial Professional Learning for Those Who Lead Collaborative Learning
Key Theme 9	Includes	Includes	Includes	Includes	Includes
A focus on student work and growth helps to keep collaborative work on track	• using student evidence to determine areas for professional co-learning	• being responsible to and accountable for data analyses and results • ensuring that data are displayed transparently and are visible (Data Walls) so all can own all the FACES • researching and formulating responses to data	• staying the course when distractions surface—and being able to articulate the "why" of staying on course • offering feedback to help move learning processes forward	• integrating many voices and choices into learning discussions • building commitment to take action on collective next steps	• knowing how to analyze data • practicing the moderation and assessment of student work samples together • knowing how to give and get Descriptive Feedback and taking action • training in conducting Learning Walks and Talks and having open to learning conversations • teaching teachers how to differentiate and personalize assessment and instruction to teach every FACE in every classroom

(Continued)

TABLE 5.3 (Continued)

Evidence-Proven Practice	Modeled Collaborative Learning	Shared Collaborative Learning	Guided Collaborative Learning	Interdependent Collaborative Learning	Beneficial Professional Learning for Those Who Lead Collaborative Learning
Key Theme 10	**Includes**	**Includes**	**Includes**	**Includes**	**Includes**
Deeper forms of collaboration for both students and educators are built on a foundation of trust and safety	• being sensitive to the learning needs and strengths of others • making learning for teachers and leaders visible and explicit	• being inclusive in the collaborative approach • valuing learning by including the contributions of all participants	• becoming skilled in establishing norms for engagement • using protocols for learning to focus conversations in a timely way	• being specific in connecting prior and evolving knowledge as learning efforts unfold	• developing working norms and using learning protocols • coaching for teams who work together to build trust and strong relationships

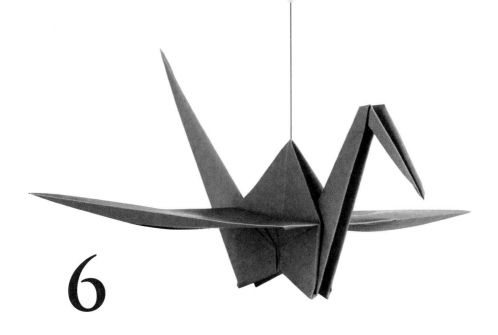

6

Teachers and Students Working Alongside Each Other

"Example is not the main thing in influencing others. It is the only thing."

Albert Schweitzer

John passed by his colleague's Grade 7 classroom and stopped briefly to watch the interaction. Student desks were not in rows but in groupings. Three students were at the whiteboard writing questions, and other students were huddled in twos and threes at computer and tablet screens. Many were standing, talking animatedly; they were engaged. He could see students had organizers or tablet/notebooks with them. John looked for the teacher, spotting him seated with two students. It was very apparent that the teacher was as engaged as the students—listening to a small group of students as they discussed something on the computer screen. He watched as his colleague moved to sit with another group. Whatever the class was working on, everyone was very "into it" and John thought maybe even excited about their work. He had to ask his colleague about the work his students were doing. Walking back into his own rather quiet classroom, John looked at his students—working alone on pages in their notebooks. John hoped his colleague had time to talk after school. "Getting kids out of their seats and working together is powerful," he enthused, albeit with the trepidation that comes from not knowing how to proceed. "I want to make that one of my Professional Learning goals for tomorrow."

Teaching Is Evolving

In this chapter we propose to answer the questions John should ask about setting the stage for the work he saw, and then fostering that work to its successful conclusion for each class and students. We know that moving from John's style of teaching—stand-up recitation—to a Collaborative Learning style is not an easy or an overnight change. It is dependent on setting the classroom "stage," "atmosphere," or learning environment similar to our discussions for creating Collaborative Learning environments for system leaders, school leaders, and teachers. So, now we shift our attention to the critical impact Collaborative Learning environments have on our students and how to get there. In the process, we will discuss learning approaches such as cooperative learning, Collaborative Learning, authentic learning, project-based learning, and what has to be in place within the classroom culture to enable the shift from classes like John's to where we all want to be.

> An important aspect of quality teaching at all levels is the ability to shift from Collaborative Learning at the staff level to leading and partnering with students in experiencing Collaborative Learning as co-work in classroom.

Knowing how to organize age-appropriate work along the cooperative to collaborative continuum is an important aspect of good first teaching (aka quality teaching) in all classrooms beginning in the

Early Years. Partnering with students begins with modeled, shared, and guided activity and moves toward independent decision making (Gradual Release of Responsibility [GRR]—as defined in Chapter 3) as students mature and become experienced in collaborative endeavors. As we have stated previously, Collaborative Learning approaches in the classroom are better understood and executed by staff who themselves are working in a culture that is open to co-learning. So let's begin by breaking down Collaborative Learning approaches in the classroom for John.

What's the Difference? Cooperative Learning, Collaborative Learning, and Co-Learning

The characteristic qualities of cooperative learning and Collaborative Learning are really a continuum of constructs. Whereas *cooperative learning* can be defined as a set of processes and structures that help people interact to accomplish a determined outcome of working together, *Collaborative Learning* is a way of learning and interacting with people (Panitz, 1997). It will not have a predetermined outcome for the group or the individual. A positive cooperative learning process, using TRIBES agreements (Gibbs, 2014) for example, can enhance both cooperative and collaborative work, as attentive listening, appreciating the input of peers with no put-downs, having the right to pass, and modeling mutual respect can help

"The qualities of co-operative learning and Collaborative Learning are really a continuum of constructs. Whereas cooperative learning can be described as a set of processes and structures that help people accomplish a determined outcome together, Collaborative Learning is a way of learning and interacting with people."

Panitz, 1997

to build strong cultures for learning along the continuum. When the class is fully immersed in the cooperative or collaborative mode with individuals and groups producing new knowledge from their research inquiries, they will generate information that is new to each other and to the teacher. Co-learning was in action at the point when John watched the teacher discuss with students what they have learned. Co-learning demands that teachers respond to the new learning in a manner that shows they have learned from students and students have learned from each other. Teaching is evolving as educators include more intentional facilitation of Collaborative Learning— activating deep learning processes and partnering with students as co-learners (Fullan, 2014).

In a Collaborative Learning culture, students feel safe to think, wonder, create, ask questions, examine multiple perspectives, and build on each other's ideas. We see Collaborative Learning as having moved beyond simple engagement to empowerment, and that cooperative and Collaborative Learning co-exist and complement each other on the continuum. Figure 6.1 depicts the integrated relationship among three powerful constructs that are foundational to deeper

FIGURE 6.1

An Integrated Relationship for Deeper Learning

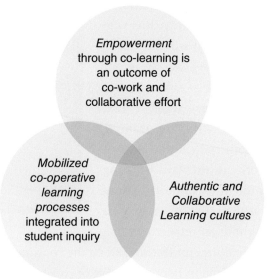

learning: (1) Empowerment through co-learning, (2) Mobilization using co-operative learning processes, and (3) Enhancement through authentic and Collaborative Learning cultures.

Authentic Collaborative Learning Matters

It's not good enough for John to have his students working on questions in their notebooks or on worksheets, even if they are working together. Part of his learning will be how to make the projects, inquiries, and questions relevant to his students using curriculum expectations as a vehicle to uncover learning and to provide fuel for having grand conversations (**Accountable Talk**—see Glossary).

There is significant and valid evidence regarding the importance of collaborative processes for students, which indicates that students learn more deeply and perform to a higher standard on complex tasks if they have had the opportunity to engage in authentic learning experiences (Darling-Hammond et al., 2008; Panitz, 1997; Zeiser, Taylor, Rickles, & Garet, 2014). *The Study of Deeper Learning: Opportunities and Outcomes—Evidence of Deeper Learning Outcomes* found that students who attended participating high schools that were part of a particular network where deeper learning processes were intentionally integrated performed better on international PISA Testing for Schools (Zeiser et al., 2014, p. vi). The report indicated more positive interpersonal and intrapersonal outcomes for students compared to students who attended non-networked schools. Graduation levels and enrollment in four-year post-secondary institutions were also higher (Zeiser et al., 2014, p. vi). Sampled network schools used a range of strategies to develop deeper learning competencies that included project-based learning, internship opportunities, and collaborative group work (p. 6). Similarly, *where environments are more conducive to supporting teacher collaboration, student learning seems to be positively impacted* (Belchetz, 2014).

Project-based learning is an inquiry-based approach to learning that integrates more authentic learning (Darling-Hammond et al., 2008). We define authentic learning as learning that is situated in processes

The following elements of co-learning are visible when teachers and students work together and are

- generating essential questions that spark curiosity and wonder,
- assessing/valuing "prior knowledge" to determine instructional starting points for each student,
- determining clear Learning Goals/Intentions from curriculum expectations,
- co-constructing Success Criteria,
- building relevant vocabulary and background knowledge,
- focusing on evidence of meaning and understanding,
- modeling "thinking aloud" as intentional teaching and learning,
- using the Modeled, Shared, Guided, Independent approach to differentiating instruction (Gradual Release/Acceptance of Responsibility—see Chapter 4),
- connecting ideas across the curriculum areas,
- actively engaging in learning,
- applying and transferring what is learned,
- giving and receiving Descriptive Feedback and following up to ensure sustained learning from the feedback,
- documenting/displaying student work as evidence of growth *and* achievement,
- sharing evidence of learning through student-chosen demonstrations of learning with authentic audiences, and
- celebrating big and small accomplishments of students and teachers learning together.

that are central to more than one subject area while being grounded and explored through real-world applications and problems that have multiple solutions. It is not enough to provide an isolated experience or a singular opportunity for students. To bring about deep learning, the planned experiences must be constructed and connected with sound assessment and instructional practices in mind to ensure all students can self-assess to learn and apply the new knowledge (Sharratt & Harild, 2015).

A strong example of this can be found in the Ontario Social Studies/ History/Geography Curriculum (Ontario Ministry of Education, 2013), which encourages students to develop concepts of disciplinary thinking—thinking like historians or geographers—while engaged in inquiries about real-world historical and geographical issues. Authenticity is also brought into the mix through intentional communication with a relevant audience (such as asking questions of Canadian astronaut Chris Hadfield via satellite communication) as a part of sharing some form of culminating work. Students choose the format that best represents their learning. You can imagine that if a project is not relevant, students will not take on the persona or fully adopt the voice required in the project.

Underpinning a dynamic classroom environment along the cooperative to collaborative continuum is a learning culture that enables and sustains relationships for deeper learning. Growing such a learning culture begins by establishing a climate for learning and the growth of relationships.

When the climate is right, teachers can create a learning culture for Collaborative Learning where

- the co-construction of knowledge thrives,
- risk taking and innovation are encouraged,
- groups of students may be researching many different questions,
- Descriptive Feedback to and from teachers and peers is sought, and
- student groups may be presenting their new learning "in voice" or personae they are not usually seen to be in.

The necessary culture is

- engaging and safe for all students;
- empowering and inclusive;
- about learning together—teachers and students, students and students;
- inquiry driven; and
- focused on social and emotional, as well as academic growth.

A continuum of developing a learning environment, illustrated in Figure 6.2, captures the big ideas in moving classroom learning spaces to enable collaborative co-learning.

FIGURE 6.2

A Continuum of Developing a Learning Environment

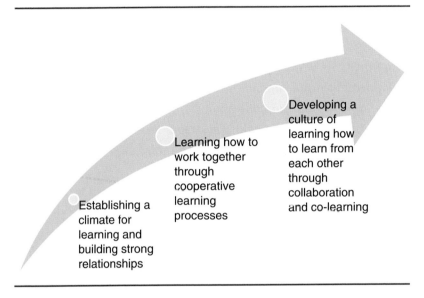

Developing a culture of learning how to learn from each other through collaboration and co-learning

Learning how to work together through cooperative learning processes

Establishing a climate for learning and building strong relationships

Constructing Knowledge Together

It is critically important to find ways to ensure that projects contain elements that enable students to believe that, while working on them, they are on the track to finding their own TrueNorth© with confidence (Sharratt & Harild, 2015). First, teachers must consider the nature of the learning tasks, and what learning processes would facilitate learning, as constructing knowledge together involves organizing, interpreting, evaluating, and synthesizing prior knowledge as well as merging new knowledge as they both apply to solving current and new problems (Newmann, Bryk, & Nagaoka, 2001). Second, the process must include rich performance tasks for students as a part of an inquiry-driven curriculum—tasks that are grounded in real-world authenticity (Darling-Hammond et al., 2008; Knight, 2013) and include

- a particular and clear focus;
- a meaningful context;
- cross-disciplinary connections;
- opportunities for critical thinking and collaborative problem solving;
- opportunities for innovation and creative thought;
- application of knowledge and skills;
- integration of disciplinary content and information; and
- skill and insight in communication, citizenship, and issues of social justice.

The teachers' quest must be to find ways to integrate academic rigor, using cognitively demanding performance tasks, at age-appropriate times to stretch all students' thinking, with learning processes that build interpersonal and interdependent learning.

Teachers as Stewards

Beyond creating the environment for Collaborative Learning and building the Learning Goals and Success Criteria for their projects, teachers, as instructors, facilitators, activators, assessors, resources, guides, and supporters of all students, are the *stewards* of successful experiences and deeper learning. As Fullan and Langworthy suggest, "the foundation of teacher quality is pedagogical capacity—teachers' repertoire and ability to form partnerships with students" (2013, p. 3). Teachers who understand the importance of deeper learning create opportunities for students to

> "Knowledge becomes most powerful when students can use information to gain deeper understanding of specific problems."
>
> Newmann et al., 2001, p. 15

- engage in work about topics that interest them,
- think critically about what they are learning and why,
- learn from different perspectives,

- engage in meaningful dialogue about discovery and investigation,
- build skills that develop growth mindsets about their own abilities,
- learn how to analyze their personal reactions to thoughts presented by peers and graciously communicate them,
- give and get constructive feedback that creates learning for other students and themselves, and
- utilize appropriate digital and social networks that reinforce that learning is a 24/7 reality.

The ultimate outcome in the classroom would be that each student is able to present her part of the project in authentic voice without anxiety that peers might react negatively to seeing her in a "different" voice. With those outcomes in place, stewardship comes alive.

Navigating Possibility While Avoiding the Rocks

> "It is becoming increasingly necessary for teachers to understand the ways in which their roles must change in order to accommodate some of the significant changes that have been bubbling under the surface for years."
>
> Todd Wright, International Consultant; personal communication, January 2015

Developing small-group work tasks for students is challenging. Research has identified three areas that must be addressed. They include developing

1. norms and working structures that allow students to work together and learn from each other,
2. tasks that are cognitively demanding and lend themselves to student cooperative work, and
3. appropriate strategies to deal with student behavior (adapted from Darling-Hammond et al., 2008).

John will want to carefully co-construct the Success Criteria with students for student interaction, analysis, and presentation quality, paying particular attention to equal participation and using shared resources in group work. An increasingly important responsibility is to help students *filter, assess, and value quality* available in the seemingly limitless arena of print and online information and activities. We do this through Descriptive Feedback. Using digital tools to actively research, analyze, apply, and communicate creates opportunities for group members to connect learning, to interact as learning partners, and to transfer growing understanding among the group members. However, feedback to students is critical in helping them to develop media literacy to

- distinguish between credible and non-credible sources,
- recognize bias and separate fact from opinion,
- select relevant or "so what?" source material, and
- learn particular skills, such as analyzing, paraphrasing, and summarizing.

There will always be a need for personal reflection and independent work to practice new work. Balancing classroom experiences with time for critical thinking and personal creative exploration is important. However, Collaborative Learning experiences can ultimately help students learn from their joint inquiries with peers about how to make better decisions, to become more critical consumers of information, and to better evaluate resources. Students learn to synthesize a great deal of information and become more innovative in their outcomes or learning products by working together.

With teacher facilitation, students can choose to demonstrate their Collaborative Learning or inquiries using a number of digital tool possibilities if they are relevant. It is critical that teachers facilitate the integration of digital literacy tools. Doing so gives students new ways to use their voices as a part of their culminating demonstration of learning, for example, using podcasts, videos, blogs, and interactive presentations. Giving students options as to how they present their thinking empowers both students and teachers. The benefits of *online learning* opportunities include

- creating authentic, real-world relevance,
- student-defined tasks and subtasks,
- complex tasks investigated over a sustained period of time,
- the inclusion of different perspectives,
- opportunities to collaborate,
- integration and application across different subject areas,
- integration of ongoing assessment (assessment-in-action) rather than artificial assignments to assess progress,
- demonstration of learning through development of valuable products, and
- multiple solutions regarding the culmination of the inquiry or project (adapted from Herrington, Oliver, & Reeves, 2003, and Sharratt & Harild, 2015).

As noted, the elements of authentic online learning above are virtually the same as those for any authentic, rich learning task.

Building a Classroom Culture Where Learning Thrives

Teachers set the tone in the classroom by believing in the potential of each and every one of their students. Those who cannot say with conviction that "All students can learn given the right time and support"—Parameter 1 (Sharratt & Fullan, 2009, 2012) will not yet have truly embraced the concept of a growth mindset (Dweck, 2006). Teachers who are able to build strong relationships with students, and who look at teaching from an asset perspective, build learning cultures where students learn to trust themselves and others. Table 6.1 is a sample of classroom teacher behaviors that build strong student learning cultures according to comments from our research respondents.

It is clear that in building strong cultures for learning, teachers need to be both skilled in understanding learning processes and in assessing the impact of their teaching on students' learning, that is defined here as how students feel about their learning, about how they learn best, and about their ability to learn. There is certainly an important relationship between the development of strong social skills, good character, and how one feels about learning and one's ability to learn (Fisher, Frey, & Pumpian, 2012; Glaze, Mattingley, & Andrews, 2013; Jensen, 2009; Sornson, 2001). As Hattie (2013) says, "Our job is to help teachers and leaders see the world through the eyes of the kids, and the great thing is when they do, teachers change."

TABLE 6.1

Classroom Teacher Behaviors That Build Strong Learning Cultures

Teachers

- set visible Learning Goals and co-construct Success Criteria that include students co-learning with other students;
- model mutual respect;
- encourage and provide multiple opportunities for student voice and choice;
- develop a culture of safety and risk taking;
- develop a culture of curiosity and wonder;
- create a culture of learning from giving and getting Descriptive Feedback;
- show concern for the whole student including their social, emotional, and academic success;
- are curious, open-minded;
- involve parents, students, and broader community partners in collaborative efforts;
- scaffold learning for students to be successful; and
- are intentional, articulate, and consistent about having high expectations for all.

Personalization and Differentiation Matters

Principles of **Universal Design** are meant to help educators recognize and remove barriers to student learning. In doing this, teachers must differentiate learning tasks and personalize individual success—by striving for three kinds of flexibility:

"Students are forces for societal change. That is how they define their humanity."

Michael Fullan, 2015, Quest Conference, York Region District School Board, Ontario

- Representing information in a variety of ways and using different forms of media,
- Providing multiple pathways for student activity and voice, and
- Providing multiple ways to engage students in interesting and motivating work (Rose & Meyer, 2002, p. 69).

The sustaining outcome of education beginning in kindergarten is learning how to learn and being able to appreciate and apply what has been learned in many different contexts and circumstances in our lives. Helping all students to achieve this requires that educators really put the FACES on their students' data in order to identify and remove barriers so all students learn.

Ultimately, employing the principles of Universal Design in our planning of individual and Collaborative Learning experiences is about finding ways for all students to access and express their learning. It is important to acknowledge that some students require more time and scaffolding. Combining Collaborative Learning and the Gradual Release of Responsibility Model (see Chapter 3) is powerful as we strive to differentiate and personalize to meet student needs. They complement each other, and both are important components of a strong teaching repertoire. And now too, teachers need to understand the power of technologies that allow students greater flexibility.

Classroom Inquiry-Based Learning: A Timely Approach

Thinking about our teacher John and how to evolve the assessment and instruction in his classroom, he needs to think strategically across subject/content areas as well as within each one to improve student learning. John needs to have a deep understanding that

- knowing all students' skill development,
- ensuring strong literacy instruction across the curriculum, and

- developing rich tasks that allow students to apply their knowledge and skills

remain the essential requirements for high-quality teaching in every classroom (Sharratt & Harild, 2015).

John needs to explore inquiry approaches that offer promise to help deepen learning by planning for teaching and learning in these three critical areas. An inquiry approach offers John and his students multiple opportunities for creative, critical, and collaborative thinking (Planche & Case, 2015) as experienced by principals, teachers, and students in the following vignette.

Student Voice and Choice Honored in an Assessment-Rich Collaborative Inquiry Process

In Adelaide, South Australia, some principals and teachers lead Year 6 and 7 students through a term-long inquiry with a culminating authentic assessment celebration known as Round Table Assessment (RTA). Students focus their inquiries on Heart–Hand–Mind: something they are passionate about, something they can do, and something they know a lot about. Students research their chosen topics in the broader community, interviewing people who can give them information and use a guided approach to critically consuming Internet resources. Teachers teach the necessary skills of facilitation, critical questioning, and self-regulation. They provide whole group, small group, and differentiated, individualized support. All projects have a culminating event, which is presenting their individual portfolios at the RTA. Students invite guests to be present to listen with some being on the RTA Presentation Panel as authentic assessors, such as those who were asked to support students through their inquiries. Six years out, this structured, Collaborative Inquiry process continues and is sustained not by the then-principal Ros Maio, but by others due to strong succession planning, shared beliefs, and a deep understanding of developing and weaving together Heart–Hand–Mind—that highlights students' voice, choice, and a "can-do," resilient attitude. Many principals and teachers continue to lead this work collaboratively. This highly impactful, inquiry-focused learning

(Continued)

strategy, driven by high expectation and anticipation, continues as students look forward to and plan for their inquiries many years in advance.

Ros Maio, Education Director of Schools and Preschools, Adelaide, South Australia; personal communication, May 29, 2015

Guiding Inquiry Learning

It is a great misconception to think that students should not be guided through inquiry, especially if they have had no prior experience with an inquiry approach. *Collaborative Inquiry is not chaos in the classroom!* There is much time and space for teaching to guide students to be ready to work interdependently on the processes involved in inquiry. Wise teachers plan for and structure the work by gradually releasing responsibility for students' learning, moving from modeling to sharing and to guiding before students become independent researchers as inquirers in the learning process. Students become assessment capable by the gradual *acceptance* of responsibility for their own learning. The purpose of inquiry is to grow depth of knowledge and to think critically through "uncovering" content rather than offering more traditional subject coverage. However, the process of inquiry still requires educators to think strategically and plan carefully where teacher intervention and guided instruction might be needed.

In planning inquiry experiences for students, teachers consider

- creating opportunities for an overarching curriculum-focused Learning Goal/Intention and a big idea to be unpacked through formulating essential questions and finding an area of focus,
- co-constructing the Success Criteria with students through a process of discovery,
- having students search for and find relevant data and information that illuminate the area of focus,
- analyzing and interpreting information or research gathered,
- evaluating the data and information and its potential interpretations,

- drawing conclusions through discussion and dialogue, and
- communicating findings involving an authentic audience in which different students may select various forms to demonstrate their learning.

Based on planning and decision making of how big ideas and curriculum expectations will be integrated into the inquiry, students engage in learning experiences that include learning how to move from one area to the next in a flexible but cyclical fashion. This is illustrated in the classroom Inquiry Framework in Figure 6.3. Practical beginnings to the work of inquiry-based teaching and learning are offered in Appendix I.

FIGURE 6.3

A Simplified Inquiry Frame for Beginning Inquiry-Based Learning

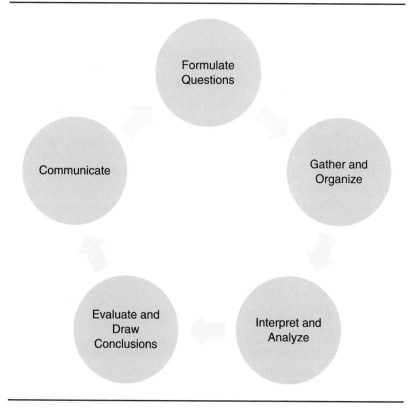

Source: B. Planche (2013b). Adaptation of the Ontario Elementary Social Studies/ History/Geography Inquiry Frame (p. 22).

Assessment Within Inquiry

In assessing the Collaborative Learning skills of their students, teachers must consider group dynamics and individual contributions by individual members as demanded in co-operative and Collaborative Learning processes. Effective group work will involve opportunities to assess learning processes and learning skills such as organization, self-regulation, and initiative while assessing individual work involves looking at how students are progressing against the co-constructed Success Criteria. Most assessment evidence must be ongoing, daily (formative), and used to inform instructional decisions the very next day. We call this responsive teaching using assessment-in-action. Formative assessment or assessment "for" learning and assessment "as" learning are presented as daily, ongoing, immediate feedback to students. However, at defined times, we look at the most consistent performance our students display and make an informed evaluation (summative assessment or assessment "of" learning) for use in reporting to parents. We have found that an effective way to report summative assessments to parents is through Student-Led Conferencing (Millar-Grant, Heffler, & Mereweather, 1995) in which students take ownership for their learning and improvement by articulating their individual Learning Goals when presenting their portfolios of work to parents (Sharratt & Fullan, 2012).

Collaborative Learning offers many opportunities for the development of self- and **peer assessment**, which we know is a high-impact learning process. Using an assessment-in-action approach, students can learn how to hold each other accountable by

- sharing learning interests,
- building on each other's ideas,
- monitoring how they apply collaborative task requirements, and
- sharing culminating learning from robust performance tasks through demonstrations, presentations, and digital productions.

One cannot over-state the power of co-constructed Success Criteria and here we reinforce that co-constructed Success Criteria for performance tasks form a matrix against which students can learn to self- and peer "assess-in-action" and mobilize feedback about their work. Appendix J outlines several types of assessment tools and processes that are relevant within inquiry approaches.

One of those assessment tools, Descriptive Feedback, clarifies next steps for learning. The waterfall chart, Figure 6.4 (Sharratt & Harild, 2015), shows how the pieces of assessment "for" and "as" learning depict this discussion and are critically dependent on each other—remove one piece and the flow of learning from assessment is halted.

FIGURE 6.4

The Dynamic Flow of Assessment For and As Learning

Source: © Sharratt & Harild, 2015. Adapted from York Region District School Board (2002–2007).

Table 6.2 illustrates what this assessment "for" and "as" learning looks like in action in planning a cross-curricular unit of study from the Ontario Curriculum Expectations for a Junior Grade (Grade 4, 5, or 6).

The teaching team at King Edward Public School in Ontario, Canada, demonstrate in the vignette on page 191 the power of assessment-in-action during a student-focused Collaborative Inquiry.

From this vignette we see curriculum content can be "uncovered" and explored in exciting ways using an inquiry approach. Teaching students to co-construct Success Criteria and to contribute Accountable Talk (see Glossary) helps them to own their learning. Through assessment-driven experiences, students and teachers can transform a compliantly engaged classroom (and in this case, a non-compliant and disengaged classroom) into an empowered one—an exciting prospect for us all.

To cause this shift from compliance to engagement to empowerment, inquiry must be flexible and collaborative with teachers and students partnering and co-learning.

At New Technology High School in Napa Valley, California, the school is organized around **project-based learning** with at least two subject teachers working together to create *integrated project-driven inquiries* combining Learning Goals across two disciplines (Planche, 2011). The outcome of the student inquiries includes a publicly presented product for an authentic audience, which keeps motivation high. The critical notion of creating a broad base of community partners supporting inquiry and project-based and experiential learning is developed further as a key theme in *Good to Great to Innovate* (Sharratt & Harild, 2015). Business, industry, and public sector partners collaborating with educators to provide authentic learning for all students is discussed and modeled. At New Technology High School, students work with and involve community partners when gathering information and sharing culminating products of their thinking.

TABLE 6.2

Planning for Assessment-in-Action

Learning Goal/Intention	Products/Processes	Success Criteria	Implications for Planning, Assessment, and Instruction
Ensuring clear information on what the Learning Goal and Big Idea are, such as "We are learning to make a good argument to influence thinking as a part of gathering support for our class eco-project on water management." **Learning Goal/Intention:** "Students will generate ideas and organize information to write and communicate for an intended purpose and audience." (Language Arts Curriculum Document, Ontario Ministry of Education)	Offering different ways learning can be demonstrated, such as • A letter • A presentation • A PowerPoint • A newspaper article or editorial • A video (with script) • An interview **Our Inquiry Question: What difference can environmental stewardship of water make in our community?**	Co-constructing what good work will look like, such as Students can: • Develop a compelling statement to open communication • State their perspective clearly • Produce their rationale and the evidence for their thinking (more than one piece of evidence from their inquiry) • Give two recommendations for next steps • Produce a summary statement that includes respectfully requesting support for their ideas	Deciding what "just in time" assessment and instruction are needed, raise questions such as: • What prior knowledge is needed? • What relevant vocabulary will be highlighted with students? • How will students be grouped for inquiry? • What sample pieces of work will we study to know how to extend students' thinking? • When will we pause to discuss and model how to interpret information?

(Continued)

TABLE 6.2 (Continued)

Learning Goal/Intention	Products/Processes	Success Criteria	Implications for Planning, Assessment, and Instruction
"Students will use the inquiry process to investigate aspects of the interrelationships between the natural environment, including climate and the way people in selected communities live." (Social Studies Curriculum Document, Ontario Ministry of Education)		• Determine how they will follow up and connect again with their authentic audience	• When and how will we guide the thinking about the interrelationships in decision making about water management? • What guidance will help students to process and to organize reference materials? • Will students need or create a template to organize information? • When will we block Social Studies and Language Arts time together to give students large chunks of time to work? • Will teachers and/or students develop a checklist for inquiry stages? • Who will determine how technology will be used?

Source: Adapted from the Ontario Language Arts Curriculum (Ontario Ministry of Education, 2006), Ontario Social Studies/History/Geography Curriculum (Ontario Ministry of Education, 2013), and Clarke (2008).

The Teapot Inquiry

At King Edward Public School, inquiry-based learning is a necessity. Ninety percent of the students live at or below the poverty line. Mental health challenges, learning issues, absenteeism, and behavior problems are the norm throughout the school, and differentiation to support the needs of all students is an absolute must. One way that we have been able to reverse that trend and to meet the needs of our students is through inquiry-based learning.

Our Grade 6 students who have typically had multiple behavior issues resulting in progressive discipline and suspensions are empowered by one simple *teapot* that is driving their learning. The class received the teapot from another school, and their mission is to send it to a school in Thailand. The teapot is to travel in one box that will have artifacts and information that will share and represent who they are as Canadians.

Not only are the students interested in learning and producing information in Social Studies for the teapot, but also the teacher has posed a wicked math problem to the class. The students in small groups must create the packaging for the teapot to safely and economically travel to Thailand. Over the course of a month, the students are creating geometric models for the box; calculating surface area, mass, and volume, and critically thinking about the best box design that will be chosen from the models the groups are building.

From one simple teapot, the students are reading and researching about Thailand, creating electronic files to send with the teapot, thinking and writing about who they are as Canadians, and, in fact, calculating lots of math!

Each day, the students in this Grade 6 class can't wait to get to school and get into class. Inquiry-based learning has created an authentic audience and a real-life, meaningful purpose for students to share their learning. The teacher ensures that there are multiple entry points for any learner to make a contribution to any component of the project. Behavior issues do not exist and during any visit, students are actively participating and sharing their voices through the work they do as they prepare to send one simple teapot to students in Thailand.

"Tea is instant wisdom—just add water," says Astrid Alauda. Similarly, inquiry-based learning is instant student empowerment—just add authentic learning that is connected to the lives and interests of students.

Lee Anne Andriessen, Principal, King Edward Public School,
Waterloo Region District School Board, Ontario, Canada;
personal communication, April 10, 2015

It's About Engagement That Leads to Empowerment

Young people are on the leading edge of technology use. Because of this, it is highly appropriate for any teacher to ask any student, "What do you think? Can you find the answer for us?"

Does it matter if it is the technology that hooks a student into searching for answers or if it is a student-relevant question that drives the student to engage with a new technology? The answer to us is that it doesn't matter. As one of our teachers shared:

> I do not think it is the technology that hooks our students into their learning. I truly feel that the students are hooked on learning when it means something to them personally or to someone else that they know. Technology helps create that connection and creates projects that go beyond the classroom. In Computer Science, technology is definitely important, but if we needed to go back to pen and paper or needed to go back to running a stack of computer cards through the computer reader, students would still be engaged if they were involved in meaningful learning. (Emily Fitzpatrick, Teacher, Orangeville District Secondary School, Upper Grand District School Board, Ontario, Canada; personal communication, February 2014)

Fitzpatrick's thoughts appear to align with Skillen's below as he reflects on his experience with a cooperative and Collaborative Learning design and its impact on transferable skills:

> When I reflect on the critical elements of teaching students transferable skills while they are learning computer programming, I have noticed that
>
> • the opportunities for substantive collaboration were provided; students were co-creating programs in Logo and were doing their math work together—not in isolation;
> • we held classroom discussions and "tiptoed back through our thinking" as we reflected on our experiences; and

- we developed a trusting and respectful environment where making one's thinking open and visible was honored and encouraged—perhaps especially when errors or bugs were detected.

We used "visible thinking" techniques that encouraged students to generate their own visible thinking strategies. (Peter Skillen, Educator, Manager of Professional Learning, YMCA; personal communication, February 19, 2014)

Ultimately it is the application and transfer of knowledge and skills with or without technology that moves learning in the direction of being more relevant and meaningful to each learner. Inquiry allows students to take on more ownership of their learning. Teachers, as guides, resources, and "just in time" instructors, create the culture in which strong learning relationships can thrive. They are partners in an intentional learning design to move students toward becoming interdependent learners—our collective goal.

Students and teachers now have the access and capability to communicate, collaborate, and think critically with unlimited access to the world's best thinkers that results in just-in-time learning. Teachers must assume the roles of risk-takers and accelerators of learning to learn from each other and from their students. Powerful learning motivators such as technology allow students to switch on to learning with, alongside, and through other students. This demands that open to learning spaces and conversations encourage wild thinking and defer judgement (Suzie Boss, in

> "Social media has become one of the most powerful ways to collaborate with colleagues near and far. Connecting with a Professional Learning Network (PLN) can help stretch our thinking, inspire us to innovate, make our ideas stronger, and help us realize that we are not alone in our way of thinking."
>
> Peter DeWitt, EdD, Author/Consultant; personal communication, June 2, 2015

Sharratt & Harild, 2015)—both skills that need to be explicitly taught *early* and *often*.

For students, social media use provides just-in-time learning that goes beyond textbook drudgery to increase informal and formal learning not only within schools but in global learning spaces. This demands that teachers, parents, and broader community partners model being critical consumers of information and technology use. The teacher's influence is vitally important in helping students navigate through the complexities of using digital media. Harnessing the power of connected learning is truly an authentic area for co-learning and collaboration among teachers and students and students with their peers (Fullan & Langworthy, 2013).

Todd Wright, a curriculum leader with strong expertise in integrating information technology seamlessly into the education landscape, reflects with us on the new roles of students and teachers.

Students as Co-Learners

It is important to consider the age and developmental level of each student when designing activities for students as co-learners. Learning can happen anywhere and with anyone. We need to understand the skills that students will need to develop to assist them in decision making and successful collaborative work. Partnering with students as co-learners can mean teacher to student, student to student, and external expert to student or teacher. In co-learning partnerships, students are becoming valid contributors to the conversation about their own learning, conversations that are concrete examples of how progress is being made. Student choice can mean different things in a truly collaborative environment. It may not be all about individual choice but more about negotiated choice. This has always been an aspect of effective teaching but now the role of technology in connecting students and teachers to other expertise requires a greater degree of organization, analysis, and communication. Increasingly, the job of students today is to learn from and with each other and assist teachers in understanding the learning approaches and tools that most benefit them as individuals.

Todd Wright, International Consultant, Toronto, Canada; personal communication, December 15, 2014

The often-raised questions about the use of technologies in education indicate real concerns about the state of current understanding of the technologies by teachers. How do we enable or keep up with online learning or online collaboration? How can digital technology assist staff in drilling more deeply into learning processes? How can we direct student inquiries? Many teachers are skilled in using digital tools and applications, yet in many jurisdictions or schools within systems, it is too soon to assess change in practice using online and social media as forms of learning. It is instructive to hear about professional experiences and reactions to them. It is critical that educators keep searching for and sharing answers to their many questions. Deborah McCallum shares her experience in the following snapshot.

In the 2013–2014 school year, I was engaged in a tech hub Collaborative Inquiry. We used technology and social media to add educational benefit to student learning focusing on literacy. Being interested in integrating a tech-enabled learning environment for students, I was amazed at what another teacher–librarian was doing in her school with literacy. It seemed we could integrate technology further and invite other students and schools into our school using technology to enhance and deepen the learning. We used technology to document the journey, we monitored and shared our learning, and I am continuing on with my own inquiry, even after the initial inquiry has ended. We had the opportunity to share our ideas, our successes, and our challenges. We were able to choose the authentic tasks that reflected the needs of our own students. Next steps will be how to take this through a Gradual Release of Responsibility Model that will support differentiation of tasks to enable students to continue with their own inquiries and allow them to use a variety of technology as learning tools. I now believe that integrating social media and Web 2.0 technologies benefit all stakeholders.

Deborah McCallum, Ontario Teacher, Simcoe County
District School Board; personal communication,
November 16, 2014

In reflecting on McCallum's experience, we are reminded that it is not the technology usage that stands out as important but how technology when used as part of the learning process engages and assists the learning. The role technology can play in engaging students and in furthering their learning is worthy of ongoing assessment and research.

Tensions between traditional approaches and new, emergent models are to be anticipated. Change tends to be evolutionary rather than revolutionary despite the rhetoric that change is needed quickly. Nevertheless, like John in our opening vignette in this chapter, we need to push forward to integrate forms of learning that are more empowering and relevant for our students. For example, becoming a lead-learner alongside students in a classroom speaks to the importance of being open to a Collaborative Learning stance as a professional.

Involving parents in understanding the shift toward a Collaborative Learning approach rather than the traditional direct teacher transmission approach is also vital. Parents benefit from becoming co-learners with teachers as they strive to develop cultures for deeper learning. Parents will support the process of inquiry if they understand its intent, application, and how it is assessed. Parent information nights become compelling and interactive when they are organized around experiences such as problem solving in mathematics or understanding inquiry-based learning—when students lead those conversations with parents. Student-Led Learning Walks embrace parents and all stakeholders in an impactful example of students' Leading Collaborative Learning.

Student-Led Learning Walks

In Figure 6.5, Greg Whitby, executive director, Parramatta Diocese, NSW, Australia, is asking Grade 1 students our five questions (see page 87) as they take him on a Student-Led Learning Walk at Precious Blood Catholic School in Ontario, Canada. Here students at all levels are articulate about their learning, the learning of others, and what success looks like for everyone at each grade level.

The vignette on page 198 describes how Student-Led Learning Walks (SLLWs) promote valuable collaboration among the principal,

FIGURE 6.5

Students Lead the Learning About Their Collaborative Inquiry

Source: Photo by Lyn Sharratt, April 15, 2015.

teachers, students, and parents as partners. SLLWs bring all aspects of Collaborative Learning together for us as a culminating event that extends learning to new levels.

Our examples in this chapter reflect the belief that "during Collaborative Learning, students develop key inquiry and innovation skills such as, creative and critical thinking, effective communication, and collaboration. It is key that educators and administrators intentionally model Collaborative Learning. Collaborative Learning leads to a very high level of student engagement in higher order thinking and doing" (James Bond, Principal, Waterloo Region District School Board, Ontario, Canada; personal communication, December 4, 2014). If we believe this, how can we not spend the time in *Leading Collaborative Learning to empower excellence in teaching and learning?*

The Student-Led Learning Walk

Precious Blood Catholic School is a Toronto, Ontario, elementary school (full-day kindergarten to Grade 8) with 480 students, 20 classroom teachers, and 15 specialty itinerant teachers.

The Student-Led Learning Walk (SLLW), as created by Principal Mirella Rossi and all staff members at Precious Blood, contextualizes learning on a continuum making it visible for all and creating a culture of learning. Initially, the school-based Professional Learning team reached out to parents with an interest in building stronger, academically focused relationships between home and school. A school-wide survey administered to gauge parents' connection and comfort level with the curriculum documents revealed an overwhelming interest and desire on the part of parents to engage more with their children's learning in relationship to curriculum expectations.

The school's learning team set out to create a culture of learning that included all stakeholders. For student learning, achievement, and well-being to be enhanced and enriched at home and school, educators and students alike collaborated and committed to make learning intentional and visible by

- aligning overall curriculum expectations with goals as outlined in the school's improvement plan;
- demonstrating and incorporating 21st century competencies;
- providing visible and specific opportunities for families to witness and understand the continuum of learning experiences and curriculum expectations from kindergarten to Grade 8 through strategic displays of student work;
- participating in Student-Led Learning Walks, where students lead their families through the school community's learning;
- participating in student, parent, and teacher conferences/interviews;
- providing a Home-Connection/Student-Led Learning Walk brochure; and
- providing hands-on experiences, resources, and classroom teachers' practical home-connection tips that go deeper into the goals of the school's improvement plan and 21st century competencies.

The goal of the Student-Led Learning Walk strategy is to make student learning visible by bringing parents and guardians into the school to "see" and "hear" their child's learning in action. SLLWs are designed to promote family educational cultures of learning as well as teacher efficacy, student engagement, achievement, and well-being.

Principal Mirella Rossi says that she introduced the concept of the SLLW to the school improvement team comprised of 10 staff members across all divisions to bring them together in a single focus. The school learning improvement team initially decided to engage in SLLWs on three occasions: during Curriculum Night, at Parent/Teacher/Student Interviews, and during Carnival Night. The staff embraced the first SLLW as an opportunity to get to know one another in a meaningful, academic, and community-centered way while familiarizing themselves with the process of the SLLW. Since engaging in the first SLLW, they have consistently increased student voice and parent engagement by inviting families to play an active role in their children's education as aligned with school goals. They have delved more deeply into community knowledge-building and positively affected teacher efficacy through displaying individual classroom strategies that support differentiated instruction.

Real data are captured so that students, staff, parents, and community partners have an opportunity to see the continuum of the school's curricular expectations, K–8; they have an opportunity to develop a common understanding of Learning Goals, related Success Criteria, and Descriptive Feedback experienced by students in classrooms. Displaying student work samples in the context of a curriculum continuum assists with parents' understanding of the curriculum expectations, in a supportive, interactive, visible, and family-friendly manner.

Most importantly, having the students lead parents through the explanations of curriculum expectations, what we learned in this project, Success Criteria, and why this piece of work was assessed as it was, have provided an authenticity that having teachers talk about the samples could not. This practice has enriched parent and guardian understanding of school in general and our school in particular. It has created a positive and inclusive learning environment, aligned instructional practices, and it has brought the community together with student learning at the center. Parents and community partners are now active participants with us. It has been an energizing and transformational experience—led by our students!

Mirella Rossi, Principal, Precious Blood Catholic School,
Toronto Catholic District School Board, Toronto, Ontario;
personal communication, April 15, 2015

Applying Our Theory of Action

Our Theory of Action for teachers like John (Figure 6.6) builds on our Collaborative Learning cycle: assessing to plan, planning to act, acting to make sense, and making sense to reflect and refine is the work that students and teachers do together. We suggest the process of partnering with students in this cycle accentuates and accelerates the co-learning process.

A Pause for Reflection

Our teacher John will have seen a very real shift in his practice if he applied the notion of students and teachers as reflective co-learners. He would have come to know this means that *building knowledge together* requires shifts in thinking about the roles of teachers and students. John would have changed his view of students as empty vessels or passive participants to that of being active co-learners. He would have seen his role as teacher refined to become collaborator, task designer, culture builder, and investigator, as well as just-in-time instructor. He would now note that there are many times students can be their own best teachers, and that he would become a vital, critical learning partner working alongside and guiding them. He would welcome in parents and members of the broader community to support student growth.

For John and other teachers, this collaborative approach must be developed through a gradual release/acceptance of responsibility, with the goal being the subsequent interdependence that develops for students and teachers. In this way, teachers conduct their own Professional Learning through Collaborative Inquiry questions and reflections on practice. As teachers, principals, and system leaders, we must engage fully in our own learning and be reflective as practitioners, to keep up with our co-learning student population. Or be left behind.

Our Culminating Event
Matrix Themes 1–10

We conclude by bringing together our 10 research themes as discussed throughout this text. They are displayed in Table 6.3 using

FIGURE 6.6

Theory of Action for Teachers Working Alongside Students and Students Working Together

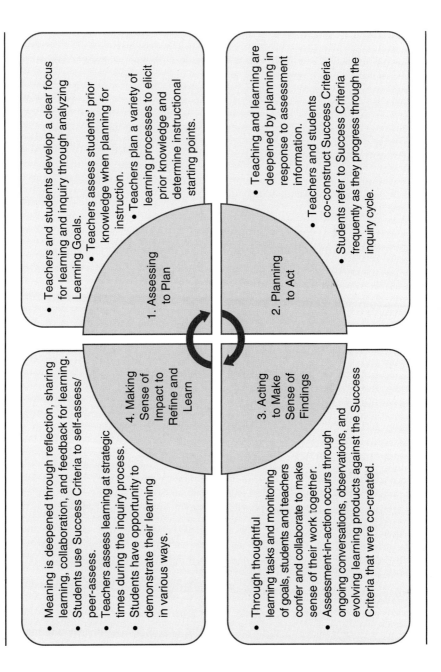

201

The Impact of Collaboration on Student Learning

A great deal of research has shown that collaborative approaches to learning are beneficial for individual and collective knowledge growth, including development of disciplinary practices (Barron & Darling-Hammond, 2008, p. 35).

For example, at East Ayr State School, North Queensland Region, Australia, learning doesn't just happen. Through their focus on working collaboratively, every staff member ensures that every day, in every classroom, every student is learning and achieving at least one year's growth in one year of schooling. How do they do that? They have a co-learning focus on precision in literacy assessment and instruction that embraces teachers' learning from each other about

- clarity and consistency (e.g., in implementing high-yield decoding strategies),
- planning in response to student reading behaviors,
- the 3 Cueing Systems,
- expected reading behaviors,
- data collection (PM Benchmarking),
- the Gradual Release of Responsibility Model,
- modeled reading– using "I" statements,
- clear expectations (for staff and students),
- their co-constructed Pedagogical Framework, and
- hosting teacher aides' Professional Learning.

This relentless focus during their initial year, 2014–2015, has resulted in students' improvement. They have doubled the number of As in Literacy/English from 5.1% to 10.3%; increased the number of Bs 8.3%, from 19.8 % to 28.1%; and decreased the number of students below standard by approximately 10%.

Their results and the research published to date allow us to make the following statements about the power of collaboration as it impacts on students' learning from teachers and each other.

1. When students own their own learning by collaboratively being involved in assessment and instruction with teachers and other students, they are empowered to articulate how and why they learn, how they can improve—and they do.

2. When students and teachers co-learn, using assessment of student work based on co-constructed Success Criteria work as their guide, students learn.
3. Students learn when teachers collaborate with students to co-construct meaning, when students demonstrate their learning, when teachers use Descriptive Feedback to set improvement goals, and when student peers provide feedback.
4. When teachers model high-impact collaborative practices such as attentive listening, open to learning conversations, and the use of relevant, cognitively demanding tasks, students are empowered to learn.
5. When teachers differentiate instruction through Collaborative Inquiries, based on data and students' interests, students learn.

The focus has gone from beyond the practical benefits of collaboration for individual learning to recognize the importance of helping children develop the capacity to collaborate as necessary preparation for all kinds of work (Barron & Darling Hammond, 2008, p. 19).

There is an apparent gap in the research literature; namely, there is a need for further intentional systemic research to explicitly correlate collaboration and student achievement. Nevertheless, this should not stop us from starting now to fundamentally change the way leaders, teachers, and students work together in schools as we have compelling evidence, compiled in this book, that we are on the right track.

the Gradual Release of Responsibility Model that *empowers excellence.* In our view, these are the 10 non-negotiables of evidence-proven Collaborative Learning practice. We must see them as pivotal in Leading Collaborative Learning—in every classroom, school, and system, globally, to bring out the "genius" in all students. Students must have the confidence to believe that they can change the world to be a better place—by Leading Collaborative Learning.

TABLE 6.3

Implementation Matrix of the 10 Non-Negotiables of Evidence-Proven Collaborative Learning Practices

Evidence-Proven Practice	Modeled Collaborative Learning	Shared Collaborative Learning	Guided Collaborative Learning	Interdependent Collaborative Learning	Beneficial Professional Learning for Those Who Lead Collaborative Learning
Key Theme 1	**Includes**	**Includes**	**Includes**	**Includes**	**Includes**
Shared beliefs and understandings solidify purpose and sustain motivation	• articulating a vision of improvement • maintaining a vision of improvement • modeling response to student data	• distributing the work and the responsibility of leading • co-constructing a vision of success • identifying improved achievement goals together	• maintaining high expectations for all • differentiating human and material resource support as needed	• reinforcing shared beliefs and understandings through co-learning • determining strategies for delivering Collaborative Learning to raise achievement for all • using research and inquiry as a vehicle to learn about deeper learning for students	• understanding the complexities of change processes • learning how to design an implementation plan • sharing leadership opportunities to deeply engage others • using student evidence of learning as a driver for co-work and co-learning

Evidence-Proven Practice	Modeled Collaborative Learning	Shared Collaborative Learning	Guided Collaborative Learning	Interdependent Collaborative Learning	Beneficial Professional Learning for Those Who Lead Collaborative Learning
Key Theme 2	Includes	Includes	Includes	Includes	Includes
Collaborative Learning is best understood as an evolving journey	• leading with purpose, passion, patience, and persistence	• rolling up sleeves and working alongside teachers and other leaders solving teaching and learning issues together • showing a passion for learning with others	• steering others toward more support as needed • scaffolding learning to meet learners where they are	• celebrating small and large wins • hosting an annual institute or symposium (Learning Fair), for example, to have educators share learning and success as well as outline areas of growth in the coming year • learning from FAIL FAST, or how to learn from failures and recover quickly • sharing learning from inquiries within and across schools during the school year	• learning how to build and sustain all learners' personal resiliency • experiencing and facilitating ongoing Collaborative Inquiry approaches • learning the lessons of personnel management and knowing how to take those who will not get "on the implementation train" off the track completely and headed toward other employment options

(Continued)

TABLE 6.3 (Continued)

Evidence-Proven Practice	Modeled Collaborative Learning	Shared Collaborative Learning	Guided Collaborative Learning	Interdependent Collaborative Learning	Beneficial Professional Learning for Those Who Lead Collaborative Learning
Key Theme 3	Includes	Includes	Includes	Includes	Includes
Some collaborative processes allow for deeper learning than others	• utilizing a co-learning stance • actively participating as a co-learner • integrating an inquiry approach to learning	• distributing leadership and learning opportunities among others	• ensuring collaborative processes include clear Learning Goals and co-constructed Success Criteria	• using high-impact learning strategies that meet the needs of all students	• co-learning strategies such as co-teaching, moderating, and assessing student work • embedding co-learning into classroom practice • establishing a growth mindset

Evidence-Proven Practice	Modeled Collaborative Learning	Shared Collaborative Learning	Guided Collaborative Learning	Interdependent Collaborative Learning	Beneficial Professional Learning for Those Who Lead Collaborative Learning
Key Theme 4	**Includes**	**Includes**	**Includes**	**Includes**	**Includes**
Practicing together using an inquiry stance can accelerate educator learning and improve outcomes for students	• embedding inquiry as a Collaborative Learning approach • posing thoughtful questions to begin learning dialogues • determining S.M.A.R.T. goals that are Specific, Measurable, Ambitious, Relevant, and Time-bound • demonstrating how to determine priorities	• having strong listening skills to hear others • paraphrasing and summarizing key points made in discussions • encouraging other opinions, questions, and reflections	• refocusing the discussion of key learning questions • helping others reach decisions about actions to be taken by building consensus	• garnering the commitment of collaborators to specific actions • determining a timeline for practice • encouraging the use of technology to assist with clear, ongoing, and collaborative communication approaches	• learning through collaborative experiences such as action research, inquiry, and moderating student work • using new technologies to accelerate learning and improve communications • learning how to use data analysis for inquiry and planning purposes

(Continued)

207

TABLE 6.3 (Continued)

Evidence-Proven Practice	Modeled Collaborative Learning	Shared Collaborative Learning	Guided Collaborative Learning	Interdependent Collaborative Learning	Beneficial Professional Learning for Those Who Lead Collaborative Learning
Key Theme 5	Includes	Includes	Includes	Includes	Includes
Leadership behaviors and organizational structures impact relationships and the depth of work collaborators can do together	• demonstrating how to work through difficulties • showing flexibility and creativity	• seeking purposeful solutions with others • addressing constraints caused by structures • applying policy and procedures in ways that move the work of schools forward	• using proactive measures to establish reasonable solutions • building consensus so decisions can be made	• including many voices in seeking the best solutions	• developing political skills in building consensus • working inclusively with diverse stakeholders
Key Theme 6	Includes	Includes	Includes	Includes	Includes
Strong collaboration includes impactful leadership and facilitation skills	• using intentional facilitation strategies to lead diverse groups	• facilitating group work with other emerging leaders	• using intuition in recognizing when to intervene to move work forward	• integrating diverse views and inviting engagement	• engaging in leadership coaching • using facilitation skills authentically

Evidence-Proven Practice	Modeled Collaborative Learning	Shared Collaborative Learning	Guided Collaborative Learning	Interdependent Collaborative Learning	Beneficial Professional Learning for Those Who Lead Collaborative Learning
Key Theme 7	Includes	Includes	Includes	Includes	Includes
Strong relationships are foundational in building a positive learning culture	• being approachable and inclusive • demonstrating a positive, growth mindset	• intentionally distributing leadership opportunities	• negotiating, navigating, and influencing when needed	• investing in his or her own learning and the learning of others	• developing emotional intelligence • being culturally responsive
Key Theme 8	Includes	Includes	Includes	Includes	Includes
Creative solutions are needed to mitigate the problem of time together	• modeling optimism that solutions can be found • mobilizing resources to support learning	• sharing the resource of time equitably • encouraging others to share ideas and work together	• influencing and guiding opportunities to work together through strategic time-tabling	• being intentional in terms of whole school, cross-divisional, and grade approaches to collaboration • developing a school ethos of co-learning • writing and sharing a thought-provoking Case Study about school improvement, so that others can learn from it	• coaching and mentoring regarding creative time-tabling • developing strong organizational skills • using new technologies to enable new, powerful, and collaborative approaches for learning

(Continued)

TABLE 6.3 (Continued)

Evidence-Proven Practice	Modeled Collaborative Learning	Shared Collaborative Learning	Guided Collaborative Learning	Interdependent Collaborative Learning	Beneficial Professional Learning for Those Who Lead Collaborative Learning
Key Theme 9	**Includes**	**Includes**	**Includes**	**Includes**	**Includes**
A focus on student work and growth helps to keep collaborative work on track	• using student evidence to determine areas for professional co-learning	• being responsible to and accountable for data analyses and results • ensuring that data are transparently displayed (Data Walls) so all can own all the FACES • researching and formulating authentic responses to data	• staying the course when distractions surface—and being able to articulate the "why" of staying on course • offering feedback to help move learning processes forward	• integrating many voices into learning discussions • building commitment to take action on collective next steps	• knowing how to analyze data • practicing the moderation and assessment of student work samples • knowing how to give and get Descriptive Feedback and taking action • training in conducting Learning Walks and Talks and having open to learning conversations • teaching teachers how to differentiate and personalize assessment and instruction to teach every FACE in every classroom

Evidence-Proven Practice	Modeled Collaborative Learning	Shared Collaborative Learning	Guided Collaborative Learning	Interdependent Collaborative Learning	Beneficial Professional Learning for Those Who Lead Collaborative Learning
Key Theme 10	**Includes**	**Includes**	**Includes**	**Includes**	**Includes**
Deeper forms of collaboration for both students and educators are built on a foundation of trust and safety	• being sensitive to the learning needs and strengths of others • making learning for teachers and leaders visible and explicit	• being inclusive in the collaborative approach • valuing by including the contributions of all participants	• becoming skilled in establishing norms for engagement participation • using protocols for learning to focus conversations in a timely way	• being specific in connecting prior and evolving knowledge as learning efforts unfold	• developing working norms and using learning protocols • coaching for teams who work together to build trust and strong relationships

Afterword

As you will have seen from the previous chapters, *Leading Collaborative Learning* is at once comprehensive and concise; big and small picture; theoretical and practical; ideas and tools in equal measure; and puts educators and students in the star roles of a great production that serves all aspects of the system. The core content chapters are deceptively seductive in making the reader realize that he or she not only has a role, but also is in fact part and parcel of the *system.*

The reader is cumulatively drawn to personal and collective action through the main Chapters 3 through 6: System Leaders Working Alongside School Leaders, School Leaders Working Alongside Teacher-Leaders, Teachers Working Alongside Teachers, and Teachers and Students Working Alongside Each Other. *Alongside* means participating as mutual learners in moving learning forward day after day.

This is a book that has crystal clear concepts, co-learning galore, guided by research, grounded in practice—all devoted to deep learning by students and adults alike. Chapter 1 established what Collaborative Learning is and is not (hint: it is a precise, focused daily devotion to learning linked to results). I love the basic premise: "Collaborative Learning cultivates *title-free* leadership" (my italics). Everyone is a leader, everyone is a learner—there is no distinction. And above all everyone is responsible for his or her own learning and for enabling the learning of others. Indeed, to do the latter is to learn oneself.

The theory of collaboration is captured early, but the real stars of the book are practitioners—by name and from around the world. They give detail to the actions that generate results, but you never get the sense that you are bogged down in descriptive accounts. The actions are clear, vivid—we know what leads to what. There is a familiar structure to each chapter: lots of vivid vignettes, two "non-negotiables" introduced in each chapter for a total of 10; use of matrixes to capture the essence of core concepts; tools for action; and a directed "pause for reflection" at the end of each chapter. The blend of scores of clear vignettes that reflect widespread take-up of the ideas, along with summary tables that specify key skills in relation to the concepts, makes for memorable images to guide follow-up.

This is a book that is brimming with ideas and specific suggestions. The appendices contain a treasure trove of tools for analysis, actions, reflection, and evaluation: practical beginnings to guided inquiry, benefits and challenges of Networked Learning Communities, and a protocol for co-learning, with and without release time, are among the many gems found in the back of the book.

It is clear that Sharratt and Planche have themselves done everything that is in the book. What is even clearer is that they have helped scores of others engage in these actions suited to their own situations. *Leading Collaborative Learning* is not a cookie-cutter solution but the concepts, themes, and strategies are cut from the same cloth. This cloth—Collaborative Inquiry—embeds non-negotiable principles and actions. There are certain sina quo nons that must be incorporated, but they guide rather than suffocate choices; they liberate rather than constrain; they focus while giving discretion.

All in all, *Leading Collaborative Learning* is a more detailed but fundamentally compatible book of action to our own recent publication, *Coherence: Putting the Right Drivers in Action* (Fullan & Quinn, 2015). Our four-part Coherence Framework—Focusing Direction, Cultivating Collaborative Cultures, Deepening Learning, and Securing Accountability—and this book readily map on to each other.

At a time when collaboration is everywhere but often superficial, it is crucial that we have serious players doing, probing, pulling out lessons, and otherwise making effective collaboration happen. Whether in Hamilton, Ontario, or Hamilton, New Zealand, or Townsville, Australia, Sharratt and Planche are bringing practitioners to the world, and vice versa. Leading Collaborative Learning is what these authors do every day of their lives. It gets better and better, more and more powerful, and it shows on every page of this book.

Michael Fullan

Professor Emeritus, University of Toronto, Canada

Appendices

Appendix A. Survey Questions

1. Please indicate the role you play in your school district.

2. If you are a teacher or teacher-leader, please indicate if you teach one or more of the following:

   ❐ Primary grades   ❐ High school

   ❐ Junior grades   ❐ Post-secondary

   ❐ Intermediate grades

3. Please indicate the name of the school district where you are employed.

4. Please indicate your home province or state and country.

	Very Important	Important	Neutral View	Not Very Important	Not Important at All
5. How important is it that formal leaders like principals and superintendents are able to articulate why collaboration is important?	❐	❐	❐	❐	❐

(Continued)

	Very Important	Important	Neutral View	Not Very Important	Not Important at All
6. How important is it that formal leaders partner with staff to establish Learning Goals for collaboration?	☐	☐	☐	☐	☐
7. How important is it that evidence of student learning be the driver for staff Learning Goals?	☐	☐	☐	☐	☐
8. How important is it for leaders (formal and informal, like teacher-leaders) to be able to build strong relationships?	☐	☐	☐	☐	☐
9. How important is it that leaders (formal and informal) are skilled in facilitation processes?	☐	☐	☐	☐	☐
10. How important is it that leaders (formal and informal) model an approach that is open to risk taking?	☐	☐	☐	☐	☐

	Very Important	Important	Neutral View	Not Very Important	Not Important at All
11. How important is it that leaders (formal and informal) model a positive growth mindset?	❑	❑	❑	❑	❑
12. How important is it that formal leaders model inclusiveness regarding participation in collaborative work?	❑	❑	❑	❑	❑
13. How important is it that formal or informal leaders be able to mediate conflict as it arises?	❑	❑	❑	❑	❑
14. How important is it that leaders, both formal and informal, model being co-learners with others?	❑	❑	❑	❑	❑
15. How important is it for formal leaders to offer frequent feedback to staff regarding their efforts to collaborate?	❑	❑	❑	❑	❑

(Continued)

	Very Important	Important	Neutral View	Not Very Important	Not Important at All
16. How important is it that formal leaders find ways to support staff efforts to collaborate?	☐	☐	☐	☐	☐
17. How important is it for principals and vice principals to mentor teacher-leaders in their efforts to Lead Collaborative Learning?	☐	☐	☐	☐	☐
18. How important is it for formal leaders such as principals or superintendents to ask for feedback from staff?	☐	☐	☐	☐	☐

19. Other thoughts regarding the role of leaders in moving Collaborative Learning forward?

20. What stands out to you as being vital to preparing leaders and teachers to collaborate using deeper processes such as Collaborative Inquiry?

21. While all of the following factors may be important, please rank the following factors from most important (1) to least important (8) to establishing a culture of collaboration.

____ Strong relationships

____ Positive school culture

____ Time to collaborate

____ Experienced facilitators

____ Shared beliefs and understandings

____ Accessible database of student learning

____ Clear goals and objectives

____ Volunteerism

22. Do you feel you are working in a Collaborative Learning environment right now?

☐ Yes, very collaborative

☐ Yes, collaboration is growing

☐ Not yet, but there is an interest

☐ No, not a very Collaborative Learning environment

Further comments:

(Continued)

23. Defining Collaborative Inquiry as a process driven by questions about the impact of our teaching on student learning, have you been part of an inquiry process to date?

   ❒ Yes, at least two opportunities

   ❒ Yes, one opportunity

   ❒ Not yet, but will have the opportunity

   ❒ No, not yet available

   ❒ Not interested in an opportunity

24. Consider the following collaborative endeavors and their impact on you as a learner. NA indicates no experience.

	Very Impactful	Impactful	Neutral View	Not Very Impactful	Not Impactful at All	NA
Collaborative Assessment of Student Work	❒	❒	❒	❒	❒	❒
Lesson Study	❒	❒	❒	❒	❒	❒
Instructional Rounds	❒	❒	❒	❒	❒	❒
Learning Walks and Talks	❒	❒	❒	❒	❒	❒
Critical Friends Study Group	❒	❒	❒	❒	❒	❒
Team Teaching	❒	❒	❒	❒	❒	❒
Staff Coaching	❒	❒	❒	❒	❒	❒
Professional Learning Community	❒	❒	❒	❒	❒	❒
Professional Learning Network	❒	❒	❒	❒	❒	❒

	Very Impactful	Impactful	Neutral View	Not Very Impactful	Not Impactful at All	NA
Online Professional Learning	❑	❑	❑	❑	❑	❑
Co-Planning, Co-Teaching, Co-Debriefing, and Co-Reflection (Inquiry)	❑	❑	❑	❑	❑	❑

25. Please indicate your agreement with the following statement: The following forms of collaborative endeavors have made a difference in terms of increasing student achievement in my work location. NA would indicate no experience.

	Very Strongly Agree	Strongly Agree	Neutral View	Somewhat Disagree	Do Not Agree at All	NA
Collaborative Assessment of Student Work	❑	❑	❑	❑	❑	❑
Lesson Study	❑	❑	❑	❑	❑	❑
Instructional Rounds	❑	❑	❑	❑	❑	❑
Learning Walks and Talks	❑	❑	❑	❑	❑	❑
Critical Friends Study Group	❑	❑	❑	❑	❑	❑
Team Teaching	❑	❑	❑	❑	❑	❑
Staff Coaching	❑	❑	❑	❑	❑	❑
Professional Learning Community	❑	❑	❑	❑	❑	❑

(Continued)

	Very Strongly Agree	Strongly Agree	Neutral View	Somewhat Disagree	Do Not Agree at All	NA
Professional Learning Network	❑	❑	❑	❑	❑	❑
Online Professional Learning	❑	❑	❑	❑	❑	❑
Co-planning, Co-Teaching, Co-Debriefing, and Co-Reflection (Inquiry)	❑	❑	❑	❑	❑	❑
Further comments:						
26. Please consider your agreement with the following statement: Emerging technologies will allow teachers to collaborate more effectively in the future.	❑	❑	❑	❑	❑	❑
Further comments:						

27. Which form of technology do you use presently to collaborate with your colleagues?

☐ E-mail   ☐ Adobe Connect

☐ Moodle   ☐ Blogging

☐ Skype   ☐ Telephone

☐ FaceTime   ☐ Blackberry instant messaging

☐ Google Docs   ☐ Texting

☐ Google Hangout   ☐ Instagram

☐ Twitter   ☐ Pictogram

Further comments:

28. Consider agreement with the importance of the following supports for teachers as they learn to engage in Collaborative Inquiry:

	Strongly Agree	Agree	Neutral View	Somewhat Disagree	Do Not Agree
Participating in an experience using an inquiry approach builds confidence.	☐	☐	☐	☐	☐
Time to work with peers during the school day is vital.	☐	☐	☐	☐	☐
A non-judgmental approach modeled for teachers helps to bring clarity to the work.	☐	☐	☐	☐	☐
Having exemplars of effective inquiries helps to bring clarity to the work.	☐	☐	☐	☐	☐

(Continued)

(Continued)

	Strongly Agree	Agree	Neutral View	Somewhat Disagree	Do Not Agree
Watching a video of Collaborative Inquiry in action brings clarity to the work.	❏	❏	❏	❏	❏
Opportunities to participate builds effectiveness.	❏	❏	❏	❏	❏
Further comments:					

29. Consider your agreement with the following strategies and their impact on the success of collaborative processes:

	Strongly Agree	Agree	Neutral View	Somewhat Disagree	Do Not Agree
Prioritizing funding supports for Professional Learning for leaders and staff	❏	❏	❏	❏	❏
Developing organizational supports that allow staff time to work together	❏	❏	❏	❏	❏
Requiring Professional Learning of leaders in the area of collaboration	❏	❏	❏	❏	❏

	Strongly Agree	Agree	Neutral View	Somewhat Disagree	Do Not Agree
Developing norms for positive engagement is vital	❑	❑	❑	❑	❑
Scaffolding supports for new teachers	❑	❑	❑	❑	❑
Integrating the use of student data as a driver for determining questions of inquiry and improvement	❑	❑	❑	❑	❑
Sustaining the use of student data as a driver for determining questions of inquiry and improvement	❑	❑	❑	❑	❑
Facilitating the placement of leaders based on schools' need to develop a strong culture of collaboration	❑	❑	❑	❑	❑
Facilitating the transfer of leaders based on schools' need to develop a strong culture of collaboration	❑	❑	❑	❑	❑
Further comments:					

(Continued)

30. If you have any powerful stories to share about Collaborative Learning and leadership from your experience, please add your contact information in the following box. Thank you for your participation!

Further comments:

Contact information:

Appendix B. A Protocol to Establish Norms of Engagement

Facilitator

- Thank the group for coming together, introduce participants if necessary—without titles—first and last names, clarify—in broad strokes—the purpose of the collaboration and the amount of time available that day, and clarify the "givens" regarding the following operating norms:

  - We all want a work environment where we feel safe and trusted.
  - We all want to be treated with respect.
  - We all want to continually improve the work we do.
  - We have a lot to learn from each other.
  - We will benefit from our work as co-learners.

- Set the tone for how participants will engage with each other—call for suggestions that must include:

  - The right to pass if asked a question that is uncomfortable
  - Agreement to listen carefully
  - Agreement to disagree respectfully
  - Agreement to clarify a question raised or offer a thought-provoking question in a respectful manner
  - Permission to laugh and enjoy the dialogue
  - Agreement to be clear and thoughtful in our responses
  - Agreement to appreciate each other's participation

Recorder

- Write up agreements and post them for review and refinement.
- Agreements will be revisited every time collaborators work together.

Facilitator

- End the collaborative time with a reflection: "This is how we agreed to work together . . . "

- "How did we do? Would we change or add anything regarding our agreements?"
- Thank the group and the host (teacher/school) as appropriate.
- Offer an opportunity for final comments and observations.

Appendix C. Inhibiting and Enabling Conditions for Collaboration

Perceived Enablers and Catalysts	Perceived Detractors and Inhibitors
A legacy of dynamic interactions, which includes • Energizing experiences • Touching the heart and hand as well as the head • Clear parameters for collective work • Collaborators working as co-investigators	**A legacy of unsatisfying past experiences, which includes** • Lack of consultation and time to work together • Build-up of resentments from less than positive experiences • Lack of skilled collaborators • Inability to clarify purpose/tasks
The involvement of flexible leadership, which includes • Warm, inviting, visible, and supportive principals, assistant principals, and teacher-leaders • Leaders as guides who facilitate • Leaders who can use humor to reduce stress • Leaders who distribute leadership to many others	**The involvement of ineffective leadership, which includes** • Formality or a lack of relationship that intimidates • New expectations perceived as one more thing to do • Forced collaboration driven by compliance • Leadership that is not visible or supportive • Leaders who have favorites
Includes intentionality by • Using student data as a focal point for collaboration • Developing shared goals together • Balancing pressure and support • Professional Learning opportunities that build in time for reflection and problem solving	**Imposing cultures and structures impacting by** • Strong norms of isolationism and teacher autonomy • Limited pockets of collaboration within a school, department, or organization • Feeling exposed—political pressures • Collaboration that is seen as "make work" rather than ultimately "less work"

(Continued)

Perceived Enablers and Catalysts	Perceived Detractors and Inhibitors
Impacted by inclusive working environments and strong personal connections, including	**Compromised by tenuous interpersonal relationships, which result in**
• A sense of camaraderie and equity as partners • Sharing of expertise • Involving individual choice and voice • Evidence of strong relational trust • Diverse opinions that are seen as a strength	• An "us and them" culture • Actively defiant and/or passively resistant • Apprehension and a fear of retribution • Interpersonal conflicts • Skepticism and a lack of regard for differing opinions
Supported by skilled collaborators with	**Unsupported collaboration resulting in**
• Ability to put others at ease • Strong communication skills • Involvement of "critical collaborators" who are influential and "knowledgeable others" • Strong skills of facilitation	• Lack of relational trust • Poor communication skills • Caution and hesitancy • Lack of focus through weak facilitation

Source: Adapted from Planche, 2004, 2008a.

Appendix D. Sample Collaborative Discussion Protocol

Peeling Back the Layers of an Issue

Facilitator's Role

- Refer participants to the norms of engagement established by the group (see example in Appendix B)
- Clarify purpose of the time together

  - Use a discussion protocol to develop a greater understanding of a complex issue by assisting each other with respectful dialogue and analysis
  - Resist the urge to begin solving the problem before it is more fully understood

- Clarify roles—facilitator, time keeper, recorder, summarizer, clarifier, encourager, etc.

  - Keep the group on track, always gently bringing the group back on topic
  - Remind the group when "advice regarding problem solving" is creeping in too soon in the process rather than allowing for full exploration of an issue
  - Work to ensure that no one voice dominates the conversation by asking for more input from others

The Process

1. **Describe.** Have designated presenters describe the problem/dilemma and ask a question to help focus the group's responses. (5 minutes)
2. **Clarify.** Clarify questions from group members to the presenters (these must be purely informational). (3 minutes)
3. **Create a time out.** Take a few minutes for reflection and gathering of thoughts. (2–3 minutes)
4. **Paraphrase.** Facilitate around the table groups where group members say—"What I heard [the presenters say] is."

(The presenters are silent and take notes.) Facilitator will ask for volunteers to start the conversation and ask for any final thoughts before moving on.

5. **Ask.** Facilitator asks (around the table groups) for assumptions about the issue or what is assumed to be true about the problem. (The presenters are silent and take notes.)

6. **Question.** Facilitate around the table groups where participants offer: "A question this raises for me is . . . " (The presenters are silent and take notes.)

7. **Check for further questions.** If needed, facilitate another round: "Further questions this raises for me are . . . " (The presenters are silent and take notes.)

8. **Check for understanding.** Facilitate further questions that check for understanding: "What if . . . ?" Or, "Have we thought about . . . ?" Or, "I wonder . . . ?" (The presenters are silent and take notes.)

9. **Review.** Presenters review their notes and say, "Having heard these comments and questions, now I think . . . " (The group members are silent and take notes.)

10. **Articulate takeaways.** Now what are the next steps? Together, the presenter(s) and group members talk about the possibilities and options that have surfaced. The facilitator asks the group to articulate what they are taking away; the presenters and the group members offer comments (with the right to pass).

11. **Debrief the process. Participants discuss:** Do we understand the complexities of the issue more fully? Do we require more time to talk about certain aspects of the issue? What about the process was useful? What was less than useful or frustrating? What do we need to change?

12. **Discuss next step(s).** When will additional time to talk be made if necessary?

13. **Name action(s).** Name the next step(s).

14. **Record** and **date** the actions.

Facilitator
- Thank the presenters and the group members.
- Refer back to the norms of engagement—ask, "How did we do?"
- "Is there anything we can improve?" Record refinements to the process.

Source: Adapted by Sharratt and Planche from the National School Reform Faculty Website—Open Source "Peeling the Onion—Developing a Problem Protocol." Available at http://www.nsrfharmony.org/system/files/protocols/peeling_onion_0.pdf

Appendix E. Benefits and Challenges of Networked Learning Communities

Benefits	Challenges
Builds trust and stronger learning relationships across a school or schools	Lack of continuity in learning if membership varies meeting to meeting, year to year
A collective capacity building vehicle for informal and formal leaders	Becomes exclusive if membership is limited to a chosen few
Clear focus, analysis of student work and courageous conversations that move learning forward	Without clear facilitation, conversations can be too broad and result in little applied change
Invitation to be a part of a learning community is a great personal Professional Learning opportunity	Perceived as important to "be seen in attendance" in terms of career advancement—may involve some personal learning but not learning for others in a school without clear responsibilities to apply learning back at the school or office
Impactful for groups of teachers within a school/across schools who are committed to co-work	Less than impactful if there are not processes in place to share the use of time and commit to actions taken—in other words, no commitment to doing the learning homework assigned
Provides growth opportunities for individuals interested in leadership	Requires a commitment to sustain personal learning as well as supporting Professional Learning of others
Utilizes specific agenda to itemize how time will be spent in the service of learning	Not productive if time together lacks common agreed-upon purpose, co-ordination, and co-operation

Appendix F. Guiding Questions for Leaders in the Establishment of a School Leadership Team

Teacher-leaders who are effective members of school leadership teams *demonstrate*

- skill in instruction and assessment;
- passion for ongoing learning;
- strong interpersonal skills and can relate to all adult and student learners;
- good listening skills;
- strong communication skills and can communicate well with peers;
- energy and high enthusiasm for being part of a collaborative team;
- risk-taking in the classroom and model an open-to-learning approach on the team; and a
- commitment to taking action together.

Important questions to ask in the selection of a school leadership team:

- ❏ Which staff members demonstrate a growth mindset?
- ❏ Which staff members are effective team members and collaborators?
- ❏ Which staff members consistently demonstrate a willingness to try new ideas?
- ❏ Which staff members are skilled in instruction and assessment and are willing to share their expertise in a non-threatening way?
- ❏ Which staff members demonstrate a belief in the talents of their colleagues and in the capability of all students?
- ❏ Which staff members have expressed an interest in learning more about Collaborative Inquiry?
- ❏ Which staff members have demonstrated an interest in leadership and in their own learning and the learning of others?

For potential teacher-leaders to become influential stakeholders, they need support in their development to understand and *to model for others* how to

- examine practice reflectively;
- hone their own assessment and instructional skills while supporting and modeling those skills for their peers;
- work with students using self- and peer-assessment processes in/with learning partners as this improves both student achievement and teacher efficacy (Hattie, 2009); and
- share the challenges and successes of holding high expectations for students and themselves as practitioners.

Appendix G. A Professional Learning Protocol: Sharing Student Work as a Driver for Co-Learning for Three to Four Participants

Setting the Context

This protocol is designed to look at a variety of student responses to a collaboratively planned lesson to deepen educator understanding of the impact of teaching on learning. It would be appropriate for grade partners or members of a teaching division to use.

Prior to the Collaborative Discussion

1. Establish norms of engagement—see Appendix B.
2. Establish an area of common teaching interest/or concern— What do student data tell you as a part of your decision making?
3. Choose a curriculum Learning Goal/Intention as a focus within a commonly agreed-upon subject area.
4. Plan a lesson collaboratively—begin with clear deconstructed Learning Goals/Intentions (developed in student-friendly language) and develop the Success Criteria that will be co-constructed with the students.
5. Decide how prior student knowledge will be assessed as part of the planning process.
6. Develop a rich performance task that directly relates to the co-constructed Success Criteria, as a culminating event.
7. Teach the lesson independently in individual classrooms.
8. Within no more than two days of teaching the lesson, each member of the collaborative endeavor chooses *three* pieces of student work from the rich performance task to bring to share and discuss. Choose work that you think represents different levels of students' thinking and understanding.

During the Collaborative Discussion
(Time needed: one and a half hours)

Alternate Roles of Debriefing, Listening, Sharing, Responding, and Ending With Reflection

- **Participant No. 1** debriefs their teaching experience and shares one piece of student work
- Participant No. 1 offers their observations as to how the work relates to the curriculum Learning Goal/Intention and the co-constructed Success Criteria—Others listen
- Participant No. 1 listens while others respond in turn and ask questions
- Participant No. 1 responds to questions and ends with a reflection

- **Participant No. 2** debriefs their teaching experience, shares one piece of student work. Participant No. 2 offers their observations as to how the work relates to the Learning Goal/Intention and co-constructed Success Criteria—others listen
- The cycle continues until *all participants* have discussed and shared three pieces of work in turn and responded to reflections from others.

Questions to Consider in the Debriefing, Discussing, and Reflecting on Student Work

1. How does the piece of student work relate to the Success Criteria that were constructed collaboratively?
2. What do we find interesting or surprising?
3. What do we see as evidence of student thinking?
4. What are the next steps for learning for the student? What Descriptive Feedback would you give each student?
5. What are the next steps for teaching that would help the student?
6. Can any of these students be grouped together for Guided Practice with you, the teacher?

Questions to Consider as a Part
of the Reflection on the Process

1. What did you learn from listening to your colleagues that was interesting or surprising?
2. What new perspectives did the experience give you?
3. What questions about teaching and assessment were raised during the process?
4. What will you take back to your classroom to try?
5. How will you build on your learning?
6. When will we meet again? What will be the focus of our discussion? Will we develop a common assessment task to assess before we come? What student work will we bring?

The Facilitator's Role

The facilitator ensures the process proceeds as outlined and that listening respectfully remains a norm. He or she paraphrases and synthesizes reflections and helps the group decide on next steps for learning.

Source: Adapted by Sharratt and Planche from open access—National School Reform Faculty—ATLAS—Learning from Student Work 2000. http://www.nsrfharmony .org/system/files/protocols/atlas_lfsw_0.pdf

Appendix H. A Protocol for the Process of Co-Learning With and Without Release Time

Scenario A–With Release Time for Three to Five Teachers	Scenario B–Without Release Time for Three to Five Teachers
Assess to Plan Collaboratively	**Assess to Plan Collaboratively**
• A host teacher will want to share his/her classroom context–class profile and instructional foci, which will make the classroom visit more relevant.	• Individual teachers will want to consider their classroom context–which students will need accommodations or modifications–which students require differentiation
• Identify and deconstruct curriculum expectation(s) into student-friendly Learning Goals/Intentions and possible Success Criteria (to be co-constructed with students)	• Identify and deconstruct curriculum expectation(s) as Learning Goals/Intentions and possible Success Criteria (to be co-constructed with students)
• Is there is any instructional vocabulary (language of the discipline) that needs to be reinforced for students?	• Is there is any instructional vocabulary (language of the discipline) that needs to be reinforced for students?
• Determine possible questions to prompt students' thinking and identify supports/anchor charts to be developed with students to help scaffold learning.	• Determine possible questions to prompt students' thinking and identify supports/anchor charts to be developed with students to help scaffold learning.
• Consider assessment points for teacher observation, and peer and self-assessment.	• Consider assessment points for teacher observation, and peer and self-assessment.
• Are there any supporting materials that have to be organized before co-learners enter the classroom, such as an observation protocol?	• Are there any supporting materials that have to be organized before the learning begins?
• Who will observe what? Who are the co-teachers if that is possible? Who will observe students' thinking and actions?	• Are there students in particular that the teacher may want to observe as "marker students" for specific reasons?

Scenario A–With Release Time for Three to Five Teachers	Scenario B–Without Release Time for Three to Five Teachers
Plan to Act and Teach Collaboratively to Make Sense of Findings	**Plan to Act and Teach Collaboratively to Make Sense of Findings**
• Host teacher explains to the class expected student behaviors and actions as well as the role of co-teachers (if present) and observers in the inquiry process: "We are here to learn to improve our teaching together."	• Explain to the class expected student behaviors and actions. • If observers are in the classroom, explain their role: "We are here to learn to improve our teaching together."
• Co-teachers (if present) make instructional decisions as a team and are the only ones who interact with students.	• Class teacher is the only one who interacts with students.
• If observers are in the classroom with co-teachers, their role is to collect observational data that describes what students are doing and saying, which indicates, in particular, student thinking.	• If observers* are in the classroom, their role is to collect observational data that describes what students are doing and saying, which indicates, in particular, student thinking. (*Observers may be a special education teacher, a paraprofessional, or the teacher-librarian, for example, who can be released without paying a supply teacher.)

Next Steps of the Protocol for Both Scenarios: Debrief Collaboratively to Make Sense Together as "Assessment-in-Action'"

- Teachers share their co-teaching experience. The conversations, observations, and the products they see students developing provide formative assessment information.
- Teachers who did not have a co-teacher share their own teaching experience with observers. The conversations, observations,

and the products they see students developing provide formative assessment information.

- Were our assumptions about student prior knowledge on the
right track?
- What stands out as needing refinement in the teaching process?
- What were the patterns that we could see in student
understanding?
- Determine and discuss: What are our next steps in teaching?
What is the specific Descriptive Feedback that students need for
their next steps in learning?

As Co-Learners: Decide What Will Be Taken
Back to Individual Classrooms and Practiced

- As we teach or act, we seek to make sense of our findings as they
apply to student learning. What did we see, hear, or observe
that we have noted in order to refine our practice?
- What would we change or adjust in the next lesson?

The Last Phase: Collaborative Reflection
to Make Sense of Our Impact to
Refine Practice and Learning

- Co-reflections are based on the experience and the feedback
that learners give each other about the teacher co-learning and
Collaborative Inquiry experience.
- What have we learned? What surprised us? What will we
change?
- How can our Descriptive Feedback help students move forward?
- Revisit our norms . . . did they work for us?
- What can we share with our colleagues? What will we share
with the school's formal leaders (if they were not present)?
- Review the appropriateness of the Learning Goals/Intentions
developed in student-friendly language from the curriculum
expectations.
- Were the Success Criteria the appropriate ones that were co-con-
structed with students?

- Can all students now set their own individual Learning Goals for this subject area? Who will support them in doing this?
- Determine another co-learning experience that would be beneficial. When will that be scheduled?
- Celebrate the collaborative effort made by participants and their evolving understanding of co-learning!

Appendix I. Practical Beginnings to Inquiry-Based Teaching and Learning

Here are a few practical considerations and questions for those who wish to begin to create a co-learning experience with students using *a guided Collaborative Inquiry approach:*

1. Begin with planning considerations

    -   What are the clear Learning Goals/Intentions from the curriculum that will be integrated?
    -   What is it that we want students to know and to be able to do at the end of the process?
    -   How will expectations be clearly communicated and visible so students can refer to them?
    -   What norms of collaborative engagement do you wish to reinforce?
    -   How can students be involved in the construction of norms?

2. Consider the background vocabulary and learning processes that will make students successful in their questioning and interpreting:

    -   What do you think students need to know ahead of time to allow them to begin their explorations?
    -   Consider the learning dispositions or learning skills that you wish to see developed through the work.
    -   How might Success Criteria be co-constructed with students to assist them in peer and self-assessment?
    -   How will students collaborate to have the opportunity to co-learn and support one another?

3. As students are beginning to experience the processes involved in inquiry, concentrate on a few outcomes rather many. Questions to consider include:

    -   How can we make Learning Goals/Intentions very accessible for students?

- How can we involve students in decisions about outcomes (Success Criteria)?

4. Use different kinds of questions in the discussions that ensue—advancing to higher-order questions as students "uncover" content.

  - For example, questions that ask students to retrieve information are lower level, while questions that ask students to clarify, represent, summarize, or develop an opposing view are higher level.

5. Limit the number of products (culminating rich performance tasks) you expect of students. We are looking for focused, in-depth thinking rather than quantity of products. We are looking for students to have choice in how they demonstrate their learning as a culminating (summative) task.

6. Consider how technologies can be infused as learning and processing tools at every stage and as appropriate to the inquiry topic.

  - Specifically, how can technologies assist students who have learning challenges?

7. Have students communicate their findings, choosing appropriately from a variety of ways, to an authentic audience.

  - How would real-life community connections reinforce their learning and value their work?

8. End the inquiry with more student-generated questions to enable another cycle to be taken up in the future by new "inquirers."

  - The message we want to leave with students is that learning is continuous for both teachers and students, and builds on the new knowledge that they have developed.

Sources: Based on 2014 material created for consulting and coaching purposes by Beate Planche; Sharratt, L., & Fullan, M. (2012); Sharratt, L., & Harild, G. (2015).

Appendix J. Assessment Within Inquiry Processes

As students discuss, research, organize, interpret, analyze, summarize, and synthesize their findings in order to share their learning—

Student and teacher assessment opportunities include gathering data (on group work and individual work) through observations, conversations, anecdotal notes, and checklists that reflect on all students, developing

- ❑ learning skills
- ❑ collaborative work skills
- ❑ listening, speaking, reading, and writing skills
- ❑ research skills
- ❑ organizational skills
- ❑ social and emotional skill development
- ❑ self-regulatory skills
- ❑ metacognition

Through observation, conversation, and application of skills, assessment opportunities include

- ❑ comprehension of key curricular concepts
- ❑ ability to think critically and creatively
- ❑ ability to communicate and share ideas
- ❑ ability to interpret and analyze
- ❑ ability to build on the ideas of others
- ❑ application of co-constructed Success Criteria built on curricular goals

Different forms of gathering assessment data for inquiry learning products and processes may include the use of the following: (These forms are most impactful when Success Criteria for their use are co-constructed with students)

- ❏ Success Criteria—co-constructed and visible in the classroom
- ❏ rubrics
- ❏ graphic organizers
- ❏ checklists
- ❏ journals
- ❏ portfolios
- ❏ learning circle discussions
- ❏ video and photographs
- ❏ note taking
- ❏ demonstrations
- ❏ performances
- ❏ presentations
- ❏ interviews
- ❏ assessment surveys
- ❏ interest inventories
- ❏ written summaries and reports
- ❏ building models or prototypes

Assessment information is feedback information for teachers as well as students. We use it to "feed forward" next steps for learning and instruction.

The Book Study

We suggest that Book Study facilitators consider asking participants the following questions, leaving plenty of time for each participant to respond to a question before moving on to the next question. Asked in series, the questions should produce rich discussions about the impact of Collaborative Learning that will strengthen each participant's classroom practice and increase all students' growth and achievement. Facilitators, remember to introduce and maintain group norms (Appendix B) to optimize discussion and learning. Feeding back the notes from the discussions will further enrich the learning for each participant.

Chapter 1

1. How closely does our definition of collaboration align with your own definition?
2. How closely does our definition of Collaborative Learning align with your experience?
3. How is collaborative leadership shared in your work setting?
4. What are the attributes of a collaborative leader in your opinion?
5. What do you think your students consider engaging and empowering school work?
6. What does student-centered, deeper learning look like in your opinion?

Chapter 2

1. What has been your own experience regarding inquiry processes?
2. What part of our four-element Theory of Action Framework do you think collaborators would find the most challenging and why?
3. What parts of the Theory of Action do you think require some intentional learning? What would you suggest?

4. How does our Theory of Action align with improvement processes best known to you?

5. What parts of the Theory of Action do you think make the biggest difference to sustaining learning and student success?

6. As a system, school, or teacher-leader, how will you put into practice the five guiding principles for leaders?

Chapter 3

1. How do system leaders best assist principals in creating strong school learning cultures?

2. How closely linked are staff learning conversations to improving classroom practice in your school or system?

3. What evidence do senior leaders need to look for in a school that indicates that school staff have worked collaboratively in their school planning processes?

4. How can system leaders best support the goals of school leaders regarding personal growth and renewal?

5. What policies, procedures, and/or practices are in place that enable the development of collaborative school learning cultures?

6. Which policies, procedures, and/or practices are in place that inhibit the development of Collaborative Learning cultures?

Chapter 4

1. Why is it so important that leaders continuously articulate a clear vision and a path forward?

2. What is the leader's role in breaking down Learning Goals into reasonable, doable actions?

3. What is the leader's role in monitoring goals as part of Collaborative Learning?

4. How does a leader best include those on staff who prefer to sit on the sidelines?

5. What are some further strategies for finding time for Collaborative Learning that can be reasonably explored?

6. How does reflecting on classroom practice move Collaborative Learning forward?

7. What beginning points are you considering to deepen the culture of Collaborative Learning in your context?

8. How might the integration of technology foster collaboration and interdependence?

Chapter 5

1. How do classroom practitioners best demonstrate a willingness to work with others?

2. What is tangible evidence of a growth mindset?

3. How do we model a sincere belief in the capability of our colleagues and students to learn and improve?

4. What do you find personally motivating about Collaborative Learning?

5. What do you find personally challenging about Collaborative Learning?

6. What suggestions would you offer to overcome the inhibiting or challenging factors that influence Collaborative Learning?

7. Collaborative Learning does not mean that individual learning is less important. What does a balance of individual and collective learning look like in the classroom or on a staff?

8. What supports do teachers need in becoming facilitators and designers of learning that empowers students?

9. How might the integration of technology help teachers to work collaboratively and foster interdependence?

Chapter 6

1. What are the characteristics of a student-centered classroom?

2. What skill sets need to be developed so that students can work together collaboratively?

3. How can we best assess the skills of learning collaboratively?

4. How can students be more involved in self-assessment and peer assessment as a critical component of collaborative work?

5. How can the co-construction of Success Criteria assist students in developing their culminating event?

6. What role might students play in the planning of Collaborative Learning and its outcomes?

7. How can students be more in control of their own learning and be of more help to each other in learning collaboratively?

8. How might integrating technology help students become both independent and collaborative learners?

Glossary

Accountable Talk: Teachers and students, and students with other students engage in dialogue to understand the meaning of their own perspectives and the perspectives of others in seeking clarity for and with each other.

Assessment: A process that takes place between teachers and students so that students can understand where they are, how they are doing, and where they are going. Assessment can be diagnostic, formative, or summative.

Assessment "for" and "as" learning (Diagnostic): Seamless integration of information about a student's learning that turns into precise instruction needed in a timely way resulting in multiple opportunities for students to demonstrate the new learning. Assessment that drives instruction is a never-ending cycle in which one informs the other daily; assessment becomes instruction that becomes assessed learning that becomes instruction and so on . . .

Assessment-in-action (Formative): Assessment is also a process that educators use to determine where improvements are needed as a part of a Collaborative Inquiry into learning. Assessment information is used to plan next steps for instruction. Assessment-in-action results in a shift or refinement of learning or teaching strategy as a response to assessment information while instruction or action is underway. Assessment-in-action fuels responsive teaching and learning.

Assessment of learning (Summative): Assessment at the end of a unit of study or a term—through observations, conversations with students, or an examination of products, comparing them against the established Success Criteria.

Authentic learning: Learning that is authentic is related to students' real-life experiences as well as their context, interests, and their culture. It is situated in processes that are central to more than one subject area while being grounded and explored through real-world applications and problems that have multiple solutions.

Co-labor-ability: The capacity of an individual member of a team from leadership at any level including informal leadership to collaborate with others from the team. Can mean the individual's capacity to participate in Collaborative Learning or Collaborative Inquiry. Can also mean the group's collective capacity to collaborate in learning or inquiry.

Co-laborers: Two or more collaborators who are interested in collaborating and working together to address specific issues of improving educational practice.

Co-learners: Two or more collaborators who are interested in learning together and in developing a shared understanding of improved instruction and student learning.

Co-learning stance: A positive attitude or position that someone holds toward learning together with a single focus.

Collaboration: In the service of Collaborative Learning, collaboration is defined as co-laboring, fostering interdependence as collaborators negotiate meaning and relevance together. Collaborators are accountable for their own learning while supporting the learning of others involved in the collaboration.

Collaborative Inquiry: Inquiry involves working with other educators who have common goals, seeking to understand and respond to issues of teaching and learning through the use of a deliberate process. Using student evidence of learning as the basis for the inquiry, those involved in the inquiry seek to solve problems or issues of practice that affect student achievement.

Collaborative Learning: It is focused understanding together with a clear goal in mind, supported by group processes and enabled when needed by facilitation. It is accountable talk grounded in trust, safety, and strong relationships.

Collegiality: Involves the cooperation and trusting relationships that develop among colleagues. Collegiality is an important aspect of the climate of effective schools.

Constructivism: A theory about the nature of knowledge that suggests that knowledge is co-constructed through social and cultural contexts.

Co-teach: Involves two or more educators who organize themselves to teach together as part of a Collaborative Inquiry into students' learning and thinking.

Co-Teaching Cycle: Also called the 4 Cs Model. Can be a formal or an ongoing, more informal process of co-planning, co-teaching (the planned lesson), co-debriefing (the outcome of the lesson as observed and assessed), and co-reflecting on the meaning of the outcomes prior to continuing the cycle with planning phase.

Deeper learning: The process through which a person becomes capable of taking what has been learned in one situation and applying it to a new situation. Through this process, students develop competencies in the cognitive, interpersonal, and intrapersonal domains (National Academies, 2012).

Descriptive Feedback: Whereas many teachers or leaders may recognize effort with high five's or a quick pat on the back, Descriptive Feedback is a response to the work done that reflects the effort against the Success Criteria. Descriptive Feedback is timely and specific assessment information that students can apply to move their learning forward.

Descriptive Feedback to students is beneficial when it is clear, timely, and useful information regarding next steps for learning. Descriptive Feedback from leaders to educators is beneficial when it involves clear, timely, and useful information regarding next steps for learning or instruction.

Differentiated instruction: An approach to instruction that aims to maximize each student's learning by assessing each student's unique need, designing instruction to match the need, and then assessing the impact of the instruction, thus moving the student's learning forward. All instruction should be thought of as differentiated instruction. It is most effective in small groups of learners with similar needs. These groups are always flexible and fluid depending on students' needs that the teacher assesses at any given moment.

FACES: FACES is not an acronym but is capitalized for emphasis. For example, we must have cognitive insights about and make emotional connections to each individual student's FACE that we teach.

Graphic organizer: A visual framework that helps students write or draw, "chunking" together their ideas or perceptions of a lesson or directions or group notes in order to make processes, concepts, and content more clearly understood.

Growth mindset: A mindset is a self-perception or deep-seated assumptions that people hold about themselves. People with a growth mindset perceive that their most basic abilities can be developed through perseverance and hard work. By contrast, a fixed mindset is one where people believe their basic abilities and talents are fixed and cannot be changed. With a fixed mindset, students (teachers, or leaders) see themselves as smart or not smart; there is rigidity in their self-perception. With a growth mindset, students (teachers, or leaders) see themselves as having the capability and willingness to improve and continue to grow. This term was first documented by Dr. Carol Dweck (1999).

Inquiry approach: An openness to new learning and an interest in solving problems and investigating solutions with others.

Inquiry-based learning: A Collaborative Learning process where students ask questions and determine a focus about real-world problems. Students then investigate and research to find answers together and in the process build shared understandings and knowledge. An important part of inquiry is the process of organizing and analyzing the inquiry's findings, a time when the teacher provides Descriptive Feedback. Finally the group communicates what has been learned, in a variety of ways, to an authentic audience for Descriptive Feedback and summative assessment. New inquiries emerge.

Leading Collaborative Learning: Leading Collaborative Learning adds the complexity of how individuals within a learning community take on the responsibility of and accountability for facilitation, resource management, mitigating challenges, and supporting the learning of others while being engaged and modeling learning themselves.

Learning Goals: Could also be termed as Learning Intentions or Learning Targets and are taken directly from the curriculum expectations. Learning Goals should be de-constructed for students, that is, students should know what they will be learning. Success Criteria—how does my level of learning measure against predetermined levels—are directly developed from the Learning Goals and are most effective when students co-construct with the teacher.

Learning protocol: A set of guidelines that aim to structure how a meeting, investigation, or inquiry will be organized to make efficient use of learning time.

Learning stance: Having an open disposition to new learning.

Leveled work: Teachers work together to examine student work against an expected learning standard or competency and decide together what level the work represents. The student's work may be at standard (perhaps a level 3) while a student's work that is approaching standard may be deemed a level 2. A student's work that is well beyond standard may be a level 4, and a student working well below standard may be a level 1. Collaborative analysis of student work allows teachers to develop shared understanding of levels of competency. The critical importance of leveling work is the resulting decisions that are made in determining the next steps in scaffolding the instruction and Descriptive Feedback to be given for the student's learning.

Observational Inquiry: Tonya Ward Singer, in Chapter 5, offers the view that inquiry can be done through simple but precise observation of, for example, a lesson being taught, an inquiry in which they are engaged, and how the students respond to it, how they learned, and what they learned from it. Equally important is what they may not have learned from the process. These factors then can form one basis for learning by the teacher and the observers in a classroom observation.

Parity: All parties involved in a collaboration have similar levels of power, such as a voice in decision making.

Peer assessment: Students, as peers, assess each other's work against co-constructed Success Criteria to give feedback to each other, which inform next steps for learning.

Personalization: Educators seek to tailor the educational environment to meet the needs, strengths, and interests of individual students. Finding ways to give students a sense of ownership of their learning is a goal of personalized learning. It is sometimes called student-centered learning. The parallel is true for school leaders and teachers as system leaders develop capacity, together, across the system.

Prior knowledge: Represents what students already know at the outset of an inquiry or a lesson. Should be assessed as a part of planning for learning or teaching new information, to allow for differentiation of instruction. No student should be sitting in lessons that they already know how to do.

Project-based learning: Closely aligned to authentic learning, project-based learning is a form of inquiry learning. It is sometimes called "learning by doing." It involves a focus on learning how to learn and integrating learning content across disciplinary lines as students investigate topic interconnections and the complexities of handling multiple pieces of a sizable project. Project outcomes normally include a focus on real-world issues and sharing the results of the findings with an authentic audience. In contrast to an assignment or a test, projects may run over several weeks and can be threaded throughout a term or semester, with several key pieces to be completed over time. The design of project-based learning integrates multiple learning standards and/or curriculum expectations as well as learning processes and curriculum content.

Reciprocity: Both leaders and followers believe they are receiving mutual benefits for their efforts in a collaboration and therefore are more willing to collaborate than if reciprocity is not evident to either leaders or followers or even within the follower group.

Reflective practice: Thinking about one's leadership or teaching practice while involved in the practice and as an ongoing habit of mind. Teachers who are reflective practitioners stop and think carefully about next steps for teaching while observing the impact of their lessons on student progress. Donald Schön (1983) saw reflective practice as a foundational characteristic of effective teaching.

Rubric: Is created to represent a consistent set of learning expectations that students need to demonstrate. Rubrics describe what low- to high-level work will look like in completing a performance task. Rubrics can be used to clarify *Learning Goals* (see above) and may also be used as assessment tools. Effective rubrics are simple and clear, and give students valuable reference guides to use during their work. Students can also use rubrics as a part of peer and self-assessment processes. In many jurisdictions, rubrics are being replaced by Success Criteria as they are more useful when co-constructed by teachers and students (Sharratt & Fullan, 2012).

Scaffolding: Supported progressive learning during which knowledge is built up. New knowledge is brought into play and is connected with prior knowledge. Learning is layered and manageable as a result. Most often seen when teachers instruct using the Modeled, Shared, Guided, and Independent approach to teaching through the Gradual Release of Responsibility Model (Sharratt & Fullan, 2009, 2012).

Scaffolds: Supports that teachers build into the learning process in order to assist students in meeting learning expectations. Some students require more scaffolds than others. They can also be displayed on classroom walls as prompts or anchor charts to support student learning. Called scaffolds as they point out to the student that "at this level," you should think about . . .

Self-assessment: Students' assessment of their own work against teacher and student co-constructed Success Criteria to determine their next steps in their learning.

Success Criteria: Very clear statements of requirement for achieving various assessment levels that are tied directly to *Learning Goals* (see above) and are developed from (clustered) curriculum expectations. Success Criteria should be visible and available in classrooms so that students can use them as a reference when they are doing their work and against which they can measure progress toward their goals. They are most effective when they are co-constructed by teachers and students.

Teacher Moderation: Also called "collaborative assessment of student work," a process of teachers working together to collaboratively assess commonly developed performance tasks to ensure consistency of practice across a grade or subject area. Through moderation, teachers work together to share beliefs and practices, enhance their understanding, compare their interpretations of student results, and confirm their judgments about each student's level of work. See *leveled work*, above.

Team teaching: Two or more teachers share the planning and instruction of students in a coordinated fashion. An example would be two Grade 6 teachers who plan together, create common assessments, and whose instructional timing and delivery is coordinated within their two classes. It may enable one teacher with greater interest or knowledge in a specific part of the curriculum to teach both sections of the class.

Theory of Action: In simple terms, a theory of action is an "If/Then" statement. For example, a theory of action may be "if teachers learn collaboratively, then student results will improve." While it is an explicit description of a sought-after outcome, it requires strategy, action or implementation, monitoring, adjustments and refinements, and is cyclical to be most effective. One inquiry should lead logically into the next.

Universal Design: A framework for designing learning environments and spaces so that they can be used by the widest range of people possible. The principles of Universal Design need to be incorporated into the way students with learning needs are served in our schools so we believe that all students can learn given time and the right support.

References and Further Readings

Abrams, J. (2009). *Having hard conversations*. Thousand Oaks, CA: Corwin.

Argyris, C., & Schön, D. (1974). *Theory in practice: Increasing professional effectiveness*. San Francisco, CA: Jossey-Bass.

Bandura, A. (1997). *Self-efficacy: The exercise of control*. New York: W. H. Freeman and Company.

Bandura, A. (2000). Exercise of human agency through collective efficacy. *Current Directions in Psychological Science, 9*(3), 75–78.

Bandura, A. (2001). Social cognitive theory: An agentic perspective. *Annual Review of Psychology, 52*, 1–26.

Barron, B., & Darling-Hammond, L. (2008). How can we teach for meaningful learning? In L. Darling-Hammond et al. (Eds.), *Powerful learning: What we know about teaching for understanding* (pp. 11–70). San Francisco, CA: John Wiley & Sons.

Barth, R. (1990). *Improving schools from within*. San Francisco, CA: Jossey-Bass.

Begley, P. (1999). Value preferences, ethics and conflicts in school administration. In P. T. Begley (Ed.), *Values & educational leadership* (pp. 237–254). New York: State University of New York Press.

Belchetz, D. (2014). *Networked learning in the York Region District School Board 2006–2014* [Unpublished document].

Bens, I. (2012). *Facilitation at a glance!* (3rd ed.). Salem, NH: GOAL/OPC.

Bentley, T., & Cazaly, C. (2015). *The shared work of learning: Lifting educational achievement through collaboration*. Melbourne, AU: Mitchell Institute for Health and Education Policy.

Berry, B., Daughtrey, A., & Wieder, A. (2009, December). *Collaboration: Closing the effective teaching gap*. CTQ–Center for Teaching Quality Brief. Retrieved from http://files.eric.ed.gov/fulltext/ED509717.pdf

Boss, S. (2012). *Bringing innovation to school: Empowering students to thrive in a changing world*. Bloomington, IN: Solution Tree.

Bruce, C., & Flynn, T. (2013). Assessing the effects of collaborative professional learning: Efficacy shifts in a three-year mathematics study. *Alberta Journal of Educational Research, 58*(4), 691–709.

Bryk, A., & Schneider, B. (2002). *Trust in schools*. New York: Russell Sage Foundation.

Calhoun, E. F. (2002, March). Action research for school improvement. *Educational Leadership, 59*(6), 18–24.

City, E. A., Elmore, R. F., Fiarman, S. E., & Teitel, L. (2009). *Instructional rounds in education: A network approach to improving teaching and learning.* Cambridge, MA: Harvard Education Press.

Clarke, S. (2008). *Active learning through formative assessment.* London: Hodder Murray.

Clay, M. (2013). *An observation survey of early literacy achievement.* Portsmouth, NH: Heinemann.

Crow, G. (1998). Implications for leadership in collaborative schools. In D. G. Pounder (Ed.), *Restructuring schools for collaboration: Promises and pitfalls* (pp. 135–153). Albany: State University of New York Press.

Dana, N. F., Tomas, C., & Boynton, S. (2011). *Inquiry: A districtwide approach to staff and student leadership.* Thousand Oaks, CA: Corwin.

Danielson, C. (2007, September). The many faces of leadership. *Educational Leadership, 65*(1), 14–19.

Darling-Hammond, L., Barron, B., Pearson, P. D., Schoenfeld, A. H., Stage, E. K., Zimmerman, T. D., Cervetti, G. N., & Tilson, J. L. (2008). *Powerful learning: What we know about teaching for understanding.* San Francisco, CA: Jossey-Bass.

Davies, A. (2007). *Making classroom assessment work.* BC: Connections Publishing Inc.

DeWitt, P. M. (2014). *Flipping leadership doesn't mean reinventing the wheel.* Thousand Oaks, CA: Corwin.

Donohoo, J. (2013). *Collaborative inquiry for educators: A facilitator's guide to school improvement.* Thousand Oaks, CA: Corwin.

Dufour, R., & Eaker, R. (1998). *Professional learning communities at work: Best practices for enhancing student achievement.* Alexandria, VA: ASCD.

Dufour, R., Eaker, R., & Dufour, R. (2005). Recurring themes of professional learning communities and the assumptions they challenge. In R. Dufour, R. Eaker, & R. Dufour (Eds.), *On common ground: The power of professional learning communities* (pp. 7–29). Bloomington, IN: National Education Service.

Dunleavy, J., Willms, J. D., Milton, P., & Friesen, S. (2012, September). *The relationship between student engagement and academic outcomes.* Research Series Report Number One. Toronto: Canadian Education Association. Retrieved from http://www.cea-ace.ca/sites/cea-ace.ca/files/cea-2012-wdydist-report-1.pdf

Dweck, C. (1999). *Self-theories: Their motivation, personality and development.* Philadelphia, PA: Psychology Press.

Dweck, C. (2006). *Mindset: The new psychology of success.* New York: Random House.

Earl, L., & Katz, S. (2002). Leading schools in a data rich world. In K. Leithwood & P. Hallinger (Eds.), *Second international handbook of educational leadership and administration* (pp. 1003–1022). Dordrecht: Kluwer Academic.

Easton, L. B. (2009). *Protocols for professional learning.* Alexandria, VA: ASCD.

Eells, R. J. (2011). *Meta-analysis of the relationship between collective teacher efficacy and student achievement* (Doctoral dissertation, paper 133, Loyola University Chicago). Retrieved from http://ecommons.luc.edu/luc_diss/133

Fink, S., & Markholt, A. (2011). *Leading for instructional improvement* (p. 158). San Francisco, CA: Jossey-Bass.

Fisher, D., Frey, N., & Pumpian, I. (2012). *How to create a culture of achievement in our school and classroom.* Alexandria, VA: ASCD.

Fullan, M. (2011). *Change leader.* San Francisco, CA: Jossey-Bass.

Fullan, M. (2013a). *Stratosphere: Integrating technology, pedagogy and change knowledge.* Toronto: Pearson Canada.

Fullan, M. (2013b). *Great to excellent: Launching the next stage of Ontario's education agenda.* Toronto, ON: Pearson.

Fullan, M. (2014). *The principal: Three keys to maximizing impact.* San Francisco, CA: Jossey-Bass.

Fullan, M., & Langworthy, M. (2013, June). *Towards a new end: New pedagogies for deep learning.* Retrieved from http://www.newpedagogies.info/wp-content/uploads/2014/01/New_Pedagogies_for_Deep%20Learning_Whitepaper.pdf

Fullan, M., & Quinn, J. (2015). *Coherence: Putting the right drivers in action.* Thousand Oaks, CA: Corwin.

Fullan, M., & Sharratt, L. (2007). Sustaining leadership in complex times: An individual and system solution. In B. Davies (Ed.), *Developing sustainable leadership.* London: Sage.

Gibbs, J. (2014). *Reaching all by creating tribes learning communities.* Windsor, CA: CenterSource Systems.

Glaze, A., Mattingley, R., & Andrews, R. (2013). *High school graduation: K–12 strategies that work.* Thousand Oaks, CA: Corwin.

Glaze, A., Mattingley, R., & Levin, B. (2012). *Breaking barriers: Excellence and equity for all.* Toronto, ON: Pearson.

Gruenert, S. (2005, December). Correlations of collaborative school cultures with student achievement. *National Association of Secondary School Principals (NASSP) Bulletin, 89*(645), 43–55. Retrieved from http://bul.sagepub.com/content/89/645/43.full.pdf+html?ijkey=jtTUMjkDW9LSs&keytype=ref&siteid=spbul

Hargreaves, A., Boyle, A., & Harris, A. (2015). *Uplifting leadership: How organizations, teams and communities raise performance.* San Francisco, CA: Jossey-Bass.

Hargreaves, A., & Fullan, M. (2013, June). The power of professional capital. *Journal of Staff Development, 34*(3), 36–39.

Hargreaves, A., & Shirley, D. (2012). *The fourth way: The inspiring future for educational change.* Thousand Oaks, CA: Corwin.

Harris, A. (2013). *Distributed leadership matters: Perspectives, practicalities & potential*. Thousand Oaks, CA: Sage.

Hart, M. (2015). Research: Collaboration is key for teacher quality. *The Journal*. Retrieved from http://thejournal.com/articles/2015/07/06/research-collaboration-is-key-for-teacher-quality.aspx?m=2

Hattie, J. (2009). *Visible learning: A synthesis of over 800 meta-analyses relating to achievement*. London: Routledge, Taylor & Francis Group.

Hattie, J. (2012). *Visible learning for teachers: Maximizing impact on learning*. New York: Routledge.

Hattie, J. (2013, Spring). Know thy impact: Teaching, learning and leading. *In Conversation, 4*(2). Retrieved from http://www.eosdn.on.ca/docs/In%20Conversation%20With%20John%20Hattie.pdf

Hattie, J. (2015a). The applicability of Visible Learning to higher education. *Scholarship of Teaching and Learning in Psychology, 1(1)*, 79–91.

Hattie, J. (2015b, June). *What works best in education: The politics of collaborative expertise*. Retrieved from https://www.pearson.com/content/dam/corporate/global/pearson-dot-com/files/hattie/150526_ExpertiseWEB_V1.pdf

Herrington, J., Oliver, R., & Reeves, T. C. (2003). Patterns of engagement in authentic online learning environments. *Australian Journal of Educational Technology, 19*(1), 59–71. Retrieved from http://www.ascllite.org.au/ajet/ajet19/herrington.html

Hill, P., & Barber, M. (2014). *Preparing for a renaissance in assessment*. Paper for Pearson; ISBN 9780992422653.

International Reading Association. (2009). *New literacies and 21st century technologies*. Retrieved from http://www.reading.org/Libraries/position-statements-and-resolutions/ps1067_NewLiteracies21stCentury.pdf

Jacobs, H. H. (2010). *Curriculum 21: Essential education for a changing world*. Alexandra, VA: ASCD.

Jensen, E. (2009). *Teaching with poverty in mind*. Alexandria, VA: ASCD.

Katz, S., & Dack, L. A. (2013). *Intentional interruption: Breaking down learning barriers to transform professional practice*. Thousand Oaks, CA: Corwin.

Katz, S., Earl, L., Jaafar, S. B., Elgie, S., Foster, L., Halbert, J., & Kaser, L. (2008, Spring). Learning networks of schools: The key enablers of successful knowledge communities. *McGill Journal of Education, 43*(2), 111–137.

Klassen, R., & Durksen, T. (2012, Summer). Teachers working together: Why collaboration really matters. *Alberta Teachers Association (ATA), 92*(4), 16–17.

Knight, J. (2007). *Instructional coaching: A partnership approach to improving instruction*. Thousand Oaks, CA: Corwin.

Knight, J. (2011). *Unmistakable impact: A partnership approach for dramatically improving instruction*. Thousand Oaks, CA: Corwin.

Knight, J. (2013). *High-impact instruction: A framework for great teaching*. Thousand Oaks, CA: Corwin.

Knight, J. (2015). *Better conversations: Coaching ourselves and each other to be more credible, caring, and connected.* Thousand Oaks, CA: Corwin.

Langer, G. M., Colton, A. B., & Goff, L. S. (2003). *Collaborative analysis of student work.* Alexandria, VA: ASCD.

Leithwood, K., & Beatty, B. (2008). *Leading with teacher emotions in mind.* Thousand Oaks, CA: Corwin.

Leithwood, K., Harris, A., & Strauss, T. (2010). *Leading school turnaround: How successful leaders transform low-performing schools.* San Francisco, CA: Jossey-Bass.

Little, J. W. (1990). The persistence of privacy: Autonomy and initiative in teachers' professional relations. *Teachers College Record, 4,* 509–535.

Lombardi, M. (2007). Authentic learning for the 21st century: An overview. *ELI Paper 1.* Retrieved from http://net.educause.edu/ir/library/pdf/eli3009.pdf

Militello, M., Rallis, S. F., & Goldring, E. B. (2009). *Leading with inquiry & action.* Thousand Oaks, CA: Corwin.

Millar-Grant, J., Heffler, B., & Mereweather, K. (1995). *Student-led conferences: Using portfolios to share learning with parents.* Markham, ON: Pembrooke.

Ministry of Education. (2014). *Investing in educational success.* Wellington: Ministry of Education. New Zealand. Retrieved May 28, 2015, from http://www.minedu.govt.nz/theMinistry/EducationInitiatives/InvestingInEducationalSuccess.aspx

Mitchell, C., & Sackney, L. (2000). *Profound improvement: Building capacity for a learning community.* Lisse, The Netherlands: Swets & Zeitlinger.

Mourshed, M., Chijioke, C., & Barber, M. (2010, November). How the world's most improved school systems keep getting better. *McKinsey & Company.* Retrieved from http://mckinseyonsociety.com/downloads/reports/Education/Education_Intro_Standalone_Nov%2026.pdf

Muhammed, A. (2009). *Transforming school culture: How to overcome staff division.* Bloomington, IN: Solution Tree.

National Academies. (2012, July). *Education for life and work—Developing transferable knowledge and skills in the 21st century.* National Research Council Report Brief. Retrieved from http://sites.nationalacademies.org/cs/groups/dbassesite/documents/webpage/dbasse_070895.pdf

Nelson, T. H., & Slavit, D. (2008). Supported teacher collaborative inquiry. *Teacher Education Quarterly,* Winter, 99–116.

Nelson, T. H., Slavit, D., Perkins, M., & Hathorn, T. (2008, June). A culture of collaborative inquiry: Learning to develop and support professional learning communities. *Teachers College Record, 110*(6), 1269–1303.

Newmann, F., Rutter, R., & Smith, M. (1989). Organizational factors that affect school sense of efficacy, community, and expectations. *Sociology of Education, 62,* 221–238.

Newmann, F. C., Bryk, A. S., & Nagaoka, J. (2001). Authentic intellectual work and standardized tests: Conflict or coexistence? Consortium on Chicago

School Research, 2001. Retrieved from https://ccsr.uchicago.edu/sites/default/files/publications/p0a02.pdf

Newmann, F. M., Smith, B., Allensworth, E., & Bryk, A. (2001). Instructional coherence: What is it and why it should guide school improvement policy. *Educational Evaluation and Policy Analysis, 23*(4), 297–321.

Ontario Ministry of Education. (2006). *Ontario language arts curriculum.* Toronto, ON: Queen's Printer.

Ontario Ministry of Education. (2010). *Collaborative teacher inquiry.* Capacity Building Series, Literacy and Numeracy Secretariat Special Edition #16. Retrieved from http://www.edu.gov.on.ca/eng/literacynumeracy/inspire/research/CBS_Collaborative_Teacher_Inquiry.pdf

Ontario Ministry of Education. (2011). *Getting started with student inquiry.* Capacity Building Series, Literacy and Numeracy Secretariat Special Edition #24 Retrieved from http://www.edu.gov.on.ca/eng/literacynumeracy/inspire/research/CBS_StudentInquiry.pdf

Ontario Ministry of Education. (2012). Ontario Leadership Framework. Retrieved from http://www.education-leadership-ontario.ca/storage/6/1380680840/OLF_User_Guide_FINAL.pdf

Ontario Ministry of Education. (2013). *Ontario social studies, history and geography curriculum.* Toronto, Canada: Queen's Printer.

Ontario Ministry of Education. (2014a). *Principals as co-learners: Supporting the promise of collaborative inquiry.* Capacity Building Series, Literacy and Numeracy Secretariat Special Edition #38. Retrieved from http://www.edu.gov.on.ca/eng/literacynumeracy/inspire/research/CBS_PrincipalsCoLearners.pdf

Ontario Ministry of Education. (2014b). *Collaborative inquiry in Ontario: What we have learned and where we are now.* Capacity Building Series, Literacy and Numeracy Secretariat Special Edition #39. Retrieved from http://www.edu.gov.on.ca/eng/literacynumeracy/inspire/research/CBS_CollaborativeInquiry.pdf

Ontario Ministry of Education. (2014c). *Specialist high skills major.* Toronto, Canada: Queen's Printer.

Pahomov, L. (2014). *Authentic learning in the digital age.* Alexandria, VA: ASCD.

Panitz, T. (1997, Winter). Collaborative versus cooperative learning: Comparing the two definitions helps understand the nature of interactive learning. *Cooperative Learning and College Teaching, 8*(2). Retrieved from http://home.capecod.net/~tpanitz/tedsarticles/coopbenefits.htm

Planche, B. (2004). *Probing the complexities of collaboration and collaborative processes.* Unpublished doctoral dissertation. University of Toronto, Ontario, Canada.

Planche, B. (2007). *A leadership perspective on the complexities of collaboration.* Paper prepared for the Simcoe County Board of Education, Ontario.

Planche, B. (2008a). Leadership perspectives on the complexities of collaboration. *The Beacon: A publication of the Pennsylvania School Study Council,* 5(1), 1–7.

Planche, B. (2008b, Summer). Improving schools: Addressing the complexities of collaboration. *Ontario Principal's Council Register, 10*(2), 14–19.

Planche, B. (2010a, Spring). Supporting teacher learning in Ontario. In *Leadership in Focus—Journal for Australasian School Leaders,* Spring, 2–7.

Planche, B. (2010b). Revisiting the Ten Conditions for Learning. Inspire, Ontario Ministry of Education Retrieved at http://www.edu.gov.on.ca/eng/literacynumeracy/inspire/classroom/10conditions.html

Planche, B. (2011). Personal notes regarding a visit to New Technology High. Napa Valley: Cal. (January, 2011).

Planche, B. (2012a, Winter). The transformative power of co-learning. *Leadership in Focus: Journal for Australasian School Leaders, 26,* 2–7.

Planche, B. (2012b). *4C's: Practising Together Changes Educational Practice.* Paper presented at the 6th International Technology, Education and Development (INTED 2012) Conference, Valencia, Spain.

Planche, B. (2013a). Today's imperative—Integrated learning. *Learning Forward Ontario* [E-Newsletter], 4(3). Retrieved from http://learningforwardontario.ca/files/LFO_Newsletter_Spring_2013.pdf

Planche, B. (2013b, May). Graphic adapted for professional learning workshop. Learning Forward Spring Conference, Niagara Falls, Ontario.

Planche, B., & Case, R. (2015, Winter). Critical, creative & collaborative thinking—A 3-sided coin? *The OPC Register, 17*(1), 8–13.

Planche B., Sharratt, L., & Belchetz, D. (2008, January): *Sustaining student's increased achievement through second order change: Do collaboration and leadership count?* Paper presented at International Congress of School Effectiveness and Improvement Conference (ICSEI), Auckland, New Zealand.

Pollack, K. (with Wang, F., and Hauseman, C.). (2014, October). *The changing nature of principals' work.* Final report for the Ontario Principal's Council. Retrieved from http://www.edu.uwo.ca/faculty_profiles/cpels/pollock_katina/OPC-Principals-Work-Report.pdf

Pounder, D. E. (Ed.). (1998). *Restructuring schools for collaboration: Promises and pitfalls.* Albany: State University of New York Press.

Rennie Center Education Research & Policy, & EdVestors. (2012). *Making space: The value of teacher collaboration.* Schools on the Move Best Practice Research. Retrieved from http://www.edvestors.org/wp-content/uploads/2014/04/EdVestors-Making-Space-The-Value-of-Teacher-Collaboration-2014.pdf

Robinson, M. A., Passantino, C., Acerra, M., Bae, L., Tiehen, K., Pido, E., . . . Langland, C. (2010, November). *School perspectives on collaborative inquiry: Lessons learned from New York City, 2009–2010.* Consortium for Policy Research in Education, Teachers College, Columbia University. Retrieved from www.cpre.org/school-perspectives-collaborative-inquiry-lessons-learned-new-york-city-2009-2010

Robinson, V., Hohepa, M., & Lloyd, C. (2009). *School leadership and student outcomes: Identifying what works and why: Best evidence synthesis.* Wellington, New Zealand: Ministry of Education.

Ronfeldt, M., Farmer, S. O., McQueen, K., & Grissom, J. A. (2015, June). Teacher collaboration in instructional teams and student achievement. *American Educational Research Journal, 52*(3), 475–514.

Rose, D. H., & Meyer, A. (2002). *Teaching every student in the digital age: Universal design for learning.* Alexandra, Virginia. ASCD.

Rubie-Davies, C. M. (2015). *High and low expectation teachers: The importance of the teacher factor.* New York, NY: Psychology Press.

Rubin, H. (2009). *Collaborative leadership: Developing effective partnerships for communities and schools* (2nd ed.). Thousand Oaks, CA: Corwin.

Schein, E. H. (1984). Coming to a new awareness of organizational culture. *Sloan Management Review, 25*(2), 5–18.

Schön, D. A. (1983). *The reflective practitioner: How professionals think in action.* London: Temple Smith.

Scruggs, T. E., Mastropieri, M., & McDuffie, K. A. (2007). Co-teaching in inclusive classrooms: A metasynthesis of qualitative research. *Exceptional Children, 73*(4), 392–416. Retrieved from http://education.ufl.edu/325t/files/2013/06/Scrugg_2007.pdf

Sergiovanni, T. J. (2007). *Rethinking leadership: A collection of articles* (2nd ed.). Thousand Oaks, CA: Corwin.

Sharratt, L. (1996). *The influence of electronically available information on the stimulation of knowledge use and organizational learning in schools* (Unpublished doctoral dissertation). University of Toronto, Canada.

Sharratt, M. (2004). *The impact of teacher leadership on students' literacy learning* (Master's thesis). University of Toronto, Canada.

Sharratt, L. (2013a). *Learning walks and talks* [Training materials]. Australia, Canada, Chile.

Sharratt, L. (2013b). Scaffolded literacy assessment and a model for teachers' professional development. In S. Elliott-Johns & D. Jarvis (Eds.), *Perspectives on transitions in schooling and instructional practice* (pp. 138–153). Toronto, ON: University of Toronto Press.

Sharratt, L. (2014). Scaffolded literacy assessment and a model for teachers' professional development. In S. Elliott-Johns & D. Jarvis (Eds.), *Perspectives on transitions in schooling and instructional practice.* Toronto, ON: University of Toronto Press.

Sharratt, L., Coutts, J. D., & Harild, G. (2015). Good to great to innovate: What matters most? *Australian Educational Leadership Journal.*

Sharratt, L., Coutts, J., Hogarth, W., & Fullan, M. (2013). Reading Recovery: A high return on investment for cost-conscious and student-achievement oriented education systems. *Journal of Reading Recovery, 13*(1).

Sharratt, L., & Fullan, M. (2005). The school district that did the right things right. *Voices in Urban Education, 9,* 5–13.

Sharratt, L., & Fullan, M. (2006). Accomplishing district-wide reform. *Journal of School Leadership, 16,* 583–595.

Sharratt, L., & Fullan, M. (2009). *Realization: The change imperative for deepening district-wide reform.* Thousand Oaks, CA: Corwin.

Sharratt, L., & Fullan, M. (2012). *Putting FACES on the data: What great leaders do!* Thousand Oaks, CA: Corwin.

Sharratt, L., & Fullan, M. (2013). Capture the human side of learning. *Journal of Staff Development, 34*(1), 44–48.

Sharratt, L., & Harild, G. (2015). *Good to great to innovate: Recalculating the route to career readiness, K–12.* Thousand Oaks, CA: Corwin.

Sharratt, L., Hine, E., & Maika, D. (2015, February). Pedagogically focused leadership: Creating reciprocal and respectful relationships. *The Register, Ontario Principals' Council, 17*(1), 35–39.

Sharratt, L., Ostinelli, G., & Cattaneo, A. (2010). *The role of the "knowledge-able other" in improving student achievement, school culture and teacher efficacy: Two case studies from Canadian and Swiss perspectives and experiences.* Paper presented at the International Congress for School Effectiveness and Improvement, Kuala Lumpur, Malaysia.

Singer, T. W. (2015). *Opening doors to equity: A practical guide to observation-based professional learning.* Thousand Oaks, CA: Corwin.

Slater, L. (2004). Collaboration: A framework for school improvement. *International Journal for Leadership in Learning, 8*(5), 1–19. Retrieved from http://iejll.journalhosting.ucalgary.ca/iejll/index.php/ijll/article/view/698t

Sornson, B. (2001). *Preventing early learning failure.* Alexandria, VA: ASCD.

Stoll, L. (2015). Using evidence, learning and the role of professional learning communities. In C. Brown (Ed.), *Leading the use of research & evidence in schools.* London: IOE Press.

Stoll, L., Bolam, R., McMahon, A., Wallace, M., & Thomas, S. (2006). Professional learning communities: A review of the literature. *Journal of Educational Change, 7,* 221–258. doi:10.1007/S10833-006-0001-8

Stoll, L., & Incorporated Association of Registered Teachers of Victoria (IARTV). (2004, August). *Leadership learning: Designing a connected strategy.* Jolimont, Victoria: IARTV. Retrieved from http://trove.nla.gov.au/work/7402226?q&versionId=8520926

Strauss, V. (2013, April 11). What teachers need and reformers ignore: Time to collaborate. *Washington Post.* Retrieved from http://wapo.st/155fSFV

Tschannen-Moran, M., Woolfolk Hoy, A., & Hoy, W. K. (1998). Teacher efficacy: Its meaning and measure. *Review of Educational Research, 68*(2), 202–248.

Vygotsky, L. S. (1978). *Mind in society: The development of higher psychological processes* (4th ed.). Cambridge, MA: Harvard University Press.

Walker, D. (2002). Constructivist leadership: Standards, equity, and learning: Weaving a whole cloth from multiple strands. In L. Lambert, D. Walker, D. Zimmerman, J. Cooper, M. Lambert, M. Gardner, & M. Szabo (Eds.), *The constructivist leader* (2nd ed., pp. 1–33). New York: Teachers College Press.

William & Flora Hewlett Foundation. (2015). *What is deeper learning?* Retrieved from http://www.hewlett.org/programs/education/deeper-learning/what-deeper-learning

Willms, J. D., Friesen, S., & Milton, P. (2009, May). *What did you do in school today?: Transforming classrooms through social, academic and intellectual development.* Toronto, ON: Canadian Education Association. Retrieved from http://www.cea-ace.ca/publication/what-did-you-do-school-today-transforming-classrooms-through-social-academic-and-intelle

Willms, J. D., & Friesen, S. (2012, September). *The relationship between instructional challenge and student engagement.* Research Series Report Number Two. Toronto, ON: Canadian Education Association. Retrieved from http://www.cea-ace.ca/sites/cea-ace.ca/files/cea-2012-wdydist-report-2.pdf

Yates, G. C. R., & Hattie, J. (2013). Experts amongst us: What do we know about them? *Journal of Educational Enquiry, 12*(1), 40–50.

Zeiser, K. L., Taylor, J., Rickles, J., & Garet, M. S. (2014). *Report 3. Findings from the study of deeper learning—Evidence of deeper learning outcomes.* Retrieved from http://www.air.org/sites/default/down loads/report/Report_3_Evidence_of_Deeper_Learning_Outcomes.pdf

Index

Notes

Notes

Notes

A SAGE Company

Helping educators make the greatest impact

CORWIN HAS ONE MISSION: to enhance education through intentional professional learning.

We build long-term relationships with our authors, educators, clients, and associations who partner with us to develop and continuously improve the best evidence-based practices that establish and support lifelong learning.

ONTARIO PRINCIPALS' COUNCIL
Exemplary Leadership in Public Education

The Ontario Principals' Council (OPC) is a voluntary professional association representing 5,000 practising school leaders in elementary and secondary schools across Ontario. We believe that exemplary leadership results in outstanding schools and improved student achievement. We foster quality leadership through world-class professional services and supports, striving to continuously achieve "quality leadership—our principal product."

Solutions you want. Experts you trust.
Results you need.

Author Consulting

AUTHOR CONSULTING

On-site professional learning with sustainable results! Let us help you design a professional learning plan to meet the unique needs of your school or district. www.corwin.com/pd

Institutes

INSTITUTES

Corwin Institutes provide collaborative learning experiences that equip your team with tools and action plans ready for immediate implementation. www.corwin.com/institutes

eCourses

ECOURSES

Practical, flexible online professional learning designed to let you go at your own pace. www.corwin.com/ecourses

Read2Earn

READ2EARN

Did you know you can earn graduate credit for reading this book? Find out how: www.corwin.com/read2earn